ReFocus: The Films of Susanne Bier

ReFocus: The International Directors Series

Series Editors: Robert Singer and Gary D. Rhodes

ReFocus is a series of contemporary methodological and theoretical approaches to the interdisciplinary analyses and interpretations of international film directors, from the celebrated to the ignored, in direct relationship to their respective culture—its myths, values, and historical precepts—and the broader parameters of international film history and theory. The series provides a forum for introducing a broad spectrum of directors, working in and establishing movements, trends, cycles and genres including those historical, currently popular, or emergent, and in need of critical assessment or reassessment. It ignores no director who created a historical space—either in or outside of the studio system—beginning with the origins of cinema and up to the present. *ReFocus* brings these film directors to a new audience of scholars and general readers of Film Studies.

Available or forthcoming titles

ReFocus: The Films of Susanne Bier
Edited by Missy Molloy, Mimi Nielsen, and Meryl Shriver-Rice

ReFocus: The Films of Corneliu Porumboiu
Monica Filimon

ReFocus: The Films of Francis Veber
Keith Corson

ReFocus: The Films of Andrei Tarkovsky
Sergei Toymentsev

ReFocus: The Films of Jia Zhangke
Maureen Turim and Ying Xiao

edinburghuniversitypress.com/series/refocint

ReFocus:
The Films of Susanne Bier

Edited by Missy Molloy, Mimi Nielsen,
and Meryl Shriver-Rice

EDINBURGH
University Press

Edinburgh University Press is one of the leading university presses in the U.K. We publish
academic books and journals in our selected subject areas across the humanities and social
sciences, combining cutting-edge scholarship with high editorial and production values
to produce academic works of lasting importance. For more information visit our website:
edinburghuniversitypress.com

© editorial matter and organization Missy Molloy, Mimi Nielsen, and Meryl Shriver-Rice, 2018
© the chapters their several authors, 2018

Edinburgh University Press Ltd
The Tun—Holyrood Road
12 (2f) Jackson's Entry
Edinburgh EH8 8PJ

Typeset in 11/13 Monotype Ehrhardt by
Servis Filmsetting Ltd, Stockport, Cheshire

A CIP record for this book is available from the British Library

ISBN 978 1 4744 2872 9 (hardback)
ISBN 978 1 4744 2874 3 (webready PDF)
ISBN 978 1 4744 2875 0 (epub)

The right of the contributors to be identified as authors of this work has been asserted
in accordance with the Copyright, Designs and Patents Act 1988 and the Copyright
and Related Rights Regulations 2003 (SI No. 2498).

Contents

List of Figures	vii
Notes on Contributors	x
Foreword by Andrew Nestingen	xiii

    Introduction: Susanne Bier's Boundary-crossing Screen Authorship   1
    Missy Molloy, Mimi Nielsen, and Meryl Shriver-Rice

Part 1 Generic and Industrial Fluidity

1. Storytelling Schemes, Realism, and Ambiguity: Susanne Bier's Danish Dramas   19
 Birger Langkjær

2. Negotiating Special Relationships: Susanne Bier's Comedies   36
 Gunhild Agger

3. Susanne Bier's Hollywood Experiments: *Things We Lost in the Fire* and *Serena*   56
 Missy Molloy

Part 2 Negotiating Identity

4. Beginning with Jewish Survival: *Freud's Leaving Home*   83
 Maureen Turim

5. Stories with Queer Identities   97
 Anders Marklund

6. Judaism and Danish Directors: The Case of Lars von Trier vs. Susanne Bier   113
Pétur Valsson

7. Gender Equity in Screen Culture: On Susanne Bier, the Celluloid Ceiling, and the Growing Appeal of TV Production   134
Mette Hjort

Part 3 Authorship and Aesthetics

8. Tracing Affect in Susanne Bier's Dramas   155
Mimi Nielsen

9. Vision and Ethics in *A Second Chance* (*En chance til*)   173
Danica van de Velde

10. The Truth is in the Eyes: Susanne Bier's Use of Close-ups in *The Night Manager*   187
Eva Novrup Redvall

Part 4 Transnational Reach

11. Cinema of the World and Women's Film Culture: Susanne Bier's Transnational Cinema   211
Belinda Smaill

12. From Local to Global: The Bier/Jensen Screenwriting Collaboration   229
Cath Moore

13. Danish Privilege and Responsibility in the Work of Susanne Bier   243
Meryl Shriver-Rice

Postscript: A Conversation with Susanne Bier   261
Interview with Susanne Bier conducted by Missy Molloy, Mimi Nielsen, and Meryl Shriver-Rice

Filmography of Susanne Bier   283
Acknowledgments   285
Index   286

Figures

1.1	Jörgen and Jacob in *Efter brylluppet / After the Wedding*	22
1.2	The motif of lying, the vulnerable human, and the open ending	26
1.3–1.5	Cæcilie and Niels in *Elsker dig for evigt / Open Hearts*	28
1.6, 1.7	Mikael Persbrandt as Anton in *Hævnen / In a Better World*	30
2.1	Sus and Sonny visiting the doctor	43
2.2	Lizzie and Niller visiting the adoption center	43
2.3	Mgala's first word in "Danish"	45
2.4	Sus in conversation with Lizzie	46
2.5	The invasion of golden fairytale dust	48
2.6	The Danish Way	49
2.7	The Italian Way	50
2.8	Lemons inaugurating the theme of the color yellow	50
3.1	Jörgen sobbing "I don't want to die" in *After the Wedding*	64
3.2	The final shot of *The Night Manager*'s Richard Roper in the back of a police van	64
3.3	Niels reacting to Cæcilie's rejection in *Open Hearts*	65
3.4	Jerry detoxing after a heroin relapse in *Things We Lost in the Fire*	65
3.5	*Sekten*'s Dr. Lack in fetal position	66
3.6	Bier's screen surrogate?	66
3.7	Jerry's frustrated desire for Audrey on display in *Things We Lost in the Fire*	69
3.8	Audrey's feelings toward Jerry are less evident	69
4.1	Close-up, arranging a guest table	85
4.2	Freud circling around her mother	85

4.3	Arrival of the older children	87
4.4	Singing "Lomir Ale Eeynem"	88
4.5	Freud's sexual initiation	91
5.1	The poster using an image from *Pensionat Oskar*'s ending	100
5.2	Absent husbands, forsaken wives in both *Pensionat Oskar* and *Den skaldede frisør*	101
5.3	*Once In A Lifetime*'s ending cuts between hope and sadness	104
5.4	Two persons enjoying the pleasures of water, and two men alarmed by the careless non-normative bathing	107
5.5	Corky poses a threat to the heterosexual hero	109
7.1	Jed receives an abusive phone call from her mother	145
7.2	Angela Burr talks to Jonathan Pine	146
8.1	Adrian, witness and confessor to Roshe's scars	159
8.2	Welcome home dinner for Jannik	161
8.3	Michael avoids looking at Niels Peter	162
8.4	Michael screams at the Taliban camp leader	163
8.5	Anton floats in the sea, caressing his slapped cheek	165
8.6	Cæcilie desperate for contact with Joachim	168
9.1	Encounter and afterimage: Andreas finds Sofus	176
9.2	Simon sees the truth	178
9.3	The fracture of the ideal family	179
9.4	Bad parents or victims?	182
9.5	"Wake up!": Addressing the viewer	184
10.1	Jonathan Pine asking questions about Mr. Hamid on the phone	193
10.2	The image of Jonathan Pine's eye spying behind a door	195
10.3	Richard Roper and Jonathan Pine/Andrew Birch in one of their "eye duels"	197
10.4a	The biometric eye scan is central to the plot of *The Night Manager*	198
10.4b	Jonathan Pine "cheats with his eyes" in the final showdown	199
10.5	Jed showering and dressing up for a new day	200
10.6	Jonathan Pine taking in the beaten face of Sophie	201
10.7	"Who are you? Everyone is attracted to you . . ."	202
11.1	Serena's descent into madness is exacerbated following her miscarriage	220
11.2	The eerie Smokey Mountains of North Carolina	221
11.3	Transitions between scenes in *Serena* consistently return to images of the mountains	221
11.4	The topography of the natural environment looms	221
11.5	*Serena* begins as a story told from George's perspective	222

11.6	Serena and Galloway hunt down Jacob and his mother, Rachel	222
12.1	The use of close-ups has become an important marker of Bier's screen aesthetic	233
12.2	Jacob says goodbye to Indian orphan Pramod	236
12.3	A South Sudanese refugee begs Anton not to help Big Man	236
12.4	Jørgen reads a bedtime story to his twin boys, Martin and Morten	237
12.5	Bier's framing highlights the legacy of violence between children and adults	239
12.6	Marianne escorts Christian to see her son Elias	240
13.1	White, blue-eyed Scandinavian protagonist	248
13.2	Clean, orderly Western space juxtaposed against Anton's South Sudan workplace in *In a Better World*	249
13.3	A young girl cries in a dust storm in South Sudan	249
13.4	Jacob and Pramod meet at eye level in *After the Wedding*	250
13.5	Close-up of unseeing animal eyes on Jørgen's walls in *In a Better World*	252
13.6	*After the Wedding*'s credits roll in India	255
P.1	Susanne Bier	262
P.2	Susanne Bier with the volume editors	281

Notes on Contributors

Gunhild Agger is a professor in the Department of Culture and Global Studies at Aalborg University. Her research areas include national and transnational film, television drama, history of media and genres, and she has published and edited several books, among them *The Aesthetics of Television* (2001), *Dansk TV-drama* (2005), and *Mord til tiden* (2013).

Mette Hjort is Professor of Film Studies at the Department of Media, Cognition and Communication, University of Copenhagen. Appointed by the Minister of Culture, she serves on the Board of the Danish Film Institute.

Birger Langkjær is Associate Professor in Film Studies at the Department of Media, Cognition and Communication, University of Copenhagen. His main research is on cognitive film theory, sound and music in film and television, and realism in Danish cinema. He has published in numerous journals, edited volumes, and he is the author of three books.

Anders Marklund is a senior lecturer in Film Studies at Lund University in Sweden and primary editor of *Journal of Scandinavian Cinema* (Intellect). His current research interests include history and remediation in contemporary cinema, (super-) popular national European films, international awards and circulation, migration and marginalized identities in mainstream cinema, and participatory cultures.

Missy Molloy is a lecturer in film at Victoria University of Wellington in New Zealand. Her work has recently appeared in *Studies in Spanish & Latin American Cinemas* (2017) and the *Journal of Popular Television* (2017), and her current research focuses on women's screen authorship, transnational media theories, and crime drama.

Cath Moore is an award-winning Australian-based screenwriter. She tutors in screenwriting at the University of Melbourne and is completing a Ph.D. on Danish screenwriting practices at Deakin University.

Andrew Nestingen is a professor and chair in the Department of Scandinavian Studies at the University of Washington, Seattle. His books include *The Cinema of Aki Kaurismäki: Contrarian Stories* (2013) and *Crime and Fantasy in Scandinavia: Fiction, Film, and Social Change* (2008). He is an associate editor of the *Journal of Scandinavian Cinema* and a review editor of *Scandinavian Studies*.

Mimi Nielsen is a Ph.D. candidate in Comparative Literature at the University of Washington, Seattle. She is currently writing her dissertation, *Playing the Edge: The Work of Affect in Emilie Flygare-Carlén's Authorship and Reception*.

Eva Novrup Redvall is Associate Professor of Film and Media Studies at the University of Copenhagen. She is the author of several books, chapters, and articles on Danish film and television, and has been a film critic for the daily Danish newspaper *Information* since 1999.

Meryl Shriver-Rice is the Director of Environmental Media at the Abess Center for Ecosystem Science & Policy at the University of Miami. She is the author of *Inclusion in New Danish Cinema: Sexuality & Transnational Belonging* (2015) and co-author of *Screen Life & Identity: An Introduction to Media Studies* (forthcoming with Hunter Vaughan). Her current media studies research focuses on digital culture and the role of visual artifacts in shaping societal values and perceptions of the environment.

Belinda Smaill is an Associate Professor in Film and Screen Studies at Monash University, Melbourne. She has published widely in the areas of women and cinema, documentary film, and Australian film and television. She is the author of *The Documentary: Politics, Emotion, Culture* (2010) and *Regarding Life: Animals and the Documentary Moving Image* (2016), and co-author of *Transnational Australian Cinema: Ethics in the Asian Diasporas* (2013).

Maureen Turim, professor of Film and Media Studies in the Department of English at the University of Florida, has published three books: *The Films of Oshima Nagisa: Images of a Japanese Iconoclast* (1998); *Flashbacks in Film:*

Memory and History (1989); and *Abstraction in Avant-Garde Films* (1985). She has published over one hundred essays in journals and books.

Pétur Valsson is a Ph.D. candidate in the Department of Scandinavian Studies and the Cinema and Media Studies Graduate Program at the University of Washington, Seattle. He holds an M.A. degree in Film Studies from Columbia University and a B.A. in History and Film from the University of Iceland.

Danica van de Velde is an early career researcher at the University of Western Australia, where she completed her doctoral thesis on the cinema of Wong Kar-wai. Her work has recently been published in *Home: Concepts, Constructions, Contexts* (2016) and a special issue of *Frontiers of Literary Studies in China* (2017) focusing on women, writing, and visuality in contemporary China.

Foreword by Andrew Nestingen

Denmark's (and for that matter Scandinavia's) most significant contributors to cinema have been enigmatic, multifaceted, and often peripatetic artists. Carl Th. Dreyer made films in Denmark, Norway, Germany, and France. After the premiere of *Day of Wrath* (*Vredens dag*, 1943), he pitched a remake of the film, "transplanted to an American milieu," to Louis B. Mayer of M.G.M. (see Wrigley 2015). While the remake never happened, perhaps it might be seen as one layer in the palimpsest of Lars von Trier's *Dogville* (2003), which reimagines *Day of Wrath*'s tortured woman (Rugg 2016) through the mythology of Hollywood. While von Trier famously has not gone to Hollywood, he has made films with international casts, including Hollywood stars, and Hollywood's myths and forms have long haunted his films. Dreyer and von Trier's Hollywood fixations have been realized by the woman who is arguably Denmark's most significant auteur of the twenty-first century, Susanne Bier. Yet as von Trier struggled, Bier became more prolific, made richer films, and received such recognition as an Academy Award, which she won for *In a Better World* (*Hævnen*, 2010). With Dreyer and von Trier she shares a body of work made in numerous countries, with multilingual casts and multinational financing. Moreover, she is a woman director who has made films, often focusing on traumatized, suffering men, in a male-centered industry. And despite her reputation for making melodramatic films, Bier revises and recombines genres to make films that are emotionally moving, aesthetically rich, and ethically thought-provoking. Despite her similarity to her cinematic colleagues, the many dimensions of her cinema, and her connections to and revisions of Scandinavian auteur cinema and its traditions, Bier has received scant attention from scholars.

ReFocus: The Films of Susanne Bier corrects this inattention by bringing together a roster of film scholars that tease out the multiple and often contradictory dimensions of Bier's films: their shifting relationship to genre, Bier's identity as a filmmaker, her status as a film author, and the transnational character of the production and aesthetics of the films. The result is a rich introduction to her work and its contexts that will serve any reader interested in Bier's films.

The artists whose work matters most to us are those who give us language and form for the questions that trouble us. Bier's film career coincides with the move to a global, digitally interconnected age of people on the move, unprecedented flows of money, and complex historical interconnections. Bier's films depict her historical moment with deft and penetrating words, comedy and drama, arresting close-ups, and contradictory scenarios. In *After the Wedding* (*Efter brylluppet*, 2006), for instance, these contrasts intersect in the collision of the saturated oranges of Jacob's (Mads Mikkelsen) home in a Mumbai orphanage and the blues of his hotel room in Copenhagen. Each of the characters in the film has their motivations and their traumas, which launch them in conflicting trajectories. The film gives us language and image for our questions. What is my responsibility to others? Does my trauma give me license to use others to heal myself? How can we be moral in a world of criss-crossing moral systems? Engaging categories of gender, sexuality, nationality, ethnicity, race, class, and generation, Bier's films put such questions to us in narratives and images that do not leave us.

ReFocus: The Films of Susanne Bier elaborates the history, aesthetics, and contexts of Bier's filmmaking. In so doing it offers the first book-length consideration of Bier's cinema, and why it matters. Bier's multidimensional films will continue to capture viewers' imaginations and emotions. This book provides readers and scholars interested in Bier with a rich entry into her cinema, and a smart companion in engaging the questions her films put to us.

WORKS CITED

Rugg, Linda Haverty (2016), "A Tradition of Torturing Women," in Mette Hjort and Ursula Lindqvist, eds., *A Companion to Nordic Cinema*, Malden, MA: Wiley Blackwell, pp. 351–70.
Wrigley, Nick (2015), Twitter post, February 6, 12.10 p.m., <https://twitter.com/shittydeath/status/563791784334348288>.

Introduction: Susanne Bier's Boundary-crossing Screen Authorship

Missy Molloy, Mimi Nielsen, and Meryl Shriver-Rice

The renaissance in Danish film during the last two and a half decades, which film scholars have dubbed the "New Danish Cinema," has produced compelling works with local and transnational appeal (Hjort 2005; Shriver-Rice 2015). Susanne Bier has been at the forefront of New Danish Cinema's international visibility since *The One and Only* (*Den eneste ene*, 1999) broke Danish box-office records and inspired an English-language remake (*The One and Only*, 2002). Despite critical accolades, including *In a Better World*'s (*Hævnen*, 2010) Academy Award for Best Foreign Language Film and significant attention from the popular press and international audiences, Bier's work has not often been the subject of scholarly discourse. In this volume we illustrate the ways in which Bier is a generically and industrially mobile screen author, one whose work has long been overlooked by film scholarship perhaps because it eludes easy classification (Smaill 2014). *ReFocus: The Films of Susanne Bier* makes significant headway toward advancing the international scholarly conversation on Bier's oeuvre and contributes to the broader conversation regarding women filmmakers currently forging viable commercial and artistic careers in a field historically dominated by men (see White 2015). It also addresses the phenomenon of directors from small nations successfully navigating competitive production contexts in an increasing global "age of media convergence" (see Hjort and Petrie 2007; Jenkins 2006).

This collection is motivated in part by the desire to parse Bier's body of work because it challenges dominant rubrics of film studies assessment, namely those fundamental to genre- and auteur-based criticism, as well as newer cinematic theories based on contemporary media's transnational dimensions. The fact that Bier, as a noted filmmaker from a small nation who is also part of a minority of globally visible female directors, could evade the attention of film scholars for a relatively long period despite her remarkable artistic and commercial achievements became for us, the editors of this volume, an irresistible enigma. What is it about Bier's work that inspires extraordinary public interest yet fails, barring a few exceptions, to stimulate scholarly criticism? Do standard approaches to film authorship sidestep idiosyncratic works and/or directors that threaten entrenched systems of determining cinematic value? These questions ground the many queries percolating through this volume. Meanwhile, the swell of attention to the problem of gender inequality in film has been an added stimulus—already certain that Bier's oeuvre would be a fruitful scholarly subject, we have been inspired by the growing sense that women's cinema, broadly yet purposefully defined, is on the cusp of unprecedented influence and expansion.

DANISH ORIGINS

There are few countries that can boast as many successful women filmmakers as Denmark (though this is starting to change: see Hjort in this volume), and it is a worthwhile venture to provide a quick overview of the innovative small-nation filmmaking context that has fostered equal production opportunities for Bier and other Danish women filmmakers. From a relatively monocultural national cinema of the 1980s, the 1990s produced two major changes to Danish film culture: a move towards Hollywoodization (recognizable in films such as *Smilla's Sense of Snow* [1997]), and the emergence of the Dogme 95 movement. Dogme inspired socially "truthful," realistic, and intimate storylines in direct opposition to highly marketable and ethically questionable Hollywood-style movies (Schepelern 2013) and was an effective, non-nationalist, and non-Hollywood response to the rapid rise of globalization. Rather than exhibit the cultural backlash of intensified localism (which might have resulted in a plethora of new Danish heritage films), Dogme directors chose to employ new digital technologies to innovate the cinematic art form (Hjort 2003: 38). As a result, Dogme spurred significant artistic development and international visibility for the directors and writers (Lars von Trier, Anders Thomas Jensen, Susanne Bier, Lone Scherfig, Thomas Vinterberg, Åke Sandgren, Annette K. Olesen, and Paprika Steen, to name a few) who have since been recognized for their contributions to New Danish Cinema.

As a production strategy involving strict rules (hence the name "Dogme" for dogmatic), Dogme challenged directors to craft superior stories using low-budget filmmaking practices that would allow for greater freedom in multiple areas of production (see Hjort 2010). One intention behind this strategy was to achieve greater cinematic "truth" through the use of imposed production parameters that included low budgets, digital cameras, and a lack of props, filters, or extra lighting (Schepelern 2006: 103). Not surprisingly, many ex-Dogme directors still favor intimate narratives that are overwhelmingly focused on the psychological and social realism that the rules of Dogme cultivated (Bondebjerg 2003: 84). Even taking into account the concerted move towards mainstream filmmaking in the last decade, Dogme's effects on New Danish Cinema are nevertheless vast, both aesthetically and philosophically (Shriver-Rice 2015).

This emphasis on story over marketability is also apparent in Danish film funding schemes. Today most Danish films are publicly funded, at least partially, through the subsidy system managed by the Danish Film Institute. The Danish system eschews solely economic evaluations of a potential film's worth, instead selecting "artistically valuable" films, which rose in number from 14–16 films a year in 1999 to 25–27 feature films by 2009 (Hjort et al. 2010: 26). The Danish film industry also encourages extraordinary screenwriting procedures unlike those common to other national cinemas. Most film scripts are co-written by the writer and director. Eva Novrup Redvall has researched the unusually prolific collaborations between writers and directors in the Danish film industry. She argues that these collaborations cultivate an environment in which the story remains the critical focus of each film (2010: 67). This distinct approach to screenwriting resembles the collaborative dynamic often exhibited by competing Danish production companies. Hjort has interpreted this unique phenomenon as a Maussian "gift culture" of film production, and it has been heralded as the creative machinery of a cinema that is tailored to nurture artistic vision over marketability (Hjort 2005: 23).

While extraordinary, this commitment to collaboration is logical for a national culture that is known to exhibit an "unshakable commitment to egalitarianism" (Hjort 2005: 4). It is within this film industry context that women directors such as Susanne Bier, Paprika Steen, Lone Scherfig, Pernille Fischer Christensen and Hella Joof have received support for their film projects. Furthermore, much of New Danish Cinema is fashioned to produce narratives of cultural, social, political, and artistic significance (Shriver-Rice 2015). This is certainly not surprising given that many Danish directors are graduates of the notoriously "socially aware" National Film School of Denmark (Stevenson 2003: 162, 201). As many high-profile film nominations and wins over the past two decades highlight, New Danish Cinema has produced compelling works with local and transnational appeal.

BIER'S DISTINCTLY TRANSCULTURAL AND EROTIC BRAND

Bier is known for her ethically ripe, timely dramas. The most successful of these, by inviting close psychological readings of their characters' complex reactions to extreme scenarios, exhibit qualities associated with psychological realism. The trio of films that have been most internationally recognized—*Brothers* (*Brødre*, 2004), *After the Wedding* (*Efter brylluppet*, 2006) and *In a Better World*—feature male protagonists responding to traumatic, life-altering events (Smaill 2014). More recently, Bier directed a television miniseries, *The Night Manager* (2016), which amassed viewing numbers that well surpass the successes of her theatrical releases. That BBC and AMC coproduced the John le Carré adaptation, combined with its categorization as a thriller, underscores Bier's generic versatility and her willingness to experiment in varied production environments and media formats. Bier has also directed several popular, critically acclaimed films classified as comedies—most significantly, *The One and Only* and *Love Is All You Need* (*Den skaldede frisør*, 2012)—and her early successes can be best described as generic hybrids. As a primary example, her first feature film, *Freud's Leaving Home* (Freud flyttar hemifrån . . ., 1991) utilizes drama and comedy to tell a Swedish-Jewish woman's coming-of-age story.

The daughter of Jewish immigrants to Denmark, Bier was born in 1960 and raised in Copenhagen as part of a minority that did not seamlessly fit into mainstream Danish culture, the homogeneity of which, in cultural and ethnic terms, can be considered the flip side of its efficient economy. Bier initially studied religion at The Hebrew University of Jerusalem and architecture at Jerusalem's Bezalel Academy of Art and Design and then continued her studies at the Architectural Association in London (danskefilm.dk; Denmark. dk). Although her application to the National Film School of Denmark appears to depart from her previous studies, Bier regards her turn to filmmaking as a natural evolution of her interests, particularly in the relationship between set design and its psychological implications, which was a dynamic that motivated her architectural studies.[1] Her application to the notoriously selective film school was accepted based on a portfolio of photographs, which Bier describes as "mini-movies," including a love story composed of images taken at an "open-air swimming spot" near the Kastrup airport on the outskirts of Copenhagen.[2] The emphasis on the impact of location on characters' experiences is apparent across Bier's eclectic works, as is the attention to romantic love or, as Bier phrased it in an interview in 2001, "eroticism at all possible levels" (Hjort 2003). While casting a wide net to cover Bier's substantial filmography, we, along with the contributors, continually reiterate elements that create a portrait of Bier as a screen author compelled by coherent interests, which are visible in the generically and industrially varied experiments that constitute her oeuvre.

Bier has been making explicitly transnational films from the start of her career, well before film studies' "transnational turn" (Kuhn and Westwell 2012). Her first feature films—*Freud's Leaving Home* and *Family Matters* (*Det bli'r i familien*, 1993)—demonstrate her interest in transnational identities and in production scenarios that complement her work's attention to characters who construct their identities in geographies that exceed national borders. Freud's *Leaving Home* is a Swedish/Danish co-production centered on a Jewish family scattered across three continents (with family members based in Israel, the United States, and Sweden), while *Family Matters* is a Danish/Swedish/Portuguese co-production that deals with the protagonist's search for his biological parents, which takes him from Denmark to Portugal. These films establish a pattern in her work that is also evident in her more prominent, twenty-first-century films, such as *After the Wedding* and *Love Is All You Need*. In addition, her recent successes with international viewers—most notably via *The Night Manager*, which was shot in six countries and sold for broadcast in at least 188 countries—can be read as fulfilling Bier's career-long goal to reach a large audience through stories with transnational relevance (Hjort 2001). Meanwhile, the Jennifer Lawrence/Bradley Cooper-starring, critical and commercial dead weight *Serena* (2014) indicates that Bier's transnational sensibility and production preferences may not lend themselves to narratives that depend heavily on specific, local meanings that are foreign to her, or where her creative autonomy is impeded by multiple stakeholders' varied investments (as argued in Chapter 3 of this volume).

Bier has been remarkably prolific, particularly when compared to research that suggests women directors often encounter notable career gaps and produce fewer films than their male counterparts (see Badley, Perkins, and Schreiber 2016). Bier has proven exceptional in this respect, directing fifteen feature-length films, a TV movie (*Luischen*, 1993), and a television series (*The Night Manager*) in the three decades since her graduation film, *The Island of the Blessed* (*De saliges ø*, 1986) won first prize at the Munich International Festival of Film Schools. Factoring in her work in television, Bier has averaged nearly one major work every other year, which makes her the most prolific in the small cohort of internationally visible women directors helming big-budget productions in contemporary film and television.

Her willingness to work in various industrial milieus and across genres has clearly increased her productivity. After *The Island of the Blessed*, which is perhaps the most classically Danish film in her oeuvre, Bier worked for several years in Sweden (on the internationally co-produced features mentioned above). Her next Danish work, the DR television drama *Luischen*, was part of a series of Danish short story adaptations intended, according to Gunhild Agger, "to educate the audience" in fulfillment of "public service obligation[s]."[3] Two years later, she premiered another film set in Sweden, *Like It Never Was Before* (*Pensionat Oskar*, 1995), which charts a middle-aged family man's surprising and transformative affair with a younger man. Her next production, *Credo* (*Sekten*, 1997), set in Denmark and classified as a psychological thriller, is a career anomaly in generic terms and was, according to Bier, not entirely successful.[4] She capped a busy decade with two features—one set in Denmark (*The One and Only*) and the other in Sweden (*Once in a Lifetime* [*Livet är en schlager*, 2000]). Both are mainstream comedies: the former a blockbuster hit considered Bier's popular breakthrough, and the latter only moderately successful and to date Bier's last film set in Sweden.

While *The One and Only* broke box-office records and won the two most prestigious Danish film awards for best Danish film in 2000 (the Bodil and the Robert awards), Bier's next film, *Open Hearts* (*Elsker dig for evigt*, 2002), is considered her international breakthrough. This Dogme film was a major critical and commercial success that significantly increased Bier's international profile and earned her another set of Bodil and Robert awards for best Danish film (in 2003) as well as a FIPRESCI special mention at the Toronto International Film Festival. These successes precipitated the trilogy of high-profile, Danish-language dramas focused on masculinity and crisis and co-authored with Anders Thomas Jensen—*Brothers*, *After the Wedding*, and *In a Better World* (the second of these was nominated for an Academy Award for Best Foreign Language Film, and the third won the 2011 Academy Award in the same category). The success of *After the Wedding* caught Hollywood's attention, and Bier was invited to direct her first Hollywood English-language film, *Things We Lost in the Fire* (2007). *Things We Lost in the Fire* was released between the second and third film of the trilogy, and despite possessing a high-profile cast that included David Duchovny, Halle Berry, and Benicio del Toro, it failed to find a significant audience. After her Oscar win, for a Danish-English-language hybrid, Bier's *Love Is All You Need* (2012), which mixes Danish, English and Italian, was a modest box-office success that scored a handful of international and Danish prizes. Returning to Danish-language drama, Bier released *A Second Chance* (*En chance til*, 2014) in the same year *Serena* premiered; *A Second Chance* is undoubtedly Bier's least successful Danish language film of the twenty-first century. Thus, 2014 represented a commercial and critical low point in Bier's career, which was succeeded by another striking success, this time in high-budget, transnational television (*The Night Manager*).

Several patterns are apparent in this brief outline of Bier's career: she has alternated with apparent ease among Swedish, Danish, and "Hollywood" productions; she is comfortable working in comic and dramatic modes (and often blends the two); she has been able to secure financing from diverse sources and is open to directing productions set in a wide variety of locations and involving multiple languages; she maintains a high rate of productivity; she is peculiarly resistant to failure (or at least bounces back quickly from it), tending to succeed with a novel project in the wake of a less successful effort; and finally, she embraces generic and industrial risks while leaning on hard-won professional skills. This volume will continually highlight Bier's willingness to adapt strategies that have proven successful in past productions to new generic, narrative, and industrial ends, while underscoring her consistent goal of reaching large audiences with challenging material rendered in a seductive cinematic style.

Additionally, the chapters in this volume address elements of Bier's cinema that have not received sufficient critical attention, including Jewish and queer themes, her navigation of distinct media industries, her long-term creative collaborations—most notably with screenwriter Anders Thomas Jensen—and her early work produced in Sweden, all of which provide insights into the cinematic preoccupations that resonate in her prominent twenty-first-century films. Collectively, contributors frame this versatile director, whose work and public persona are difficult to codify, in the context of a fluid, competitive media environment that requires filmmakers to take advantage of emerging opportunities in early stages of their critical comprehension. Furthermore, the call across the field of media studies for greater attention to transnational cinematic elements affords opportunities to utilize novel critical lenses regarding the work of this idiosyncratic filmmaker, who identifies with the concerns of Jewish diasporic directors, is inspired by Hollywood more than European cinema, and has recently become a vocal advocate of women's screen authorship despite her sustained attention to masculinity on screen and her long-standing nonchalance regarding being a woman filmmaker in a male-dominated industry (Bier 2016).

Obviously, we are enthusiastic about Bier's screen authorship, yet the analyses in this volume are as attentive to challenging as they are to seductive elements of her work. Therefore, this filmmaker's tendency to foreground masculinity is a recurring subject of critical attention, particularly in chapters that deal directly with gender. On a related note, the sense that the term "melodrama," despite its high frequency in discourses involving Bier, obstructs the process of critically analyzing her work was pervasive while the volume took shape. Consequently, a critical stand against the usefulness of the term melodrama as applied to Bier's work has evolved through the process of authoring this collection. While this position is by no means relevant to every topic discussed in this volume, it nonetheless steers our editorial approach to establishing a foundation on which to build future work on Bier's complex authorship.

BIER'S MULTIFACETED AUTHORSHIP

Part One traces Bier's complicated maneuvers through independent, popular, and art cinemas, which involve ambiguous classificatory territories as she transitioned from nationally and regionally to globally targeted productions. The chapters stress that Bier's work often challenges generic categorization as a result of its innovations; therefore, the authors collectively emphasize the distinctive features of her work that have been consistently singled out for praise and censure. Because Bier's films are often referred to as melodramas yet are, in fact, generically diverse, the section parses the generic elements of her films and the way classification impacts her work's visibility, reception and cultural status in Denmark and abroad.

This section grapples with relevant complexities in its treatment of films that are narratively and industrially diverse. In "Storytelling Schemes, Realism, and Ambiguity: Susanne Bier's Danish Dramas," Birger Langkjær connects Bier's approach to genre with Danish cinema's gradual shift, apparent since the 1990s, from realism and folk comedy to mainstream genres with greater international appeal. Langkjær suggests that Bier's romantic comedies and dramas evidence this broader shift, which he locates in a preference for "tight narrative structures" observable in Danish cinema during the last several decades. In Chapter 2, "Negotiating Special Relationships: Susanne Bier's Comedies," Gunhild Agger highlights Bier's directorial range by analyzing her comedies, which, Agger argues, borrow from and innovate characteristics derived from distinct romantic comedy traditions. Finally, Chapter 3, Missy Molloy's "Susanne Bier's Hollywood Experiments: *Things We Lost in the Fire* and *Serena*," looks into the production contexts and results of Bier's "Hollywood" films, stressing their capacity to illuminate the strengths and limitations of Bier's direction.

The chapters in Part Two foreground issues related to identity on and off screen. Despite Bier's reluctance to discuss such issues—barring the profound impact of her Jewish heritage on her worldview—her films' receptions are nonetheless impacted by the fact that she is a Jewish woman from Denmark, a small country with a strong film culture that is known for unusual cultural perspectives on gender and sexuality. Therefore, the chapters in this part spotlight aspects of her identity that inform Bier's approach to storytelling and address her public persona, status in Danish and international film communities, and on-screen treatments of marginalized social groups.

Chapter 4, Maureen Turim's "Beginning with Jewish Survival: *Freud's Leaving Home*," closely analyzes the complex references to Jewish heritage in Bier's first feature-length film and situates them in the context of contemporaneous films that feature diasporic Jewish families in cultural transition. In "Stories with Queer Identities," Chapter 5, Anders Marklund analyzes representations of queer characters in *Like It Never Was Before*, *Once in a Lifetime*, *Love Is All You Need*, and *The Night Manager*, concluding that Bier's transition from modest to big-budget, mainstream filmmaking has resulted in less nuanced, more stereotypical queer characters. In Chapter 6, Pétur Valsson's "The Case of Lars von Trier vs. Susanne Bier," von Trier's controversial remarks about Judaism and Bier motivate Valsson's comparison of the directors' divergent cinematic approaches to Jewish characters and culture in their films. Finally, Mette Hjort's "Gender Equity in Screen Culture: On Susanne Bier, the Celluloid Ceiling, and the Growing Appeal of TV Production" reflects on Bier's shifting responses to the challenges posed by both her gender and nationality and connects them to broader conversations in film and television studies.

Part Three examines issues of aesthetics and agency within Bier's oeuvre. The *Historical Dictionary of Scandinavian Cinema*'s entry on Bier reads: "She is known for emotional dramas 'with a visual rawness' and for her ability to bring out strong and sensitive performances from her actors" (see Sundholm et al. 2012: 78). Leaning heavily on frequent, tightly framed close-ups, Bier's aesthetic utilizes the camera's gaze to explore subtle components of her characters' experiences. Her ability to incite empathy for characters in extreme situations facilitates readings of her films' complex ethics, which this section fleshes out in close readings of particular films as well as in broader discussions of the narrative and stylistic gestures that cohere her works. Thus, contributors pinpoint Bier's signature visual and narrative tendencies, while additionally foregrounding the affective dimensions of Bier's aesthetic and its stylistic anomalies.

Mimi Nielsen's "Tracing Affect in Susanna Bier's Dramas," Chapter 8, straddles questions of genre and classification, as found in this anthology's first chapters, and those pertaining to aesthetics and authorship. Nielsen, in support of her dual argument that Bier's films evidence a preoccupation with "affect-as-intensity," as it moves "across and through bodies, especially male bodies," draws from four feature films that span much of Bier's directorial career. In Chapter 9, "Vision and Ethics in *A Second Chance* (*En chance til*)," Danica van de Velde establishes *A Second Chance* as a particularly poignant example of how Bier's work forefronts the "intertwining of image and psychology." Van de Velde suggests that Bier's approach functions as "a visual strategy that, among other things, highlights the dynamic between spectatorship and ethics," thereby evoking a critical stance that questions the reliability of the image. The final chapter in the third section, Eva Novrup Redvall's "The Truth is in the Eyes: Susanne Bier's Use of Close-ups in *The Night Manager*," analyzes Bier's recent and extremely successful foray into serial television drama, taking extensive note of Bier's use of close-ups as a means to "explore character depth and the spaces between utterances." Redvall applies theoretical discourses on the close-up and studies of Bier's stylistic traits in previous work, as she reflects on the "remarkable array" of eyes and the close-ups of objects in *The Night Manager*.

The fourth and final part of this collection features the global nature and transnational reach of Bier's film practices and reception. Bier's work outlines useful strategies for circumventing limitations related to gender and nationality, and demonstrates opportunities for screen authors willing to take risks in competitive, global media environments in states of flux. This section investigates Bier's work and its industrial connotations through various theoretical frames related to scale. In Chapter 11, Belinda Smaill employs a feminist lens to situate women filmmakers within a wider "world cinema" context in which women's cinema illustrates distinct views on resources, space, and mobility. Smaill focuses on *Serena* to comment on Bier's unique position in transnational women's cinema. In Chapter 12, "From Local to Global: The Bier/Jensen Screenwriting Collaboration," Cath Moore draws attention to the unique Danish co-writing process that most Danish directors employ in which a director and screenwriter collaborate on scripts and share writing credit. Bier's most successful films have been co-written with Anders Thomas Jensen; with a focus on the Bier/Jensen trilogy, Moore delineates the creative divergences between Bier's solo work and Jensen's dark satirical and absurdist self-written and directed films. In the final chapter of this collection, "Danish Privilege and Responsibility in the Work of Susanne Bier," Meryl Shriver-Rice situates the Bier/Jensen trilogy within a wider trend of contemporary Scandinavian narratives of guilt, examining postcolonial criticism to argue that the trilogy stresses the failures of employing universal moral systems in different socio-cultural contexts.

Our interview with Susanne Bier in November 2016 functions as the volume's postscript; it foregrounds the topics covered in the volume and touches on provocative readings of her films advanced by contributors. Because of the timing of the interview, contributors—other than the editors—did not have access to it as they wrote their chapters. Therefore, Bier's responses provide material for future discussion, particularly in the overlaps they reveal between contributors' interests and Bier's. Finally, and crucially, the interview includes Bier's thoughts on many issues addressed in the volume, thus inviting the director to collaborate on this first major push to lay down a critical foundation for understanding her as a significant screen author who, we predict, will inspire substantial critical attention in the future—perhaps in response to interpretive threads the analyses included herein no doubt leave hanging.

NOTES

1. Bier suggested as much in our interview with her in November 2016, which functions as the final chapter of this volume.
2. This statement is based on the same interview.
3. Gunhild Agger provided her recollections regarding *Luischen* via email on June 7, 2017.
4. This statement is also based on a comment Bier made during our interview with her in Copenhagen in November 2016.

BIBLIOGRAPHY

Badley, Linda, Claire Perkins, and Michele Schreiber, eds. (2016), *Indie Reframed: Women's Filmmaking and Contemporary American Independent Cinema*, Edinburgh: Edinburgh University Press.

Bier, Susanne (2017), "TV is opening the door to female directors—film needs to catch up," <https://www.theguardian.com/commentisfree/2016/mar/05/tv-film-female-directors-susanne-bier-the-night-manager-le-carre> (accessed November 14, 2017).

Bondebjerg, Ib (2003), "Dogme 95 and the New Danish Cinema," in Mette Hjort and Scott Mackenzie (eds.), *Purity and Provocation: Dogme 95*, London: British Film Institute, pp. 70–85.

Hjort, Mette (2003), "Dogme 95: A Small Nation's Response to Globalization," in Mette Hjort and Scott Mackenzie (eds.), *Purity and Provocation: Dogme 95*, London: British Film Institute, pp. 31–47.

Hjort, Mette (2005), *Small Nation, Global Cinema: The New Danish Cinema*, vol. 15, Minneapolis: University of Minnesota Press.

Hjort, Mette (2011), *Lone Scherfig's* Italian for Beginners, Seattle: University of Washington Press.

Hjort, Mette, and Ib Bondebjerg, eds. (2003), *The Danish Directors: Dialogues on a Contemporary National Cinema*, Bristol and Chicago: Intellect Books.

Hjort, Mette, and Duncan Petrie, eds. (2007), *Cinema of Small Nations*, Edinburgh: Edinburgh University Press.

Kuhn, Annette, and Guy Westwell (2012), *A Dictionary of Film Studies*, Oxford: Oxford University Press.

Redvall, Eva Novrup (2010), "Teaching Screenwriting in a Time of Storytelling Blindness: The Meeting of the Auteur and the Screenwriting Tradition in Danish Film-making,' *Journal of Screenwriting* vol. 1, no. 1: 59–81.

Schepelern, Peter (2006), "The American Connection: Inspiration and Ambition in the New Danish Cinema," in Højbjerg, Lennard and Henrik Søndergaard (eds.), *European Film and Media Culture*, Vol. 4, Copenhagen: Museum Tusculanum Press.

Shriver-Rice, Meryl (2015), *Inclusion in New Danish Cinema: Sexuality and Transnational Belonging*, Bristol and Chicago: Intellect Books.

Smaill, Belinda (2014), "The Male Sojourner, the Female Director, and Popular European Cinema: The Worlds of Susanne Bier," *Camera Obscura* vol. 29, no. 1, 85: 5–31.

Stevenson, Jack, (2003), *Dogme Uncut: Lars Von Trier, Thomas Vinterberg, and the Gang That Took on Hollywood*, Santa Monica: Santa Monica Press.

Sundholm, John, et al. (2012), "Historical Dictionary of Scandinavian Cinema," *Historical Dictionaries of Literature and the Arts*, Lanham, MD: Scarecrow Press.

Sundholm, J., I. Thorsen, L. G. Andersson, O. Hedling, G. Iversen, and B. T. Møller (2012), *Historical Dictionary of Scandinavian Cinema*, Lanham, MD: Scarecrow Press.

"Susanne Bier," Denmark.DK: The Official Website of Denmark <http://denmark.dk/en/meet-the-danes/great-danes/film-makers/susanne-bier> (accessed November 14, 2017).

"Susanne Bier," Danskefilm.dk. <https://danskefilm.dk/skuespiller.php?id=11587> (accessed November 14, 2017).

PART I

Generic and Industrial Fluidity

Part 1 Introduction

Bier's generic flexibility is striking. It has allowed her to be successful in multiple genres and to combine generic elements in a way that constitutes one of her authorial signatures: the integration of extremely dramatic scenarios with a close attention to character psychology that is inflected with irony and humor. Moreover, the qualities associated with the two genres Bier is known for—drama and romantic comedy—often overlap in her individual works. For example, her first feature, *Freud's Leaving Home* (*Freud flyttar hemifrån . . .*, 1991), is an often comical treatment of a tragic circumstance, in which a family confronts the impending death of its matriarch, Rosha, while gathered to celebrate her sixtieth birthday; in addition, the film foregrounds the youngest daughter's delayed coming of age and cultivation of a first love affair. Meanwhile, *Love Is All You Need* (*Den skaldede frisør*, 2012) is classified as a romantic comedy, yet deals with the radical life changes Ida initiates while in limbo between breast cancer treatment and results, which include leaving her husband of more than twenty years and falling in love.

Romantic and erotic undercurrents are conspicuous elements of Bier's storytelling regardless of generic classification, as is sensitivity to human vulnerability and absurdity, which generates humor in situations that might lend themselves more easily to drama. The chapters in this section grapple with relevant complexities in their discussions of films with diverse generic, narrative, and industrial elements. Their arguments underscore the productive potential of questions related to genre while providing multiple frames for understanding Bier's generic mobility, as well as its impact on efforts to construct a coherent portrait of Bier as a screen author.

In "Storytelling Schemes, Realism, and Ambiguity: Susanne Bier's Danish Dramas," Birger Langkjær connects Bier's approach to genre with Danish cinema's gradual shift, apparent since the 1990s, from realism and folk comedy to mainstream genres with greater international appeal. Langkjær suggests that Bier's romantic comedies and dramas evidence this broader shift, which he locates in a preference for the "tight narrative structures" observable in Danish cinema during the last several decades. Langkjær narrows his focus to Bier's dramas, including *Open Hearts* (*Elsker dig for evigt*, 2002), *Brothers* (*Brødre*, 2004), *After the Wedding* (*Efter brylluppet*, 2006), and *In a Better World* (*Hævnen*, 2010), which have attracted significant international attention and praise, while also provoking criticism, particularly of their melodramatic and/ or 'schematic' properties. Langkjær scrutinizes such criticism by examining the narrative structures of Bier's dramas in relation to art and realism. He specifically highlights the tension between "the macro-structures of melodramatic story-telling and film realism" and the films' evocations of "a psychological intimacy with [their] characters and the trivialities" of their everyday lives. It is precisely this tension, he concludes, that distinguishes Bier's dramas from traditional Danish realism and the formulas conventionally associated with melodrama.

In "Negotiating Special Relationships: Susanne Bier's Comedies," Gunhild Agger highlights the diversity of Bier's films by analyzing her comedies, which, Agger argues, borrow from and innovate characteristics derived from distinct romantic comedy traditions. Agger reads Bier's *The One and Only* (*Den eneste ene*, 1999) as a modern take on a template established by classical Hollywood films. Meanwhile, Agger connects *Love Is All You Need* to trends in romantic comedy that are visible in more recent British and American films, most notably *Four Weddings and a Funeral* (1994), which inspired a number of transatlantic co-productions targeting the massive audience it attracted. In outlining key features of these films, Agger highlights that *Love Is All You Need* is significantly more cross-cultural and transnational than *The One and Only* and explicitly utilizes formal and narrative devices to cite its American and British predecessors. She also stresses that while the film is mainly in Danish, it includes aspects of English and Italian languages and cultures as part of its appeal to transnational spectators.

In the section's final chapter, "Susanne Bier's Hollywood Experiments: *Things We Lost in the Fire* and *Serena*," Missy Molloy explores the lackluster responses to Bier's first English-language productions, often referred to as her "Hollywood films." Molloy surveys a variety of sources related to the films' productions and receptions to reveal the challenges Bier faced transitioning to new production contexts. This chapter proposes that, while the films demonstrate Bier's willingness to experiment with unfamiliar genres and production conditions, they also reaffirm her attractions to specific cinematic subjects, images, and narrative scenarios. Thus, these less successful films provide information relevant to the project of tracing Bier's authorial influence across a body of extremely varied works. Furthermore, the fact that her authorial influence was somewhat muted in her first 'Hollywood' films—due to her signing on late in pre-production, as well as complications that arose during post-production— indicates that in Bier's case, early involvement allows her to affect the characters and narratives to the extent that they reflect career-long preoccupations, which manifested in *Things We Lost in the Fire* and *Serena* to a degree that didn't significantly appeal to either her domestic or international audience. The chapter complements Langkjær's and Agger's attentions to more successful films by highlighting that Bier's approach to genre is expansive, even when it does not produce desirable results. Molloy concludes that less effective elements of Bier's cinematic strategies are results, at least partly, of bad timing. She further argues that reception prejudices played a role in *Things We Lost in the Fire* and *Serena*'s failures to land with audiences.

CHAPTER 1

Storytelling Schemes, Realism, and Ambiguity: Susanne Bier's Danish Dramas

Birger Langkjær

Susanne Bier is part of a movement in New Danish Cinema beginning in the 1990s that explored genres other than popular folk comedy and engaged with realism and art films, transforming traditionally episodic narratives into a tight dramaturgical form. In this historical context, Bier made a modern and very popular comedy, *The One and Only* (*Den eneste ene*, 1999); she embraced central elements of realist art films with *Open Hearts* (*Elsker dig for evigt*, 2002); and she made a potent drama with melodramatic features, *Brothers* (*Brødre*, 2004). As such, she epitomizes this movement in Danish cinema towards tight narrative structures across several genres and modes. A surprising number of these films have travelled across borders due to a combination of their generic and narrative features and national peculiarities making them comprehensible yet evocatively different to an international audience.

This chapter will focus on five of Bier's Danish dramas. In this context, 'drama' is broadly defined as films about intimate relations in conflict presented in a serious or mainly non-comic manner.[1] Even though her dramas have been successful with audiences and have received a series of nominations and awards, it is not unusual to find critiques of these films that scorn their schematic structure (Sklar 2011) or mock them as "compassion porn" (Taylor 2011). Whether or not one agrees with such judgments, there is no doubt that Bier strives to maximize contrasts and character dilemmas in order to enhance the emotional impact on audiences. This has placed her films within the categories of the melodramatic and the popular. Yet the schematics of the narrative macrostructure such as sudden reversals, unsolvable dilemmas, stark contrasts, and extraordinary moral challenges combine—as I will demonstrate—with realism and art film.

Therefore, Bier's dramas are not melodramas only. Films such as *Open*

Hearts, Brothers, After the Wedding (*Efter brylluppet*, 2006), *In a Better World* (*Hævnen*, 2010), and *A Second Chance* (*En chance til*, 2014) sustain a particular tension between the macrostructures of melodramatic storytelling and a realism anchored in a psychological intimacy with characters and the trivialities of family life. Furthermore, these interactions between melodrama and realism are systematically embedded within an ambiguously subjective as well as a "supra-diegetic" level that belong to an art film mode. As such, Bier's dramas are structured within a triangle of melodrama, realism, and art film, a combination of filmic modes that may explain the variety of critical receptions.

MELODRAMATIC STORYTELLING AND STYLE

Louise Kidde Sauntved rightly points out how, in the Dogme 95 film *Open Hearts*, Bier, in collaboration with scriptwriter Anders Thomas Jensen, "developed a virtual formula for storytelling: she establishes an idyllic world full of love and security and then, seemingly out of nowhere, disaster strikes, shattering the worlds of all involved. Lives are put on hold while characters try to cope with overpowering feelings" (Sauntved 2011: 26). This reversal of fortunes through sudden disaster is a classic melodramatic formula, as is the emphasis on "overpowering" emotions. The "sudden impact" (the title of Sauntved's article) can strike in different forms: being paralyzed in a traffic accident (*Open Hearts*), being shot down in a helicopter (*Brothers*), being diagnosed with terminal cancer (*After the Wedding*), or finding your newborn baby dead (*Another Chance*). *In a Better World* varies this formula: personal decisions (infidelity, violent acts, and indirect involvement in a killing) prompt the reversal of fortunes, rather than something happening to the character outside their control.

These disasters (or disastrous acts) seriously affect the central characters and their close relations. They suddenly face dilemmas that can be paraphrased in terms of questions: can an honest love relationship be sustained while one party has terminal cancer or is bound to a hospital bed for the rest of his life? Can a man who has killed or has committed other ethically compromising actions integrate the knowledge of what he has done and live a normal life? The conflicts that result from these sudden changes in circumstances are mostly inner conflicts. For example, Meryl Shriver-Rice writes that Michael, the older brother in *Brothers*, is "struggling to come to terms with his own actions" (Shriver-Rice 2009: 16). That is, his ethical struggle results more in introverted suffering than outright action. To a large extent, these films are "male melodramas" (Smaill 2014: 13) because Bier's narratives tend to focus on guilt-ridden men who face dilemmas. The combination of sudden disasters and the moral and emotional dilemmas that follow creates the kind of heightened emotionalism that has often been associated with melodrama (Elsaesser 1985/1972; Neale 2000: 179–204; Singer 2001; Langford 2005: 30-42).

These epic and emotional reversals and dilemmas are further enhanced by strong contrasts, especially those between places, characters, and dramatic situations. Despite being films about Danish and, sometimes, Swedish characters, *Brothers*, *After the Wedding*, and *In a Better World* open in faraway places—Afghanistan, India, or somewhere in Africa. By contrasting two major locations, the films introduce a close "here" and a distant "there." Whereas the familiar "here" and the exotic "there" are often established through signposted geographic and cultural markers, *A Second Chance* establishes its two spaces through social markers.[2] Moreover, characters are contrasted: the bullied Elias with the hard-hitting Christian in *A Better World*; the duty-bound big brother with the slacker little brother in *Brothers*; the rich, goal-driven patriarch with the failed idealist in *After the Wedding*; the impassioned Cæcilie to the hateful Joachim in *Open Hearts*; and the altruistic policeman Andreas to the self-centered junkie Tristan in *A Second Chance*. Finally, dramatic situations often carry strong contrasts in emotional tone and dramatic implications. A wedding's happy promise for the couple's future is contrasted with the lost father/unknown daughter reunion theme in *After the Wedding*, and two lovers' routine "see you" precedes a fatal accident within the same scene in *Open Hearts*.

Moreover, contrasts may not only be between elements within the three categories mentioned. They can also be between categories. For example, the contrast between character and place can be underlined by music that does not fit with the scene. In *After the Wedding*, a female hotel clerk with no sign of human warmth routinely shows Jacob the rooms and features of his luxury hotel apartment. The soundtrack lingers on Indian musical elements in reference to what Jacob, apparently temporarily, has left behind, emphasizing that he feels like a stranger in the clean minimalism of the hotel, which the dark-gray color scheme governing the filming of the scene further underlines. This music is also heard when Jacob arrives (too late) for the wedding, once more emphasizing his estranged position.

Bier's emphasis on similarities further enhances these three forms of contrast: place, character, and dramatic situation. When Michael's helicopter is shot down and hits the water in *Brothers*, there is a cut to his wife, Sarah, in a bathtub. The difference in situation (Michael facing death, his wife relaxing in the bathtub) is emphasized; yet the edit connects the two scenes, implying that they are somehow causally connected, and foreshadows the crash's impact on Sarah. Moreover, the water and dusk motifs as well as the silence connect the scenes. This technique is emblematic of Bier's maximization of similarity and difference, analogy and contrast, between two adjacent scenes.

These narrative and stylistic features are excessive in their insistence on a hidden meaning in a manner described by Elsaesser (1985/1972) and Brooks (1995/1974) as reflecting melodrama's conception of the world as a Manichean contrast between good and evil. In what follows I will argue that this melodramatic macrostructure of narrative form and style in Bier's dramas combines with recurrent micro-level depictions of the everyday and a psychological realism on the level of characters and their interactions in ways that complicate Manichean concepts of right and wrong.

ORDINARY PEOPLE IN EXTRAORDINARY SITUATIONS: A TENSION BETWEEN REALISM AND MELODRAMA

Belinda Smaill notes that "Bier's films consistently focus on the psychodynamics of family" (Smaill 2014: 9). Many of Bier's characters are ordinary people leading ordinary lives, involved in common social settings such as homes, schools, and workplaces; or they are misfits, like the confrontational younger brother Jannik in *Brothers* and Jacob in *After the Wedding*, who appears hostile to anything connected with his native Denmark (Figure 1.1). In either case, there is nothing extraordinary about most of her characters. What is extraordinary is the kind of challenges they meet: having your fiancé paralyzed in a traffic accident, being forced to kill somebody, or facing death. The films combine the complexity of psychological realism at the level of character with the extremes of melodrama at the level of plot and dramaturgy.

Figure 1.1 Facing death and keeping it a secret. Jörgen (Rolf Lassgård) and Jacob (Mads Mikkelsen) in *Efter brylluppet/After the Wedding* (2006).

There is a long critical tradition of connecting realism not only with a mimetic relation to the world (Aristotle 1996; Auerbach 1957) but also to a mimesis of the everyday; realism is concerned with the ordinary rather than the spectacular. Northrup Frye distinguishes between high mimetic genres such as tragedies about noblemen and low mimetic genres about ordinary men (Frye 1957: 33–70). Within film criticism and theory, André Bazin has written the most influential essays on realism (especially Italian neorealism), in which he emphasizes the ordinariness of the characters and their problems (Bazin 1971). The films depict non-spectacular stories that, like *The Bicycle Thief* (1948), do not have enough material "even for a news item: the whole story would not deserve two lines in a stray-dog column" (Bazin 1971: 50).

In Danish cinema, there is a long tradition from the 1940s until today of social and psychological realism (Langkjær 2002) that depicts ordinary people in dramas elevated from everyday situations. In psychological realism, the conflicts have to do with lovers, friends, and families. In social realism, the conflicts have to do with institutions or different forms of social circumstances such as alcoholism, neglect, and poverty (see Langkjær 2012). In a sense, the National Danish Film School transformed the mimetic intent of these forms of realism into a particular formula, which teaches "the natural story" (Philipsen 2005a). This refers to stories that take ordinary events as their point of departure—most outrageously, a birthday party in *The Celebration* (*Festen*, 1998)—or use environments that involve routines and habitual actions, what early cognitive theories called "scripts" (Schank and Abelson 1977). Scripts are what we usually do in certain kinds of situations, such as going to a restaurant, giving a gift, or introducing someone. Obviously, dramatizing such "scripts" provides recognizable situations to which audiences can relate.

Bier's dramas are full of such depictions of the ordinary: families or friends around dinner tables, kids going to school or playing with other kids, parents doing their job or seeing friends. Many conflicts are played out within or on the edge of these scripted everyday routines, and they usually involve people lying to themselves or others. As the sociologist Erwin Goffman pointed out, most people are not only keen to control how they appear to others in social settings, they also regularly lie (Goffman 1959). Thus, pretending and, sometimes, lying are what social agents do—that is, it is part of the ordinary. However, in Bier's dramas, lying is a way of coping with a fundamental dilemma that results in feelings of shame and guilt. The denial or lie comes at great cost, and contaminates the person's idea about himself or herself. This contamination is enhanced by the idealism of the characters. They do humanitarian work in *After the Wedding* and *In a Better World*, or they are protective of others' welfare and/or the social order such as doctors, soldiers, and policemen in *Open Hearts*, *Brothers*, and *A Second Chance*. The main characters do not only lie about facts that are socially unacceptable, for instance cheating on loved ones, or are decisively fatal, such as having killed someone or having a deadly disease, but the fissure between front-stage social performance and what is denied and kept backstage results in extreme situations. In *Brothers*, for example, Michael is the morally straight father, husband, and soldier who ends up lying about the fact that he was forced to kill a fellow soldier to save his own life when imprisoned in Afghanistan (probably by Taliban forces). He lies to the military authorities, to his own wife, and to the widow of the man he killed. His bad conscience even drives him to visit the widow, who is now left alone with a small baby. He gives her false hope by telling her that he has seen her husband. He pretends to engage in an honorable social role, emotionally participating in someone else's mourning—yet, due to his previous acts and his omission of the central facts (his lies), it is a painful pretense.

The motif of lying replicates a script from everyday interactions and anchors the drama in the ordinary. One might object that lies are default motifs in many genres—for example, crime fiction and comedies. Nevertheless, most genre films focus on instrumental lies: the criminal wants to hide his identity and/or his crime; in comedy, the lie involves a scheme—for example, when two men disguise themselves as women in order to get a job and escape some criminals in Billy Wilder's *Some Like It Hot* (1959). In Bier's dramas, however, characters lie because their self-identity is being challenged. Lying does not serve an instrumental purpose in the outer worl,d but hides an inner conflict between ideals and actual deeds. Lying is giving oneself time to cope with something at an existential crossroad. As such, psychology does not only motivate character actions but becomes a study in its own right. This adds aspects of psychological realism to Bier's narratives and anchors the characters and their otherwise spectacular stories in an ordinary world. In this way her dramas combine familiar situations to which the audience can relate with excessive dramatization and conflict that pushes her characters out of the ordinary and into an existential void.

SUPERSIZING THE ORDINARY: DILEMMAS, TRAUMA, AND THE THEME OF VULNERABILITY

> Anton: "I will show the kids that I am not afraid of you, that you cannot do me any harm."
> Lars: "But that is exactly what I can do. I can seriously harm you."

This exchange from *In a Better World* takes place just before the violent car mechanic, Lars, hits Anton in the face in front of his kids. The idealistic Anton, a doctor and humanitarian aid worker, has brought his kids with him to demonstrate that there is no need to be afraid of Lars. But there are certainly reasons to fear what some people are capable of doing to you and your loved ones, and to also fear what such experiences in and of themselves will do to you. As the story progresses, Anton's son and his best friend decide to take revenge by detonating a bomb under the mechanic's car. Anton himself, passively but decisively, allows a crowd of people in Africa to kill a man in revenge. These shifts from ordinary family life to extraordinary events and actions create dilemmas and provoke characters to act in ways that are incommensurable with their ideas about themselves, which results in trauma for the male protagonists, and by extension their loved ones. With reference to *Brothers*, Gorm Larsen writes that, if the characters "act evil, then it is not because they are evil but because they do not possess the power to do the right thing" (Larsen 2010: 3, my translation). This narrative form demonstrates the central theme or implied meaning[3] in Bier's melodramas: human beings are vulnerable.

According to Thomas Fuchs (2013), trauma arises from experiencing a limit situation such as, for example, death, disease, or loss, which evaporates the everydayness of the world. Traumatic events have fundamental implications for people because they are incongruent with their personal story: "The trauma becomes a singularity; it produces a radical discontinuity of the inner life story, i.e. of the subjectivity construed as a narrative" (Fuchs 2013: 4). It is because of trauma's "radical discontinuity" that Bier's male characters often appear psychologically paralyzed. The event, such as a death or a traumatic injury, creates a present that the character cannot integrate with his prior self-concept, that is, his self-narrative.

Therefore, it is not surprising that Bier's dramas do not have straightforward happy endings. *Open Hearts* ends on a bittersweet note, with no reconciliation of lovers or broken families in sight. This open ending ties it closer to a realist art film tradition than other films by Bier. That said, in the end, most characters in Bier's films will forgive each other, and themselves, as well. In *Brothers*, Michael's denial of what happened in Afghanistan finally results in his violent nervous breakdown and imprisonment; yet his wife's ultimatum, "If you do not tell me about it, then you will never see me again!" makes him confess (Figure 1.2); in *After the Wedding*, the death of the patriarch, Jörgen, and the family's mourning compel Jacob to wrap things up in India and join his new family in Denmark, which is a moderately positive ending; in *In a Better World*, sons, parents, and best friends are reunited; in *A Second Chance*, the protagonist is all by himself, but is somehow redeemed because the baby that he once stole as a substitute for his own dead baby appears to have developed into a healthy child. Even though the characters are being upended by traumatic events and react by denial and lying, they ultimately accept and admit to themselves and others what has happened. Their final reconciliation with their loved ones is not a straightforward happy ending but appears as a

Figure 1.2 The motif of lying, the vulnerable human, and the open ending. Michael (Ulrich Thomsen) about to confess to his wife Sarah (Connie Nielsen) in *Brødre / Brothers* (2004).

new beginning, yet on very different terms and in ways not fully explicated by the plot.[4]

These stories grow out of realistic everyday situations, and are mostly grounded in recognizable "scripts" of everyday life. The family is the central but destabilized unit; and in this respect Bier, through her depiction of intimate relations within families, including marital and parent-child conflicts, carries on the tradition of psychological realism in Danish cinema. This ordinary world is challenged by extraordinary events. In this way, there is a contrast between a macro-level of melodramatic storytelling and a micro-level of psychological intimacy with characters; yet they also mutually inflect each other. Whereas the classical melodrama seeks "moral and emotional truths" (Williams 1998: 42), the sudden disasters in Bier's drama suspend any pre-given ideas about what or who is evidently right or wrong. Also, Bier's characters are more complex than in classical melodrama and often more indecisive, but her narratives are more strongly fueled by major negative events to which the character needs to act than is the case within the tradition of psychological realism. In these ways, melodrama and psychological realism interact and modulate each other. I will now turn to a third element in Bier's films, their art film imagery.

OPEN HEARTS AS AN EARLY PROTOTYPE: SUBJECTIVE INTIMACY AND AMBIGUITY

Bier's Dogme 95 film *Open Hearts* not only introduced storytelling schemes along melodramatic lines, but also combined a series of art film features that would again show up in her later films. Several critics have pointed out these stylistic features in Bier's films (Shriver-Rice 2009: 17; Sauntved 2011: 25; Marklund 2012: 80; Smaill 2014: 12). *Open Hearts* depicts actions that are inconsistent with the rules otherwise governing the film's fictional world. For example, after Cæcilie turns out the lights in the hospital room, she lies down and looks at her paralyzed fiancé, Joachim. Music begins, and three blurred shots follow: one of Joachim, another of her, and a third of Joachim, who slowly turns his head and looks towards her. The action in these shots is inconsistent with the fictional world that the film has previously established: it is intercut since the shots are juxtaposed with the normally lit shots that are without music, and in which Joachim is paralyzed. The question is: how do we explain the apparent co-existence of two realities? Is it Cæcilie who is imagining a smiling Joachim? Are these Joachim's mental images? Or is it that these incongruent shots have nothing to do with any of the characters' wishful thinking? Are they instead an authorial interruption, intended to make the emotions of the characters visible to us, to then brutally contrast them with the reality of the fictional world?

This technique of using shots that are inconsistent with the film's fictional world results in ambiguity about whether they represent an objective, subjective, or authorial form of narration. According to David Bordwell (1988/85), such ambiguity characterizes the art film as a mode of narration. While classic narration, including melodrama, creates a consistent fictional world in which style is always in the service of making the plot clear to the audience, the art film typically deploys elaborate stylistic patterns with no straightforward narrative purpose. It is not clear whether art films depict the fictional world objectively, subjectively through a character, or in the form of some authorial comment: "In short, a realistic aesthetic and an expressionist aesthetic are hard to merge. The art cinema seeks to solve the problem in a sophisticated way: through ambiguity" (Bordwell 1988/85: 212).

There are indications in later scenes that the alternative reality is anchored in a particular mind. For example, Niels offers Cæcilie an apple in the hospital's cantina. While they both eat, he looks at her, and two grainy shots follow: one super-close-up of her mouth, another of one of her eyes. By adopting a point-object/point-glance editing pattern (Carroll 1998: 283–8) that moves between shots of someone looking and someone or something being looked at, the scene seems to denote something subjective and connected to the doctor's experience of Cæcilie. Yet the shots are not necessarily seen from his angle, and their extreme close-up is much more intimate than is implied by the situation: two people in a public place who do not know each other very well. The device may or may not be motivated in part by character or situation, but the reality status (objective, subjective, authorial) remains unclear.

Figures 1.3–1.5 A sequence of shots in which the third shot (bottom) disrupts the style of previous shots and creates an ambiguity as to what motivates this deviation. Cæcilie (Sonja Richter) and Niels (Mads Mikkelsen) in *Elsker dig for evigt/Open Hearts* (2002).

In later films, the extreme close-up is frequently aligned with the subjective view of the characters. In *After the Wedding*, the bride praises her parents during her wedding toast for their honesty in telling her that her dad, Jörgen, is not her biological father. This scene is accompanied by extreme close-ups of her parents, Jörgen and Helene, and of her biological father, Jacob, of a mouth or a single eye. In this way, extreme close-ups of facial parts are used to enhance an emotional intensity connected to the subjective experience of the central characters. Furthermore, intimacy with another person despite physical distance is often implied. In *Brothers*, for example, an extreme close-up of Michael's wife's mouth, while she is in Denmark, is followed by a straight cut to an extreme close-up of Michael's eye, at a point when he is still in Afghanistan. In these cases, the intimate shots and the editing may indicate objective causality, express subjective distortions, or present as authorial interventions. As such, they create a formal ambiguity concerning the narrative premises, that is, the perceptual mode of an art film.

SUPRA-DIEGETIC MOTIFS BALANCING MELODRAMA AND ART FILM

Scholars and critics differ in how they categorize Bier's dramas. Smaill points out that "Bier's films, their critical reception, and her director's statements frequently indicate a position between the worlds of art cinema and popular cinema" (Smaill 2014: 11), but that this has also "led to divergent perceptions of her cinema as largely mainstream in a local European context and as European arthouse cinema in English-speaking cultures" (Smaill 2014: 12). Gunhild Agger (2015) also seems to place Bier within this dualism of mainstream versus art film, whereas, with reference to *Brothers*, Meryl Shriver-Rice emphasizes "Bier's Nordic art-film style" (Shriver-Rice 2009: 17). Heidi Philipsen situates *Brothers* and New Danish cinema within a "combination of realism and genre experiments" (Philipsen 2005b, my translation), and Sauntved states that it "is exactly this mix of events bordering on the melodramatic and quotidian settings that is a Bier trademark" (Sauntved 2011: 26). In other words, there is some indeterminacy about which of three categories to pick: mainstream genres, art film, or realism. I have complicated a dualistic approach to categorizing Bier's dramas by suggesting that she uses all three modes as structural components in her dramas. In this last subsection, I will address her use of "supra-diegetic" depictions as part of an art film narrative strategy and as something that interlocks the modes of art film and melodrama.

In *In a Better World*, one scene depicts the doctor, Anton, jumping into the water to calm his mind. A close-up of his face in the water slowly, very slowly, dissolves into a shot of the sky above. The scene is accompanied by ambient

Figures 1.6 and 1.7 Visual layering: A slow dissolve from Anton to sky (upper) and Anton looking through the mirror plane that reflects the sky (lower). Mikael Persbrandt as Anton in *Hævnen/In a Better World* (2010).

music that adds to the flowing, ethereal quality. The slowness of the dissolve results in a visual layering or simultaneity of human face and sky. Later, Anton is seen looking at the sea through a window, a shot that layers his image with the reflections of the sky in the windowpane. In these ways, humans are embedded in nature, that is, something beyond human will.

Through these evocations of some larger nature around as well as within humans, the film is signposting its narrative agency. The film insistently connects these motifs through an audiovisual form that is not motivated by character action. It is an extra layer, a kind of artifact or artistic expressivity, that underlines the film's implied themes of human vulnerability in a very direct and abstract form. Actually, the integration of diegetic action and pictures of nature in the scene from *In a Better World* is not the default procedure. Usually, they appear in isolated sequences with no humans in sight. These devices may be subsumed under the term "supra-diegetic" motifs, a feature of the narrative that is neither simply diegetic nor non-diegetic but something in between that extends the film's melodramatic imagination, yet also aligns them with an art film mode.

The term "supra-diegetic" is not new. Rick Altman has suggested it in reference to the simultaneous interaction between diegetic song and non-diegetic music in the musical. It typically occurs when fictional characters sing to orchestral underscoring, a mixture and coordination of narrative realities that creates the idealized supra-diegetic space of romance (Altman 1987: 70). I will use the term slightly differently. The supra-diegetic, metaphorically speaking, is "above" the fiction, yet still part of it. There are many examples in Bier's films—also in her early dramas: The slow-motion images of massive sea waves in *Like It Never Was Before,* or the many shots of nature in the form of sky, earth, trees, and water in *Brothers, After the Wedding, In a Better World,* and *A Second Chance.* These sequences of two to five shots typically occur between scenes of action, that is, they are inserts between events and apart from human life. They present things that happen without intentional purpose, but result from natural laws. These natural events are also presented in a highly stylized form thanks to low camera angles, wide-angle lenses, color filters, and so on. In other words, the artificial quality is emphasized. Technically, these sequences *are* diegetic, but they function in a different way. They do not exactly depict a particular place; rather, they typify it. For example, the desert pictures of *In a Better World* are not explicitly mapped onto the central locations, but could be any place nearby. They are metonymically connected to the fictional world; they are part of it and, therefore, really diegetic. These non-action spaces impose themselves as something "extra," a presence of an authorial intentionality that insists on making the specific story part of a universal story of human nature. In Bier's films, this supra-diegetic intervention becomes an *intrinsic* norm, something we expect thanks to its repetition. As the films regularly display sequences of nature—including at least three of the four elements in ancient Greek thinking (earth, water, air), and of cyclical alterations such as the change of light, migrating birds, or images of animal nature, like those of spiders in their web, or bones from an ox—they invite the audience to make sense of these motifs as a symbolic supra-level that frames the human interactions in diegetic space.

This authorial presence that embeds human drama within a stylized rendering of universal nature is an auteur feature across Bier's films, but it is also a form of storytelling that aligns itself with an *external* norm shared by art film and melodrama alike. Several scholars have pointed to the kind of stylistic excess that characterizes melodrama (Elsaesser 1985/1972; Langford 2005). Yet art cinema is also characterized by stylistic excess. David Bordwell (1988/1985) has demonstrated how style has a life of its own in the art film and is not necessarily connected to diegetic events. Torben Grodal (2009) has described how the art film disconnects from singular actions and tends to evoke ideas of eternal essence, and András Kovács (2005) has established the presence of melodramatic features in the art film modernism of the 1960s. Therefore it comes as no surprise that Bier can balance melodrama and art film. Supra-diegetic elements, as I have termed them, fit melodrama and art film equally well. Bier's films present non-specific places or stylized aspects of the fictional world in ways that disconnect them from everyday human interaction. These excessive presentations of Nature embed the characters in something that they cannot defeat. Melodrama and art film are both concerned with eternal forces and values, though the ambiguity of meaning is more pervasive in the art film. In Bier's dramas, the characters do not face nature in the way the idealistic heroes of romanticism do, overwhelmed and excited by the divine powers of nature. Nature is an authorial aside for the audience to contemplate, as that mysterious something beyond human control. While the subjective intimacy that I have already touched on in the previous subsection creates a formal ambiguity in relation to the narrative premises, as it poses the question "who is telling?," the supra-diegetic inserts constitute an interpretive ambiguity on the level of meaning or understanding that concerns the significance of what is told.

Belinda Smaill has argued that "[n]egative evaluations of Bier's work seem to suppose that popular, mass cultural elements and art cinema modernism or realism cannot successfully coexist in a single film or oeuvre, or even film tradition" (Smaill 2014: 15). In the case of Bier's dramas, the structural elements of melodrama, realism, and art film do co-exist. This composite nature of her movies may at least partially explain their diverse reception. Each audience will find things they like and things they dislike, depending on generic preferences.

CONCLUDING REMARKS

This article has focused on Bier's Danish dramas. However, one may speculate on whether her less successful Hollywood productions failed due to something cultural lost in translation. I think a more reasonable suggestion would be that the films simply do not follow the kind of narrative structure that has made her Danish dramas efficient narratives. *Things We Lost in the Fire* (2007) does deploy some of Bier's signature features. It has the fatal incident: a father is killed, and his family is left on its own. It also has the motif from *Brothers* and *After the Wedding* of a man who has failed in life but responds to sudden death by stepping into character and helping others. Yet the fatal incident does not produce any ethical dilemmas or reasons to lie or deny anything, no painful pretense. The characters are not pushed by external circumstances to act in ways that contaminate their self-understanding. *Serena* (2014), on the other hand, has no ordinary world to begin with but is a historical epic in the high mimetic mode of classical tragedy (Frye 1957) with special and extraordinary characters: the characters, the location, and the mood of the film signify myth. This is just to say that the Danish melodramas made in collaboration with scriptwriter Anders Thomas Jensen have some recurrent structural features that are different from her American melodramas, made with two different scriptwriters, neither of whom is Jensen.

I have argued that Bier's Danish dramas are not melodramas only but are composed within a triangle of melodrama, psychological realism, and art film. The realism anchors the characters and stories in an ordinary world of routines, stable relations, and a familiarity that provides a feeling of ontological security. This is the world to which the characters strive to return after being hit by some major challenge. As such, the films are narratives about the precariousness of the ordinary when it is challenged by sudden events outside any individual's control. A final component is the ambiguously motivated rendering of subjective and supra-diegetic events, an authorial intervention that is part of the fictional world, yet not integrated with human action. This aligns her dramas with an art film tradition. The result of this triangular composition is a kind of super-sized naturalism that, through a fundamental rupture, extends the small, the familiar, and the intimate into a story of human vulnerability.

NOTES

1. Actually, Bier's films in the 1990s, which were mostly produced in Sweden, often combined drama and comedy – with the thriller *Sekten* as an exception. The Danish comedy *The One and Only* ushered in a more distinct tone in her films, whether inclined towards the serious or the comic. This does not exclude funny moments in her dramas or serious moments in her comedies, but the dominant tone in each film is more definitive from 1999 onwards.
2. Another difference from previous dramas by Bier is that the narration in *A Second Chance* is mainly aligned with one character (the policeman). This withholding of central information creates uncertainty about the true nature of the wife's actions and adds elements from the thriller.
3. By understanding "theme" (*dianoia*) as the thought or idea of a novel, I follow Northrup

Frye: "When a reader of a novel asks, 'How is this story going to turn out?' he is asking a question about the plot [...] But he is equally likely to ask, 'What's the *point* of this story?' This question relates to dianoia [theme]" (Frye 1957: 52). In other words, theme is the implied meaning of a novel (or a film).
4. This narrative pattern aligns these ordinary characters to some extent with the heroes of classical tragedies since the plot roughly follows the Aristotelian scheme of a sudden reversal of fortunes (*peripeteia*), suffering (*pathos*), and final insight (*anagnorisis*). See Aristotle (1996).

BIBLIOGRAPHY

Agger, Gunhild (2015), "Strategies in Danish Film Culture—and the Case of Susanne Bier," *Kosmorama* 259 (March 11), <http://www.kosmorama.org/Artikler/Susanne-Bier.aspx> (accessed November 14, 2017).
Altman, Rick (1987), *The American Film Musical*, Bloomington: Indiana University Press.
Aristotle (1996), *Poetics*, trans. Malcolm Heath, London: Penguin Books.
Auerbach, Erich (1957), *Mimesis: The Representation of Reality in Western Literature*, New York: Anchor Books.
Bazin, André (1971), *What is Cinema? Vol. II*, Berkeley: University of California Press.
Bordwell, David (1988 [1985]), *Narration in the Fiction Film*, London: Routledge.
Brooks, Peter (1995 [1974]), *The Melodramatic Imagination: Balzac, Henry James, Melodrama, and the Mode of Excess*, New Haven, CT: Yale University Press.
Carroll, Noël (1998), *A Philosophy of Mass Art*, Oxford: Oxford University Press.
Elsaesser, Thomas (1985 [1972]), "Tales of Sound and Fury: Observations on the Family Melodrama," in Bill Nichols (ed.), *Movies and Methods, Vol. II*, Los Angeles: University of California Press, pp. 165–89.
Frye, Northrup (1959), *Anatomy of Criticism*, Princeton, NJ: Princeton University Press.
Fuchs, Tomas (2013), "Existential Vulnerability: Toward a Psychopathology of Limit Situations," *Psychopathology* vol. 46: 301–8.
Goffman, Erwin (1957), *The Presentation of Self in Everyday Life*, New York: Anchor Books.
Grodal, Torben (2009), *Embodied Visions: Evolution, Emotion, Culture, and Film*, Oxford: Oxford University Press.
Kovács, András Bálint (2005), *Screening Modernism: European Art Cinema, 1950–1980*, Chicago: University of Chicago Press.
Langford, Barry (2005), *Film Genre, Hollywood, and Beyond*, Edinburgh: Edinburgh University Press.
Langkjær, Birger (2002), "Realism in Danish Cinema," in Anne Jerslev (ed.), *Realism and "Reality" in Film and Media*, Copenhagen: Nordic Lights/Museum Tusculanum Press, pp. 15–40.
Langkjær, Birger (2012), *Realismen i dansk film*, Copenhagen: Samfundslitteratur.
Larsen, Gorm (2011), "Overlevelsesinstinktets skam og skyld—Et temas transformationer: Om Susanne Biers film *Brødre*, Jim Sheridans adaption *Brothers* og Morten Ramslands roman *Hundehoved*," in P. E. Ljung and C.-G. Holmberg (eds.), *Översättning—adaption, interpretation, transformation*, IASS 2010 Proceedings, 28:e studiekonferensen, Lund.
Marklund, Anders (2012), "Skandinaviska filmer i världen," *Folia Scandinavica* vol. 4.
Neale, Steve (2000), *Genre and Hollywood*, London and New York: Routledge.

Philipsen, Heidi (2005a), *Dansk films nye bølge. Afsæt og aftryk fra Den Danske Filmskole*, Ph.D. dissertation, Odense: Syddansk Universitet.
Philipsen, Heidi (2005b), "En familiefar bliver til fare for familien," *16:9 filmtidsskrift*, vol. 3, no. 12 (June).
Sauntved, Louise Kidde (2001), "Sudden Impact," *Film Comment* vol. 47, no. 2 (March/April): 24–7.
Schank, Roger, and Robert Abelson (1977), *Scripts, Plans, Goals and Understanding: An Inquiry into Human Knowledge Structures*, Mahwah: Lawrence Erlbaum.
Shriver-Rice, Meryl (2009), "Adapting National Identity: Ethical Borders Made Suspect in the Hollywood Version of Susanne Bier's *Brothers*," *Film International* vol. 9, issue 2: 8–19.
Singer, Ben (2001), *Melodrama and Modernity: Early Sensational Cinema and Its Contexts*, New York: Columbia University Press.
Sklar, Robert (2011), "In a Better World," *Cinéaste* vol. 36., no. 3 (Summer 2011): 47–9.
Smaill, Belinda (2014), "The Male Sojourner, the Female Director, and Popular European Cinema: The Worlds of Susanne Bier," *Camera Obscura* vol. 29, no. 1, 85: 5–31.
Taylor, Ella (2011), "In a Better World: Oscar-Feted Compassion Porn," *Voice* (March 30).
Williams, Linda (1998), "Melodrama Revised," in Nick Browne (ed.), *Refiguring American Film Genres*, Los Angeles: University of California Press, pp. 42–88.

CHAPTER 2

Negotiating Special Relationships: Susanne Bier's Comedies

Gunhild Agger

INTRODUCTION

An exhibition of diversity, Susanne Bier's oeuvre shows that the same director can master a variety of strategies, genres, and media. Transnational elements have undoubtedly contributed to her innovative oeuvre. Bier's work comprehensively illustrates the options available to filmmakers in small national cinemas participating in an increasingly transnational production environment.

In Agger (2015), I outlined five viable strategies in Danish film culture vis-à-vis national traditions and transnational challenges. Bier's work exemplifies all five possibilities: (1) Art films in Danish, embracing Danish as well as international auteur film traditions. The Dogme film *Open Hearts* (*Elsker dig for evigt*, 2002) is an excellent case study of a Danish art film, exploring two families' traumatic change of partners. (2) Danish genre films in Danish, primarily relying on the domestic audience for support. The Danish-language comedy *The One and Only* (*Den eneste ene*, 1999) represents this strategy. It marked Bier's popular breakthrough in Denmark at a time when original Danish comedies were hardly appreciated. It is worth noting that several of Bier's earliest films are in Swedish, such as *Freud's Leaving Home* (*Freud flyttar hemifrån*, 1991), *Like It Never Was Before* (*Pensionat Oskar*, 1995), and *Once in a Lifetime* (*Livet är en schlager*, 2000). These films transcend national borders within the Nordic region, thus paving the way for the third strategy: (3) Cross-cultural and transnational mainstream films primarily in Danish, intentionally combining film traditions, cultural traditions, and languages. *Brothers* (*Brødre*, 2004), *In a Better World* (*Hævnen*, 2010), and *Love Is All You Need* (2012) are cross-cultural, transnational, and mainstream films in Danish that demonstrate this strategy. (4) Original English-language art films of an international standard that primarily target an international art film audience without excluding the domestic audience. Bier's *Things We Lost in the Fire* (2007) may be an example, although it may fit better into the last strategy: (5) English-language mainstream and genre films of an international standard. Good examples of this strategy are the Hollywood production *Serena* (2014) and the British *The Night Manager* (BBC, 2016). In addition, Bier has also varied her formats and media: she directed the short films *Island of the Blessed* (*De saliges ø*, 1986) and *Letter to Jonas* (*Brev til Jonas*, 1991); *Luischen* (1993) is a TV film; and the spy thriller *The Night Manager* is a television miniseries.

This chapter will focus on the negotiations between Danish and British-American comedy traditions in two of Bier's most successful comedies. It will examine and compare the changing markers of transnationality in *The One and Only* and *Love Is All You Need* (*Den skaldede frisør*, 2012). I argue that the former is a classical Hollywood-style screwball comedy that innovates Danish film comedy traditions, whereas *Love Is All You Need* is a markedly transnational, mainstream take on romantic comedy conventions associated with American and British traditions (aspects that facilitated its successful international distribution). To make this argument, I will briefly discuss some prevalent characteristics of the three main comic traditions Bier negotiates—Danish, British, and Hollywood. Whereas the Dogme movement prohibited the use of genres and its figurehead Lars von Trier tends to deliberately deconstruct genres (Agger 2014), Bier has assumed a more flexible approach to genres, magnifying certain generic traits and critically commenting on others. In my view, this approach to genre stems from Bier's persistent interest in drawing from different film traditions, mainly Danish, Swedish, British, and Hollywood. Moreover, transnational elements have become more distinct in her recent work, a development that carries with it the risk of increased mainstreaming.

DANISH COMEDY TRADITIONS

Danish film historians generally agree that Bier's *The One and Only* and Danish director Lone Scherfig's Dogme film *Italian for Beginners* (*Italiensk for begyndere*, 2000) led the way for the new Danish comedy breakthrough at the turn of the 21st century (Schepelern 2010; Grodal 2003: 24 and 2004: 121; Eigtved 2003: 235). What Schepelern labels "populist" comedies adhered to an older tradition of so called "folk comedies"; they prospered because they matched prevalent tastes in the domestic audience, and they received financing as a result of the Danish Film Institute's 50/50 scheme.[1] Bier's and Scherfig's comedies innovatively combined reflection and humor to address contemporary dilemmas. With Danish box-office sales amounting to 843,472 admissions, *The One and Only* became one of the most popular comedies in Danish film history. It was also critically acclaimed, winning both the Robert and Bodil prizes for best film in 2000. Its international potential was tested by a British-French remake *The One and Only* (Simon Cellan Jones, 2002) that replaced Copenhagen with Newcastle. The remake's box-office success was limited.

Bondebjerg's (2006) analysis of Danish comedy traditions during the period 1940–72 suggests that these films possess a particularly close relationship to American screwball and romantic comedy traditions.[2] However, there has not yet been sufficient accounting for the character of the innovations that have occurred since the turn of the twenty-first century. According to Grodal (2003: 24), one main reason for the success of the new comedies was the rejuvenation of canonical film narratives represented by Hollywood mainstream film. Grodal considers the reflectivity inherent in the new comedies part of a well-established tradition in the screwball tradition—a reflectivity reinterpreted by the new Danish comedy (2004: 124).

Eigtved's analysis provides two additional points. First, he stresses "the challenge of Danishness and the search for a new (Danish?) identity deriving from it" (Eigtved 2003: 235, my translation). He draws attention to the fact that people from other nations increasingly represented foreign and innovative views of the ways in which New Danish Cinema mirrored the Danes. *In China They Eat Dogs* (*I Kina spiser de hunde*, 1999), a comedy written by Anders Thomas Jensen, who later became Bier's favorite screenwriter, exemplifies this trend. The second trait that Eigtved draws attention to is "the breach of the norm as a norm" achieved by mixing "absurdism, harsh humor and quite direct representations"—with humor as a decisive factor (ibid.). Eigtved's observation highlights the role of satirical elements in pointing out the absurdities of everyday life. Bondebjerg, Grodal, and Eigtved have one observation in common: the significance of the international comedy tradition at this time, be it as a search for reflectivity or used as a platform to indicate what is or is not foreign, thereby enabling it to pinpoint features representing national and cultural identity.

These innovative changes in Danish cinema spurred a remarkable comedy renaissance, which blossomed into a variety of subgenres with diverse twists. For instance, Anders Thomas Jensen's *Flickering Lights* (*Blinkende lygter*, 2000), *The Green Butchers* (*De grønne slagtere*, 2003), *Adam's Apples* (*Adams æbler*, 2005), and *Men & Chicken* (*Mænd og høns*, 2015) experimented with black comedy conventions, disrespectfully but effectively exhibiting the breach of the norm as a norm. Masculine comedy or "homme-Com" (McDonald 2009), a subgenre characterized by a penchant for exhibiting naked bodies and fragile souls in a variety of embarrassing situations, was epitomized in Casper

Christensen's *Klovn—the Movie* (2010) and its sequel *Klovn forever* (2015), in which Casper Christensen went to Hollywood.[3] Recent queer comedies have also relied on familiar rom-com conventions to portray the emotional and psychological similarities between heterosexual and gay couples, as is the case in Hella Joof's *Shake It All About* (*En kort, en lang*, 2001). The choir comedy *Oh, Happy Day* (2004), also directed by Hella Joof, exemplifies the variation possible within classical comedy that stressed the importance of music. Each of these subgenres delivers case studies that are interesting to examine in connection with the overall question of negotiations between national and international traditions. However, before proceeding, I shall take a closer look at dominant British and Hollywood comedy traditions.

BRITISH AND HOLLYWOOD COMEDY TRADITIONS

One of the main driving forces in the renewal of Danish cinema was a more direct and audacious way of negotiating British and Hollywood genre traditions. This trend affected multiple genres. These generic adaptations were part of a rebellion against realism, which, in different forms, had been a dominant tradition in Danish cinema that had affected the choice of themes as well as style (Langkjær 2012). Combining the war genre with the family film, Bier's *Brødre* is an excellent example of generic experimentation.[4] *Brødre* integrated American genre references and recognizable Danish realities, and thus became a catalyst for New Danish Cinema; genres could be deliberately used to pinpoint current dilemmas in society. Danish filmmakers began making use of genres, instead of avoiding them as prescribed by the realist tradition.

In Hollywood, the screwball comedy had its heyday during the 1930s, whereas the romantic comedy dominated during the 1940s and 1950s. According to Abbott and Jermyn (2009), the romantic comedy genre has since struggled to be taken seriously. Finally, the 1990s presented a variety of innovations. Wes Gehring (2008) regards screwball and romantic comedy as two distinct forms. He proposes a number of key differences. First and foremost, the attitude to love differs in each subgenre: "Though romantic comedy has its fair share of funny scenes, it is dead serious about the importance of love" (Gehring 2008: 67). Consequently, whereas the male hero in screwball comedies tends to be an incompetent and rather childish professor type who plays opposite an independent, brilliant woman (as seen in the prototypical *Bringing Up Baby* [Howard Hawks, 1938]), the characters in romantic comedies are less contrived and more realistic. Additionally, the dialogue in screwball comedy must be witty, whereas romantic comedy dialogues can simply be "fun." Discussing remakes such as Howard Hawks' *Monkey Business* (1952) or Peter Bogdanovich's *What's Up, Doc?* (1972), as well as "makeovers" such as the

British *Four Weddings and a Funeral* (1994), *Notting Hill* (1999), and *Bridget Jones' Diary* (2001), Gehring concludes: "Though a critic might be tempted to interpret this English connection as a major genre makeover, these movies merely reinforce the most basic of screwball values" (2008: 146). Gehring then proceeds to highlight the constancy of the genre from the Golden Age of Hollywood to the beginning of the twenty-first century, but he does not consider the special relationship between British and American comedies or the development of subgenres as major aspects of genre evolution. Besides pinpointing the basics of the two types of comedy, Gehring's approach is fairly narrow.

However, significantly, Gehring establishes Hollywood cinema as the main influence on European film culture, an influence that is evident in large as well as small European nations.[5] Among the larger European nations, the U.K. in particular has developed tight cinematic relationships with the U.S.A., as noted by Higson (2015). Even if U.K. films do exceptionally well on the European market, the major British production companies keep looking to the West rather than to the East for co-financing and co-production: "U.K. film policy has long been dominated by schemes designed to attract inward investment from the major Hollywood players, which is seen as a much more lucrative means of creating a vibrant film economy than co-operating with Europe and European co-production partners" (Higson 2015: 132).

In "A special relationship?" (2009), Roe examines the British film company Working Title (established in 1983) as an interesting example of cooperation between productions companies based in the U.K. and U.S.[6] Working Title is the main production company behind the romantic comedies that contributed to the remarkable success of British film around the turn of the century: *Four Weddings and a Funeral* (1994), *Notting Hill* (1999), and *Love Actually* (2003).[7] Significantly, *Four Weddings and a Funeral* (1994) was initially released in the U.S.A. Having proved successful there, it was released in Britain as "America's No. 1 Smash Hit Comedy" and subsequently developed into an international success (Roe 2009: 82). Since 1999, co-operation between Working Title and Universal resulted in the greenlighting of up to five British films a year.

Thematically, it is striking that the financial cooperation between U.S. and U.K. production companies resonates with this era of romantic comedy's preoccupation with romantic relationships between characters from the U.K. and the U.S.A. Romantically hopeless Englishmen and self-assured American women form couples that mirror the British and American film industries, thus confirming their special relationship. This transatlantic alliance demonstrates the significant resources many films require to achieve commercial success. As co-productions between major production corporations in the U.S. and production companies in smaller European nations are more rare, a happy ending is harder to imagine on a European level. However, the comparable romantic

Danish-English liaison in *Love Is All You Need* compels consideration of Europeanness vis-à-vis transnationality.

TRANSNATIONALITY AND EUROPEANNESS

The concept of transnationality is often used to characterize a dominant movement in film and television that transcends national traditions and languages. According to Hjort (2010), transnationality should be utilized "as a scalar concept allowing for the notion of strong or weak forms of transnationality" (Hjort 2010: 13). Hjort goes on to propose a distinction between marked and unmarked transnationality as well as further clarifications related to production, distribution, reception, and textual elements that impact a film's transnationality. I apply the term transnationality somewhat differently, concluding that it is "a concept implying strong negotiations and dialogues with national and local traditions of all types" (Agger 2016: 87).

The anthology *The Europeanness of European Cinema: Identity, Meaning, Globalization* (2015) critically investigates the many challenges of developing a shared perspective on Europeanness. European co-productions are often considered a viable path with notable disadvantages. Liz (2015) discusses the term "Euro-pudding" and its negative impact, drawing attention to the prevailing image of mainstream European productions as art films, unable to appeal to broader audiences. Jäckel confirms that there is no easy way to develop Europeanness in European film, but concludes that EU programs and schemes do make a difference. Jäckel also contradicts Europe's art film image by stressing that a "large number of European co-productions supported by Pan-European programs and/or awarded European prizes are essentially concerned with social and moral issues" (Jäckel 2015: 70). In New Danish Cinema, according to Shriver-Rice, moral concerns and ethical choices are the rule rather than the exception, a claim that particularly resonates with Bier's films. Equating European film with art film has confused audiences and critics alike. In the case of Bier, Smaill asserts that "the dual markers of *arthouse* and *popular* have led to divergent perceptions of her cinema as largely mainstream in a local European context and as European arthouse cinema in English-speaking cultures" (2014: 12). Smaill finds the concept of transnationality more relevant than that of Europeanness to the work of a cohort of female filmmakers born between 1945 and 1960, including Bier.

The successful dynamic between the British and American film industries has led many European film producers to choose English as their preferred language. This does not mean that the native languages in domestic film production vanish, but it means that each year a certain number of films are produced in English. Drawing on quantitative analysis of film production in selected European countries, Kulyk conducted a survey on the use of English instead of the native language in films in nine European countries during the period 1990–2010. At the beginning of the 1990s, to a certain extent, English was used in films from Spain, the Netherlands, and Greece. Since 2003, more countries began to produce English-language films. Although, already in the mid-1990s, a remarkable increase in English-language films occurred in the Nordic countries: "their number increased: up to seven in Sweden in 2006, up to four in Denmark in 2008. Even more remarkable is the fact that most countries had at least one title per year—indeed, from 2008 to 2010 the five Nordic countries produced at least one film in English" (Kulyk 2015: 176). This move to English-language film production further attests to the difficulties of making European films and the relative advantages of the English-American-transnational strategy.

THE ONE AND ONLY

The One and Only was produced by Sandrew Metronome, a Swedish-Danish distribution company, in cooperation with Danish Metronome Productions. The cast and crew were primarily Danish, as was the language, although some Italian and mixed Italian/Danish phrases were used. The Swedish actor Rafael Edholm played the Italian character Sonny; thus, Danishness with a touch of Swedishness dominated on the production level. *The One and Only* jump-started scriptwriter Kim Fupz Aakeson's career as a feature film manuscript writer.

Bier's comedic point of departure is the common situation of two unhappy couples: Niller (Niels Olesen) and Lizzie (Søs Egelind), and Sus (Sidse Babett Knudsen) and Sonny. Both couples are childless, but their motivation for desiring or not desiring a child differs. Sonny clearly expresses his need for a child as rooted in his traditional Italian background,[8] whereas Sus suspects that his interest in her will dwindle if she becomes pregnant (Figure 2.1). Due to Niller's shortcomings regarding semen quality, Lizzie cannot become pregnant. Consequently, the couple agree to adopt a child, and they experience all the obstacles and difficulties involved in adoption (Figure 2.2). Adoption, as well as poor semen quality, is given a comical treatment.[9] The same is the case with pregnancy.

On the stylistic level, a vertical and horizontal wipe effect[10] in the opening sequence is used to place the main characters both as parallels and in mutual opposition. During the three-act structure, we follow the ups and downs of Niller and Sus, the two main protagonists, supported by Knud (Lars Kaalund) and Stella (Paprika Steen), the protagonists' job partners and single sidekicks. The structure of parallel and opposition is emphasized on the plot level, where

SUSANNE BIER'S COMEDIES   43

Figure 2.1 Sus and Sonny visiting the doctor who reveals that Sus has cheated on Sonny, avoiding pregnancy by pretending that she did not know the most elementary facts of life.

Figure 2.2 Lizzie and Niller visiting the adoption center with the aim of acquiring approval as fit parents.

the most apparent innovation is the inversion of the traditional narrative of romantic comedies—with a twist. This comedy begins where most romantic comedies end—after the wedding, quoting a later Bier title.

The first act focuses on parallels, aesthetically highlighted by identical scenes in comparable situations. However different their backgrounds, both couples have to overcome the problems involved in becoming parents. The first act ends with a solution: Mgala (Vanessa Gouri) is welcomed into Niller and Lizzie's household, and Sus takes four tests that confirm her pregnancy. The second act involves the disappearance of the two "wrong" partners, Lizzie and Sonny. Immediately after Mgala's arrival, Lizzie is hit by a car and dies.[11] This puts the adoption in jeopardy. The adoption center persuades Niller that Mgala may be best off at the children's home back in Burkina Faso. Similarly, Sus and Sonny's marriage breaks up. As expected, Sonny has an affair with a slim young blonde, and Sus tries out all the usual remedies. Having made love with Niller and facing a divorce, she decides on an abortion. The third act represents the great climax. Niller realizes that he needs Mgala—as well as Sus. Together, Niller and Mgala set out to prevent Sus from having the planned abortion. Sonny gains credit by supporting their efforts. Sus finally opts for a life with Niller, Mgala, and the expected baby. The wedding at the end hints at the romantic comedy—but the screwball tradition prevails.

In connection with *Love Is All You Need*, Susanne Bier has explicitly referred to the comedies of Richard Curtis as an inspiration: "Despite the fairytale English settings, the characters are authentic . . . He reinvented the romantic comedy by being pretty real" (Goodridge 2012). Since *The One and Only* includes a funeral, a divorce, and a wedding inaugurating the next two weddings at the end,[12] the British *Four Weddings and a Funeral* can be recognized as an influence on Bier's plot. However, where *Four Weddings and a Funeral* is a typical upper-class comedy, Bier dispenses with fairytale settings. Everybody but Sonny has a working-class or middle-class background. As expressed in Niller's recurrent kitchen metaphors, the value of working life is solidly accentuated, contrasted with Mulle's (Sofie Gråbøl) vain claim to insight, gathered during the seven years she spent studying psychology. Despite their ridiculously exaggerated behavior, the characters in *The One and Only* are recognizable from everyday life.

The One and Only renewed the Danish comedy tradition by importing elements from the British romantic comedy, adapting them to Danish society, and in the process combining it with the Hollywood screwball tradition as well as with an ironic attitude towards current ways of life, stereotypes, and sociological clichés. The title of *The One and Only* is intentionally banal, clearly alluding to the dream of "love at first sight." The comical approach is announced from the very beginning, by the choice of names: "Niller" for Niels, "Sus" for Susanne, "Sonny" for Andrea, and "Mulle" for Merete. These nicknames are linguistic signs of screwball comedy, followed by wittily constructed dialogue that has since been frequently quoted in Danish cultural contexts, such as "Bare ærgerligt, Sonny Boy" ("Too bad, Sonny Boy"), and Niller's use of "f***," echoed first by Mgala, and subsequently by the social worker from the adoption center (Hella Joof). The latter presumes that it is an African expression (Figure 2.3). Also, when Sus sees the wrong handyman in the door, she

Figure 2.3 Mgala's first word in "Danish".

comments "Meget mærkeligt firma" ("A very strange company"), which has become yet another classic quote from the film.

Additionally, the wittily constructed dialogue critiques current sociological understanding in sentences such as "Hvis jeres ægteskab er en bil, hvad er det så for en?" ("If your marriage were a car, which one would it be?"), delivered by the social worker from the adoption center. This line ironically references *Hvis din nabo var en bil / If Your Neighbour Were a Car*, a popular Danish sociology textbook by Henrik Dahl (1997). Much to Lizzie's dissatisfaction, Niller's honest answer to the question is "a delivery van." Similarly, Mulle's line "Du er uegnet" ("You are unsuitable") refers to Peter Høeg's novel *Borderliners* (*De måske egnede*, 1993), which, in its time, raised a debate about discipline, normality, and education, including the prevailing understanding of being suited or unsuited to society—in this case, as adoptive parents.

Moreover, cultural markers are negotiated by exhibiting national stereotypes, most obviously the virile Latin lover and professional soccer player versus the Danish carpenter with poor semen quality. Although the sympathy belongs to the latter, the Danish way of life is challenged by the perspectives of characters from Italy and Burkina Faso. The linguistic humor so essential to screwball comedy is at work in these negotiations. Mgala's first word in "Danish" is *f****, which signals marked transnationality and ironically comments on "Danglish" expressions. She quickly sides with Niller by accepting the black doll, which Lizzie rejected because of its postcolonial equivalency to *Little Black Sambo*; her actions therefore suggest that the African child understands more than meets the eye.

Another example of ongoing cultural negotiation occurs in the constant linguistic surveillance of Sonny by Sus. As Sonny lives up to all the common prejudices about macho types, we side with her. However, where language is concerned, we cannot help noticing her domineering attitude towards Sonny. She is annoyed that Sonny's Danish is marked by a heavy Italian accent. Their

Figure 2.4 Sus in conversation with Lizzie: "Jeg synes, der lugter sådan af løg" (It seems to me there is a smell of onion).

quarrels are characterized by her natural linguistic superiority. She seems more preoccupied with correcting his Danish than considering the meaning of his words. Sonny does not master the irregular declension of verbs. When he says: "Jeg bedragede dig" ("I deceived you" [weak declension]), she emphatically exclaims: "Nej, du bedrog mig!" ("No, you deceived me!"—insisting on the correct strong declension). No wonder his final line of dialogue is: "Forza Italia!"

Similarly, Sus becomes less brilliant as she enacts a number of stereotypes associated with pregnancy. Among them is a sensitivity to certain smells—in Sus's case, particularly the smell of onion. This smell has the role of sidetracking the plot. The onion theme is introduced in the scene where Lizzie meets Sus to help her with choosing a new kitchen (Figure 2.4). The issue of the smell of onion is further pursued when Stella gives her trivial advice: she should try to make Sonny jealous in order to win him back. The smell functions as a warning signal during the planned abortion to stop and reconsider. In the end, Sus is rescued by this stereotype—as well as by Niller's final development into a mature person who is willing to take on responsibility. The incongruity between these factors is funny.

The One and Only shows that a comedy can negotiate national and gender-based stereotypes at several levels, confront them, and laugh at them, drawing on traditions from the screwball comedy and implying the genre conventions of the romantic comedy. Bier uses the opportunity to comment on traditional romantic comedies by inversion—starting where the romantic comedy usually ends, adding the twist that the ending represents the beginning of new romances. The main characters can be compared to prominent types in screwball comedy. Niller and Sonny represent socially incompetent and rather childish types who play opposite Sus, an independent, brilliant woman. But clichés and conventions from British and Hollywood comedy traditions are also critically exhibited; for instance, via the sidekick's direct comments on adopting when it is so easy to "get laid" somewhere in town. The outspoken linguistic humor and the witty dialogue so typical of screwball comedy help *The One and Only* to acquire its special status with the Danish audience.

The clichés of romantic as well as screwball comedy are turned around in a slew of negotiations and twists. However, the classical overall purpose is retained—the "right" couples should get together. On this level, *The One and Only* copies the norms known from the preceding "populist" Danish as well as the English-American comedy tradition. This is also the case in *Love Is All You Need*. More interesting, however, are the striking differences between the two.

LOVE IS ALL YOU NEED

Despite its Danish title (which literally means "The Bald Hairdresser"), *Love Is All You Need* is a romantic comedy involving all the traditional ingredients of the genre—with some twists, which will be accounted for later. Compared to *The One and Only*, *Love Is All You Need* involves a significant development of marked transnationality. It is a transnational co-production with participants from Zentropa companies in Sweden, Germany, and France, as well as Arte, DR, and STV, among others. Support was obtained from diverse European and national funding institutions, including the DFI, SFI, and the Italian Ministry of Culture. The film was widely distributed by international distribution companies, theatrically and via DVD. *Love Is All You Need* received the prize for Best European Comedy at the European Film Awards in Berlin in 2013. Thomas Anders Jensen is the screenwriter, and while most actors were also Danish, the cast included Pierce Brosnan in the leading role as Philip, Swedish Stine Ekblad as a doctor, and the Italian actors Cire Petrone (Alessandro) and Marco D'Amore (Marco). Similarly, the crew was composed of mixed nationality. With 644,681 admissions, the comedy was Denmark's second most watched film in 2012.

In an interview with Liz Hoggart, Bier points out what romance means to her: "*Love Is All You Need* is unashamedly romantic. It says: 'Yes, we do believe in love.' You have to stop worrying about good taste. There is an intellectual timidity when you don't want to deal with things because they will become very colorful, but you can't be ashamed of big emotions if you make movies" (Hoggart 2013). This feeling of being "unashamedly romantic" is emphasized by the English title and the adoption of "That's Amore" as part of the soundtrack. The fairy-tale dust at the beginning and end of the film provides a nod to Disney's *Cinderella* (Figure 2.5). Where *The One and Only* avoided "fairytale English settings" (Goodridge 2012), *Love Is All You Need*

Figure 2.5 The invasion of golden fairytale dust.

deliberately embraces a fairy-tale setting—admittedly not English, but Italian. In contrast, the Danish title points out the apparent paradox that a hairdresser can be bald. In leaving the spectator to ask why, it paves the way for the subtheme of the film—breast cancer. Serious issues lurk under the surface of the fairy tale.

Following the conventions of British and Hollywood romantic comedy, the main narrative element in the plot is a wedding. During a three-act structure, we follow preparations, doubts, and obstacles. In the first act, the first person to be introduced is Ida (Trine Dyrholm), the bride's mother, a fact that points out her special status in the film. We meet her at the hospital, in a follow-up situation after her treatment for breast cancer. She is unaccompanied, and although she looks scared, she has no questions after the doctor's statement and suggestions. In this way, she is characterized as a woman who does not want to bother anyone with anything. We are also introduced to Philip, the groom's father, busily occupied by his successful trade in vegetables, and Leif, the father of the bride (Kim Bodnia). The latter has an affair with Thilde (Christiane Schaumburg-Müller), a young woman of the same age as his own daughter. Very quickly, the bride's family is broken up as Leif leaves his wife in favor of Thilde. A less conspicuous couple are Astrid (Molly Blixt Egelind) and Patrick (Sebastian Jessen), the bride and groom, who have invited the whole family from both countries to join them at Patrick's father's place in Sorrento, neglected since the death of Patrick's mother.

Following a well-known pattern in the romantic comedy genre, several obstacles occur during the second act. The young engaged couple appears to be happy, but are they really? Meeting Alessandro, his Italian friend from his childhood, sparks Patrick's doubts about his sexuality; he finds himself more and more emotionally attached to Alessandro, who is gay. Astrid has her premonitions. The arrival of the whole family including Benedicte (Paprika Steen), Philip's sister-in-law, and Thilde at Sorrento only increases the complications. In the meantime, Philip and Ida, originally adversaries, experience a growing affection for one another.

The last act is a game-changer. In spite of its romantic splendor, Sorrento Bay turns out not to be a place of celebration, but of reflection and reconsideration. The engaged young couple, Astrid and Patrick, break up. Already on their arrival, the untraditional proportions of their relationship were demonstrated: the beautiful tall woman carried her tiny fiancé over the threshold into his father's house.

The traditional theme of wrong partners in the romantic wedding comedy is thus repeated—with a double twist. The planned wedding must be cancelled, and all the guests must return home without a happy ending. But a romantic comedy cannot end in this way. The first twist is the replacement of the wedding between the young Danish couple by an intercultural gay constellation, an alliance between "Italy" (Alessandro) and "Denmark/England" (Patrick). The second twist is caused by the older generation; the romance between the parents follows a similar path, as the Danish hairdresser settles in Sorrento with her English partner, living up to a revised Cinderella fairy tale—and to the intercultural liaison in English romantic comedies, mirroring the "special relationship" in the preferred alliance between unequal partners.

This leads us to the question about national versus transnational markers. Italianness plays quite a different role in *Love Is All You Need* compared to *The One and Only*; national stereotypes and all they represent are reversed. Where Italian qualities in *The One and Only* were associated with stereotypes such as the Latin lover, they play a liberating role in *Love Is All You Need*. From the beginning, the score "That's Amore" indicates that Bier embraces Italy as well as Hollywood. In *Love Is All You Need*, worn-out Italian clichés such as "That's Amore" are given a sparkling afterlife, confirming Bier's appetite for mixing traditional ingredients in new ways.

A major theme is the comical renegotiation of opposition. Danishness is contrasted to Italianness, but in *Love Is All You Need* the latter is favored (Figures 2.6 and 2.7). With its grey everyday life and its modest gardens and flowers, Copenhagen is unfavorably compared to Sorrento Bay with its blue water, bright colors, lemons and oranges, breathtaking views, and exquisite

Figure 2.6 The Danish Way.

Figure 2.7 The Italian Way.

cultural traditions. Not only the setting, but even the characters are depicted via national stereotypes. In the social settings contrasting northern and southern Europe, some of the Danes are characterized by excessive drinking and casual sexual habits. The Englishman who settled in Denmark retains a stiff upper lip, never showing his feelings—if indeed he has any. By way of contrast, the Italians dare to show their emotions and act accordingly. Italy serves as a catalyst in disrupting stereotypical Nordic behavior, and opposites meet in a shared love of lemons, reflecting the yellow color that first set the atmosphere in the film.

The color yellow is central to the very first action we see in the film: a grey hospital building in Copenhagen is painted yellow as if by magic, inaugurating a change of genre—from grey realism to romantic comedy. The color yellow alludes not only to romantic comedy, but also to golden fairy tales, and the style corresponds to this change—clear colors and clear-cut takes dominate. The color yellow exemplifies the film's consistent style and provides a leitmotif that links the entire narrative (Figure 2.8). Lemons figure on large posters in the background when we first meet Philip at the surprise birthday party organized by Benedicte. Lemons roll out of Ida's basket when she comes home to find Leif having sex with Thilde on the sofa. Ida's car is lemon-colored. Sympathy arises between Philip and Ida for the first time in the lemon grove in Italy. From a superior uphill position he watches her swim in the sea, and

Figure 2.8 Lemons inaugurating the theme of the color yellow.

although she is vulnerable because of her illness, she appears in harmony with nature and herself. We watch her nakedness from his perspective and get a glimpse of her post-operative breast. She is bald, having left her wig on the sand. The dialogue between Philip and Ida in the following scene stresses that orange trees can be changed into lemon trees when grafted, so the nature of things can change, a suggestion that resonates with the changes Ida is experiencing through cancer treatments. Consequently, Philip can change, too.

The clear-cut style with its bright colors and its emphasis on yellow enhances the prevailing theme of the film—the option of change for better or worse. People can change, and feelings can change, anger and sorrow may follow, but change inevitably implies development. This development is seen in the light of opposite cultural markers and negotiations between Danishness, Englishness, and Italianness. In the end, the universal theme is underlined: it is imperative to be true to deeply felt emotions rather than conventions. The wedding, the chief attraction of the romantic comedy, does not take place, which, like the cancer theme, is unconventional in this genre, but the film does end with a future wedding prospect—ironically for the older couple. Seen from a perspective of strategic alliances in the film industry, it is striking that the Danish-English liaison uses Italy as an intermediary.

CONCLUSION

From the beginning of her career, Susanne Bier's films have been simultaneously domestically and transnationally oriented. Producing at home and abroad, she has made genre films as well as art films that are appreciated by domestic and international audiences. Bier is often considered a director with a special preference for family drama in a melodramatic vein. However, her interest in exploring a diversity of genres has become more pronounced over time. Today, her oeuvre's generic range encompasses family films and war films, comedies and thrillers, contemporary narratives, and films set in the past. Often she mixes a dominant genre with elements of other genres.

Taking up the traditions presented by British-American comedies, international relationships are investigated in *The One and Only* as well as in *Love Is All You Need*. Both intentionally combine domestic and European-Hollywood comedy traditions, cultural references, and multiple languages. *The One and Only* is a Danish genre film in Danish, and while primarily targeting a domestic audience, it does not exclude international audiences. With its witty and satirical dialogue, *The One and Only* draws most obviously from the screwball comedy tradition. Thematically and linguistically, it plays with Italian and Danish references, comically negotiating stereotypes and sociological clichés in a way that has appealed to the broad public and to sophisticated audiences alike. Figures from the Danish Film Institute confirm that it is impossible to reach a box-office sale amounting to 843,472 admissions in Denmark without this double appeal.[13] Its fresh take on outdated traditions in Danish film comedy, such as stereotypical gender roles, flat characters, and plots without an edge, can hardly be overestimated.

Love Is All You Need is a cross-cultural mainstream film that primarily uses Danish as its language, but also includes spoken English and Italian. Corresponding to a current trend in films produced in Europe's smaller countries, the intentional transnational impact at all levels is much stronger in *Love Is All You Need* than in *The One and Only*. This is clearly demonstrated by production details as well as by the choice of themes, languages, and not least, location. Between 1999 and 2012, Bier gained ample international experience, undertaking experiments with a variety of films, including Academy Award-winner *In a Better World*. *Love Is All You Need* is a classical romantic comedy that emphasizes the necessity of making love a priority, and of giving way to emotions despite social or cultural obstacles. While national stereotypes of Italianness are very bluntly presented in *The One and Only*, Italianness in *Love Is All You Need* is seen as a vehicle for liberating emotions and, in spite of the pain they produce, for being true to them. Thanks to this all-pervasive message and its negotiations of Italian, English, Danish, and universal values, *Love Is All You Need* is more closely related to British-American co-productions than to *The One and Only*. As a result, it is a more transnational mainstream film. *The One and Only* strikingly innovated Danish film comedy, while *Love Is All You Need* rather aims to lift a Danish everyday life out of its boredom, combining the best of the American Disney fairy-tale tradition with British romantic comedy conventions. In *Love Is All You Need*, love is a serious matter.

I started this article by maintaining that Bier's work illuminates the strategies available to filmmakers from countries with small national cinemas in an increasingly transnational production environment. The development in Bier's comedies illustrates an increasing transnational orientation in her work. *The One and Only* was more successful with domestic audiences, but *Love Is All You Need* was more widely distributed, showing that a Danish comedy with a combined British-American mainstream inspiration is in a better position to win international acclaim.

NOTES

1. The 50/50 scheme allowed the Danish Film Institute (DFI) to support one half of the film's total budget up to a certain limit, provided a commercial film company would finance the other half. Cf. Bondebjerg 2006.

2. In his analysis of the commercial Danish comedy during the 1930s, Niels Hartvigsson (2002) confirms an international inspiration in the use of music, songs, and sounds.
3. Preceded by a popular TV show 2005–10.
4. Cf. Gemzøe 2013 and Shriver-Rice 2015. Both focus on cultural negotiations between Danish and American traditions but with diverging conclusions.
5. Cf. Elsaesser 2005, Bondebjerg and Redvall 2015.
6. The title quotes Winston Churchill's speech "Sinews of Peace" (March 5, 1946), where he coined the phrase "a special relationship" to describe relations between the British Commonwealth and the United States: "Neither the sure prevention of war, nor the continuous rise of world organization will be gained without what I have called the fraternal association of the English-speaking peoples. This means a special relationship between the British Commonwealth and Empire and the United States" (<http://www.nato.int/docu/speech/1946/s460305a_e.htm>). Since then, the extent and implications of this "special relationship" have been frequently debated. This also goes for film scholarship.
7. Richard Curtis was the scriptwriter of the first and writer/director of *Love Actually*.
8. This view is not confirmed by Italian birth rate statistics.
9. Cf. Fisher 2013: 237.
10. One shot is replaced by another by traveling from one side of the frame to the other.
11. This sudden but convenient death is anticipated by Mulle, Lizzie's sister, who in a moment of absent-mindedness barely avoids being hit by a car.
12. Stella and Knud, Mulle and the vicar.
13. *Den eneste ene* figures as number 10 on a list of the 25 bestselling films in Denmark since 1976. The list is topped by *Olsen-banden ser rødt* (1976), which sold 1,201,293 tickets, cf. <http://www.dfi.dk/Tal-og-fakta/Noegletal.aspx> (accessed January 6, 2017).

BIBLIOGRAPHY

Abbott, Stacey, and Deborah Jermyn (2009), *Falling in Love Again: Romantic Comedy in Contemporary Cinema*, London: I. B. Tauris.

Agger, Gunhild (2014), "Fra dystopi til apokalypse: *Dogville* og *Melancholia*," in Kim Toft Hansen and Peter Kaj Pedersen (eds.), *Terminus i litteratur, medier og kultur*, Aalborg: Aalborg Universitetsforlag, pp. 127–60.

Agger, Gunhild (2015), "Strategies in Danish Film Culture—and the Case of Susanne Bier," *Kosmorama* 259 (March 11), <http://www.kosmorama.org/Artikler/Susanne-Bier.aspx> (accessed November 14, 2017).

Agger, Gunhild (2016), "The development of transnationality in Danish Noir—from *Unit One* to *The Team*," *Northern Lights: Film & Media Studies Yearbook* vol. 14, no. 1 (June 2016): 83–101.

Bondebjerg, Ib (2006), *Filmen og det moderne*, Copenhagen: Gyldendal.

Bondebjerg, Ib, and Eva Novrup Redvall (2015), "Introduction: Mediated Cultural Encounters in Europe," in Ib Bondebjerg et al. (eds.), *European Cinema and Television*, Basingstoke: Palgrave Macmillan, pp. 1–22.

Eigtved, Michael (2003), "Folkekomedien tur/retur," in Anders Toftgaard and Ian Halvdan Hawkesworth (eds.), *Nationale spejlinger: Tendenser i ny dansk film*, Copenhagen: Museum Tusculanums Forlag, pp. 225–42.

Elsaesser, Thomas (2005), *European Cinema: Face to Face with Hollywood*, Amsterdam: Amsterdam University Press.

Fisher, Lucy (2013), "The Reproduction of Mothering: Masculinity, Adoption, and Identity in *Flirting with Disaster*," in Andrew S. Horton and Joanna E. Rapf (eds.): *A Companion to Film Comedy*, Oxford: Blackwell, pp. 236–47.

Gehring, Wes D. (2008), *Romantic vs. Screwball Comedy*, Lanham, MD: Scarecrow Press.

Gemzøe, Lynge A. (2013), "*Brødre* vs. *Brothers*: The Transatlantic Remake as Cultural Adaptation," *Academic Quarter*, fall: 283–96. <http://www.akademiskkvarter.hum.aau.dk/pdf/vol7/19a_LyngeAggerGemzoee_BroedreVsBrothers.pdf > (accessed November 14, 2017).

Goodridge, Mike (2012), interview, DFI's magazine *FILM*, May 10, <http://www.dfi.dk/service/english/news-and-publications/film-magazine/artikler-fra-tidsskriftet-film/75/a-true-romantic.aspx> (accessed November 14, 2017).

Grodal, Torben (2003), "De bløde følelser: Filmfortællinger og den nye danske film," in Anders Toftgaard and Ian Halvdan Hawkesworth (eds.), *Nationale spejlinger: Tendenser i ny dansk film*, Copenhagen: Museum Tusculanums Forlag, pp. 23–56.

Grodal, Torben (2004), "Stille eksistenser finder lykken—*Italiensk for begyndere*," in Ove Christensen (ed.), *Nøgne billeder: De danske dogmefilm*, Holte: Medusa.

Hartvigsson, Niels (2007), *1930'ernes danske filmkomedie i et lyd-, medie- og genreperspektiv*, Københavns Universitet, <http://nordicom.statsbiblioteket.dk/ncom/files/39339/ph.d.afhandling_Niels_Henrik_Hartvigson.pdf> (accessed November 14, 2017).

Higson, Andrew (2015), "British Cinema, Europe and the Global Reach for Audiences," in Ib Bondebjerg et al. (eds.), *European Cinema and Television*, Basingstoke: Palgrave Macmillan, pp. 127–50.

Hjort, Mette (2010), "On the plurality of cinematic transnationality," in Natasna Durovicova and Kathleen Newman (eds.), *World Cinemas: Transnational Perspectives*, London: Routledge, pp. 12–33.

Hoggart, Liz (2013), interview with Susanne Bier, *The Guardian*, April 14, <http://www.theguardian.com/theobserver/2013/apr/14/susanne-bier-love-all-you-need> (accessed November 14, 2017).

Jäckel, Anne (2015), "Changing the Image of Europe? The Role of European Co-Productions, Funds and Film Awards," in Mary Harrod, Mariana Liz, and Alissa Timoshkina, *The Europeanness of European Cinema: Identity, Meaning, Globalization*, London: I. B. Tauris, pp. 59–71.

Kulyk, Laëtitia (2015), "The Use of English in European Feature Films: Unity in Diversity?" in Mary Harrod, Mariana Liz, and Alissa Timoshkina, *The Europeanness of European Cinema: Identity, Meaning, Globalization*, London: I. B. Tauris, pp. 173–81.

Langkjær, Birger (2012), *Realismen i dansk film*, Copenhagen: Samfundslitteratur.

Liz, Mariana (2015), "From European Co-Productions to the Euro-Pudding," in Mary Harrod, Mariana Liz, and Alissa Timoshkina, *The Europeanness of European Cinema: Identity, Meaning, Globalization*, London: I. B. Tauris, pp. 73–85.

McDonald, Tamar Jeffers (2009), "Homme-Com," in Stacey Abbott and Deborah Jermyn (eds.), *Falling in Love Again: Romantic Comedy in Contemporary Cinema*, London: I. B. Tauris, pp. 146–59.

Melgaard, Max (2012), "Den eneste 2," *Nordjyske Kultur*, September 6.

Roe, Anabelle Honess (2009), "A 'Special Relationship'? The Coupling of Britain and America in Working Title's Romantic Comedies," in Stacey Abbott and Deborah Jermyn (eds.), *Falling in Love Again: Romantic Comedy in Contemporary Cinema*, London: I. B. Tauris, pp. 79–91.

Schepelern, Peter (2010), "Danish Film History 1990–1999," <http://www.dfi.dk/Service/

English/Films-and-industry/Danish-Film-History/1990-1999.aspx> (accessed November 14, 2017).
Schepelern, Peter (2010), "Danish Film History 2000–2009," <http://www.dfi.dk/Service/English/Films-and-industry/Danish-Film-History/2000-2009.aspx> (accessed November 14, 2017).
Shriver-Rice, Meryl (2009), "Adapting National Identity: Ethical Borders Made Suspect in the Hollywood Version of Susanne Bier's *Brothers*," *Film International* vol. 9, issue 2: 8–19.
Shriver-Rice, Meryl (2015), *Inclusion in New Danish Cinema: Sexuality and Transnational Belonging*, Bristol and Chicago: Intellect Books.
Smaill, Belinda (2014), "The Male Sojourner, the Female Director, and Popular European Cinema: The Worlds of Susanne Bier," *Camera Obscura* vol. 29, no. 1, 85: 5–31.

CHAPTER 3

Susanne Bier's Hollywood Experiments: *Things We Lost in the Fire* and *Serena*

Missy Molloy

INTRODUCTION

In an interview published in *Kosmorama* in 2010, Eva Novrup Redvall asked frequent Susanne Bier collaborator Thomas Anders Jensen[1] to comment on the differences between European and American film industries on one hand, and Danish on the other (Redvall 2010: 86). He replied, "the main difference is that you do not get a chance abroad. You get one go. What you deliver must really be in order. In Denmark, you can present something in progress that you involve people in, get feedback on, and discuss. That you cannot do with producers abroad" (Jensen quoted in Redvall 2010: 86, my translation).

Yet Bier's experiences abroad contradict Jensen's evaluation; she has gotten several chances to direct English-language, U.K./U.S. co-productions despite notable setbacks. The British-produced, American-distributed *Things We Lost in the Fire* (2007),[2] starring Halle Berry and Benicio del Toro, received tepid reviews on release and was dismissed as "awards bait" that failed to replicate Bier's then-recent successes with English-speaking audiences via the Danish-language films *Open Hearts* (*Elsker dig for evigt*, 2002), *Brothers* (*Brødre*, 2004), and *After the Wedding* (*Efter brylluppet*, 2006) (Holden 2007; Smith 2007; Whipp 2007). The film's theatrical run yielded only fifty percent of the film's production cost, and, despite generating positive reviews (for del Toro's performance in particular), *Things We Lost in the Fire* failed to generate the award nominations which, according to some critics, motivated its production. Furthermore, several reviews of the film specifically criticized stylistic features that had been praised in Bier's Danish-language international hits (Whipp 2007; Ebert 2007), which indicates that strategies that worked for her in past productions were not as effective in the new context.

Things We Lost in the Fire's underwhelming response appears enthusiastic in comparison to Bier's next "Hollywood" production, *Serena* (2014), a commercial failure that generated the worst reviews of her career and is distinguished as the only Jennifer Lawrence/Bradley Cooper collaboration not to have generated a profit.[3] Thus, while it can be said that as Bier's international reputation blossomed she savvily managed directing opportunities, in the process overcoming setbacks related to her nationality and gender, *Things We Lost in the Fire* and *Serena* stand out as conspicuous anomalies in the career of a filmmaker otherwise known for successful generic and industrial fluidity (Agger 2015). While neither film was produced by a major Hollywood studio, I refer to them as Bier's Hollywood films because they are widely understood as such. Hence until recently, the Wikipedia page on Bier featured the statement, "Bier has been praised as being a director capable of making films that appeal to an international market (although she has yet to make a successful transition to Hollywood filmmaking)." While the sentence has been edited in the wake of Bier's massively successful BBC/AMC event miniseries, *The Night Manager* (2016), it nonetheless points to intriguing aspects of Bier's complex, transnational career, which this chapter will parse by addressing the following: Bier's desire to reach a large audience, and how her status as a female filmmaker from a small nation has challenged and abetted that goal; narrative and tonal overlaps between *Things We Lost in the Fire* and what Belinda Smaill refers to as Bier's "trilogy"—*Brothers*, *After the Wedding*, and *In a Better World*—that augment crucial differences between the two; and finally, *Serena*'s fraught production process, which resonates with Jensen's statement on disparities between the Danish and American film industries in regards to experimentation, collaboration, and risk.

Definitive reasons why *Things We Lost in the Fire* and *Serena* were not successful in the manner of Bier's Danish films from the same time period are elusive, which makes this chapter partly speculative. However, integrating analytical methods associated with auteur theory and industry studies reveals overlaps between her U.S./U.K. productions and her other industrially diverse works. Furthermore, examining *Things We Lost in the Fire* and *Serena* for evidence of Bier's influence yields interesting details about the films and their paratexts that impacted the extent to which Bier was able to make her authorial mark visible in bigger-budget productions featuring Hollywood stars. Because she entered both projects at relatively late stages in the production process, her authorial mark is more visible in the films' styles than in their narratives, yet even the latter resemble other works in Bier's oeuvre. Therefore these films, which have been interpreted as failed efforts to transition to different industrial milieus, provide information regarding what Kaja Silverman calls "the 'scene' of authorial desire," the "cluster of fantasies" that "gives a particular group of films," in this case Bier's, "their libidinal coherence" (1988: 216).

This chapter reads *Things We Lost in the Fire* and *Serena* as Bier's efforts to find her footing in production contexts that challenged her creative ethos, which, while not synonymous with a Danish ideal (in that her work breaks with Danish cinematic traditions in key respects), relies on spontaneity and instinct as well as craft and confidence regarding the intended result. From Bier's perspective, *Serena* in particular was characterized by uncertainty regarding the desired end result, which frustrated the process of producing a successful film.[4] In effect, these less successful films provide valuable insights into the stories Bier is drawn to tell, as well as the conditions that best enable their telling.

BIER'S POPULIST ASPIRATIONS

Bier's comment, "I don't see a conflict between art and commerce, but I do see one between boredom and commerce," is widely circulated, appearing most prominently on the "Official Website of Denmark" (Denmark.dk). Her statement is explicitly provocative, an admission that she is aware, on the one hand, that her work has been criticized for being too commercial, popular and/or "American" in Denmark, where the cinematic culture champions singular artistic vision and risk-taking (for instance, see Redvall 2012). On the other hand, her first film to attract significant international attention, *Open Hearts*, was received by English-language audiences as an art film, and in Denmark is often discussed as her most aesthetically distinct and unconventional film, though it has also been referred to as a melodrama whose stylistic features mitigate its generic qualities (for instance, see Langkjær 2012). Tracing the application of the term "melodrama" to Bier's work reveals that critics, particularly in popular press publications, often connect the dramatic content of her dramas centered on family and intimacy to Bier's own gender in problematic ways; the result is that her work's melodramatic properties are imprecisely diagnosed, both in reviews that praise and fault Bier for her evocative portrayals of family trauma. Furthermore, Bier criticism often pejoratively links melodrama with a perceived desire to reach and affect viewers.

For example, Jack Stevenson's *Dogme Uncut* (2003), published a year after *Open Hearts* premiered, dismisses the significance of both *Open Hearts* and Lone Scherfig's *Italian for Beginners* (*Italiensk for Begynderne*, 2000) on the basis of their directors' genders and the films' perceived sentimentality (for Stevenson, the two are causally linked): "The fellows made the raw, hard-edged films that were transgressive, ground-breaking, and experimental, while the women made, well . . . 'women's pictures,' that promulgated a more sentimental set of values and which tapped into a potentially much larger audience" (2003: 150). Interestingly, Stevenson appears to hold the fact that *Open Hearts* and *Italian for Beginners* were "massive hits" against their directors (2003: 150).

His statements have been frequently cited (see, for instance, Aaron 2007 and Bainbridge 2007), no doubt due to the high level of bias against women filmmakers they brazenly convey; yet a similar sensibility pervades many reviews of Bier's films, even those that praise her use of "realistic" techniques to mitigate "melodramatic" elements. For instance, Terry Lawson's review of *Things We Lost in the Fire* reads, "Though it flirts with melodrama to the tipping point, the movie, like the characters played by [Halle] Berry and Benicio del Toro, ultimately makes connections too honest, hopeful and human to induce guilt on the part of any open-hearted moviegoer" (Lawson 2007). One of the statement's subtexts, which equates melodrama with artificiality, is apparent in assessments of Bier's work suggesting that her films inflate everyday experiences and emotions to an extent that would make them unappealingly artificial (i.e. "women's pictures") were it not for the sincerity of the emotions represented, which is positively attributed to Bier's direction and the actors' performances. When the drama is perceived as unconvincing, as it was by most critics that reviewed *Serena*, Bier and melodrama are blamed. In sum, popular press treatments of Bier's work treat melodrama as a dangerous representational mode, which Bier, as a woman, must exert extra effort to control.

A number of film scholars have argued against dismissing Bier's films on account of their melodramatic properties; for instance, in *Realismen i Dansk Film*, Birger Langkjær cites Anne Jerslev's opinion of *Open Hearts*, which he shares, that the film involves a "special form of realism" which is framed as melodrama's antidote (Langkjær 2014): "The realistic effort in *Open Hearts* is, for me, to stage a filmic universe without narrative or aesthetic superstructure, without embedding the characters in a story or stylistic expression greater than them, and without giving any overarching explanation for their actions and reactions" (Jerslev quoted in Langkjær 2014, my translation). Although I find Jerslev's and Langkjær's interpretations of *Open Hearts* convincing, I suggest that instead of pitting realism against melodrama—in other words, "legitimate" expressions of emotion against sentimentality, thereby weighing "soft" and "hard" elements of Bier's films to determine whether authenticity outweighs excess—scholars and critics should reassess the interpretative frameworks and terminology through which they judge films' values, particularly films made by women working in dramatic modes historically associated with female viewers and that appeal to large audiences. In "The Male Sojourner, the Female Director, and Popular European Cinema: The Worlds of Susanne Bier," Belinda Smaill proffers a related claim: "The terms on which [Bier's] films are negatively assessed frame the popular dimensions of the work pejoratively as feminine" (2014: 15).

Many have commented on the irony that Kathryn Bigelow became the first woman to receive the Academy Award for Best Director for *The Hurt Locker* (2009), a war film that focuses almost exclusively on men (see, for instance,

White 2015: 3). Bier's Academy Award winner (for Best Foreign Language Film), *In a Better World*, also raises social and ethical questions related to masculinity and violence. In addition, Bier's recent Emmy win was for *The Night Manager*, a spy thriller focused primarily on two men: the hero, Jonathan Pine, and villain, Richard Roper. These facts underscore gender inequalities in media industries and criticism, which continually stoke conditions in which representations focused on men and masculine cultural issues are judged most legitimate. Consequently, women directors must carefully modulate their generic, narrative, and stylistic choices according to the prejudiced assessments to which their works will be undoubtedly, and perhaps unconsciously, subject. In Bier's case, her consistent interest in masculinity lends her work legitimacy in some quarters, whereas her focus on extreme emotional states is met with greater skepticism. That many of her works evince both of these qualities makes her a difficult screen author to classify.

The lack of critical consensus regarding Bier's work is partly the result of prejudices in film criticism, both in Denmark and elsewhere. Furthermore, her consistently reiterated aspiration to appeal to broad audiences has been subject to a special form of criticism, which is symptomatic of continuous cultural debates regarding popular culture and social and/or artistic value. Therefore it is important to note, in assessing *Things We Lost in the Fire*'s and *Serena*'s failures to land with audiences, that evaluations of Bier's work are slippery and highly dependent on context—a fact Bier alluded to during the Q&A that directly followed *The Night Manager*'s premiere at the 2016 Berlinale when she called her own work "mainstream," stating, as an aside, that her Danish-language films were not treated as such abroad only because they were in Danish. Furthermore, she appeared entirely comfortable with the label she adopted for her work.[5] Clearly, the challenges Bier experienced transitioning to U.S./U.K. production environments do not result from a lack of awareness on her part regarding inconsistencies in film reception, which are likely familiar to other women directors emerging from small national cinemas to global platforms.

On the contrary, Bier demonstrates an unusually canny sense of negotiating audiences' and critics' varied and contradictory expectations, and has been open about her ambition to achieve popular success from early in her career. In an interview with Mette Hjort published in 2001, Bier states, "I think of film as a kind of mass communication, and I care about reaching a lot of people, or particular kinds of people" (Bier quoted in Hjort 2001: 246). The interview doesn't include an explicit elaboration on the statement's intriguing final phrase, which makes me wonder if Bier's qualifier was the result of uncertainty regarding her target audience or an acknowledgment that her individual works appeal to different audiences. Both possibilities are relevant to Bier's Hollywood experiments, which reflect her desire to reach new, untested audiences and, specifically in *Serena*'s case, her willingness to work in genres she had little experience with. Therefore, she should be considered a filmmaker who takes risks, though not of the class most frequently celebrated in film criticism, which, in my view, consistently favors aesthetic experimentation and formal innovation above other creative risk-taking. Skimming the titles of scholarly monographs dedicated to individual filmmakers, in which Danish director Lars von Trier, for example, is well represented, supports this conclusion.

The Official Website of Denmark's page on Bier implicitly addresses the backlash Bier's popularity abroad stimulated in her home country: "Denmark's leading female film director Susanne Bier is very conscious that cinema is not only art but also entertainment. Her ability to balance art and entertainment is exactly the quality that has made Bier a popular director in both Europe and Hollywood." This promotional language situates Bier's intentionality as a defense against attacks on her work based on its commercial appeal. In regard to Bier's mixed reception, Smaill remarks, "The categorization of art cinema and popular cinema is not fixed but rather relies on a dynamic between transnational and national that is influenced by the terms of production, popular reception, and criticism" (2014: 14). Additionally, Gunhild Agger highlights Bier's creative versatility when she uses Bier's filmography to outline five production strategies available to Danish filmmakers, including art, mainstream, and genre films in Danish and English (2015: 10). Agger categorizes *Things We Lost in the Fire* and *Serena* as examples of what she labels the "fifth strategy," "English/American language mainstream and genre films of an international standard" (2015: 10).

In drawing attention to the strategy Bier has found most challenging, I stress that her goal of reaching a wide, international audience required the productive flexibility Agger notes, which also exposed Bier to risk. Furthermore, *The Night Manager*, exceptional in her body of work in many respects, demonstrates the successful adaptation of her directorial strengths to big-budget, mainstream, Hollywood-style production, albeit in television. That success, however, was predicated on previous efforts to produce "English/American language mainstream and genre films of an international standard," such as *Things We Lost in the Fire* and *Serena*, that did not pay off in conventional ways.

Interestingly, Bier experienced popular success working in romantic comedy with *The One and Only* and *Love Is All You Need*, the latter an intriguing hybrid of characteristics associated with Danish and American cinema that is relatively big-budget and definitely mainstream. Meanwhile, her experiments with English-language drama indicate a tougher learning curve. However, one of the most consistent aspects of Bier's work is the revelation of humor in unexpected, tragic circumstances, a characteristic that makes her films generically complex; this skill is apparent in her earliest feature film, *Freud's Leaving Home*

(*Freud flyttar hemifrån* . . ., 1991), and is particularly notable in the unique approach to Ida's illness in *Love Is All You Need*, which accounts for much of the romantic comedy's dramatic charge. And, to cite a relevant example from one of her internationally successful Danish-language dramas, Jannik's character transformation in *Brothers* generates extremely funny moments in an otherwise serious film. Thus, while Bier is definitely the Danish director whose work best illustrates the range of production options Agger outlines, her generic fluidity is apparent not only among her films, but in the films themselves, which consistently draw attention to humor in traumatic situations and drama in the everyday regardless of generic classification. Therefore, her work aligns with Christine Gledhill's concept of "melodramatic modality" because Bier tends to work in a mode "not identified with any one genre" (2000: 240) that employs "heightened contrasts and polar oppositions to make the world morally legible" (Peter Brooks quoted in Gledhill 2000: 234)[6].

TRAUMA, MASCULINITY, AND CRISIS, CONTINUED: *THINGS WE LOST IN THE FIRE*

Smaill explains that her "trilogy" reference connotes *Brothers*, *After the Wedding*, and *In a Better World*'s shared interest in "masculinity and dilemmas facing male culture and sociality." These films, she continues, "draw on the codes of melodrama to emphasize the ways in which the complex backdrop of war, globalization, and politics supplement and compel family dynamics" (2014: 16). *Things We Lost in the Fire* also stresses the revisionary impact of trauma on family and intimacy, thus foregrounding the same issues Smaill notes in the trilogy. I will quickly summarize *Brothers* and *Things We Lost in the Fire* to propose overlaps between the trilogy and Bier's first Hollywood production.

In *Brothers*, Michael's apparent death and imprisonment while serving in Afghanistan motivates the main characters' transformations. Thus, the film crosscuts between his traumatic experiences in Afghanistan and his family's efforts to adjust to his loss in Copenhagen. The title, *Brothers*, previews the major contrast, which the film immediately establishes, between Michael and his never-do-well brother, Jannik. In Michael's absence, Jannik steps into his shoes, providing emotional support to Michael's wife Sarah and their daughters, Natalia and Camilla. Later, when Michael unexpectedly returns home, the family must readjust to include him, having found a working emotional dynamic in his absence, one that includes an attraction between Jannik and Sarah. The film's third act builds to a physical confrontation between the brothers in which Jannik must protect Michael's family from him because Michael has come home too emotionally damaged to care for them (or himself). In the film's final scene, Sarah visits Michael in prison to present him with an ultimatum—either reveal his trauma, or never see her or his children again. In the final shot, Michael begins to recount what happened to him in Afghanistan, the film thus concluding on the possibility that he might recover with her support.

Things We Lost in the Fire has a remarkably similar dramatic arc, except the death that motivates the character transformations is not mistaken; Audrey's husband, Brian, is shot and killed in the film's first act after he intercedes in a public altercation between an abusive husband and his wife. Prior to his death, the film had set up a contrast between Brian's successes as a father and husband and the failures of Jerry, his best friend, who is a long-term heroin addict with whom Brian maintains a friendship despite their extremely different social statuses. Brian is a successful real estate agent whose wealth is obvious from the upscale suburban home he shares with Audrey and their two children, while Jerry is unemployed and nearly homeless, surviving on minimal resources. After Brian's death, Audrey reaches out to Jerry for emotional support even though she had resented him in the past, regarding him as unworthy of her husband's friendship and trust. The film thus engineers a character contrast reminiscent of *Brothers*, focusing, in this case, on the never-do-well character, as the husband is only present via flashbacks after the first act. *After the Wedding* also centralizes such a contrast, in that case between Jacob and Jörgen, as does *A Second Chance* (*En chance til*, 2014), though in the latter film, the contrast between Andreas and Tristan is much more stark and thus inspires less compelling moral questions.

Obviously, given that Jensen is not the writer on *Things We Lost in the Fire*, it seems clear that one of Bier's main interests is juxtaposing divergent forms of masculinity. In my view, she is particularly energized by revealing the vulnerabilities of apparently successful men, thus exposing masculine models of power and privilege as hollow. Meanwhile, her less socially successful male characters discover unexpected strengths and lighten the dramatic weight of her dramas. The "money shots" in her films are men breaking down: both the successful and unsuccessful men in her films do so, the shared vulnerability to trauma thus equalizing their superficial differences. In this context, Silverman's account of authorial desire is relevant: "Insofar as authorial desire manages to invade a particular corpus, it will be organized around some such structuring 'scene' or group of 'scenes'" (1988: 217). The "structuring scene" that pervades Bier's "corpus" exposes traditional masculine models of success as tenuous and revels in the sights and sounds of vulnerable men.

Dramatic representations of men in extremely vulnerable states include Jörgen sobbing, "I don't want to die," in *After the Wedding* (Figure 3.1); the final shot of Richard Roper in the back of a police van (about to be brutalized by his captors) in *The Night Manager* (Figure 3.2); Niels reacting to Cæcilie's

Figure 3.1 Jörgen sobbing, "I don't want to die" in *After the Wedding*.

Figure 3.2 The final shot of *The Night Manager*'s Richard Roper in the back of a police van.

rejection in *Open Hearts* (Figure 3.3); and Jerry detoxing after a heroin relapse in *Things We Lost in the Fire* (Figure 3.4). An interesting variant of the scene appears in Bier's B-side from the 1990s, *Sekten* (1997)—her first experiment in the psychological thriller subgenre—which, unlike the films noted above, features a female protagonist. The film follows Mona's efforts to save her best friend Anne from the seductive appeal of a rogue psychiatrist, Dr. Lack, the leader of a cult. In the film's climax, Mona and Anne lock Dr. Lack in a torture

Figure 3.3 Niels reacting to Cæcilie's rejection in *Open Hearts*.

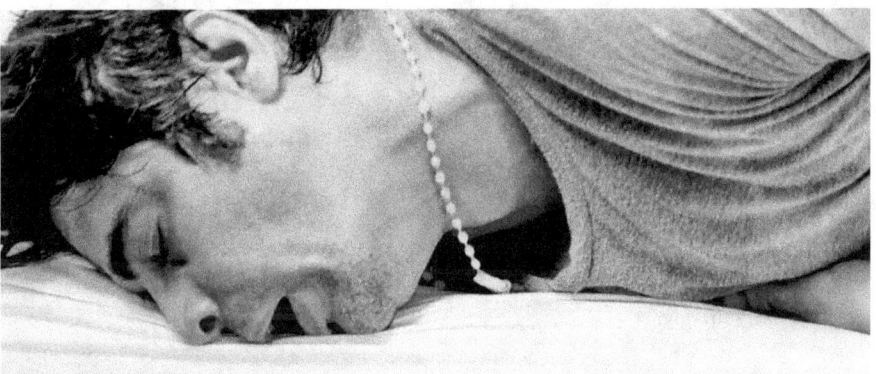

Figure 3.4 Jerry detoxing after a heroin relapse in *Things We Lost in the Fire*.

chamber, Anne pumping up the lights and screeching sounds (engineered to "reset" his followers' personalities) to maximum before she and Mona flee. The following shot reveals Dr. Lack curled in the fetal position, screaming in pain (Figure 3.5). The climax thus highlights the extreme reversal of a hypnotically powerful man suddenly subject to the vulnerability he had until that point systematically inflicted on others. The final shot of the sequence, in which his wife and professional partner, Karen, observes impassively, suggests Karen as a potential screen surrogate for Bier (Figure 3.6).

Figure 3.5 *Sekten*'s Dr. Lack in fetal position.

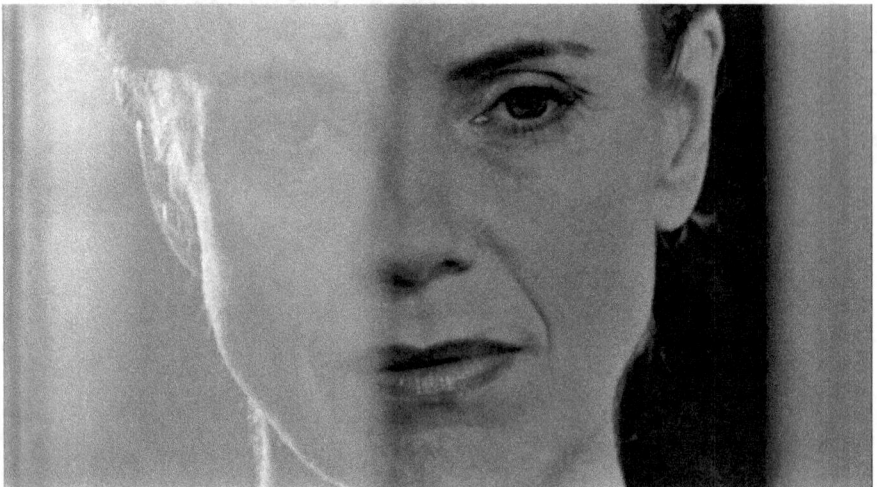

Figure 3.6 Bier's screen surrogate? Lack's wife and professional partner, Karen, impassively observes him suffering.

Silverman asks the following questions of Italian director Liliana Cavani's body of work: "What desire finds expression through this constant return to and preoccupation with male subjectivity? And what dream is fulfilled through the stipulation that this subjectivity be impaired in some radical way?" (220–1). The same questions apply to Bier's cinematic preoccupations, which take shape in her consistent attention to various, seemingly disparate forms of masculinity, the dramatic scenarios in her films bearing down on the characters to expose their fragility. These "impaired" masculinities take purest form in films Bier co-created with Jensen, though it is fascinating that they appear, to some extent, in all of her works.

Thus, the similarities between *Things We Lost in the Fire* and the trilogy beg the question of why the former was not as successful as the latter films, which also dramatize opposing forms of masculinity and spectacularize the vulnerability of men experiencing traumas. For one thing, the film doesn't stress "the complex backdrop of war, globalization, and politics" that Smaill identifies as crucial to the trilogy (2014: 16). *Things We Lost in the Fire* is apolitical in that it focuses mainly on Jerry's efforts to fight his addiction and become someone who others can depend on. For another, *Things We Lost in the Fire* backed off, somewhat, from developing the relationship between Audrey and Jerry, which appeared to be one of the film's main promotional selling points; instead, Audrey fades into the background as Jerry's struggle to stay clean commandeers the plot. Because Berry had been a significant part of the film's promotion (for instance, in her image's prominent placement in posters advertising the film), her vague supporting role as the grieving widow reaching out, somewhat bizarrely, to her husband's childhood friend was surprisingly underdeveloped and difficult for viewers to parse.

Nevertheless, the emphasis on Jerry's struggle to balance his individual desires and weaknesses with the needs of the family Brian left behind is consistent with Bier's other dramas, in particular *Brothers* and *After the Wedding*, Jerry's arc paralleling Jannik's and Jacob's efforts to nurture strong, supportive relationships. However, Bier signed on to *Things We Lost in the Fire* late in pre-production with the screenplay complete and the main roles nearly cast, while in the films highlighted above, she developed the story concept with Jensen, who then wrote the screenplay. Therefore, she helped shape the trilogy's characters and narratives from the start.

In an interview promoting *Things We Lost in the Fire* before its release, Bier explains her initial attraction to the project, which she perceived as both familiar and exotic in relation to her previous work:

> I was interested because . . . I felt very familiar with the subject matter, and I was kind of wondering, is it too much like something that I've already done? But then I felt that I hadn't dealt for a very long time with a female lead, which I thought was really interesting . . . and then I had never dealt with addiction. For somebody [who doesn't] really have any addictive traits, it's very fascinating, and it's kind of scary . . . and I was very compelled by that. (Sloan 2007)

Her statement is revelatory regarding her approach to selecting new projects. She first considers her familiarity with the material, i.e. whether her skill set complements it. At the same time, she is careful that the project is not *too* similar to what she has "already done." In this case, she decided the female lead and the focus on addiction made the material novel enough to offer creative challenges. However, Bier doesn't elaborate much on what would be interesting about working with a female lead for the first "in a very long time,"[7] which resonates with the film's shift in focus from Audrey to Jerry. Meanwhile, Bier's fascination with addiction is apparent in the film, which may explain Audrey's relegation from lead to supporting character.

In fact, the film seems a bit at a loss regarding what *else* to do with Audrey and/or her relationship with Jerry beyond observing the strain addiction causes those close to an addict. Initially, Audrey's role involves grieving; then she convinces Jerry to live in her garage for obscure reasons; next, after encouraging a relationship between him and her two small children, she evicts him on an emotional whim, which contributes to his relapse; finally, she commits to supporting his recovery. Unfortunately, the specific actions that elaborate her character are at best careless: for example, accusing Jerry of stealing without grounds and kicking him out because she feels threatened by the fact that he gets along well with her kids. In sum, the film represents Audrey as an enigma, her actions too opaque to shed much light on her psychology.

In that sense, she resembles *Open Hearts*' Cæcilie, who is also gradually overshadowed by a male character whose behaviors are more transparent. Although *Open Hearts* follows Cæcilie's experiences from the start and the music she listens to while wandering Copenhagen functions as a framing device for the film's opening and closing, viewers are not privy to the nuances of her psychological motivations to the same extent that they are to those of Niels, the married doctor with whom Cæcilie begins an affair after her fiancé is paralyzed in a car accident involving Niels' wife and teenage daughter. In contrast, *Sekten* centralizes female friendship and passes the well-known Bechdel test with flying colors[8]; many scenes highlight the intimacy between Mona and Anne, thereby generating interest in their relational dynamic as well as in the motivations behind their actions. In other words, that the protagonist is a woman seems central to *Sekten*'s plot and primary to its development. Similarly, *Love Is All You Need*'s protagonist is undoubtedly Ida, and her transformation in the wake of cancer treatment inspires those of the supporting characters. I conclude that Bier's success with female characters depends on their orientations to the plot as well as to how well they align with Bier's cinematic fixations in particular films.

In Audrey's case, the film passes her by en route to other fascinations. According to Bier, Audrey and Jerry fell in love and should have consummated their relationship: "I actually did think it should have been a love story ... [But] it was so much not part of the project, and the producers and the writers ... when I came into it, it was not a love story, so it wasn't an argument I could really win."[9] This statement recalls one Bier made in the interview with Hjort: "I'm enormously interested in eroticism at all possible levels, and this is reflected in everything I do. I don't mean sex, but rather a kind of underlying erotic drive or erotic frustration, which I think is very important"

Figure 3.7 Jerry's frustrated desire for Audrey on display in *Things We Lost in the Fire*.

Figure 3.8 Audrey's feelings toward Jerry are less evident.

(2001: 246–7). Jerry's frustrated desire for Audrey is painfully apparent in *Things We Lost in the Fire*, though her feelings for him are less evident (Figures 3.7 and 3.8).

The differing perspectives on Audrey and Jerry's relationship are evident in the film's hesitation regarding which direction to develop it. Several reviews comment on "false note[s]" in the characters' interactions: Kirk Honeycutt (in a mainly complimentary review) astutely states that "Audrey['s] insist[ence] that Jerry come to her bed one night and hold her as Brian once did . . . makes sense on no level—especially given her antipathy for him at this time—and the movie takes a while to recover" (Honeycutt 2007), while Roger Ebert hints, "There is only one scene between them that is ill-advised, and indeed unbelievable, and you'll know the one I mean" (Ebert 2007). These two reviews present complementary accounts of the film's strengths and weaknesses, which resonate with Bier's statements about her interests in the story and her alternative perspective on the character dynamics. Honeycutt praises the casting, "dramatic intensity and keen observation," yet calls the film an "unstable mix of ... tearjerker, junkie-recovery story and odd-couple pairing." Meanwhile, Ebert singles out Del Toro's performance as "key" to the film's effectiveness, but comments on the "strangeness of [Audrey's] asking a heroin addict to live in her garage." Their evaluations suggest that particular aspects of the film are impactful, yet inconsistencies in the plot and character developments nonetheless undermine the film's effect. In conclusion, Ebert calls the film "an engrossing melodrama [with] its heart in the right place," while Honeycutt half-heartedly states, "Despite the challenges of blending a European sensibility into a Hollywood production, the film holds together not all that badly." In my opinion, the film registers Bier's urge to take the story in directions not originally intended by the screenwriter or producers, as well as her unique skill at observing extreme and ambivalent emotions; however, this combination in a new production environment had mixed results, which left viewers uncertain what to make of the film despite intriguing characters and several notable and compelling scenes.

Although North American critics were selective regarding what worked in *Things We Lost in the Fire*, most praised the performances, which reiterate Bier's success with actors and demonstrate its industrial portability. Indeed, del Toro's performance stands out in the actor's filmography as a striking evocation of the difficulty of fighting addiction. Regardless, scholarship on Bier's work, which though minimal has begun to develop of late, barely addresses the film except as a side note. In sum, the film resembles several of her most internationally successful films, was sandwiched between *After the Wedding* (an Academy Award nominee for Best Foreign Language Film) and *In a Better World* (an Academy Award winner for Best Foreign Language Film), and shares many narrative and stylistic features with both films and *Brothers*, yet it failed to generate much interest despite a higher budget and Hollywood stars. In fact, the film cost more to produce, at approximately $16 million, than the three films in the trilogy combined. Thus, in that respect at least, the film highlights the economy of the Danish production model Jensen compares favorably to Hollywood's.

Regarding Hollywood production environments, Bier, recalling her first impressions of *Things We Lost in the Fire*'s set, commented: "I felt it was like a camping site, and it was all the trailers that had to do with the set, lots more makeup artists and hairdressers and strange cappuccinos. There's a different layer [to] it" (Sloan 2007). The Hollywood production model presumes a budget most Danish films don't come anywhere near, even in the wake of significant successes in Danish cinema post-Dogme. And as Bier's recollections indicate, directing in this budget range involves other, unfamiliar layers to which directors from other film cultures must quickly acclimate in order to succeed. Nonetheless, Bier apparently found strength in the challenge, concluding that "as a filmmaker, what you do is the same always. You are telling a story, and you should concern yourself with that, and I decided that I wasn't going to be overwhelmed by all of it" (Sloan 2007).

A 2012 interview with Bier conducted by the Directors Guild of America confirmed her commitment, post-*Things We Lost in the Fire*, to reaching "the masses" via English-language, Hollywood productions:

> [Bier] learned from making *Things We Lost in the Fire*, as well as from having her 2004 war drama *Brothers* remade by Jim Sheridan, what it's like to reach the masses as only a Hollywood-produced film can. "Of course you want to do English-language films," says Bier . . . "My movies have been very successful in Europe. But if you feel that you've got some stories to tell which are going to interest, amuse, or entertain, you want to address a bigger audience." (Rochlin 2012)

THE *SERENA* QUAGMIRE

Bier's next Hollywood experiment, *Serena*, is more international from a production standpoint and less so in the context of its narrative, which depends heavily on regional and historical connotations far afield of Bier's comfort zone. The narrative charts the downfall of George Pemberton, the co-owner of a North Carolina timber company, who is simultaneously beset by two severe challenges: changing attitudes toward the logging industry in Depression-era Appalachia, and the ruthless ambitions of his new wife, Serena. *Serena* was much less successful than *Things We Lost in the Fire*,[10] and further attests to Bier's attraction to generic experimentation and predilection for risk-taking, her strengths as a director and collaborator, and the conditions least likely to offset them. Commenting on connections across her works, Bier stated, "I think I can create moments of extreme presence, of extreme intimacy, not just in intimate scenes but also in bigger scenes, which is pretty visible in all my work, even the works that are not entirely successful. And then, in the works that are less successful, there are less of those moments."[11] Multiple factors contributed to *Serena*'s implausibility and lack of intensity, including challenges reminiscent of *Things We Lost in the Fire*.

Various stakeholders in *Serena* cite collective confusion regarding what kind of film they were making as a key contributor to production and post-production difficulties. This situation was exacerbated by the skyrocketing careers of the lead actors, in particular Lawrence's, which occurred after *Serena* was filmed but well before its release following two years of editing that failed to entirely satisfy any creative parties. Initially, the global success of Lawrence and Cooper's *Silver Linings Playbook* stimulated interest in Bier's project. However, post-production delays and reticence to discuss the film on the part of main creative players significantly diminished expectations. By the time *Serena* premiered quietly at the BFI London Film Festival in 2014, the then buzz-less film met drastically reduced expectations.

Serena appears a victim of bad timing to an even more extreme extent than *Things We Lost in the Fire*. Again, Bier did not participate in the early stages of the project. When I interviewed *Serena*'s screenwriter, Christopher Kyle, in December 2016, he explained that the screenplay had already passed through various hands and been workshopped with multiple cinematic partnerships in mind, most notably as a Darren Aronofsky film starring Angelina Jolie, before Aronofsky (and Jolie) moved on, making Bier's involvement possible. Consequently, Bier inherited a project with a screenplay that had already been through multiple revisions and the title role recast. Jolie is well suited to hard-edged, driven characters whose psychological motivations are unclear, as her well-regarded performances from *Gia* (Cristofer, 1998) to *Wanted* (Bekmambetov, 2008) to *Maleficent* (Stromberg, 2014) illustrate—which makes her a logical choice to play Serena, whose interiority is not fleshed out in the novel by Ron Rash and who functions instead as a provocative villain, wreaking havoc on the lives around her. On the other hand, Lawrence was manifestly too young for the role at the time of shooting; although the novel doesn't specify Serena's age, biographical details indicate that she is at least in her early thirties. Additionally, Lawrence is skilled at revealing the vulnerability and naiveté of characters struggling to understand their power over others. However, from the novel's outset, Serena has clearly had considerable experience exercising power. For example, in the novel's first scene, she calmly observes her new husband, George, murder the father of his former lover, Rachel, who is present and visibly pregnant with George's child. Serena then hands Rachel the hunting knife used to gut her father, recommending that she "sell it . . . That money will help when the child is born. That's all you'll ever get from my husband and me" (Rash 2008: 10). Lawrence performs Serena as vulnerable in a manner that sharply departs from the novel's characterization. From the start, casting Lawrence diminished Serena's credibility, which was critical to the film's because her character propels much of its plot (a fact reflected in the title of the novel and film).

Furthermore, forging a feature film from the sprawling, literary, and regionally specific novel was an extremely ambitious undertaking. From the vantage of the present, one can imagine a successful series based on the novel, several recent adaptations, such as HBO's *Olive Kitteridge*, Hulu's *The Handmaid's Tale*, and Bier's *The Night Manager* having demonstrated the miniseries as an appropriate format for complex, lengthy novels. Additionally, odd adaptive decisions undercut the film narrative's plausibility. For instance, the novel alternates between the perspectives of George and Rachel, the characters most strongly subject to the extremity of Serena's love and hate; however, the film whittled Rachel's role down to its bare minimum. Obviously, novels must lose weight to fit the parameters of feature films; in this case, the shedding process too drastically trimmed material that ensured comprehensibility.

Bier cites the sudden fame of Lawrence and Cooper as a significant post-production challenge. As concerns regarding public image and star persona mushroomed, the film's producers became increasingly hesitant to tell the story as originally envisioned, wanting instead to forge a romantic drama from footage connoting tragedy. In the end, the novel's characterizations did not survive the transfer to screen. In 2014, *The Hollywood Reporter* stated that *Serena* had been screened multiple times for potential buyers without success: "Says one top buyer, 'The film was so edited, it made no sense.'" Another called the performances "uneven, particularly Lawrence's [descent into madness] as the childless wife of a timber baron" (Siegel 2014). Regarding Lawrence as Serena, Bier mused, "It might possibly be that a character who does such horrific things and is played by someone as lovable as Jennifer Lawrence—it was difficult making that whole story work." She sums up the protracted editing process as disastrous:

> We must have done 120 edits or something. And I can't edit that much; I can probably do ten edits. Part of my life is I've got a compass, which is right or wrong, and with an audience, I can tell if the beats are working or not. And that sort of intuitive, sharp sense of "Is this working?" goes away. You kind of go, "I don't know." I was numb. After edit number eight I was completely numb. And I think that was edited for like two years. (Bier quoted in the final chapter of this volume)

Published information regarding the production, most significantly the statements of those most closely involved in the project, indicates that the intentions motivating the adaptation at the start were no longer central at its completion. Bier concludes that making *Serena* was "hugely educational. I think it was probably one of the things that has [taught] me the most, because I'm never going to do that again. I'm never going to venture into something and then end up in a process where I can't remember why I wanted to do it."

I conclude that *Serena* is an interesting failure whose production setbacks are more illuminating than the completed film—particularly in charting Bier's experiments with genre and industry. The story dramatizes an arc as seen in earlier Bier successes by featuring a successful man made vulnerable by tragedy. Furthermore, *Serena* could have enabled Bier to centralize a complex character who, like *After the Wedding*'s Jørgen, orchestrates the lives of those around her according to her vision. Additionally, *Serena* centers on an enigmatic, extremely powerful woman who mesmerizes most of those she comes in contact with and plays an extremely active role in the plot, in contrast to female characters in Bier's films who react to the men around them (for example, Sarah in *Brothers* and Marianne in *In a Better World*) or to the difficult circumstances they find themselves in (for example, Cæcilie in *Open Hearts* and Ida in *Love Is All You Need*). Serena acts—often selfishly and aggressively—and other characters, including George, *re*act. She thus descends from a narrative lineage of powerful women, imagined by male authors, who inspire a hero's downfall (including Euripides' Medea and Shakespeare's Lady Macbeth). By directing *Serena*, Bier tackled a project in which a woman has a narrative influence typically reserved for men in the Bier/Jensen collaborations.

In the novel, Serena is the catastrophe that incites the plot, inspires character transformations, and pushes the drama to its traumatic climax. Consequently, adapting *Serena* for the screen could have struck Bier's ideal creative balance by demanding that she direct simultaneously familiar and exotic material. Moreover, Bier has cited the novel's attention to the destruction of nature as a fascinating, foreign element of the project's initial appeal. However, the transnational production shot mainly in the Czech Republic with primarily European actors fails to animate the local specificity that made the novel compelling, especially its evocation of the historical conflict between the logging industry and the U.S. federal government at the start of its National Park initiative, which illustrates the opposition between industrial avarice and environmental protection that remains central to contemporary U.S. and global politics.

CONCLUSION

Criticisms levied against *Things We Lost in the Fire* and *Serena* oddly resemble commentary on her most successful films. Since her international breakthrough, Bier's predilection for highly dramatic situations has been consistently noted, and film critics have habitually referred to her films as melodramas tempered by realism, the former's emotional excesses regulated by the latter. Popular press reviews of Bier's Hollywood films imply that *Things We Lost in the Fire* and *Serena* lack the realism necessary to tip the scale in favor of authenticity; the films, in other words, subject viewers to unregulated emotional excesses. And in *Serena*'s case, plot and character inconsistencies further undermine the credibility necessary to affect viewers. Regardless, these dramatic experiments reaffirm Bier's attraction to "big emotions," strong personalities, and extreme circumstances, all of which constitute her perception of reality, which contradicts traditional notions of cinematic realism:

My feeling is that in Scandinavia there's been a tendency to emphasize a certain naturalism, and I must say that I don't actually experience the naturalism in question as particularly true or as particularly descriptive of how people really live together. My characters are always a little more crazy. I'm sure that other people wouldn't describe them as naturalistic characters, although they *are* authentic, because they're emotionally authentic. (Bier quoted in Hjort 2001: 241)

The Night Manager undoubtedly demonstrates that Bier can helm commercially viable work in Hollywood-style production conditions. The miniseries, her second most expensive production (after *Serena*) and most commercially oriented project, has already drawn more viewers than her previous films combined; its final episode averaged 6.6 million viewers in the U.K. (BBC News 2016), and the series has been broadcast in 180 countries and counting, attracting at least 40 million views in China alone (Wiseman 2016). Bier's career to date uniquely illustrates the challenges and opportunities of a woman film director from a small nation whose goal is popular and artistic success in a male-dominated field. Focusing on her less successful features exposes the limits of auteur-based film criticism, which ascribes more power to a film's director than she, in many cases, is able to exercise. Such criticism is therefore particularly unsuited to a film that represents a director's first or second effort to transition from a small national cinema context to a big-budget production with global ambitions. In the cases of *Things We Lost in the Fire* and *Serena*, Bier's authorial control over the end result was limited to a much greater extent than in the case of, for instance, *Open Hearts*, which she created with Jensen from the ground up.

These case studies outline and clarify Bier's skills as a screen storyteller and their potential limits: it appears that a historical novel adapted as a feature-length film may not demonstrate her key competencies, and centralizing a female character like Audrey in *Things We Lost in the Fire* requires Bier to modify strategies that have proven successful in her works focused on men. I have emphasized throughout that Bier's less successful films provide valuable information regarding her directorial strengths as well as the preoccupations that fuel her craft. Thus, my interpretations stress that *Things We Lost in the Fire* and *Serena* provide unique data regarding what fascinates Bier, as well as the conditions in which her cinematic vision thrives.

In conclusion, these films demonstrate Bier's willingness to take risks and to fail, which, in my opinion, is the flip side of her greatest triumphs. Her grace in acknowledging her less successful efforts suggests that she will continue to experiment with projects that push her into new creative terrain, a prediction supported by the recent announcement of a project in development: an adaptation of *Out of Africa* produced by NBC International for television.

Additionally, Bier's current project, *Bird Box*, exposes her to the special industrial conditions of Netflix's current phase of feature-film development, represents a genre novel to Bier (the post-apocalyptic thriller), and features a female lead (played by Sandra Bullock). To create effective screen versions of *Out of Africa*, composed of a woman narrator's recollections of colonial Africa, and *Bird Box*, which is also adapted from a book, Bier will undoubtedly draw on her hard-earned experience as well as her sophisticated narrative and stylistic skills to confront, head-on, genre and gender issues that have proven challenging for her in the past.

NOTES

1. Bier and Jensen share "story by" credit for, and Jensen is credited as screenwriter of, six films directed by Bier: *Open Hearts* (*Elsker dig for evigt*, 2002), *Brothers* (*Brødre*, 2004), *After the Wedding* (*Efter brylluppet*, 2006), *In a Better World* (*Hævnen*, 2010), *Love Is All You Need* (2011), and *Second Chances* (*En chance til*, 2013).
2. The film was produced by Neal Street Productions (U.K.) and distributed by DreamWorks Pictures (U.S.).
3. Jennifer Lawrence and Bradley Cooper have collaborated on four films: *Silver Linings Playbook* (2012), *American Hustle* (2013), *Serena* (2014), and *Joy* (2016). *Serena* grossed only about $4 million on an estimated $25–30 million budget, while *Silver Linings Playbook* grossed $236 million on a $21 million budget (according to online estimates).
4. I'm paraphrasing statements Bier made in an interview in November 2016 conducted by the editors of this volume (Molloy, Nielsen, and Shriver-Rice). A transcript of the interview is included as the final chapter.
5. I base these observations on my memory of Bier's statements after the world premiere of *The Night Manager*'s first two episodes, which I attended in Berlin on February 18, 2016.
6. Mette Hjort makes a similar claim about Lone Scherfig's work in *Lone Scherfig's Italian for Beginners* (2011).
7. Bier's Danish romantic comedies, *The One and Only* (1999) and *Once in a Lifetime* (2000), center on female characters (Sus and Mona). Additionally, her Dogme film, *Open Hearts* (2002), debatably has a female protagonist (Cæcilie). The main characters in her next two films are men: Michael (*Brothers*) and Jacob (*After the Wedding*).
8. Originating in 1985 (and attributed to Alison Bechdel), the Bechdel Test comprises three criteria: "(1) [a film] has to have at least two women in it, who (2) talk to each other, about (3) something besides a man" (<http://bechdeltest.com/>). References to the test have become increasingly common, along with debates about gender equity behind and in front of the camera.
9. I again refer to the November 2016 Bier interview included as this volume's final chapter.
10. The title of *The Telegraph* review of *Serena* aptly represents the film's critical reception in the popular press: "*Serena*, review, 'intensely unlikeable,'" <http://www.telegraph.co.uk/culture/film/filmreviews/11182717/Serena-review-intensely-unlikeable.html> (accessed November 14, 2017).
11. I again refer to the November 2016 Bier interview included as this volume's final chapter.

BIBLIOGRAPHY

Aaron, Michele (2007), *Spectatorship: The Power of Looking On* (vol. 35), London: Wallflower Press.

Agger, Gunhild (2015), "Strategies in Danish Film Culture—and the Case of Susanne Bier," *Kosmorama* 259 (March 11), <http://www.kosmorama.org/Artikler/Susanne-Bier.aspx> (accessed November 14, 2017).

Bainbridge, Caroline (2007), *The Cinema of Lars Von Trier: Authenthicity and Artifice*, London: Wallflower Press.

BBC (2016), "*Night Manager* finale beats Queen at 90 by 1m TV viewers," *BBC News*, March 28, <http://www.bbc.com/news/35910724> (accessed November 14, 2017).

Ebert, Roger (2007), "*Things We Lost in the Fire*," RogerEbert.com, October 18, <http://www.rogerebert.com/reviews/things-we-lost-in-the-fire-2007> (accessed November 14, 2017).

Gledhill, Christine (2000), "Rethinking genre," in Linda Williams and Christine Gledhill (eds.), *Reinventing Film Studies*, New York: Bloomsbury Academic, pp. 42–88.

Hjort, Mette (2011), *Lone Scherfig's* Italian for Beginners, Seattle: University of Washington Press.

Hjort, Mette, and Ib Bondebjerg, eds. (2003), *The Danish Directors: Dialogues on a Contemporary National Cinema*, Bristol and Chicago: Intellect Books.

Holden, Stephen (2007), "An Addict and a Widow With a Lot of Pain to Heal," *The New York Times*, October 19, <https://mobile.nytimes.com/2007/10/19/movies/19thin.html> (accessed November 14, 2017).

Honeycutt, Kirk (2007), "*Things We Lost in the Fire*," *The Hollywood Reporter*, October 8, <http://www.hollywoodreporter.com/review/things-we-lost-fire-159210> (accessed November 14, 2017).

Jerslev, Anne (2004), "Elsker dig for evigt-lige nu," in *Nøgne Billeder-De Danske Dogmefilm*, Medusa.

Langkjær, Birger (2012), *Realismen i dansk film*, Copenhagen: Samfundslitteratur.

Lawson, Terry (2007), "Review: *Things We Lost in the Fire*," *Detroit Free Press*, October 19, <http://www.popmatters.com/article/a-few-words-with-things-we-lost-in-the-fire-star-benicio-del-toro/> (accessed June 1, 2017).

Rash, Ron (2008), *Serena*, New York: HarperCollins.

Redvall, Eva Novrup (2010), "For mig har det altid bare handlet om film," *Kosmorama* 246: 77–88.

Redvall, Eva Novrup (2012), "Encouraging artistic risk-taking through film policy: The case of New Danish Screen," in Mette Hjort (ed.), *Film and Risk*, Detroit: Wayne State University Press.

Rochlin, Margy (2012), "Susanne Bier: Small World," *Directors Guild of America Quarterly*, Winter, <http://www.dga.org/Craft/DGAQ/All-Articles/1201-Winter-2012/Indie-Voice-Susanne-Bier.aspx> (accessed November 14, 2017).

Siegel, Tatiana (2014), "Lost Jennifer Lawrence–Bradley Cooper movie: It "made no sense,'" *The Hollywood Reporter*, September 17, <http://www.hollywoodreporter.com/news/lost-jennifer-lawrence-bradley-cooper-733113> (accessed November 14, 2017).

Silverman, Kaja (1988), *The Acoustic Mirror: The Female Voice in Psychoanalysis and Cinema*, Indianapolis: Indiana University Press.

Sloan, W. (2007), "Burning questions for Susanne Bier," *The Varsity*, October 15, <https://thevarsity.ca/2007/10/15/burning-questions-for-susanne-bier/> (accessed November 14, 2017).

Smaill, Belinda (2014), "The Male Sojourner, the Female Director, and Popular European Cinema: The Worlds of Susanne Bier," *Camera Obscura* vol. 29, no. 1, 85: 5–31.

Smith, Kyle (2007), "Going down in flames," *New York Post*, October 19, <http://nypost.com/2007/10/19/going-down-in-flames/> (accessed November 14, 2017).

Stevenson, Jack (2003), *Dogme Uncut: Lars von Trier, Thomas Vinterberg, and the Gang That Took on Hollywood*, Solana Beach, CA: Santa Monica Press.

"Susanne Bier," Denmark.DK: The Official Website of Denmark <http://denmark.dk/en/meet-the-danes/great-danes/film-makers/susanne-bier> (accessed November 14, 2017).

Whipp, Glenn (2007), "*Fire* draws its heat from Del Toro," *Los Angeles Daily News*, October 19, <https://web.archive.org/web/20071222043105/http://www.la.com:80/movies/10652576.html> (accessed November 14, 2017).

White, Patricia (2015), *Women's Cinema, World Cinema: Projecting Contemporary Feminisms*, Durham, NC: Duke University Press.

Wikipedia (2017), "Susanne Bier," <https://en.wikipedia.org/wiki/Susanne_Bier> (accessed November 14, 2017).

Wiseman, Andreas (2016), "*The Night Manager*'s 40m views in China highlights growing drama opportunity," *Screen Daily*, September 15, <http://www.screendaily.com/news/the-night-managers-40m-views-in-china-highlights-growing-drama-opportunity/5109468.article> (accessed November 14, 2017).

FILMOGRAPHY

The Hurt Locker, film, directed by Kathryn Bigelow (USA: Voltage Pictures, 2009).
Italian for Beginners, film, directed by Lone Scherfig (Denmark: Zentropa, 2000).

PART 2

Negotiating Identity

Part 2 Introduction

While Bier has been unusually attentive to marginalized social and ethnic identities on screen from the start of her film career, she often appears reluctant, in interviews, to discuss identity politics except when directly related to her Jewish heritage, which she has consistently credited as pivotal to her worldview (see for instance Hjort 2000 and Johnson 2011). Quite possibly, Bier, like other women successful in film, has been wary of stressing her exceptional status as a woman filmmaker to protect the reception of her work on its own terms. The chapters in this section stress the influence of identity on film production and reception, and collectively indicate that films are rarely, if ever, evaluated without factoring it in. The section is therefore attentive, in equal measure, to how Bier approaches identity on screen as well as to how others perceive her work in light of her off-screen persona. Thus, this collection of chapters illuminates Bier's evolving creative and paratextual responses to particular identities.

Maureen Turim's "Beginning with Jewish Survival: *Freud's Leaving Home*" is a close reading of the complex references to Jewish heritage in Bier's first feature-length film. Turim employs a psychological lens to assess the film's distinct blend of comedy and tragedy, most particularly in its evocations of Freud's delayed maturation, Rosha's impending death, and their intense, ambivalent mother-daughter bond. The chapter further situates *Freud's Leaving Home* in the context of contemporaneous films by Jewish directors that represent diasporic Jewish families in cultural transition.

In "Stories with Queer Identities," Anders Marklund analyzes representations of queer characters in Bier's films *Like It Never Was Before* (*Pensionat Oskar*, 1995), *Once in a Lifetime* (*Livet är en schlager*, 2000), and *Love Is All You Need* (*Den skaldede frisør*, 2012), and in her television series *The Night*

Manager (2016). Marklund argues that Bier's career shift from 'modest-sized Swedish productions to larger international ones' parallels a movement away from nuance and toward broad stereotyping in her work's approach to queer characters. He connects this shift to each film's specific context and intended audience, linking, for instance, *Like It Never Was Before* to Sweden's gay rights movement in the 1990s and considering *The Night Manager*'s Corky according to the series' function as mainstream, heteronormative entertainment. Marklund concludes that Bier's more recent and 'elegant transnational productions' re-marginalize queer characters in a manner reminiscent of earlier problematic film stereotypes.

"The Case of Lars von Trier vs. Susanne Bier" focuses on the public conflict between Denmark's leading international film directors, which has developed almost entirely through von Trier's defamation of Bier in widely published, anti-Semitic statements. In this chapter, Pétur Valsson outlines the history of von Trier's and Bier's relationship, which includes personal and professional ties that illustrate the closely knit nature of the Danish film industry. Valsson then questions the role of Jewish identity in each director's work and professional persona, concluding that Bier's more direct experience of Jewish culture contrasts with von Trier's fetishization of Jewishness, which was challenged by his late-in-life discovery that his biological father was not Jewish as he had thought. Valsson suggests that the simultaneity of Bier's career ascendance and von Trier's discovery of mistaken identity unfortunately resulted in von Trier's very public misogynist and anti-Semitic comments, to which Bier refused to respond, characterizing them as ridiculous.

Finally, Mette Hjort's "Gender Equity in Screen Culture: On Susanne Bier, the Celluloid Ceiling, and the Growing Appeal of TV Production" reflects on Bier's career in light of the "unprecedented attention" recently directed at gender inequality in the film industry. Hjort foregrounds, in particular, the fact that Bier's success involved her overcoming challenges posed by both her gender and her nationality. The chapter stresses that Bier's shifting perception of such challenges is provocative, specifically Bier's increasingly vocal support of gender equity in screen industries. Hjort concludes by predicting likely effects of "a broader involvement of women in the film industry," which Bier's career harbingers.

CHAPTER 4

Beginning with Jewish Survival: *Freud's Leaving Home*

Maureen Turim

Freud's Leaving Home (Freud flyttar hemifrån ..., 1991) has a most provocative title; "Freud" in this instance refers to the twenty-five-year-old daughter of a Swedish-Jewish family, Angelique Cohen, who has earned her familial nickname by infusing discussions with psychological analyses. Of course, the title serves as double entendre, suggesting that leaving home is always fraught with psychoanalytical significance. More specifically, it recalls the opening of Freud's 1909 essay, "The Family Romance":

> The liberation of an individual, as he grows up, from the authority of his parents is one of the most necessary though one of the most painful results brought about by the course of his development. It is quite essential that liberation should occur and it may be presumed that it has been to some extent achieved by everyone who has reached a normal state. Indeed, the whole progress of society rests upon the opposition between successive generations. On the other hand, there is a class of neurotics whose condition is recognizably determined by their having failed in this task. (237)

Angelique, at the film's outset, embodies just such failure; apparently past adolescence, her bedraggled appearance and discomfort with her braces, and her retreat to her bedroom (from which she argumentatively phones in questions and complaints to her mother, who is in other rooms of their apartment), play humorously with a portrait of an adult who can't leave home or childhood. She is fixated on being annoying by engaging in numerous small rebellions. The film uses comedy to treat dramatic and even tragic circumstances, which I will here discuss not only in relation to Freud's theories, but those of Melanie Klein, Alice Miller, and Marianne Hirsch.

Susanne Bier renders screenwriter Marianne Goldman's narrative as a comic and poignant investigation of a post-Holocaust Jewish family in Sweden. As Bier's first feature film, it won a series of prizes that generated the possibility for her future success. It has also been called 'the first feature film in Sweden to depict Swedish-Jewish culture' (Solia 1998: 219), and a detailed description of the film figures in Rochelle Wright's *The Visible Wall: Jews and Other Ethnic Outsiders in Swedish Film*, in which the author notes its striking focus on the range of Jewish identities within the same family, while it does not primarily focus on interactions with non-Jewish Swedes, as is the case with other films in her corpus.

The wartime connection between Jews in Denmark and Sweden offers an intriguing background to this collaboration between the Swedish-Jewish Goldman and the Danish-Jewish Bier. As Nathaniel Hong examines in his book *Occupied: Denmark's Adaptation and Resistance to German Occupation 1940–1945*, the military conquering by Germany of Denmark on April 9, 1940 was followed by the Danish government agreeing to collaborate with their occupiers in order to maintain its presence. For the next three years, Danish authorities actively aided the Germans in suppressing resistance. At only around 8,200 persons, the relatively small population of Danish Jews were well integrated into Danish society and were not subject to the increasingly repressive measures taken against Jews in other occupied countries, until a Nazi crackdown following general strikes and active resistance in 1943. In *Countrymen: The Untold Story of How Denmark's Jews Escaped the Nazis*, Bo Lindegaard chronicles how in April of 1943, the Resistance saved several thousand Jews from Denmark by evacuating them to neutral Sweden from fishing villages by boat.

Bier's own family's survival was tied to these efforts to save Danish Jews from the Holocaust. Bier's father, Rudolf Salomon Bier, a German Jew who left for Denmark in 1933, and her mother, Hennie Jonas, a descendant of Russian Jews who resettled in Denmark to escape pogroms, were among those survivors. "Being Jewish is a determining thing in how one sees the world," Bier has said. "I have a very strong catastrophe gene, and that has influenced my storytelling. The family thing also has to do with being Jewish—that imminent sense of the impossible happening" (Johnson, Mcleans). Let's pause on that phrase, "the imminent sense of the impossible happening" offered here as explanation of "the family thing." The situational comedy explored in *Freud's Leaving Home* is largely familial, depending on the ironies of past secrets and deep fears that surround each interaction. The narrative permits itself numerous brushes with the "impossible," here evidenced by the highly concentrated iterations of explosive events, and in Freud's impetuous reactions.

Figure 4.1 Close-up, arranging a guest table.

Figure 4.2 Freud circling around her mother.

As the film opens, Freud's mother Rosha Cohen is preparing for her sixtieth birthday celebration; the credit sequence traces in close-up the meticulous homemaker arranging place settings, as she gives a last polish to her silver cutlery (Figure 4.1). Finally the camera pulls back to reveal the elegantly dressed Rosha, enlisting the aid of her daughter to fetch butter knives (Figure 4.2). Surprisingly, the daughter brandishes two butter knives that she has been holding, as she asks "These?" Dismissively, Rosha says "no, the silver ones." Clearly the daughter is expected to be a domestic helpmate, though she proves inept at the simplest tasks, failures of performance that betray her unwillingness to fulfill the assumed subservience of a dutiful daughter. Freud chides her mother's precipitate preparations, noting that they still have three days left to prepare, but clearly Rosha is obsessed with arranging the place cards this far in advance. With great economy of exposition, the tenor of their relationship is displayed.

It will instantaneously turn more vicious. In a tight two-shot, Rosha begs her daughter not to wear her braces for the party: "You look like a monster," she suggests, with a smile on her face, as she pinches her daughter's cheek, possessively. A moment later she chides Freud's clothing as an unsightly "gray tent," wondering why her daughter doesn't "help nature along." A third comment on Freud's appearance is more indirect, as she asks Freud to model the shoes she recently bought her, but her daughter refuses, saying "they hurt," while proclaiming that one more word about her looks will mean she won't come to the party. Rosha digs in, saying "perhaps that's best. You ruin everything with your silly psychic talk." As the camera cuts to a close-up of Freud, we witness her resistance, correcting her mother, who meant to say "psychological." As we return to a countershot on Rosha, the women's squabbling is interrupted by the father, Ruben, appearing behind Rosha to her right. This is characteristic of the framing and reframing of intimate, yet often hostile exchanges in the first half of the film. Insofar as there is love in these familial bonds, it is laced with incessant confrontation. Thus Rosha turns her attention to critiquing her husband's clothing choices, to which Freud objects, claiming her mother always abuses her father; for his part, Ruben quickly defends his wife, saying these exchanges are just their habit. Both daughter and father exit the shot in opposite directions, leaving Rosha alone, inviting us to contemplate her being.

The exaggerated portrayal of Rosha as a demanding and self-involved person, who feels the price owed her for her housework is having others conform to her taste and submit to her tongue-lashings, sets her up as a stereotyped vision of the overbearing Jewish mother. The humor of the scene is misanthropic and dark; none of the characters emerges as particularly likable. It is interesting to compare this scene to that of an American sitcom, to the dysfunctional family such as it developed in the 1970s with *All in the Family* to continue in the late eighties with *Rosanne*, and many more iterations. Bier's film does not have as many nor as developed situational gags of those episodic television offerings. Instead, the comic scenes are closely observed confrontations that, except for their hyperbole, might occur in drama.

Rosha's two diasporic children—David, a gay man living in Florida, and Deborah, an Orthodox Jew living with her family in Israel—are returning home for the occasion of their mother's birthday party. We crosscut their setting out on their journeys with images of Ruben working in his small antique shop, in which he communicates with his co-owner brother only by handwritten notes. That the two brother-partners live in tense resentment of each other will only be explained and developed in later dialogue. This is characteristic of the film's exposition, initially withholding information, then post facto revealing what was at stake in earlier scenes.

For the elder Cohen children, the journey home is clearly traumatic. First we are introduced to David as he fumbles the slides that he will take to show his family, then as, embarrassed, he tries to explain his family to his male lover, including why he is not honest with them about his homosexuality. Deborah leaves her husband and three young children in Israel to board an airplane in which she suffers while sitting next to a businessman who is smoking, then throws up into a plastic bag that turns out to be his, presumably filled with his belongings. This gag, dependent on the last gasp of smoking sections on airplanes, becomes linked to her familial anxiety, as she explains to the businessman: "My sister would say it is psychological. Tension."

Their anxiety is echoed on the home front in the next scene as Rosha pauses in her party preparations, looking dizzy. Her glance at the crystal chandelier displays it in a canted angle precariously turning, a reflection of her uneasy state, just as a phone call interrupts. Answering this call from her older children, who have just arrived at the airport, she tells them not to sit together nor talk to each other on the bus home, a residual worry held over from a time in which Jews were less safe in Europe than at the moment the film is set (though terrorism has renewed such fears in parts of Europe). A close-up of Rosha in profile has her whisper comfortingly to herself, "No accidents. They've both landed." On first viewing this scene simply fits with the overwrought character already established for Rosha, but in retrospect the intensity of her physical state may be seen as prefiguring not only her illness, but also obliquely introducing her legacy as a Holocaust survivor, which will subsequently be revealed.

From here, the film addresses Jewishness, particularly for an audience knowledgeable of Jewish custom, more directly. The Hebrew prayer "Avinu Shalom Alechim" is sung by the father to greet the arrival at the door of the apartment of the elder children, the tumultuous reunion towards which the previous scenes were building (Figure 4.3). It will be followed by the first of his half-finished Jewish jokes, a running ploy in the film to not fulfill any expectations of verbal Jewish humor, but to present instead the rituals of joke-telling as so repetitive that the children already know the supposed punchline.

Figure 4.3 Arrival of the older children.

"Avinu Shalom Alechim" traditionally welcomes the Sabbath (Shabbat), wishing for peace; it was written in the sixteenth century by the Kabbalists of Safad, an ancient Jewish city in what is now Israel, then spread throughout the Jewish diaspora. The song makes reference to angels in the Kabbalist tradition, giving its use in the film an ironic reference to Freud's given name, "Angelique," the name suggesting that she is perhaps not the good angel of Shabbat observance, but a more troublesome evil angel that the song was first composed to vanquish.

From the outset, this return of the older children is rendered mockingly, for they stumble into a context that suits neither one of them. For Deborah, who has embraced Orthodoxy, her Swedish family is not observant enough, while for her brother who is living in a non-Jewish context in Orlando, Florida, it is an awkward reminder of all that he has left behind.

Later, the Yiddish "Lomir Ale Eeynem," a song for toasting, is offered at the end of the first dinner of the reunited family, comically set at the kitchen table to which they are confined, due to the party preparations occupying the larger and more elegant dining room (Figure 4.4). The song is prompted by the surprise entrance of two guests, who will miss the upcoming birthday party; they arrive with flowers and a bottle of champagne for an impromptu early celebration, and it is the champagne that motivates the group to sing. These two songs unfolding in comic scenes directly mark the film with complex references to Jewish heritage. General audiences might not be aware of the inclusion of two different Jewish languages, but for those who are, the film strikingly includes a Yiddish language tradition that may becoming more rare amongst contemporary generations of European Jews. It connects this family to the Ashkenazi Polish and Russian Jewish immigration that characterizes Bier's own family, in contrast to earlier North European Jewish populations of Holland, Denmark, and Sweden, who were more likely to be connected to

Figure 4.4 Singing "Lomir Ale Eeynem."

Sephardic traditions following the Spanish and Portuguese Jewish diaspora after expulsion of Jews from those countries in 1492. "Lomir Ale Eeynem" is a twentieth-century song, written in 1911 by a Lithuanian Jew, Mordkhe Rivesman, that represents the celebration of family, of gathering together, including in its lyrics "mekabl-ponem zayn!," a toast to each person or group participating in the assembly, so that its use at the Cohen family's reunion dinner signifies a gesture of reintegration after the family's most recent voluntary diaspora from the Swedish adopted homeland to the U.S. and Israel. Yet both the preparatory difficulties we have already witnessed and the ensuing squabbles that will soon follow undermine this gesture of family unity.

A round robin of different dialogue exchanges, pairing each family member with another in quick succession, propels the film. Rosha and Freud talk over the phone as an effort to create distance, even though Freud is at home in her bedroom. Freud begins questioning her mother aggressively on not breastfeeding her children, as if channeling Melanie Klein's investigation of childhood development in connection to the absence of the breast revisited in "Notes on Some Schizoid Mechanisms" in its relationship to aggression. Expanding Klein's theories while addressing their development and paradoxes, Edith Frampton looks at actual breastfeeding scenes in contemporary women's literature to note how women authors depict intersubjectivity, "realising within their formal narrative structures the psychosomatic processes that Klein theorised" (Frampton 2004: 363). Bier and Goldman's strategy is different: they are interested in tracing the later, residual effects of a felt lack of physical warmth from Rosha by Freud, while hinting at, yet satirizing, the feminist psychoanalytic deciphering of such a case history. Freud aggressively questions her mother, even as she tries to figure out a potential psychoanalytical origin of her own aggressive desires. She is the daughter caught in an unresolved longing for her mother, a longing all the more poignant as she has become, as we shall learn, her mother's caretaker, and the two are codependent.

While they are talking, Rosha finally opens the letter from her doctor, long after Freud handed it to her in an earlier scene, with the command "open it" unheeded. This delay is a pattern in the family that infuriates Freud. as denial or fear causes David, Deborah, Rosha, and Ruben to avoid facing and talking about many of their secrets and concerns, while Freud plunges into the role of demanding more openness and directness, often in the rudest possible manner. Throughout the film, carefully composed close-ups on objects and crowded family groupings trace the tragi-comic handling of this trajectory. It is across their entirely unnecessary telephone call—given that they are but feet from each other—that Rosha finally informs Freud of the battery of tests she needs, tests that will eventually diagnose her cancer. While Rosha is still holding the phone, Freud enters the shot with her mother to offer a warm embrace. The space between them will be the subject of cinematic exploration from now on: How much distance will Freud seek, or conversely, how will this ominous diagnosis and Freud's willingness to confront it directly tighten the physical depiction of the two in the filmic frame?

At Rosha's hospital bed, the family surrounds her as her doctor tries to explain her medical condition. Deborah introduces gifts, light-hearted banter ensues, and the doctor is unable to finish his explanation. Freud sets out to discover the truth from the doctor, yet her quest is treated comically, as the doctor is not to be found. Freud's aggression at this absence takes the form of badgering a nurse into revealing his phone number. More of Freud's impetuousness is thus displayed, her intensity treated mockingly, but the tone shifts as, once home, she learns from her phone call to the doctor the seriousness of her mother's diagnosis.

A swirling camera depicts Freud's first encounter with her siblings and father after hearing of her mother's terrible prognosis. The others chatter at the Shabbat dinner table, still set up in the kitchen. "I spoke with the doctor," Freud finally asserts. Deborah literally plugs her ears with her hands, hiding behind a religious conviction in Shabbat as joyful: "Don't discuss bad news on Shabbat!" Freud visibly has become the bearer of bad news as the only one willing to face their family crisis directly, but her own response is yet another demand and more moody behavior: "You two stay here for the summer," she demands of her siblings, yet she herself then leaves their parents' apartment abruptly for an uncharacteristic night out.

Freud heads to a bar, orders a large whisky, and attempts to attract the interest of a tall blond man, literally the first man she sees. Her approach is direct: "I've come to lose my virginity," she says, determined to begin this affair as overdue rebellion, or, following one psychoanalytic logic, replacing the lost good breast with a penis substitute. What would be believable behavior in a teenager, in fact behavior reminiscent of the rebellious teenagers in Catherine Breillat's early film *36 fillette* (1988), is here made more comic as Freud is in her mid-twenties. That she acts as the determined seductress during her mother's hospitalization and in the midst of the family's returning becomes another petulant acting-out. From the outset, luckily, the man, Adrian, seems less some cad poised to take advantage of her than a rather gentle free spirit who wants to help her through her distress. A comical sex scene transpires in a tower-like structure that Adrian inhabits next to a railroad (Figure 4.5): Freud, in dialogue, mocks Adrian's fixation with trains, and the film echoes this decidedly Freudian mockery in a Hitchcock-inspired cut to a trellis outside that stands in for a tunnel.

Yet as Freud phones the hospital the next morning, the comedy seemingly gives way to a more serious tone. "Really? That's the worst thing I ever heard," Freud says to her interlocutor, whom we presume to be a nurse. The audience is led to believe that the news is terrible, even that her mother has died. Instead

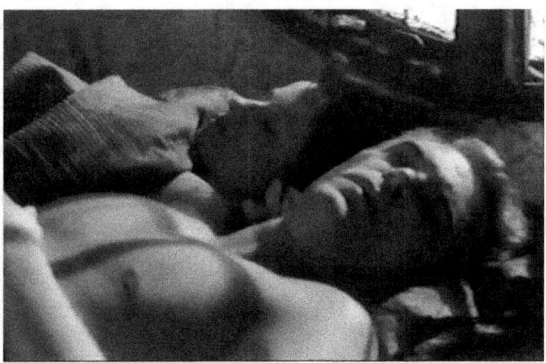

Figure 4.5 Freud's sexual initiation.

we are offered Freud's monologue: "For twenty-five years I have listened to her anxiety attacks, held her hand and said, 'There are no Germans here, no Germans anywhere.'" As her new boyfriend enters the shot, kissing her in the golden light, she continues, "Not in the chandelier nor in the painting. I tried to fight World War II again by myself, with the aid of cards, walks, quarrels, and talks. Now the hospital says she slept all night on one and a half Valium." This is the soliloquy of a "gifted child" in the terms introduced by Alice Miller: a sensitive, intelligent daughter who has been solicited as her mother's confidant and caretaker, and whose own psychological problems stem from inheriting the pain of an earlier generation while still very young. Comically, Freud laments her years of service to her mother supposedly being futile, as drug therapy can be so easily substituted, evoking with ironic humor the larger substitution of psychoanalytic practices with drug-based therapies, and thus a challenge to her Freudian obsessions.

If this monologue is comic, it re-covers the same territory of intergenerational Holocaust memory I have traced elsewhere across the body of Chantal Akerman's films. Akerman, like Bier, was a second-generation Holocaust survivor, and gradually she addressed those issues in several of her films, though certainly not in her earliest work. It is only in retrospect that *News from Home* (1977), with its soundtrack reading by Akerman of the letters her mother wrote her when she first left Belgium for New York with no warning, becomes even more poignant when we realize that the artist-daughter was fleeing not just a possessive mother, but a childhood laced with special constraints that derived from her mother's fears. With her last film, *No Home Movie* (2015), Akerman is able to embrace her mother and her Jewish heritage with great tenderness. Bier, unlike Akerman, decided to start her career with a film that directly takes on this heritage, ironically under the guise of a mother dying of cancer, which would finally become Akerman's mother's fate. Yet the comedic mode that Bier and her scriptwriter adopt represents a struggle with the seriousness of the second-generation aspect of this tale, a tone only taken once by Akerman, in a brief reference to the mother being a Holocaust survival in her comedy *Golden Eighties* (Window Shopping, 1986). For Bier, a director who will become famous for her hard-edged dramas, though she will certainly make other comedies that cement her reputation in Denmark, we can see a certain continuity of film style and material in both modes. Bier's comedies are filled with the confrontational wrangling of social issues, as are her dramas, though this is the only one to consider the Shoah and Jewish culture. Asked about this, Bier says: "I do think that life is a balance between tragedy and comedy. My earlier work, including the comedies, does have a sadness to it." Further, elsewhere she links her focus throughout her body of films on interpersonal and familial communication to her Jewishness, when asked about *Freud's Leaving Home* being her only Jewish film:

> I would love to make a film with a Jewish theme again at some point. It's clear that I know that world concretely and can easily describe it as a result. In my mind having a definitive cultural background and also a very strong family background is a source of tremendous strength. The implications of this milieu for my work as a filmmaker are probably that I'm able to draw on certain styles of communication. The way that my family communicates is reflected again and again in my extreme characters.

It helps to see *Freud's Leaving Home* then in the context of loss and recovery found in other Bier films, such as *Family Matters* (1993), *Open Hearts* (2002), *After the Wedding* (2006), *Things We Lost in the Fire* (2007), and *In a Better World* (2010), asking in what sense, following on Bier's interviews, her body of work may be seen as that of a second-generation Holocaust survivor and a Jewish filmmaker. For as she herself suggests, she dwells in the matters of loss and heart-breaking grief, made all the more intense by the troubles that existed in relationships prior to death or loss reverberating for the survivors.

Further, we may place *Freud Leaving Home* in the context of other recent films by Jewish directors worldwide that trace family reunions and parental deaths, including Didier Martiny's *Pique-nique de Lulu Kreutz* (*Lulu Kreutz's Picnic*,1999), from a script by Yasmina Reza; Zac Braff's *Garden State* (2004); Alejandro Springall's *Morirse está en Hebreo* (*My Mexican Shiva*, 2007); Ronit Elkabetz's and Shlomi Elkabetz's *Shiva* (2008); Shawn Levy's *This is Where I Leave You* (2014); and Jerome Cohen-Olivar's *L'Orchestre de minuit* (*Midnight Orchestra*, 2016). In addition, Mike Mills's *Beginners* (2010) follows a similar structure of investigating a parent's life after his death, though with greater ambiguity regarding Jewish heritage. Exploration of first closeted, then acknowledged, homosexuality also links this film to David's character in *Freud*

Leaving Home, though here it is the deceased father who finally lived his life as a gay man. The film is less specifically Jewish than the others, though the lead character's mother, five years deceased, was a Jew before she converted, and as symbolic homage to her legacy, the protagonist becomes involved with a young Jewish woman he meets through this journey of familial discovery. In the other films, exploring and retrieving Jewish heritages becomes the core. *Midnight Orchestra* explores Jewishness in a Moroccan context of musical performance, while *My Mexican Shiva* foregrounds the blending of Jewish customs with Mexican culture.

All of these films may be seen as trying to work through the meaning of Jewish ritual in the context of assimilated and sometimes religiously blended families. In *Freud Leaving Home*, it is Deborah's adoption of Orthodoxy that receives sharply negative treatment. From the beginning, as they are first reunited in Deborah's return home for the birthday celebration, Rosha chastises her daughter's wearing of a wig that some Orthodox Jewish sects substitute for traditional head-coverings. Later, her sister Freud will actually tear her wig off as the culmination of an argument against her turn to Orthodoxy, one that reveals Deborah's drug arrest in Morocco as a young woman. Deborah, in distress, confides to her tormenting siblings that she is pregnant, but does not wish to have this fourth child, giving Freud more ammunition against her sister's Orthodoxy by screaming that she should accept abortion as a viable solution to her anguish. Earlier, the role of the Orthodox in Israeli politics and the refusal of many to serve in the armed forces becomes part of the family's banter, aimed at challenging Deborah; while the family seems sympathetic to Israel, there is no support for Deborah's having moved there, unlike the pride some diaspora Jews take in children who "make aliyah," moving to Israel as an act of commitment. This is all a prelude to Deborah's own transformation and reconciliation to her past. When Rosha is ill from chemotherapy, Deborah seeks to purchase a non-kosher rotisserie chicken, though it is "against her beliefs." Then she goes further to actually steal the last remaining chicken from another customer, when he ignores her urgent pleas to let her buy it. After one happy bite, Rosha can't eat Deborah's pilfered offering, so the daughter's efforts on her mother's behalf end in a tragi-comic tableau of the reunited family witnessing their impending loss.

Eventually, Deborah will confide her just-accomplished abortion to her dying mother, who gently embraces her daughter's choice, advising her to tell her husband that she suffered a miscarriage, a consolation that Deborah gratefully accepts. Perhaps the most transformational moment for Deborah, though, is her encounter with an old boyfriend, as it is he who removes her wig gently as prelude to an embrace signaling their reconciliation, for the first time facing the demise of their earlier relationship due to the drug arrest, and offering their mutual acknowledgment of the lingering longing they each bear for their past love. In other words, Deborah serves in the film as testimony to the assimilated values of Swedish Jews, for as she appears at the end, naturally coiffed and happy at the party the family holds for their dying matriarch, she has softened to their way of life and become a model of the usefulness of a psychoanalytical working-through of the trauma of the past.

David's trajectory of seeking a more honest relationship with his family is initiated with Freud's implicit acceptance of him, as she acts on her brother's insistence that she needs to experience sexual freedom in order to leave her emotional imprisonment at home. Yet for David himself, an argument with his father, portrayed in tight two-shots, brings into sharp focus the way he has been hiding his sexuality and desires from his parents, fearing their disapprobation. Indeed, Ruben vents complete disapproval of David's life, his work at Disney as a character actor, and very directly, his homosexuality. *Open Hearts* hinges on just such a revelation of homosexuality by a very young son to his more understanding father, who simply tells his son "you have to wait until you're twelve to come out." Meryl Shriver-Rice discusses how this film builds an intimacy through lighting (36–7), and I would like to suggest that it answers to Ruben's harsh rejection of his son's homosexuality by choosing this different shot style. Homosexuality and a character's coming out to his family also figure in Bier's *Pensioniat Oskar* (*Like It Never Was Before*, 1995), in which a family's troubled attempt to salvage the parents' marriage by undertaking a vacation together comes up short when the father falls for a young man, Petrus. Clearly, homosexuality in Bier's films becomes an issue for the family, a challenge to the understanding of family members. Ruben fails that test, unable to stop inflicting wounds that his son clearly feared were coming.

In contrast to the tension between Ruben and David, Rosha, after her diagnosis, lets David know she knows he is gay, and begins to show interest in learning about his lover. Yet this new understanding by his mother makes her loss more unbearable for David, who decides to leave rather than witness her end.

Indeed, Rosha's evolution towards greater sympathy with her children begins when she forgives Freud's escape from the family on the night of Rosha's hospitalization. Rosha understands that Freud "wants to prove she is free."

Adrian, seeking Freud, who is not home, ends up visiting the bedridden Rosha, who has returned home to die. Rosha shows him a scar from a shoulder operation that she confesses to have been "paid for by Germans." This is the first we know of the reparations for which she, as a survivor, would have been eligible. It is a most curious scene, recalling shots of Adrian and Freud together in the railroad tower, and he is shown offering her the same compassion that he extended to Freud there and during their intervening camping idyll. As the sole major character who is apparently non-Jewish, Adrian offers a portrayal of sympathetic understanding and quiet comfort. Rather abruptly, the film stages its ending with Rosha holding her postponed party. Adrian is introduced to Rosha, and both feign that they are meeting for the first time, but Rosha's newfound sympathy for her daughter extends to her welcoming this lover. Rosha collapses in the midst of the party, and will later die in Freud's arms in her bed. The shot of their embrace links back to Adrian's visit, which in turn links back to Freud and Adrian's first sexual encounter. The film thus connects sexuality and empathy, seeking in the intimate encounter the moments in which characters exposing their bodies and then touching acts as a salve to past hurts and grievances.

After Rosha's funeral, the last shot is of Freud burdened with suitcases, descending the staircase. Of course this is how the film, given its title, must end visually. Bier has created an absurdist comedy, though rather than in the abstracted setting favored by theater of the absurd, she situates hers in the detailed trappings of a bourgeois Jewish family whose family secrets include brushes with financial precariousness, and for whom Holocaust reparations served to provide basic needs. Indeed, the film may be seen in the context of Marianne Hirsch's *The Mother/Daughter Plot: Narrative, Psychoanalysis, Feminism* (2009) as part of a larger literature devoted to the reworking by women authors of the centrality of the mother-daughter relationship. Freedom for Freud comes not simply with her mother's death, but as a process that involves the entire family in the weeks between diagnosis and death, as her mother's late openness to and honesty with her children leads to their reconciliation with her.

BIBLIOGRAPHY

Frampton, Edith (2004), "Fluid objects: Kleinian Psychoanalytic Theory and Breastfeeding Narratives," *Australian Feminist Studies* issue 45, vol. 19: 357–68.

Freud, Sigmund (1909), "The Family Romance," in James Strachey et al. (eds.), *The Standard Edition of the Writings of Sigmund Freud*, London: Hogarth Press, pp. 235–42.

Hirsch, Marianne (2009), *The Mother/Daughter Plot: Narrative, Psychoanalysis, Feminism*, Bloomington: Indiana University Press.

Hjort, Mette, and Ib Bondebjerg, eds. (2003), *The Danish Directors: Dialogues on a Contemporary National Cinema*, Bristol and Chicago: Intellect Books.

Hong, Nathaniel (2012), *Occupied: Denmark's Adaptation and Resistance to German Occupation 1940–1945*, Copenhagen: Frihedsmuseets Venners Forlag.

Johnson, Brian (2011), "The best in the world," *Macleans.ca*, April 12, <http://www.macleans.ca/culture/the-best-in-the-world/> (accessed November 14, 2017).

Klein, Melanie (1946), "Notes on Some Schizoid Mechanisms," *International Journal of Psycho-Analysis*, vol. 27: 99–110.

Lindegaard, Bo (2013), *Countrymen: The Untold Story of How Denmark's Jews Escaped the Nazis*, New York: Knopf.

Miller, Alice, and Ruth Neils Ward (1997), *The Drama of the Gifted Child: the Search for the True Self*, New York: BasicBooks.

Shriver-Rice, Meryl (2015), *Inclusion in New Danish Cinema: Sexuality and Transnational Belonging*, Bristol and Chicago: Intellect Books.

Soila, Tytti, Astrid Söderbergh-Widding, and Gunnar Iversen (1998), *Nordic National Cinemas*, London: Routledge.

Wood, Jason (2005), "Susanne Bier interviewed," *Projections 13: Women Filmmakers on Filmmaking*, London: Faber and Faber, pp. 96–106.

Wright, Rochelle (1998), *The Visible Wall: Jews and Other Ethnic Outsiders in Swedish Film*, Carbondale and Edwardsville: Southern Illinois University Press.

CHAPTER 5

Stories with Queer Identities

Anders Marklund

Susanne Bier's interest in contemporary stories, identities, and situations is evident in the three films and one television series with queer characters and elements that will be discussed here. Two are Swedish films made before her international breakthrough: *Like It Never Was Before* (*Pensionat Oskar*, 1995) and *Once in a Lifetime* (*Livet är en schlager*, 2000). One is a Danish film with a clear international approach in story, setting and characters: *Love Is All You Need* (*Den skaldede frisør*, 2012). The most recent production, *The Night Manager* (2016), is a six-part British-American television series with no Scandinavian affinities at all. The shifting national/transnational contexts not only illustrate how Bier's career has taken her from rather modest-sized Swedish productions to larger international ones, but also corresponds with a lesser attention to local, not only Scandinavian, contexts. A parallel shift can be seen in how attuned the films are to queer concerns, with the two earlier films developing queer characters and themes in a more foregrounded and nuanced way.

LIKE IT NEVER WAS BEFORE

Both *Like It Never Was Before* and *Once in a Lifetime* were written by Jonas Gardell, a Swede, who already at this time, in Scandinavia, was a very well-known writer and stand-up comedian. He was also, at the time, one of the few gays to be a public figure, and whose sexual identity was common knowledge. His significance as a gay role model can hardly be overstated, a fact made all the more poignant by the release of these two films that foreground queer identities, undermine heteronormative hegemony, and thematize marginalization

(Hamrud 2013). *Like It Never Was Before* tells the story of Rune, a middle-class and middle-aged family man who, during a summer vacation with his family at a seaside inn, gets more and more involved with Petrus, a younger man working at the inn. Initially Rune does not clearly understand his attraction to Petrus, but eventually he breaks with his habitual life and embraces change. *Once in a Lifetime* is about Mona, a care assistant who gets accepted to the Swedish Eurovision Song Contest qualifications. While homosexuality is not foregrounded in the same way in this film, a discourse on normality and marginalization is nevertheless highlighted—primarily through Mona's transvestite brother, Candy Darling, and Daniel, whom Mona assists and who has cerebral palsy (CP). In addition to this, the Eurovision itself was already at this point, around the turn of the twenty-first century, an arena open for camp and queer perspectives (see Rosenberg 2005).

Like It Never Was Before was made directly after, and possibly influenced by, the films of the New Queer Cinema in the early 1990s. At this time in Sweden, Bier's film was rather alone in foregrounding queer themes; the Swedish-Norwegian high school coming out film *Sebastian* (1995) premiered later the same year, and the queer character Zac was a central character in the very successful *Änglagård/House of Angels* (1992 and 1994) films, but otherwise there was little else. A few years later, large audiences in both Sweden and Denmark embraced two films foregrounding homosexual couples—*Show Me Love* (*Fucking Åmål*, 1998) and *Shake it All About* (*En Kort en Lang*, 2001), marking a significant mainstream breakthrough. In contrast to the works by Bier discussed in this chapter, the films by Moodysson and Joof included non-heteronormative happy endings.[1] *Like It Never Was Before* is different from all these films, being a somewhat unconventionally narrated drama-comedy exploring the problems with taking conventional lifestyles for granted. Rune's coming out story underscores some of the complexities in the process of discovering and accepting a new identity, and it avoids a rosy ending where everything appears settled.

Like It Never Was Before was made at an important moment in the gay rights movement. It was shot during the summer of 1994, when the Swedish parliament debated a new law granting same-sex couples the right to registered partnership, and it premiered in March 1995, three months after this law entered into force. In the parliament, there were conservative and liberal politicians who raised concerns about challenges to the nuclear family and stressed the need for a stable (heterosexual) couple to secure reproduction and a safe sphere for children. Fredrik Reinfeldt, later Prime Minister and at this point one of only a few conservatives who supported the law, said, "I share the concern about the nuclear family breakdown. But I think the reasons for this can be traced to a growing lack of heterosexual love and mutual respect, rather than the existence of homosexual love" (Sveriges riksdag 1994). Also in *Like It*

Never Was Before the two (unrelated) questions share the same story regarding, on the one hand, the breakdown of the nuclear family, including lacking love and respect, and, on the other hand, homosexuality, gay love, and gay rights. The film encourages viewers to observe characters' relationships and consider whether traditional and external views on what is a good relationship and a good life are valid for any individual at any point. And it encourages the freedom to reconsider one's life.

Long before Rune begins realizing his attraction towards Petrus, and that he is gay, the film makes it clear that he is dissatisfied. He is caught in a life that has stagnated, does not suit him any longer, and offers no particular joy, freedom, or success. This is foregrounded in a variety of ways: from non-pleasurable daily routine and conformity to missed career chances. When explicitly asked what he wants to do with his life—possibly an unusual question to a man of his age, as if his life was not already predetermined by previous choices—Rune responds that he would like to be an actor.[2] He reveals that he, a long, long time ago, was accepted to a prestigious theater school, but chose a safer alternative and finished his engineering exam instead. This, he says, seemed most reasonable—probably reasonable both to the minds of others and to his own internalized norms. As a consequence, he finds himself in a life that is reasonably good, but not one in which he pursued what he most desired. As underlined by Gardell in an interview, the main theme of the film is achieving freedom (Sveriges television 1995), and this is what Rune eventually pursues. For Rune this is about accepting a new sexual orientation identity; but more universally, *Like It Never Was Before* encourages everyone to strive for a bit more "freedom and lunacy," as suggested by the film's tag line.

While reconsidering his current life and assessing his feelings, Rune hesitates, wondering if it is too late, or merely lunacy, for him to change. His conclusion is that it is not, and he returns to the seaside inn for Petrus. The film's striking poster shows these concluding moments of the film: unable to find Petrus, the film ends with Rune standing in the stormy ocean—on the border between the firm land he has left behind him, and one step into the unknown life ahead of him. The poster's image stresses his courageous decision, aiming to be true to himself rather than to social conventions, but it also leaves him with his new desires unfulfilled (Figure 5.1).

Closing the story on such a note is in line with Michael Bronski's article on coming out films, where he suggests that those films are more valuable that go beyond providing "easy affirmation and positive images" (Bronski 2001: 25). This is partly the case with *Like It Never Was Before*. It offers no easy affirmation, but rather foregrounds both confusion and difficulty on a number of occasions.[3] As Rune stands in the water without Petrus he is confounded. Although Rune has achieved something—realizing who he is, making a decision about his life, choosing change and freedom—he

Figure 5.1 The poster using an image from the film's ending: Rune has chosen the open ocean ("freedom and lunacy," as the poster's tag line, also taken from this scene, reads) rather than his earlier, no longer fulfilling life. However, Rune's courageous decision is not rewarded with newly found love—the joyful seaside days he shared with Petrus (right) are now gone. Instead the film stresses his continuous fatherly care for his son Victor. (*Pensionat Oskar*, Sveriges television, 1995).

is not rewarded with a happy ending. One might have wished for him (and Petrus) to get what the elderly lesbian couple visiting the inn have achieved—a loving and harmonious relationship, in stark contrast to the film's two rather dysfunctional heterosexual families. In a sense, then, the story pauses before it reaches an entirely positive image. It leaves viewers with reason to reflect on what Rune has achieved, but also what remains for him to resolve.

It is noteworthy that Petrus is not present on the film's poster, but that Rune's young son Viktor is. A while after the vacation Rune realizes that he must trust his feelings. He then reveals them to his wife, and leaves his home and the life he led so far. Viktor comes with him, and then, standing in the ocean, Rune gives Viktor a big hug. It is equally reassuring for both of them, but it also appears as if they now only have one another to hold on to. Bronski stresses the value of films that focus on the effect the coming out process has on a larger group of people (Bronski 2001: 25). Here the group of people effected by Rune's coming out may not be very large, but it does include his family. The closing images of father and son illustrate a family that has been divided, but where there are still strong bonds and a continuous degree of caring. For Bier, it was important that the film could grant Rune his freedom, but without forgetting or sacrificing the children. The film is not, she asserts, an "anti-marriage" film, but rather the "family breaks down because they have

Figure 5.2 Absent husbands, forsaken wives. In both *Pensionat Oskar* (upper) and *Den skaldede frisør* (lower)—and to some degree also in *Livet är en schlager*—the films initially construct a normal, somewhat dull and monotonous suburban life in order to disrupt it. A table routinely or denyingly set also for the husband who will not return; scattered lemons—in this film, lemons symbolize zest for (non-normative) life—after Ida surprises her husband with another woman. Both films trace a hesitant movement away from these lives (*Pensionat Oskar*, Sveriges television, 1995; *Den skaldede frisør*, Zentropa, 2012).

always conformed to conventions" (Sveriges television 1995). In a sense, the film suspends progression at around the same point as the Swedish parliament did, entangled in a discourse on family "lack of heterosexual love and mutual respect, rather than the existence of homosexual love"—acknowledging gay love and gay rights, but without the promise of easy affirmation or positive images.

ONCE IN A LIFETIME

Once in a Lifetime offers a comprehensive undermining of normative lifestyles and identities—encouraging openness towards others and towards the possibilities of unfolding one's own potential. Similarly to Rune in *Like It Never Was Before*, the protagonist, Mona, feels caught in a life that is not for her. Among the first things she says is, "sometimes I feel like a prisoner . . . four kids and a husband on ninety-five square meters." In this the film is similar to *Like It Never Was Before* but the approach is different. The task of unbalancing traditional roles and normative identities is shared between at least four characters. Mona, who works as a care assistant, seizes the opportunity to pursue her interest in popular *schlager* music, and comes out as a *schlager* queen during the Swedish Eurovision qualifications. Mona's partner is unemployed and unable to assume the role of the male breadwinner, thus he initially appears indolent, before engaging in the role as supporting husband. Moreover, in online sex chats with a man (played by Jeanne-Pierre Barda, well known to a wide audience from the pop band Army of Lovers and for being openly non-heteronormative) he will accidentally meet later, he playfully poses as a young woman. Further, Mona's brother is a transvestite, calling herself Candy Darling, explicitly referencing the 1960s New York transgender actress, whereas the young man for whom Mona is a care assistant, Daniel, has a cerebral palsy (CP) disorder. Both challenge ideas of normality. The film thus foregrounds a variety of roles, bodies, and identities and promotes the attitude that everyone should take the chance to achieve their own goals, and that this should be both respected and supported. This is orchestrated through everyone's contribution to the main storyline that leads to Mona's successful Eurovision performance; Daniel writes the music, Candy Darling makes the dress, and Mona's husband and family support her as best they can. Somewhat dreamily, perhaps, the story confirms the film's original title that *Life is a schlager*—and that everyone is involved in the performance.

The film flaunts the diverse, and asks probing questions about being true to one's identity. Candy Darling tells Mona's children what a "transa" (trannie) is, demystifying and glamorizing it, while Daniel self-consciously exaggerates his CP condition in order to provoke anxious reactions from presumably normal individuals. A few years earlier, Gardell touched upon similar moments of highlighted diversity and emphasized the importance of making visible those who are marginalized. In a stand-up monologue concerning how many people have a dangerously cautious approach towards disabled persons, Gardell opposed the general stance that "You are not allowed to make jokes [about disabled people]. You shouldn't talk about them either. Actually, you shouldn't know they exist," before provocatively concluding, "If a developmentally disabled person is not even allowed to be developmentally disabled, what is he then? A goddamn neutral. The danger is not in being joked about. The danger is in being rendered invisible" (Gardell 1993).[4] In this monologue, as well as in *Once in a Lifetime*, disability is foregrounded, and reminds audiences of the importance of noticing and respecting other people for who they are—not more, not less—and not merely tolerating or pretending not to notice them. Two years earlier, in *Fucking Åmål*, the groundbreaking film for queer representation in mainstream Swedish cinema, Lukas Moodysson centrally featured a disabled character, further thematizing marginalization. There are similarities between the disabled Daniel and queer Candy Darling, highlighted in a scene where Candy Darling says how she understands Daniel when he feels betrayed and alone. When Daniel asks, "If you could re-live your life, would you be a transvestite?" Candy Darling returns the question: "Would you be CP?" Daniel must respond that he would, because "otherwise I would not be me." Candy Darling gives the same answer: "Otherwise I would not be me." The film presents a collage of identities and shows how they are circumscribed by misguided understanding of what is normal and possible, while also emphasizing the positive (essential) core of everyone's identity.

While the overall mood in the film is lighthearted, there are also moments of melancholy and tragedy related to even more disrupting matters than misunderstood and marginalized identities. Early in the film Candy Darling returns back from hospital, but is clearly not well; she is coughing, she has a temperature, and her new medication is not working. When Mona says she wishes life should be like a *schlager*, Candy Darling ends the sentence with "and not like a fucking requiem." It is suggested, but never explicitly confirmed, that Candy Darling has AIDS. The representation of the character Candy Darling is located midway between the AIDS epidemic igniting the New Queer Cinema, and Gardell's book and television series *Don't Ever Wipe Tears Without Gloves* (*Torka aldrig tårar utan handskar*, 2012), which captures the disrupting AIDS period in honest detail. In *Once in a Lifetime* the mode is more melodramatic and comic and less direct, not really attempting to repeat what Monica Pearl suggests the films of the New Queer Cinema achieved, namely to authentically represent the experience of living with the virus and "[provide] meaning that does not change or sanitize the experience" (Pearl 2004: 33). Possibly *Once in a Lifetime* did just what could be achieved in a film of this mainstream character at this time: it secured honesty in its representation, but embedded it within a story that was overall more positive.

With her last efforts Candy Darling is able to reconcile everyone, and to finish Mona's stage dress in time for the Eurovision qualification. Even though the closing sequence at the qualification makes an overall happy ending possible, this sequence is intercut with emotional moments of Candy Darling passing away—she is lying in a spangle-covered hospital bed, emotionally savoring her sister's achievement. While there is an oscillation between hope and sadness, the editing between Eurovision and Candy Darling's hospital room place more emphasis on success than on disruption—despite the death of Candy Darling, the closure's main focus is on happiness. In this, the ending is illustrative of the film's overall comical-melodramatic mode of inserting more serious moments of queer characters' lives into a mainstream-oriented experience (Figure 5.3).

Figure 5.3 *Once In A Lifetime*'s ending cuts between hope and sadness: between Eurovision, where Mona wins the qualification, and the hospital room where her transvestite sister Candy Darling silently passes away after seeing Mona's success. Waiting for the results, Mona stresses that no matter what happens, the important thing is that they have done this together. Still, the film places more emphasis on (heterosexual) happiness and success than on (queer) sadness and death. (*Livet är en schlager*, Sveriges television and Nordisk film, 2000).

LOVE IS ALL YOU NEED

Regarding transvestites and gay characters in French cinema around the year 2000, Darren Waldron has observed that "the films' endings may be said to return to hegemonic conceptualisations of sexual desire and relationships through the formation of heterosexual couples" (Waldron 2006: 358). This return can also be seen in both *Once in a Lifetime* and *Love Is All You Need*, two films that close with happy heterosexual couples/families.[5]

The film's main character, Ida, is straight, but an important part of the film's constant queering of the everyday. *Love Is All You Need* is a vast departure from Bier's earlier queer characters, as the constantly uncertain gay character in *Love Is All You Need* is the least convincing aspect of the film's queerness. The film opens with Ida receiving hopeful but still uncertain information about her recently completed breast cancer treatment. The film then traces a hesitating movement from her gray, suburban life in a semi-detached house with a cheating husband, to the promise of love and life in an exotic seaside nature-embedded villa in southern Italy; still, however, with some uncertainty lingering regarding her cancer.

In the film, cancer serves both to encourage and to characterize Ida's life-embracing and generally non-normative attitude. Her cancer involves bodily changes, including losing her hair (as foregrounded in the original title, "The Bald Hairdresser"), worries about whether the just-concluded chemotherapy treatment will remain effective, and the surgical removal of one of her breasts. When she is invited to consider breast reconstruction surgery, she spontaneously declines—rather than wishing to reconstruct a "normal" body, she prefers to continue her life in her body as it now is.

Ida is ready to accept changes and embrace life, something that is not initially the case with the two men she is about to meet: her daughter Astrid's fiancé, Patrick, and his father, Philip. Both are wary of change, but both will eventually "come out." In this context, the Danish expression *"springe ud"* concretely refers to the parachute jump Philip's employees gives him on his birthday, but also to their wish that he comes out in life, and, finally (and mistakenly), that he should come out of the closet. Instead, Philip will come out from the self-isolation he has chosen since the tragic death of his wife. Thanks to Ida, he will change his workaholic approach to running his business, and instead find other meanings in his life and engage with other people, including his son.

Patrick will come out as gay—at least to himself, his fiancée Astrid, and his new friend Alessandro, although not necessarily to the expectant wedding guests. His closeting is scantly motivated. The explanation suggested by the film is, it seems, that he has never suspected he was gay. While Patrick clearly hesitates about marriage and avoids having sex with Astrid, it seems to be because he is nervous or possibly not in love with Astrid after all, rather than due to the fact that he is gay. There is a narrative necessity to mislead the audience to expect a story leading up to the wedding, and in retrospect one may assume that Patrick is more aware of his sexual orientation that the film can reveal. This does not, however, fully explain why he, in contemporary Denmark and surrounded by unprejudiced persons, should need to conceal his identity and get married to a woman. Patrick is characterized as someone who is unaware of his own desires, or at least disregards them at the expense of others'. The film indicates that the engagement was originally Astrid's idea. Now, three months after their first meeting, they are getting married, and Patrick hopes to fulfill her dreams to live in the countryside and have six children. It is not only Astrid's dreams that Patrick aims to fulfill, as he explicitly says that he wishes to please his father, but is not sure how to do that. His father could not care less about his son's studious efforts, and instead encourages him to focus on himself. Here—and by foregrounding that Patrick's father was very absent from his life after Patrick's mother died in a car accident—the film resonates with somewhat troublesome ideas that relate homosexuality with a problematic father-son relationship, or overall with unstable parenting (see Benshoff and Griffin 2006: 187–8; Frisch and Hviid 2006: 543–4). However, after having attempted to accommodate both Astrid and his father, Patrick seems to find pleasure for himself when he learns that Alessandro is attracted to him. He immediately goes to Alessandro, and they kiss passionately. After an otherwise faint characterization of Patrick, with brief lines of dialogue and uncommitted actions, his and Alessandro's intense kiss is a clear statement. At least retrospectively, viewers may make sense of Patrick and realize that they have seen a coming out story.

Just as in *Like It Never Was Before*, the coming out story ends with the coming out. There are no further indications of what may happen with Patrick and Alessandro. Instead, as in *Once in a Lifetime*, *Love Is All You Need* foregrounds another storyline and a happier ending, presumably more fitting to a romantic comedy. As Debra Moddelmog observes regarding how same-sex passion "is typically subordinated to the heterosexuality of the film" (Moddelmog 2009: 164), here the heterosexual union between Ida and Philip is established in front of a magnificent view of the sun setting over the Mediterranean. In this fashion, gay characters and stories are, to some degree, marginalized.

What *Love Is All You Need* does not develop regarding the main homosexual character and his coming out, it compensates for to some degree by an overall queer discourse. This is, however, done in a playful, metaphorical way—not necessarily a way most viewers will think much about. Apart from the polysemic notion of "coming out" and the implications of cancer and accepting/adjusting to bodily changes mentioned earlier, the film presents an interesting discourse on lemons and oranges which destabilizes clear-cut

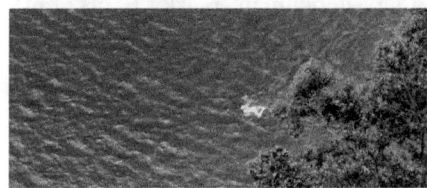

Figure 5.4 Two persons enjoying the pleasures of water, and two men alarmed by the careless non-normative bathing: too rainy, too cold or too strong currents. What both men really react to is the naked person in front of them, to whom they will later develop strong romantic/sexual attraction. The relative novelty in these films lies in the nude bodies they look at (seemingly without great interest): in *Pensionat Oskar* another male body, with a transgressive homosexual relationship looming, and in *Love Is All You Need*, a body reconfigured by breast cancer treatment, with the transgression being the undermining of established norms of what bodies are worthy of being seen as attractive in a mainstream film. In both films, however, the men looking are able to disregard whatever upset them at first and form close attachments (*Pensionat Oskar*, Sveriges television, 1995; *Den skaldede frisør*, Zentropa, 2012).

categories. Lemons are an important motif in the film. They are visually associated with Ida (her dress, car etc.), adding color, taste, and something exotic to her life—or at least reflecting her wish for this. Likewise, the title sequence's concrete buildings are magically given a lemon color, transforming the gray and dull, and placing her in more welcoming surroundings. Later (in the most significant moment of queering) in his orchard in Italy, Philip fascinates Ida with a discourse on lemon trees. He explains that the lemon trees around them were actually originally orange trees, and now, after being pruned with lemon and becoming lemon trees, they need to be nurtured so they don't return to oranges. Ida loves the thought of trees able to grow both lemons and oranges. He further adds that, botanically speaking, lemons are not fruits but berries. Highlighting the performativity of these trees and challenging their seemingly obvious categorization, Philip is clearly queering lemons. And, one may add, since lemons are associated with life, the film appears to advocate a more general queering of life itself. More so, in fact, than the film is queering sexual orientation identities.

THE NIGHT MANAGER

The Night Manager (2016) is Bier's six-part miniseries produced by BBC and AMC, based on John le Carré's thriller from 1993. The novel has been altered and adapted to contemporary world problems and sensibilities; for example, by using an Arab Spring backdrop, and by casting the leading intelligence officer as a woman instead of a man. The series is now a contemporary story about illegal arms trade and the individuals and groups that engage in this trade. Jonathan, the hero, infiltrates a circle of cynical arms traders run by Richard Roper. Within this group there is also a gay henchman, Corky (Corkoran). This gay character is not, however, updated to contemporary sensibilities, but rather seems to belong to an even earlier era than when the novel was written.

Corky poses a threat to the heterosexual hero, and is consequently disposed with, in a fashion that is well in line with observations of queer representation during earlier periods (Dyer 1993; Russo 1987). Corky (correctly) suspects that Jonathan cannot be trusted, and watches him closely. He also notices Jonathan's romance with Roper's young girlfriend Jed, seemingly with a sense of jealousy. Corky is thus a threat to Jonathan, both in his project to bring Roper to justice and in his romantic pursuits. In particular, two scenes stand out. In an elegant restaurant in the third episode, Corky is unruly, both in etiquette and according to normative sexuality. He rudely complains about the service disturbing other guests before he grabs Jonathan both by the butt and the crotch in a fellatio-like position. In Corky's last scene towards the end of the fifth episode, he has caught Jonathan sneaking out from the camp, and during the fight that follows Corky is killed by Jonathan. This is partly, it seems, because of his own sexuality; towards the end of the physical struggle Corky has clearly gotten the better of Jonathan, hitting his head repeatedly as he sits astride him. Instead of killing Jonathan, which he just said he was going to do, he instead proceeds to unbuckle his belt, allowing Jonathan to counter and kill him. The role of Corky is thus a familiar one in heteronormative mainstream cinema and television: a tragic and marginalized person who threatens the straight male hero, both sexually and otherwise, and who eventually ends up dead.[6] Another name to add to Vito Russo's necrology of queer characters killed by mainstream cinema (Russo 1987: 347–9) (Figure 5.5).

CONCLUSION

The films discussed here are quite distinct and there is no coherent way to summarize how they represent queer identities. Instead, I would like to offer two brief comparisons between earlier works and later works, with the general

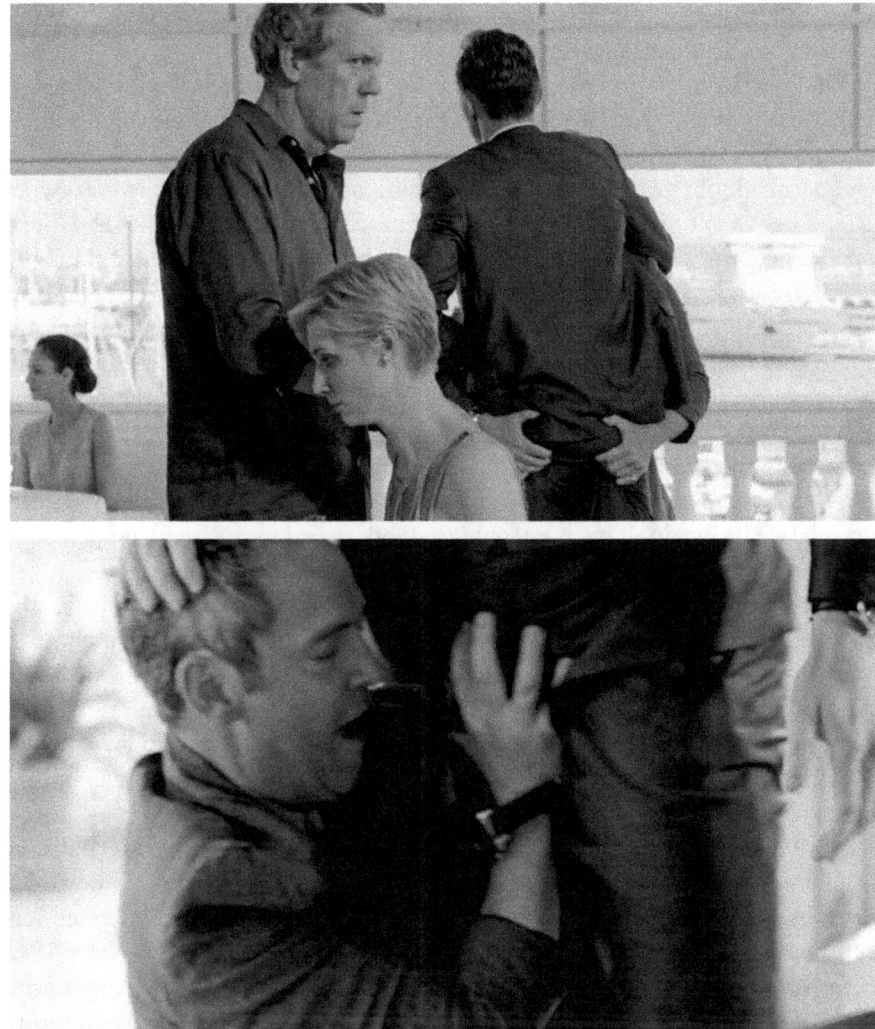

Figure 5.5 Corky poses a threat to the heterosexual hero, revealed with great clarity in the restaurant scene of the third episode. Corky threatens to expose Jonathan's relationship with Roper's girlfriend, Jed—exposure which would have Jonathan killed. Further, being attracted to Jonathan himself, Corky grabs Jonathan both by the butt and the crotch in a fellatio-like position, thus compromising the hero's hetrosexuality (*The Night Manager*, BBC and AMC, 2016).

point being a change from two local films with modest budgets, but with a clear and nuanced focus on queer characters, to two elegant transnational productions where the representations are not equally strong. Suffice to say, a sample of four productions is not enough to draw any conclusions, and there are many ways to explain any trend that may be discerned. Still, it seems that when contrasted with Bier's earlier films, her more recent projects show signs of queer re-marginalization and re-stereotyping.

First, in *Love Is All You Need*, the major point of focus is the contrast between a normal, prescribed, and predictable way of living, and a more life-affirming existence. An example of this message is played out when Ida goes for a swim. Philip sees her from afar, calling out to her that she is crazy and urging her to get out because of the current. She explains that the sea is just wonderful, and when he says the water is cold, she responds that it is fresh. In similar scenes from *Like It Never Was Before*, it is Petrus who swims in the stormy ocean and Rune who calls out how crazy and dangerous it is. At this point, like Philip, Rune is still unchanged—and has not yet come out—but at the end of the film he will walk into the waves, embraced by the sea. And by life. The difference between the two films is that *Like It Never Was Before* explicitly foregrounds Rune's homosexual coming out story, whereas *Love Is All You Need* merely lets Philip come out as a heterosexual man, finally ready to embrace life again. This is encouraging, but it also means that compared to Bier's earlier films, the queer identities have been re-marginalized.

Second, when Candy Darling dies in *Once in a Lifetime* it is within a distinctly Swedish cultural context, and within a more general queer context, including references to the AIDS trauma of the 1980s and 1990s. In stark contrast, when Corky dies in *The Night Manager*, his death occurs in an anonymous Middle Eastern non-place. In the former film it is a nuanced characterization, whereas the latter falls back on problematic stereotypes belonging to earlier eras. In this juxtaposition one may sense a re-stereotyping of queer identities.

Such a pattern of re-marginalization and re-stereotypicalization would be troublesome if it were indeed a larger pattern. Regarding these four works made by Bier, one might suggest that to her and to her audiences, the extended and nuanced representations of queer identities made in *Like It Never Was Before* (1995) and *Once in a Lifetime* (2000) came at a particularly important time, and that there may not be a similar need for such stories at a later point, in *Love Is All You Need* (2012) or *The Night Manager* (2016). If so, one could also suggest that Susanne Bier's interest in contemporary stories, identities, and situations has now found new subjects to include.

NOTES

1. For concise introductions to these contexts see Bendjelloul (2012) and Shriver-Rice (2015).
2. Rune's wish to be an actor also signals that he is ready to assume another identity/role—and that he is a good match with Petrus, who aspires to be a magician. Here I will not mention potentially rewarding readings related to the biblical name Petrus (St Peter), foregrounded as they are by the film, for example concerning fishing, rocks, and possibly even Petrus as gatekeeper of heaven.

3. There are many scenes that illustrate this. Some include Petrus's magic skills, which make it even more difficult for Rune, and the viewer, to understand and verify his feelings. A characteristic example is the first sex scene. Petrus has conjured up an egg that he places in the bewildered Rune's mouth, after which a close-up captures the mixed feelings of sorrow and pleasure in Rune's face as he reaches orgasm, and the egg breaks.
4. Similar concerns are raised among queer theorists; of particular relevance here is Ambjörnsson (2016: 62–3).
5. A brief reminder of *Like It Never Was Before* is the reappearance of the actors Stina Ekblad and Philip Zandén. In *Like It Never Was Before*, their characters (Rune's wife and the inn owner) came across as guardians of the status quo and of conflict avoidance. Here, they turn out to be cancer specialists, assisting Ida in her dealings with the life-changing experience of breast cancer. To some degree they still aspire to maintain a status quo, but when that is no longer possible, they are now more supportive and respectful of her worries and decisions.
6. To be fair, while it is a stereotypical portrait, it is still not without nuances. Jessica Kiang has commented that the "initially worrisomely portrayed gay character gets to largely lay those worries to rest by delivering Corkoran's [Corky] enjoyably spiky dialogue with such relish" (Kiang 2016). Apart from his sharp lines of dialogue (also present in the novel), Corky attracts audience sympathy through the viewer's sense of social justice. His suspicions about Jonathan were right, but he was undeservedly outmaneuvered and blame was falsely placed upon him. When Jonathan kills him, viewers are likely to wish it had been someone else.

BIBLIOGRAPHY

Ambjörnsson, Fanny (2016), *Vad är queer?*, 2nd ed., Stockholm: Natur och Kultur.
Bendjelloul, Wanda (2012), "Bortom garderoben," *Flm* 17/18 (October 6), <http://www.flm.nu/2012/10/bortom-garderoben/> (accessed November 14, 2017).
Benshoff, Harry, and Sean Griffin (2006), *Queer Images: A History of Gay and Lesbian Film in America*, Lanham, MD: Rowman & Littlefield.
Bronski, Michael (2001), "Positive images and the coming out film," *Cineaste* 26.1: 20–6.
Dixelius, Kalle (2004), "Schlagern kommit ut ur garderoben," *Dagens nyheter*, February 19, <http://www.dn.se/kultur-noje/schlagern-kommit-ut-ur-garderoben/> (accessed November 14, 2017).
Dyer, Richard (1993), *The Matter of Images: Essays on Representation*, London and New York: Routledge.
Frisch, Morten, and Anders Hviid (2006), "Childhood Family Correlates of Heterosexual and Homosexual Marriages: A National Cohort Study of Two Million Danes," *Archives of Sexual Behavior* 35, 5: 533–47.
Gardell, Jonas (1993), "En finstämd kväll med Jonas Gardell," stage show, Intiman, Stockholm, <https://www.youtube.com/watch?v=GqolTKleEkg> (accessed November 14, 2017).
Gardell, Jonas (2012), *Torka aldrig tårar utan handskar*, Stockholm: Norstedts.
Hamrud, Annika, and Jonas Helling (2013), "Fönstret har utsett: Sveriges 30 största gayförebilder genom tiderna," *Fönstret*, <http://www.fonstret.se/Artikelarkivet/Reportage/kom-ut/> (accessed November 14, 2017).
Kiang, Jessica (2016), "Berlin Review: Susanne Bier's 'The Night Manager' Starring Tom Hiddleston & Hugh Laurie," *IndieWire*, February 19, <http://www.indiewire.

com/2016/02/berlin-review-susanne-biers-the-night-manager-starring-tom-hiddleston-hugh-laurie-268230/> (accessed November 14, 2017).

le Carré, John (2016 [1993]), *The Night Manager*, London: Penguin Books.

Moddelmog, Debra A. (2009), "Can Romantic Comedy Be Gay?: Hollywood Romance, Citizenship, and Same-Sex Marriage Panic," *Journal of Popular Film and Television* 36: 162–72.

Pearl, Monica B. (2004), "AIDS and New Queer Cinema," in Michele Aaron (ed.), *New Queer Cinema: A Critical Reader*, Edinburgh: Edinburgh University Press, pp. 23–35.

Rosenberg, Tiina (2005), "Schlager, känslor och svensk homokultur," in Don Kulick (ed.), *Queersverige*, Stockholm: Natur och Kultur, pp. 336–62.

Russo, Vito (1987), *The Celluloid Closet: Homosexuality in the Movies*, revised ed., New York: Harper & Row.

Shriver-Rice, Meryl (2015), *Inclusion in New Danish Cinema: Sexuality and Transnational Belonging*, Bristol and Chicago: Intellect Books.

Sveriges riksdag (1994), "Protokoll 1993/94: 119," in *Riksdagens snabbprotokoll*, June 7, <http://www.riksdagen.se/sv/dokument-lagar/dokument/protokoll/riksdagens-snabbprotokoll-199394119-tisdagen_GH09119/html> (accessed November 14, 2017).

Sveriges television (1995), "Jonas Gardell om Susanne Bier (2008/1995)," interview, <https://www.youtube.com/watch?v=EwxX-WmJkz>E> (accessed January 29, 2017).

Waldron, Darren (2006), "New clothes for temporary transvestites? Sexuality, cross-dressing and passing in the contemporary French film comedy," in *Modern & Contemporary France* vol. 14, no. 3: 347–61.

FILMOGRAPHY

Änglagård/House of Angels, film, directed by Colin Nutley (Sweden: Memfis film, 1992).

Änglagård II—andra sommaren/House of Angels—Second Summer, film, directed by Colin Nutley (Sweden: Memfis film, 1994).

En kort en lang/Shake it all about, film, directed by Hella Joof (Denmark: Angel Production, 2001).

Fucking Åmål/Show me Love, film, directed by Lukas Moodysson (Sweden: Memfis film, 1998).

När alla vet/Sebastian, film, directed by Svend Wamb (Norway and Sweden: Mefistofilm, 1995).

Torka aldrig tårar utan handskar/Don't Ever Wipe Tears Without Gloves, television series, directed by Simon Kaijser (Sweden: Sveriges television, 2012).

CHAPTER 6

Judaism and Danish Directors: The Case of Lars von Trier vs. Susanne Bier

Pétur Valsson

Susanne Bier and Lars von Trier are arguably the most internationally successful contemporary Danish directors.[1] While radically different stylistically, both directors regard themselves as outsiders within the Danish cinematic tradition, describing their styles as "un-Danish" and on multiple occasions setting themselves apart from their fellow Danish directors.[2] In part, this "outsider" sentiment is connected to their being a part of the Jewish minority in Denmark and subsequently growing up with a feeling of being different, although von Trier found out as an adult that his Jewish identity was mistaken. Perhaps as a result of his mistaken identity, von Trier has openly expressed distaste for Bier and her films and even referred to her and her Jewishness in his now infamous rant at the Cannes film festival in 2011.[3]

Both Bier and von Trier have benefitted from the "transnational turn" in Danish film production, gaining access to international financing, international film stars, and audiences; most importantly, it has allowed them to address topics, interests, and concerns that are not bound by national culture and language. Through a change in the Danish film laws in 1989, the definition of Danish film was broadened, which, for example, allowed films in languages other than Danish to be granted support from the Danish Film Institute (Bondebjerg 2005: 121). Von Trier was instrumental in bringing about this change by challenging established film policies with his English-language film *The Element of Crime* (1984). The new film policy was a denationalizing act, in a sense, that opened the door for international co-productions to apply for funding. Whereas previous film law considered a film Danish only if the language and majority of talent were Danish, after 1989 it was enough for a film have a Danish producer and be in Danish or contribute to film culture in Denmark (Hjort 2005: 12).[4] The establishment of the Nordisk Film &

TV Fond a year later, along with pan-European funds like Eurimages (1988) and MEDIA Programme (1991), provided further incentives for Scandinavian filmmakers to make films with funds culled from various transnational sources. For instance, Bier's first film, the Swedish-language *Freud's Leaving Home* (*Freud flyttar hemifrån* . . ., 1991), and von Trier's English- and German-language *Europa* (1991) both received funds from the Danish Film Institute as well as from multiple other Scandinavian or European sources. The new opportunities these production initiatives offered helped boost the Danish film industry in the 1990s, thus creating what Mette Hjort has termed "The New Danish Cinema." Without the help of newly established funding schemes, big-budget productions such as von Trier's *Breaking the Waves* (1996) and *Dancer in the Dark* (2000) could not have been made. Meanwhile, Bier's films were transnational in nature from the start of her career, her first two features set in multiple countries with international casts.

Mette Hjort has pointed out the plurality of the term "transnational cinema," which can come in different forms and promote different values, whether they be economic, artistic, cultural, social, or political. While it has become a ubiquitous phenomenon, it is also an open one, "with the potential to develop in many different directions" (Hjort 2010: 30). For a small film industry like Denmark's, economic necessity might be the most common reason for transnational productions, but with it comes the pressure to make films with appeal beyond the national. Denmark has one of the smallest spoken languages in the world and few outside the country speak or understand it. As a result, von Trier has mainly produced English-language art films with casts consisting of well-known international and Scandinavian actors. This strategy, while mainly targeting international arthouse audiences, has also ensured that domestic audiences are not excluded.[5] However, Bier has employed a number of strategies throughout her career to attract an international audience. Already at the beginning of her career she alternated between making Swedish- and Danish-language genre films, displaying her interest in reaching audiences beyond Denmark. Since the early 2000s her directorial output has become more varied, but these films fall mainly in two categories according to Gunhild Agger: "cross-cultural and in this sense transnational mainstream films primarily in Danish, intentionally combining film traditions, cultural traditions and to a certain degree languages," and "English/American language mainstream and genre films of an international standard."[6] Bier's most successful films, such as *After the Wedding* (*Efter brylluppet*, 2006) and *In a Better World* (*Hævnen*, 2010), fall into the former category, which has been interpreted as part of what Ib Bondebjerg refers to as the "Hollywoodization" of Danish cinema in which filmmakers make "Hollywood-style mainstream films, adding a European, Nordic tone to them" (Bondebjerg 2005: 131–2). In 2005, von Trier harshly criticized this tendency, saying that in "many of the new Danish films some minor stories have just been expanded to stress a similarity to American films." He adds that "Danish film has become more sentimental, furnished with more cheap tricks,"[7] and blames prolific Danish screenwriters like Bier's frequent collaborator Anders Thomas Jensen for this trend.[8] Von Trier has, for example, called Bier's and Jensen's *Brothers* (*Brødre*, 2004) "meaningless shit"[9] even though he served as a consultant on the film.[10]

Denmark is a small nation of fewer than six million people, and while its film industry has been thriving in recent history, only around two dozen feature films are currently released per year (*Facts and Figures* 2016: 4). The community of Danish filmmakers is thus a small one, and the majority of active directors know each other, especially since many of them graduated from the National Film School of Denmark. Although von Trier graduated five years prior to Bier,[11] he dates their acquaintance back to the 1980s: "I have problems with Susanne Bier and she has problems with me, we went to school together, and we always had these problems."[12] However, it is unclear whether his statement refers only to their private life or also to their professional relationship. Bier's graduation film, *The Island of the Blessed* (*De saliges ø*, 1986), thanks von Trier in the credits (as Lars Trier), and the film was produced by Peter Aalbæk Jensen, von Trier's longtime producer and co-owner of Zentropa since 1992. Having established a working relationship with Bier during their school days, Aalbæk Jensen has partly credited her for his becoming a film producer: "She persuaded me to move over to production . . . She is an extremely loyal person. I learned a lot from her" (Macnab and Swart 2013: 14). Zentropa has produced most of Bier's Danish-language films, starting with *Family Matters* (*Det bli'r i familien*) in 1993, and Aalbæk Jensen remains the main professional link between Bier and von Trier.[13]

The two have more in common than the fact that they are contemporaneous Danish directors. Each won an award at the Munich Filmschool Festival for their graduation film, which helped launch their careers. More importantly, though, they were both raised as part of the small Danish-Jewish minority,[14] although their connections to Judaism were quite different. Ulf Trier, who von Trier grew up believing was his biological father, descended from an old Danish Jewish family that had been "atheists for generations" (Koplev 2003: 182), while Bier grew up in the active Jewish community in Copenhagen.

Bier's mother was of Russian-Jewish decent, but was born in Denmark, while her father's family fled Germany when he was a young child. Her primary education was at a Jewish school, but because she was not Orthodox, she did not feel a strong sense of belonging within the Jewish community: "It's always been a slight problem if you feel a cultural Jewish identity but don't feel super religious. Then it's not easy to be Jewish in Denmark, because there's no natural kind of environment for you to be part of," she says.[15] Bier also notes that even though she didn't notice any anti-Semitism growing up, she felt different from her non-Jewish friends, "who were deeply physically rooted in the country."[16] Bier's choice of words indicates that she felt somewhat like an outsider growing up, not quite belonging among the mostly Orthodox Jewish community or ethnic Danes.[17]

Bier's first feature, *Freud's Leaving Home*, is a Jewish family drama, and her next project, the short film *Letter to Jonas* (*Brev til Jonas*, 1992), confronts the Jewish diasporic experience; in the film two Danish girls go to Israel to be kibbutz volunteers, and while one remains faithful to her boyfriend in Denmark, the other begins a passionate relationship with an Israeli boy. Although Bier's later films do not include explicitly Jewish themes or characters, her films reflect a point of view that is informed by her Jewish background and history. Commenting on her work relationship with screenwriter Anders Thomas Jensen, she said that they "met through my own very strong personal sense of potential catastrophe. I think that this has to do with being Jewish and having a sense of history where the impossible is a possibility. I think Anders also has this sense of potential catastrophe so this was very close to us" (Wood 2004: 98). Thus, the impression that something bad could happen at any moment is a motif in her work that Bier connects to her Jewish heritage, and which is particularly apparent in her collaborations with Jensen.[18] This is not only a characteristic of Bier's later dramatic films but also of her early comedies, which address taboo issues or include characters facing impending disasters.[19]

In most of Bier's films, the family is at the center of the drama, and Bier connects its importance directly to her Jewish heritage: "I think that being Jewish has generated an extremely strong sense of the importance of family . . . If I look at my Scandinavian colleagues, they don't have that urgency about family. All my movies are about that."[20] Her films typically explore the impacts of "potential catastrophe," which function as crucial plot motivators in many of her films, on the family—for instance, the sudden and horrible loss of a child in *Island of the Blessed* or *A Second Chance* (*En chance til*, 2014) and the gradual decline of a sick parent in *Freud's Leaving Home* and *After the Wedding*. The urgency in Bier's work frequently manifests in characters willing to go to great lengths to protect or repair the family unit; for example, Jørgen arranges for Jakob to fill his role in the family before he dies in *After the Wedding*, and Andreas replaces his dead child with another in *A Second Chance*.

Bier has repeatedly expressed the will to return to Jewish subjects and cites her family and their way of communicating as a source of inspiration for her characters:

> I would love to make a film with a Jewish theme again at some point. It's clear that I know that world concretely and can easily describe it as a result. In my mind having a definitive cultural background and also

a very strong family background is a source of tremendous strength. The implications of the milieu for my work as a filmmaker are probably that I'm able to draw on certain styles of communication. The way that my family communicates is reflected again and again in my extreme characters. (Hjort and Bondebjerg 2001: 242)

Family is front and center in *Freud's Leaving Home*, a contemporary depiction of a Jewish family in Stockholm. The film, with its distinctly Jewish focus and characters, addresses the Jewish experience to an extent that is rare in Scandinavian cinema. However, the film was made at a time when there was a minor wave of films on Jewish topics produced in Sweden. In her book on the portrayal of Jews and other ethnic minorities in Swedish films, Rochelle Wright identifies five films and one co-production made between 1990 and 1993 that focus on the Jewish experience (Wright 1998: 323). Like Denmark, Sweden has a small Jewish population, and while it produces slightly more films annually than Denmark, the number of films addressing the experiences of Jewish characters in such a short time span is noteworthy. Wright points out that in the early 1990s there was an increased interest in Jewish history and culture in Sweden, probably because of changing dynamics in the Swedish Jewish community. The children of Jewish immigrants who had fled or survived the Holocaust had reached adulthood, and many were examining their roots and heritage in a Swedish context (ibid. 324). The Jewish-Swedish writer Marianne Goldman, who wrote the screenplay for *Freud's Leaving Home*, says that her family, while "extremely Jewish," had emphasized assimilation. However, many second-generation Jewish Swedes were later driven to draw attention to their Jewish identity to address their place in Swedish society. Goldman commented at the time that "[a] new generation working in theater and film has grown up and longs to bring out this part of their identity. Our generation demands the right to take up space" (quoted in Wright 1998: 327). This drive to tell stories that reflected their unique experiences and culture was common among Jewish filmmakers of the period and manifested in many diasporic communities around the world.

The sudden surge of Swedish Jewish-themed films in the 1990s was a part of a global wave of Jewish filmmaking exploring Jewish identity and culture. This was similar to the change in Jewish representation in American cinema of the 1960s and 1970s. Although Jewish moguls had been influential in Hollywood since the mid-teens, Jewish representation on the screen was sporadic and Jewish characters were often "de-Semitized"—that is, portrayed by non-Jews and with Jewish characteristics eliminated (Abrams 2012: 5). As middle-class, educated, second-generation immigrants, emerging Jewish-American filmmakers defined their heritage differently from their parents. While more assimilated than earlier generations, they clearly felt a need to assert distinctive Jewishness in "multicultural" post-WWII America. In his book on Judaism in contemporary cinema, Nathan Abrams says that this produced "a dialectical tension *between* assimilation and multiculturalism. The more Jews become accepted, therefore, the more their difference must be defined" (ibid. 9, emphasis in original). It wasn't until the 1990s that this cinematic shift in the portrayal of Jewish people and Jewishness became global. Abrams states, "[b]eyond North America, there was renaissance, or even birth in some cases, of Jewish filmmaking, clearly signaling similar trends to those in the United States" (ibid.). Historian Lawrence Baron connects this change to a widespread acceptance of ethnic, racial, and religious differences in previous decades, which had stimulated the production of films with more distinctively Jewish themes (Baron 2011: 6).[21]

Freud's Leaving Home portrays a Jewish family in Stockholm that undergoes a crisis after the mother is diagnosed with cancer amidst preparations for her sixtieth birthday. Each member of the family represents a different way of being Jewish and has a different connection to her or his heritage. The parents come from different backgrounds; the mother, Rosha, is a Holocaust survivor still dealing with traumatic memories, while her husband Ruben, who continuously cracks Jewish jokes, is from an old Jewish-Swedish family.[22] The oldest daughter, Deborah, lives in Jerusalem with her husband and three children and has converted to Orthodox Judaism, while the son David, who is gay, lives in Miami with his partner and is a secular Jew who does not take religious traditions or customs too seriously. The youngest daughter Angelique, nicknamed Freud, who still lives at home and is extremely close to her mother, represents the tradition of Jewish intellectualism. Freud acts as a mediator and a kind of therapist for the family, while struggling to extricate herself from her codependent relationship to Rosha. Rosha's impending death signifies a loss of tradition and values that is compounded by the fact that Judaism is matrilineal, and by the family's minority status in Sweden. Goldman says that for her the film is about "the disintegration of the Jewish family, what happens to the Jewish world when the mother dies. The mother is a central figure. She's in the home and the Jewish religion is practiced in the home" (quoted in Wright 1998: 372). Each family member embodies a different aspect of Judaism, and the mother is the family's unifying figure. With the impending death of the matriarch as the preserver of Jewish tradition, the family is uncertain about how family customs will be maintained in the future.

The emphasis on tradition in the film reflects its importance for Bier's and Goldman's generation. With a Jewish screenwriter and a director, as well as a number of Jewish actors in the cast, the film strives to authentically represent contemporary Jewish experience. Therefore it provides insights into the complexities of being part of an ethnic and religious minority in a homogeneous society.[23] Bier later said that she thinks the film "had clarity and a personal feel to it. I was extremely excited when making it. Exhilarated. It wasn't until it was finished that I realized that it is actually quite difficult to make a film" (Goodridge 2012: 36). Her experiences growing up in Copenhagen as a part of the Jewish minority enabled her to draw out cultural nuances that directors from other backgrounds would not have been able to portray.

Freud's Leaving Home is exemplary of the post-1990 global trend of Jewish filmmaking that both Abrams and Baron describe. The film has a distinctly Jewish narrative, was produced in a country with a small Jewish minority, and was welcomed by audiences; it was well received both in Sweden and abroad, and won several international film awards.[24] Already, with her first feature film, Bier established a distinct position within the mostly male-dominated world of Danish filmmakers.

Whereas Bier grew up in a Jewish family, went to a Jewish school, and had a bat mitzvah, Lars von Trier was raised in a non-religious household where the attitude toward Judaism was fairly relaxed and Danish identity was primary. However, while his family did not observe religious traditions, he felt a cultural connection to Judaism. For example, von Trier recalls no shortage of Jewish jokes at home and "a sense of security in 'Jewishness'" (Björkman 2003: 8). Despite not being Jewish in the traditional religious sense—as Jewish status is transferred through matrilineal descent or conversion—von Trier felt a sense of belonging with Judaism and Jewish culture: "All Jews were Family. I had the feeling I had a family, and that I belonged" (Koplev 2003: 184). Moreover, his sense of Jewish people as outcasts surely enhanced von Trier's attachment to Jewish identity:

> First of all it's really cool to be among the ones who were always persecuted. Say what you want, but you have to admit it's really cool and it has some kind of aura to it . . . I've always seen myself as something of an outsider and felt a little persecuted and then it's very nice to belong to a club of persecuted people. (ibid. 183)

Part of identifying with Judaism, for von Trier, was linked to his sense of being different. In other words, belonging to a minority group that had experienced discrimination throughout history validated von Trier's outsider sensibility. As a consequence, von Trier experienced quite a shock when his mother confessed on her deathbed in 1989 that his biological father was Fritz Michael Hartmann, rather than Ulf Trier. Apart from the confusion this news likely inspired, it also meant that his Jewish identity was built on a lie: "Not a Jew? Not a part of the great 'victims' of the world? I was devastated," von Trier said in 1998 (Roman 2003: 138). At the Cannes press conference in 2011, von Trier referred to and elaborated on this incident, connecting it oddly to Bier: "I thought I was a Jew for a long time and was very happy being a Jew. Then later on came Susanne Bier and then suddenly I wasn't so happy about being a Jew." Following this statement he infamously claimed to "understand Hitler" and said, "I'm really a Nazi, because my family was German."[25] Although many have interpreted these remarks as evidence of von Trier's anti-Semitism, they could be viewed to more productive ends in the context of von Trier's family history. Resentment towards the parents who had lied to him about his ancestry and his biological father, who, when von Trier contacted him, denied paternity,[26] could help explain his ill-conceived comments. Although he had never practiced Judaism as a religion and had converted to Catholicism when he first got married (Björkman 2003: 104), this revelation deeply affected him, inspiring an identity crisis. The knowledge of his true paternity's effect is also evident in his films. After *Europa*, which was in pre-production when his mother disclosed von Trier's paternity, he replaced a controlled technical style with a more chaotic, emotional approach to filmmaking.[27]

The most overt references to Judaism in von Trier's films are the Jewish characters in his early films, produced before his mother's confession. These characters, often minor characters portrayed by von Trier or a relative, often reflected Jewish stereotypes and were not given names but identified by recognizable cultural and ethnic markers.[28] For example, von Trier's character in *The Element of Crime* (1984) is called "Schmuck of Ages," where the use of the Yiddish-derived derogatory term (which originally referred to the circumcised penis) points to the stereotypical nature of the characterization. Stereotypes can, as Homi Bhabha suggests, offer secure points of identification (Bhabha 1994: 99). Perhaps because of the lack of Jewish role models in von Trier's life, he turned to negative and pejorative stereotypes to express what he considered the Jewish part of his identity.

The evocation of pejorative Jewish stereotypes is perhaps most evident in von Trier's early short *The Orchid Gardener* (*Orchidégartneren*, 1977), where he plays a Jewish artist named Victor Marse who is dealing with his identity and sexual frustration. After becoming consumed by his love for a nurse at the sanatorium he is staying at, Marse starts behaving strangely. His antics include dressing up in a Nazi uniform, ripping the head off a live bird to use as rouge when dressing up in drag, and staging his own hanging. In the film's preface a narrator describes Marse, whose real name is Felimann von Marseburg, as "a Jew and big nosed as they are." The narrator recites the story of how Marse's ancestors had been "chased down the streets by rock-throwers," but that he did not know anything about this and "didn't want to know anything about his heritage." While the Jewish character, ignorant of the history of Jewish persecution and dressed up in a Nazi uniform, was certainly meant to provoke, it also reflects von Trier's struggle with his identity. Trier later claimed he had exposed himself in the film and that it was "the expression of a young man who was in really, really bad shape" (Hjort and Bondebjerg 2001: 212). Marse is in a way von Trier's alter ego, the struggling artist in search of identity, and he uses the character to represent his own lack of knowledge about his heritage.

Two of von Trier's films take place in the aftermath of World War II: his graduation film, *Images of a Relief* (*Befrielsesbilleder*, 1982), which doesn't address the treatment of Jews during the war,[29] and *Europa*, in which von Trier appears as a Jewish character. In *Europa*, a young American goes to Germany to help with the reconstruction but instead becomes entangled in a pro-Nazi terrorist conspiracy. Von Trier's character, simply identified as "Jew," appears in a scene where he is called upon to testify on the behalf of business mogul Max Hartmann, who is accused of being a Nazi collaborator. The "Jew" exonerates Hartmann and claims that he is a friend who hid him in his cellar during the war. Afterwards, it becomes apparent that he was handsomely rewarded for giving false testimony about Hartmann's participation with the Nazi regime during the war. Von Trier's character cares more about money than he does about bringing those who aided the Holocaust to justice. This negative portrayal of a Jewish character, as in *The Orchid Gardener*, could again be interpreted in light of von Trier's struggle with his identity. About this character, von Trier said, "I wanted to identify myself as part of the family I thought I belonged to . . . I've always had a certain weakness for all things Jewish. At the same time, it's a portrait of a wretched, faithless Jew who turns up to give false testimony" (Björkman 2003: 138–9). Von Trier had written the script for *Europa* before his mother's disclosure, and was in the middle of pre-production when he learned about his true paternity. Von Trier subsequently changed the name of the German tycoon and Nazi collaborator in the film to Hartmann, after his own biological father who had denied the paternity. The scene in *Europa* can be read, in a way, as a therapeutic act, a "letting go" of the Jewish identity and an attempt to come to terms with his real ancestry. As the "wretched, faithless Jew," von Trier, having just learned that he is not a Jew after all, exonerates a character that is a surrogate for the father who wouldn't acknowledge von Trier as his son. When regarded in the context of this scene, von Trier's comments at Cannes in 2011 that he thought he was a Jew and then "found out [he] was really a Nazi" are not about his personally being anti-Semitic; instead, these comments reveal his feelings towards his mother's deceit and his biological father's rejection. At the end of the scene von Trier's character is heard saying: "No more! I won't do it again," indicating that the character will not bear false witness any more for Nazi collaborators. This can also be interpreted as von Trier's declaration that he will not perform the part of the "Jew" again, a promise that he has so far kept.

Comparing the influence of Judaism on the works of Bier and von Trier illustrates how differently Jewishness manifests in their films. While it would be erroneous to consider Bier simply as a "Jewish director," because her work is too varied for such a simplification, her films are informed by growing up within the Jewish community in Denmark. For example, she successfully explores the subtleties of Jewish family life in *Freud's Leaving Home* and attributes some of the tropes in her films to her Jewish identity. On the other hand, despite regarding Jewishness as an important part of his identity, von Trier had very little experience of the traditions of Jewish family life and was brought up in a home where "the subject [of religion] was more or less forbidden" (Björkman 2003: 104). Thus, Judaism in von Trier's films is mostly reflected through Jewish characters who are based on pejorative Jewish stereotypes and portrayed by von Trier himself. Although we can regard these characters as reflections of von Trier's self-exploration, the characterizations are obviously anti-Semitic. Although this suggests von Trier's ignorance, the purposely anti-Semitic stereotypes might well be an attempt to highlight prejudice through satire.

While accusations about anti-Semitism first arose after von Trier's remarks in 2011,[30] critics have frequently described his films as laden with other types of prejudice, in particular misogyny, and have even accused von Trier of being a sadist.[31] Since *Breaking the Waves*, with the exception of *The Boss of It All* (*Direktøren for det hele*, 2006), all of von Trier's films have focused on female characters who undergo suffering or degradation. News stories about his manipulative relationships with actresses such as Björk and Nicole Kidman are considered further proof of a misogynistic perspective apparent in many of his successful films. Thus, one critic claims that von Trier "seems to get a kick out of putting his screen women in jeopardy or in violent situations,"[32] and *Antichrist* (2009) received a special anti-prize at the Cannes film festival for being "the most misogynist movie from the self-proclaimed biggest director in the world."[33] Von Trier dismisses such charges, claiming that these women represent his own feminine side: "I've always been the female characters in all my films."[34] In October 2017, as multiple women accused Hollywood producer Harvey Weinstein and other influential men in the entertainment industry of sexual misconduct, Björk released a statement in which she described multiple incidents of sexual harassment by an unnamed Danish director. Both von Trier and producer Aalbæk Jensen denied the allegations,[35] but since then multiple former female employees at Zentropa have come forward accusing Aalbæk Jensen of sexual misconduct, sparking an investigation by Danish authorities into allegations of "sexual harassment, degradation and bullying" at the company.[36] Although von Trier was not named in these allegations, the descriptions of sexually degrading behavior within Zentropa strongly indicates a misogynist working environment within the company co-owned by Aalbæk Jensen and von Trier. Film scholars have been divided on the issue of von Trier's misogyny, some rightly arguing that the extreme suffering of his female characters is problematic while others have defended von Trier's work by suggesting that his representations of women are more complex.

In her essay on *Breaking the Waves* Alyda Faber argues that through the characterization of Bess, von Trier idealizes feminine masochism and legitimates male dominance, and insists that the film "is not just man's 'masochistic *fantasy*' but a part of a persistent male creation of women's social reality" (Faber 2003: 74, emphasis in original). Paula Quigly finds von Trier's depiction of female suffering "so excessive that it can no longer function as cathartic. Consequently, these representations are much more resistant to being recuperated as 'positive'" (Quigly 2012: 156). On the contrary, Caroline Bainbridge argues that von Trier's films can be seen as familiar cultural constructs of femininity, albeit not feminist, and suggests that they "capture elements of the socio-cultural formation of femininity and its silences and enable them to be articulated" (Bainbridge 2007: 120). Bainbridge acknowledges von Trier's association of femininity with masochism, but argues that he could be responding to cultural assumptions about how femininity is understood and thus his films can "be seen to draw attention to the way femininity often secedes the boundaries imposed on it by patriarchal systems" (ibid. 138). Linda Badley similarly suggests that with *Breaking the Waves* and *Antichrist*, von Trier simultaneously exploits and "confronts the taboo by unearthing a persistent, half-conscious misogyny that passes without comment in a glib, consumerist 'post-feminist' era, exposing it for what it is" (Badley 2010: 149). Badley has also pointed out *Antichrist*'s connection to Nordic paganism. The film, like some works of Carl Th. Dreyer and Ingmar Bergman, explores a tension between Nordic pagan beliefs and modern Christian/secular points of view and "a commingled fear of and desire for the return of the repressed pagan code while often empathizing with the (female) witch's point of view" (Badley 2013: 15). She also argues that "the film confronts a misogyny unspeakable precisely because it is as ancient and ingrained as the distinction between Christian and pagan, 'Man' and 'Nature,' self and Other" (ibid. 28). These interpretations indicate the complexity of the representations of women in von Trier's works, which should be considered in the contexts of both the socio-cultural formation of femininity and Scandinavian history. Despite this, von Trier's repeated use of female suffering and degradation in his films to the point that female sexuality is equated with masochism remains deeply problematic, whether or not these female characters are a reflection of his own psyche.

In contrast to von Trier, Bier usually focuses on male characters in her films, and has claimed in interviews that she identifies more easily with men than women.[37] Writing on the character of the male sojourner in Bier's films, Belinda Smaill points out that men undergo the most extreme challenges and emotional transformations in Bier's work, which leads Smaill to categorize them as "male melodramas" (Smaill 2014: 13). Even though Bier's films have sometimes been negatively assessed in terms that describe feminine attributes pejoratively,[38] Smaill argues that "there is no overt or essential quality to these films that proclaims a female authorial stamp" (ibid. 18). Both Bier and von Trier's most successful films transgress the gendered subject-position their director occupies, a fact that resonates with Kaja Silverman's conceptualization of the cinematic "mise-en-scène of desire":

> [T]his libidinal masculinity or femininity must be read in relation to the biological gender of the biographical author, since it is clearly not the same thing, socially or politically, for a woman to speak with a female voice as it is for a man to do so, and vice versa. All sorts of cultural imperatives dictate a smooth match between biological gender and subject-position, making any deviation a site of potential resistance to sexual difference. (Silverman 1988: 217)

Von Trier made his Depression trilogy films[39] to deal with his own depression, and thus characters such as Justine in *Melancholia* (2011) and the unnamed female character in *Antichrist* embody, in a sense, von Trier's authorial desire. Bier's male characters similarly reflect a part of Bier's own personality. She claims that she identifies with Jörgen in *After the Wedding* because she feels and recognizes "a certain extreme sense of responsibility and a certain extreme sense of feeling he has that he has to make sure everything is okay".[40] This sense of responsibility is a personality trait common to many of Bier's male characters, such as Anton in *In a Better World* and Brian in *Things We Lost in the Fire* (2007). Even more common are characters like Jannik in *Brothers*, Jakob in *After the Wedding*, and Jerry in *Things We Lost in the Fire*, who, in the face of disasters, must step up and attempt to assume responsibility. Both directors clearly identifying with characters of the opposite gender suggests transgender "libidinal" identifications according to Silverman's theory of authorial desire. However, this manifests quite differently in their films. Von Trier's authorial desire could be described as masochistic and highly sexual, especially in *Nymphomaniac* (2013), while Bier's often quite vulnerable male characters demonstrate masculinity in terms of responsibility and care rather than, for example, aggressiveness or power.[41] Bier's cross-gender authorial identification results in films that emphasize the positive aspects of masculinity. On the other hand, von Trier's feminine alter-ego manifests in representations that degrade femininity. Early in his career von Trier used negative Jewish stereotypes to represent his own self-image, but moved on to female characters for the same purpose in his later films. In either case, von Trier—who is firmly in a privileged social and historical position as a white ethnic Danish male—uses historically marginal groups to express personal frustrations and psychological difficulties. If his intentions are not fueled by anti-Semitism and misogyny, von

Trier's representations of these historically marginalized groups still exhibit lack of understanding and respect and remain no less offensive.

It was twenty years after von Trier's last appearance as a Jewish character in *Europa* that he made his controversial "jokes" about Jews and Nazis during the *Melancholia* press conference at Cannes. Immediately afterwards, in a smaller press conference held for Scandinavian journalists, von Trier was asked what he thought Bier would think about his statements, to which he responded, "I'm sure that Susanne Bier will love them. She will put "Fiddler on the Roof" on the record player and dance around." When asked if he planned to apologize, he said that he had already "apologized more than plenty to Susanne Bier. I have apologized to the whole world. Now it's enough with apologies. I don't want to apologize more."[42] The self-proclaimed provocateur expressed no regrets about his words, but continued his insults against his fellow countrywoman. The image he conjured of Bier dressed up and dancing to the music of *Fiddler on the Roof* was obviously meant in a derogatory way and was more overtly anti-Semitic than anything he had said at the first press meeting. Bier has always been reluctant to comment on von Trier's remarks or his alleged hostility towards her. When asked about their relationship in 2014, she responded, "It's much more interesting when he talks about his relationship with me . . . I have quite a humorous perception of him. I think he is a brilliant filmmaker, and I think he at times says things which are hugely inappropriate."[43] Bier elaborated on the incident in an interview on BBC in 2016, admitting that while she considered von Trier's remarks ridiculous, they had been hurtful. She stated that she had never confronted von Trier about them, saying "certain attacks you don't want to respond to because they are so utterly repulsive. I must admit that I found those remarks repulsive and stupid and in no way felt compelled to react to them." She further explained, "if you react to any aggression, you also become somehow vulnerable. I didn't particularly want to feel vulnerable."[44] None of Bier's statements on the matter indicate that von Trier apologized for his remarks about her and she did not confront him privately or publicly about the subject. She also did not let the controversy affect her working relationship with Zentropa, which has continued to produce her Danish-language features.

Von Trier's Jewish characters indicate that while his Jewish heritage was important to him, he relied on Jewish stereotypes rather than personal experience to integrate it into his work. Interviewed by Jewish-Danish journalist Martin Krasnik at the end of 2014, von Trier emphasized the sense of belonging he had felt being Jewish and how tough it had been when he found out that he did not in fact belong: "I miss the part, which I don't have anything to do with after all. The Jewish part, I miss it like nothing else. It was very identity-creating for me back then" (Skadhauge and Tønde 2016: 33). And while von Trier graciously accepted Karsnik's invitation to participate in the ritual of lighting the Hanukkah menorah, he evidently had not only never taken part in such a ceremony but also seemed to lack any knowledge about it.[45] Von Trier's connection to Judiasm appears superficial; while he sought comfort in belonging to the group, he never made much effort to gain an understanding of the religion. In comparison, representations of Jewish characters in Bier's *Freud's Leaving Home* are more authentic and insightful, which reflects the director's and screenwriter's personal experiences of Jewish family life. In addition, in her later films, Bier has emphasized families facing impending disaster, connecting both the importance of family and the sense of potential catastrophe to her Jewish identity. Thus, while she has only made one feature film with a distinctly Jewish theme, her oeuvre is informed by a Jewish sensibility far more intricate and profound than the stereotype-based Jewish characters in von Trier's films. That the arrival of Bier as a distinctly Jewish voice on the scene of Danish film coincided with the revelation of von Trier's paternity very likely sparked his initial resentment towards Bier. As her profile has risen, both at home and abroad, Bier has gained prominence within Zentropa and challenges von Trier's position as the company's biggest name, which seems to have fueled von Trier's discontent.

In order to fully understand von Trier's anti-Semitic and misogynist remarks, one must take into account his personal history as well as the ambivalence toward both Judaism and women that is visible in his films. After learning about his true paternity, von Trier replaced the self-portrayed Jewish characters in his early films with female main characters, who he acknowledges are a reflection of his psyche. From a privileged position as an ethnic white Danish male von Trier repeatedly puts himself in the role of disadvantaged people, either presenting himself as a part of the Jewish minority or claiming that he is the female characters in his films, without any first-hand knowledge or experience of how it is to live as a part of underprivileged social group. This is certainly problematic, as he continues to exploit marginalized cultural groups of which he is not part in order to cope with his own personal frustrations, depression, and anger. His dismissive responses to criticism are at best culturally insensitive, but might also indicate that he is ignorant of his own privileged position.

The public conflict between von Trier and Bier, which is somewhat one-sided as Bier has only reluctantly responded when pressed about it in interviews, is both strange and complex, as it seems to be rooted in von Trier's personal family history. Von Trier has always used provocation as a self-marketing tool, whether through his public statements or the controversial subject matter of his films. The conflict, and von Trier's reluctance to apologize, could certainly be regarded as a part of his constant self-marketing, a way to keep his name constantly in the media. A second feud with another of his fellow Danish filmmakers, Nicolas Winding Refn,[46] seems to substantiate this.

Although von Trier hardly imagined that he would become *persona non grata* at Cannes following his remarks in 2011, *Melancholia* subsequently received plenty of news coverage and did well in theaters worldwide.[47] The controversy surrounding von Trier's and Bier's conflict has, for better or worse, helped to keep the spotlight on Danish filmmaking—proving perhaps that negative press is better than no press at all.

NOTES

1. A number of other Danish directors have enjoyed international success in recent decades, including Bille August, Nicolas Winding Refn, Lone Scherfig, and Thomas Vinterberg. However, in terms of international prominence and recognition, Bier and von Trier are still the most widely known Danish filmmakers.
2. In an early interview von Trier described contemporary Danish films as being unintelligible, boring, and insipid (Michelsen 2003: 8), and Bier has said that she has "absolutely no relation to the Scandinavian tradition of cinematic representation, with its very direct correlation of inner feeling and external appearance" (Hjort and Bondebjerg 2001: 242).
3. Referring to his mistaken Jewish identity, von Trier said, "for a long time I thought I was a Jew, and I was happy to be a Jew. Then later on came Susanne Bier, and then suddenly I wasn't so happy about being a Jew . . . and then I found out I was really a Nazi." Later, he stated, "I am not against Jews, not even Susanne Bier." Available at <http://www.festival-cannes.fr/fr/mediaPlayer/11391.html> (accessed March 28, 2016).
4. There is no clause in the law about how to accomplish these goals, making virtually any film with a Danish producer that might have artistic merit applicable for support. New film laws were again passed in 1997, retaining the same qualifications but raising the maximum support from fifty percent to sixty percent.
5. It is worth noting that Danish films in English are rarely successful at the domestic box office, and even though von Trier has become an internationally recognized brand, only a few of his English-language films have attracted large audiences in Denmark.
6. Available at <http://www.kosmorama.org/Artikler/Susanne-Bier.aspx> (accessed February 1, 2017). Agger identifies five main strategies that Danish filmmakers have resorted to in order to negotiate national and transnational appeal: Danish-language art films, Danish-language genre films with international appeal, multi-language mainstream films, English-language art films, or English-language mainstream and genre films.
7. Quoted in Agger, available at <http://www.kosmorama.org/Artikler/Susanne-Bier.aspx> (accessed February 1, 2017).
8. Available at <http://www.ekkofilm.dk/artikler/drillepinden/> (accessed February 1, 2017).
9. Available at <http://www.ekstrabladet.dk/flash/filmogtv/film/article3042740.ece> (accessed February 1, 2017).
10. Anders Thomas Jensen calls von Trier's criticisms absurd, as "many of the ideas were his own!" (Redvall 2010: 86).
11. Von Trier graduated from the National Film School in 1982, Bier in 1987.
12. Available at <http://www.indiewire.com/2011/05/

lars-von-triers-last-cannes-q-a-stupid-statements-melancholia-i-am-not-a-nazi-dunst-cruz-185454/> (accessed March 29, 2016).
13. In addition to professional ties through Aalbæk Jensen and Zentropa, there are also some personal connections between Bier and von Trier through their children, as their daughters are friends. See <https://youtu.be/IH8qdq6f7YU> (March 28, 2016).
14. It is worth noting that only 0.12 percent of the Danish population identified as Jewish in 2014, according to the Jewish Virtual Library's "Jewish Population of the World" resource: <http://www.jewishvirtuallibrary.org/jewish-population-of-the-world> (accessed March 29, 2016).
15. Available at <http://forward.com/schmooze/176187/a-different-kind-of-cancer-story/> (accessed February 1, 2017).
16. Ibid.
17. In *Small Nation, Global Cinema* Mette Hjort uses a direct translation of terms used in public debates about multiculturalism in to distinguish between "new Danes," people living in Denmark who are of a different, race, religion, or ancestry than the majority of the population, and "ethnic Danes," who are Caucasian, Protestant, and "whose ancestral connections to Denmark have an antiquity going beyond at least two generations" (Hjort 2005: 237–8).
18. Talking about her grandparents when they still lived in Germany, Bier said, "They had a lot of non-Jewish friends. And then suddenly society turned against them. I think the lack of automatically feeling, 'Yes, the future is going to be like the present'—that is very much a Jewish thing." Available at <http://www.nytimes.com/2007/03/25/movies/25gold.html> (accessed January 13, 2018).
19. For example, the lead character of *Family Matters* unknowingly has an incestuous relationship with his own sister; the protagonist of *Like It Never Was Before* (*Pensionat Oskar*, 1995) is a closeted family man who has an affair with a younger man during a family holiday; one of the supporting characters in *Once in a Lifetime* (*Livet är en schlager*, 2000) is transgender and going through the final stages of AIDS; and finally, in the romantic comedy *The One and Only* (*Den eneste ene*, 1999), death and adultery make the romantic relationship of the two main characters possible.
20. Available at < http://www.nytimes.com/2007/03/25/movies/25gold.html> (accessed April 4, 2016).
21. Instead of minimizing Jewish stereotypes or Jewish elements of narratives, the ethnic, racial, and religious dimensions began to be accentuated. This phenomenon has not only been noted in Jewish films; the surge in global migration led to more self-consciously ethnic films being made in Western and Central Europe.
22. Ruben's constant need to tell Jewish jokes could be viewed not only as a light-hearted performance of identity but also as an expression of the difficulties associated with integration.
23. For an expansion on this subject, see Maureen Turim's chapter in this volume.
24. *Freud's Leaving Home* received several nominations for the 1992 Guldbagge Awards, the Swedish equivalent of the Academy Awards, and Gunilla Röör won the best actress award. At the Robert Awards, the Danish Film Academy prize, the film was particularly successful; actresses Ghita Nørby and Jessica Zandén both won awards for their performances, and Marianne Goldman received the best screenplay award. The only film that was more celebrated at the Robert Awards that year was von Trier's *Europa*, which snatched the best picture award as well as a number of technical prizes.
25. Available at <http://www.newyorker.com/culture/richard-brody/lars-von-trier-the-melancholy-dane/> (accessed February 1, 2017). Although von Trier immediately

professed that he had been joking, the comments made headlines around the world and made him *persona non grata* at the festival.

26. Contrary to von Trier's controversial claim, "I'm really a Nazi," because of his paternity, his father was active in the Danish resistance during World War II. See <http://modstand.natmus.dk/Person.aspx?43138> (accessed April 5, 2016).
27. Von Trier radically changed his style with the TV series *The Kingdom* (*Riget*, 1994–7), which eschewed the controlled style of his early films, with its meticulously storyboarded and complex camera action, in favor of a handheld camera and often improvised action. In his subsequent feature films, he focused on excessively emotional female characters, such as Bess in *Breaking the Waves* (1996) and Selma in *Dancer in the Dark* (2000), instead of the emotionally restrained male characters of his early films.
28. Carl-Henrik Trier's character in the shorts *The Orchid Gardener* and *Menthe – den lyksalige* (1979) is simply referred to as "Old Jew" or "Jew," and von Trier's character in *Europa* is likewise only named "Jew."
29. The film caused some controversy at the time due to von Trier's somewhat sympathetic depiction of a German Nazi officer and the use of documentary footage showing Danish mobs assaulting Nazi collaborators.
30. In his essay on the representation of the Holocaust in *Europa*, Udi E. Greenberg notes that some contemporary critics saw the film as anti-American or anti-German, but makes no mention of criticism of the film as anti-Semitic. Greenberg only briefly mentions von Trier's portrayal of the Jew and regards it as "a self-reflexive move that implicates cinema history in racial hiding" (Greenberg 2008: 49).
31. Available at <https://www.theguardian.com/film/2003/oct/12/features.magazine> (accessed September 30, 2016).
32. Available at <http://www.telegraph.co.uk/culture/film/starsandstories/5843594/Lars-Von-Trier-Antichrist-Or-just-anti-women.html> (accessed February 1, 2017).
33. Available at <http://www.independent.co.uk/arts-entertainment/films/features/is-antichrist-anti-women-1755616.html> (accessed February 1, 2017).
34. Available at <http://www.independent.co.uk/arts-entertainment/films/features/lars-von-trier-its-good-that-people-boo-1692406.html> (accessed February 1, 2017).
35. Available at <https://www.theguardian.com/music/2017/oct/17/bjork-reveals-more-details-of-alleged-sexual-harassment-by-director> (accessed November 16, 2017).
36. Available at <https://www.theguardian.com/film/2017/nov/13/nine-women-allege-sexual-harassment-and-bullying-at-lars-von-triers-production-firm> (accessed November 16, 2017).
37. Available at <http://awfj.org/blog/2007/03/30/jennifer-merin-interviews-susanne-bier-re-after-the-wedding/> (accessed February 1, 2017).
38. Smaill notes some negative comments from reviewers who characterize Bier's work "as 'apparent and schematic' and overly emotionalized, with 'soap-operatic background noise' and back-patting platitudes. David Edelstein describes *In a Better World* as 'an Oprah movie'" (Smaill 2014: 15).
39. The Depression trilogy consists of *Antichrist* (2009), *Melancholia* (2011), and the two-part *Nymphomaniac* (2013).
40. Available at <http://awfj.org/blog/2007/03/30/jennifer-merin-interviews-susanne-bier-re-after-the-wedding/> (accessed February 1, 2017).
41. Usually characters that display their masculinity in terms of aggressiveness and power in Bier's films remain minor characters, such as Big Man and the bully mechanic in *In a Better World*, with the exception of Michael in *Brothers*.

42. Available at <http://ekstrabladet.dk/flash/filmogtv/film/article4099517.ece> (accessed March 29, 2016).
43. Available at <https://youtu.be/IH8qdq6f7YU> (accessed March 28, 2016).
44. Available at <http://www.bbc.co.uk/programmes/b073q99k> (accessed April 15, 2016).
45. Available at <https://youtu.be/8PCgMpnQVH4> (accessed February 15, 2017).
46. In a 2017 interview, von Trier complained that Winding Refn didn't defend him after the Cannes controversy, calling him an "opportunist in an unpleasant way." Available at <http://www.indiewire.com/2017/04/lars-von-trier-nicolas-winding-refn-feud-1201809072> (accessed April 28, 2017).
47. *Melancholia* grossed roughly 16 million USD worldwide according to Box Office Mojo, twentyfold that of *Antichrist*, although still far behind *Dancer in the Dark*'s 40 million USD worldwide gross. Available at <http://www.boxofficemojo.com/movies/?id=melancholia.htm> (accessed April 28, 2017).

BIBLIOGRAPHY

Abrams, Nathan (2012), *The New Jew in Film: Exploring Jewishness and Judaism in Contemporary Cinema*, London: I. B. Tauris.

Agger, Gunhild (2015), "Strategies in Danish Film Culture—and the Case of Susanne Bier," *Kosmorama* 259 (March 11), <http://www.kosmorama.org/Artikler/Susanne-Bier.aspx> (accessed November 14, 2017).

Badley, Linda (2011), *Lars von Trier*, Urbana: University of Illinois Press.

Badley, Linda (2013), "*Antichrist*, Misogyny and Witch Burning: The Nordic Cultural Contexts," *Journal of Scandinavian Cinema* 3.1: 15–33.

Bainbridge, Caroline (2007), *The Cinema of Lars von Trier. Authenticity and Artifice*, London: Wallflower Press.

Baron, Lawrence (2011), "Introduction: Wandering Views," in L. Baron (ed.), *The Modern Jewish Experience in World Cinema*, Waltham, MA: Brandeis University Press, pp. 1–21.

Bhabha, Homi K. (1994), *The Location of Culture*, New York: Routledge.

Björkman, Stig (2003), *Trier on von Trier*, trans. Neil Smith, London: Faber and Faber.

Bondebjerg, Ib (2005), "The Danish Way," in A. Nestingen and T. G. Elkington (eds.), *Transnational Cinema in a Global North: Nordic Cinema in Transition*, Detroit: Wayne State University Press, pp. 111–39.

Brody, Richard (2011), "Lars von Trier: The Melancholy Dane," *The New Yorker*, May 19, <https://www.newyorker.com/culture/richard-brody/lars-von-trier-the-melancholy-dane> (accessed November 14, 2017).

Bryant, Jacob (2016), "'Serena' Director Susanne Bier Says Movies 'Will Die Out' If They Don't Reflect Diversity," *Variety*, March 16, <http://variety.com/2016/film/news/susanne-bier-slams-movie-industry-lars-von-trier-1201730519/> (accessed November 14, 2017).

"Conférence de presse de 'MELANCHOLIA' de Lars VON TRIER" (2011), *Festival de Cannes*, May 18, <http://www.festival-cannes.fr/fr/mediaPlayer/11391.html> (accessed March 28, 2016).

Faber, Alyda (2003), "Redeeming Sexual Violence? A Feminist Reading of *Breaking the Waves*," *Literature & Theology* 17.1: 59–75.

Facts and Figures, Production and Exhibition (2016), Copenhagen, The Danish Film Institute.
"Fritz Michael Hartmann," *Frihedsmuseets Modstandsdatabase*, <http://modstand.natmus.dk/Person.aspx?43138> (accessed November 14, 2017).
Gold, Sylviane (2007), "A Director Comfortable With Catastrophe," *New York Times*, March 25, <http://www.nytimes.com/2007/03/25/movies/25gold.html> (accessed November 14, 2017).
Goodridge, Mike (2012), *FilmCraft: Directing*, London: Ilex.
Greenberg, Udi E. (2008), "The Holocaust Repressed: Memory and the Subconscious in Lars von Trier's *Europa*," *Film & History: An Interdisciplinary Journal of Film and Television Studies* 38.1: 45–52.
Gritten, David (2009), "Lars Von Trier: Antichrist? Or just anti-women?" *The Telegraph*, July 16, <http://www.telegraph.co.uk/culture/film/starsandstories/5843594/Lars-Von-Trier-Antichrist-Or-just-anti-women.html> (accessed November 14, 2017).
Guardian music (2017), "Björk reveals more details of alleged sexual harassment by director," *Guardian*, October 17, <https://www.theguardian.com/music/2017/oct/17/bjork-reveals-more-details-of-alleged-sexual-harassment-by-director> (accessed November 16, 2017).
Hjort, Mette, and Ib Bondebjerg, eds. (2003), *The Danish Directors: Dialogues on a Contemporary National Cinema*, Bristol and Chicago: Intellect Books.
Hjort, Mette (2005), *Small Nation, Global Cinema: The New Danish Cinema*, Minneapolis: University of Minnesota Press.
Iversen, Ebbe (2003), "Tracing the Inner Idiot," in J. Lumholdt (ed.), *Lars von Trier Interviews*, Jackson: University Press of Mississippi, pp. 125–9.
Johnston, Sheila (2009), "Is Antichrist anti-women?" *The Independent*, July 21, <http://www.independent.co.uk/arts-entertainment/films/features/is-antichrist-anti-women-1755616.html> (accessed November 14, 2017).
"Jewish Population of the World" (2017), *Jewish Virtual Library*, <http://www.jewishvirtuallibrary.org/jewish-population-of-the-world> (accessed November 14, 2017).
Kastrup, Kim (2005), "Von Trier:—Susanne Biers 'Brødre' er lort," *Ekstra Bladet*, May 19, <http://www.ekstrabladet.dk/flash/filmogtv/film/article3042740.ece> (accessed November 14, 2017).
Kastrup, Kim (2011), "Lars von Trier håner igen Susanne Bier," *Ekstra Bladet*, May 18, <http://ekstrabladet.dk/flash/filmogtv/film/article4099517.ece> (accessed November 14, 2017).
Koplev, Kjeld (2003), "9 A.M., Thursday, September 7, 2000: Lars von Trier," in J. Lumholdt (ed.), *Lars von Trier Interviews*, Jackson: University Press of Mississippi, pp. 170–204.
"Lars von Trier—'Deadline' Interview—Dec. 19, 2014," (2014), <https://youtu.be/8PCgMpnQVH4> (accessed November 14, 2017).
"Lars von Trier—'It's good that people boo'," (2009) "Lars von Trier—'It's good that people boo'," *The Independent*. May 28, 2009, <http://www.independent.co.uk/arts-entertainment/films/features/lars-von-trier-its-good-that-people-boo-1692406.html> (accessed November 14, 2017).
"Lars von Trier: Melancholia, Cannes and press conferences," (2001) "Lars von Trier: Melancholia, Cannes and press conferences," *The Culture Show*, BBC Two, September 30, 2011, <http://www.bbc.co.uk/programmes/p00l7wqt> (accessed November 14, 2017).
Macnab, Geoffrey, and Sharon Swart (2003), *FilmCraft: Producing*, New York: Focal Press.

Melancholia, Box Office Mojo, <http://www.boxofficemojo.com/movies/?id=melancholia. htm> (accessed November 14, 2017).

Merin, Jennifer (2007), "Susanne Bier chats with Jennifer Merin re 'After the Wedding,'" *Alliance of Women Film Journalists*, March 30, <http://awfj.org/blog/2007/03/30/jennifer-merin-interviews-susanne-bier-re-after-the-wedding/> (accessed November 14, 2017).

Michelsen, Ole (2003), "Passion Is the Lifeblood of Cinema," in J. Lumholdt (ed.), *Lars von Trier Interviews*, Jackson: University Press of Mississippi, pp. 5–12.

Mumford, Gwilym (2017), "Danish authorities investigating claims of sexual abuse at Lars Von Trier's studio Zentropa," *Guardian*, November 13, <https://www.theguardian.com/film/2017/nov/13/nine-women-allege-sexual-harassment-and-bullying-at-lars-von-triers-production-firm> (accessed November 16, 2017).

Quigly, Paula (2012), "The Spectacle of Suffering: The 'Woman's Film' and Lars von Trier," *Studies in European Cinema* 9: 2+3, pp. 155–68.

Redvall, Eva Novrup (2010), "'For mig har det altid bare handlet om film': Anders Thomas Jensen," *Kosmorama* 246 pp. 77–88, <http://video.dfi.dk/Kosmorama/magasiner/246/kosmorama246_077_artikel7.pdf> (accessed November 14, 2017).

Roman, Shari (2003), "Lars von Trier: The Man Who Would be Dogme," in J. Lumholdt (ed.), *Lars von Trier Interviews*, Jackson: University Press of Mississippi, pp. 133–43.

Schleier, Curt (2013), "A Different Kind of Cancer Story," *The Assimilator: Intermarrying High and Low Culture*, May 14, <http://forward.com/schmooze/176187/a-different-kind-of-cancer-story/> (accessed November 14, 2017).

Sharf, Zack (2017), "Lars von Trier Keeps His Nicolas Winding Refn Feud Alive, Calls Him "An Opportunist In An Unpleasant Way,'" *IndieWire*, 25. April 2017, <http://www.indiewire.com/2017/04/lars-von-trier-nicolas-winding-refn-feud-1201809072> (accessed November 14, 2017).

Shoard, Catherine (2011), "Cannes film festival bans Lars von Trier," *The Guardian*. May 19, <https://www.theguardian.com/film/2011/may/19/cannes-film-festival-2011-lars-von-trier-banned> (accessed November 14, 2017).

Silverman, Kaja (1988), *The Acoustic Mirror: The Female Voice in Psychoanalysis and Cinema*, Bloomington: Indiana University Press.

Skadhauge, Troels, and Lars Tønde, transl. (2016), "An Invitation from Lars von Trier—Transcript of the First TV interview since the Cannes Press Conference, with Martin Krasnik, Danish journalist," in B. Honig and L. J. Marso (eds.), *Politics, Theory, and Film: Critical Encounters with Lars von Trier*, New York: Oxford University Press, pp. 23–41.

Smaill, Belinda (2014), "The Male Sojourner, the Female Director, and Popular European Cinema: The Worlds of Susanne Bier," *Camera Obscura* vol. 29, no. 1, 85: 5–31.

"Susanne Bier, Film Director" (2016), *HARDtalk*, BBC News, March 15, <http://www.bbc.co.uk/programmes/b073q99k> (accessed November 14, 2017).

Thompson, Anne (2011), "Lars von Trier's Last Cannes Q & A: 'Stupid' Statements, Melancholia, 'I Am Not a Nazi,' Dunst, Cruz," *IndieWire*, May 26, <http://www.indiewire.com/2011/05/lars-von-triers-last-cannes-q-a-stupid-statements-melancholia-i-am-not-a-nazi-dunst-cruz-185454/> (accessed November 14, 2017).

Wise, Damon (2003), "No Dane, No Gain," *The Guardian*, October 12, 2003, <https://www.theguardian.com/film/2003/oct/12/features.magazine> (accessed November 14, 2017).

Wood, Jason (2004), "Susanne Bier interview," in I. Weibretcht et al. (eds.), *Projections 13: Women Film-makers on Film-making*, London: Faber and Faber, pp. 96–106.

Wright, Rochelle (1998), *The Visible Wall: Jews and Other Ethnic Outsiders in Swedish Film*, Carbondale: Southern Illinois University Press.
"ZFF Masters 2014: Susanne Bier" (2014), <https://youtu.be/IH8qdq6f7YU> (accessed November 14, 2017).

FILMOGRAPHY

Europa, film, directed by Lars von Trier (Denmark: Nordisk Film, 1991).
The Orchid Gardner (*Orchidégartneren*), film, directed by Lars von Trier (Denmark: Filmgruppe 16, 1977).

CHAPTER 7

Gender Equity in Screen Culture: On Susanne Bier, the Celluloid Ceiling, and the Growing Appeal of TV Production

Mette Hjort

Susanne Bier, undoubtedly, is a major figure in the landscape of contemporary cinema. Global visibility of the kind enjoyed by this director generally invites questions about the reasons for success. But, let us be frank: success is all the more intriguing in this particular instance. After all, Bier is a woman. And she is a citizen of a small nation. In Bier's success, there appears to be tantalizing evidence of a woman's ability to deal effectively with the challenges of both gender and small nationhood, and this in the context of a global film industry that is, to put it bluntly, dominated by men, and, by virtue of the sheer clout of large-scale capital investments, big nations. Bier's is a story that does indeed tell us something about the fissures in the celluloid ceiling. However, it also highlights its continued existence.

When seeking to pinpoint the factors shaping Bier's contributions, their global recognition, and her emergence as a star director, various lines of inquiry are relevant. These include broadly institutional types of analysis, where it is a matter, for example, of grasping the role played by the National Film School of Denmark in developing Danish talent, or the place of art and commerce in the business models and strategic positioning of Zentropa, the production company behind Bier's best-known films. Creative processes, including team-based cinematic authorship, as evidenced in Bier's long-term collaboration with scriptwriter Anders Thomas Jensen, also warrant consideration.[1] Questions of genre, style, and narrative focus are anything but trivial, for Bier's character-based, issues-oriented filmmaking springs from a commitment to ensuring that the moving images on our screens bring something of value to our lives. In her engaging and entertaining stories, there is often an invitation to reflect on the nature of citizenship and a good society, on duties and responsibilities that extend well beyond national borders, and on the connections between apparently personal actions and a larger global order. The underlying "philosophy" of filmmaking, it seems, is one with considerable appeal. Finally, there is the issue of how Bier, as a citizen of Denmark and native speaker of one of the world's minor tongues, has negotiated the challenges of moving beyond national borders and onto the terrain of English-language filmmaking with international stars.

Emphasizing practitioner's agency, in this instance the subjective rationality of Bier, this chapter looks at the director's changing self-understandings in the course of her career. Now in her mid-fifties and with three decades of experience to reflect on following graduation from the National Film School of Denmark in 1987, Bier's narrativization of her career over a longer period of time offers a good deal of insight into the problems facing women filmmakers. Emerging from conversations with critics and journalists, the reflexive story points to a strategic shift from film to TV production as a means of circumventing recurring and ever more frustrating challenges. Bier's status as a winner of an Emmy (for the TV miniseries *The Night Manager*), an Oscar for Best Foreign Language Film and a Golden Globe (both for *In a Better World* [*Hævnen*, 2010]), and an Audience Award at Sundance (for *Brothers* [*Brødre*, 2004]) makes the purported experience of gender-based constraints all the more telling.

In what follows, I begin by sketching a larger context for looking at one woman's experience of how gender limits the opportunities that success typically yields. At no time in the history of film, it seems, have the unfavorable conditions facing women filmmakers been as much of a source of mobilization as in the second decade of the twenty-first century. Reflecting increasingly rigorous, evidence-based analyses of women's ultimately limited participation in the world of film, initiatives all around the globe offer hope for change. Highly public and difficult to ignore or dismiss, these interventions undoubtedly inform Bier's more recent pronouncements and thus require some discussion. Following a brief evocation of especially noteworthy projects initiated outside Denmark, I go on to look at ongoing policy-oriented discussions about women and film in Denmark. Here, as we shall see, Bier's success, somewhat surprisingly at first blush, does not necessarily register as purely positive. In the final parts of the chapter, I trace changes in Bier's self-understandings and make a case for seeing the move from Denmark to the United States as a significant factor. I claim that gender politics has come to assume a more significant place in Bier's thinking, as the constraints of gender, even in the wake of significant success, have become more apparent and more frustrating. Bier's shift from feature film production to the production of a miniseries for TV (*The Night Manager*, based on John le Carré's eponymous novel) should, I contend, be seen as a successful attempt to circumvent limiting yet widespread understandings of what women can and cannot do with film. I conclude by looking at Bier's *The Night Manager*, the aim being to identify concrete examples of the kind of difference that women can be expected to make, if given the opportunity to assume far greater responsibility for the storytelling on our screens. In this case, the differences are apparent on the small screen, through the format of the TV miniseries. Yet there is every reason to assume that the relevant conclusions have a significant degree of generalizability, and thus implications for the screen culture of feature filmmaking as well.

TIME FOR CHANGE—INTERVENTIONS AROUND THE WORLD

That gender equity is lacking in the film industry is by no means a new finding. Indeed, data documenting the unequal participation of women in film has been available for some time. The "Celluloid Ceiling Report" has, for example, "tracked women's employment on the top grossing films for the last 18 years" and is described as the "longest-running and most comprehensive study of women's behind-the-scenes employment in film available" (Lauzen 2016a: 1). An initiative of Martha M. Lauzen, executive director of the Center for the Study of Women in Television and Film at San Diego State University, the analysis of employment data relating to women's involvement in the top 250 films of 2015 identifies a significant degree of inequality: "91% of films had no female directors" (Lauzen 2016a: 1). Lauzen's efforts have also focused on the independent sector, where, intuitively, women's participation rates should be higher. Analysis of women's representation, as independent directors, at twenty-three U.S.-based film festivals does in fact produce a higher figure (28% in 2015–16), but here too it is the significant lack of parity that is ultimately striking (Lauzen 2016b: 2). Lauzen also seeks to pinpoint the consequences of women's inclusion in the film industry, her findings in the context of the analysis of the independent film sector serving to underscore that the gender effects of women assuming a position of executive control are nontrivial:

> Films with at least one woman director also had higher percentages of women writers, editors, and cinematographers. In films with at least one female director, women comprised 74% of writers vs. 6% on films directed exclusively by men. In films with women directors, women accounted for 43% of editors compared with 15% on films directed exclusively by men. In films with women directors, women comprised 20% of cinematographers versus 8% on films directed exclusively by men. (Lauzen 2016b: 2)

Facts, even in an era of "alternative facts," are hard to ignore and certainly a powerful force for change, especially in contexts where the comfort zones, habits, and networks of dominant groups are more likely to explain exclusion than explicitly held commitments to systematic discrimination on the part of companies, funders, and individual decision-makers. Yet isolated reports by academics cannot, it would appear, produce the collective will to effect significant change.

There is cause for hope, however, in the striking proliferation in recent years of much more high-profile interventions on behalf of women more generally, and female film practitioners more specifically. Speaking on behalf of the HeForShe campaign as a United Nations Goodwill Ambassador, celebrated British actress Emma Watson made the case for gender equity as such. At the same time, her statement to the effect that "if we do nothing it will take seventy-five years, or for me to be nearly a hundred before women can expect to be paid the same as men for the same work," also registered as personal, as it is highly relevant to the industry in which she has become a global star—in her speech she referred to herself as "this Harry Potter girl" (Watson 2014). In 2015 the Directors Guild of America (DGA) published its first ever "Feature Film Diversity Report," offering figures on the gender and ethnicity of feature film directors who, in 2013 and 2014, made films for companies that are signatories of the DGA collective bargaining agreement. In addition to highlighting inequity along the lines of the "Celluloid Ceiling Report," the DGA's analysis brought attention to the (unmeasured) cultural costs of inequity: "What this report does not reflect is what people who love film—even our culture as a whole—are missing when such a disproportionate percentage of films are directed by one gender or one ethnicity" (DGA 2015). Using big data, "automated algorithms that measure screen and speaking time of characters by their gender," the Geena Davis Institute on Gender in Media, in partnership with Google and the University of Southern California, analysed the top 100 grossing films of 2014 and 2015. The automated results showed that men enjoyed twice as much screen time as women, and three times as much if the lead was a man. The results for speaking time were almost identical. The researchers also investigated the implications of women's enhanced presence for the bottom line of production companies. Films with women as leads, it turned out, generated 15.8% higher returns at the box office, a result suggesting that there are pragmatic reasons, above and beyond issues of fairness, for supporting an increase in the number of leading roles for women (Geena Davis Institute, nd).

Sweden has assumed an especially prominent role in effecting change, with Anna Serner, CEO of the Swedish Film Institute, having announced in 2011 that, moving forward, gender parity would be a parameter for the allocation of funding for film production. In 2011, women were receiving a mere 26% of the SFI's funding, and three years later Serner was able to report significant progress: in 2014 half of the SFI-funded films were directed by women, the participation rates of women writers and producers being even higher, at 55 percent and 65 percent respectively (Heckel 2016). Critics voiced concerns about diminished quality, but Serner was able to provide counter-arguments, pointing to the films' capacity to meet esteem measures such as festival screenings and the garnering of nominations and awards. Funding parity has worked in synergy with other equity-oriented measures aimed at changing the practices of the film industry. The Swedish rating system is now designed in such a way as to discourage gender bias. Films, more specifically, can only achieve an A rating if they pass the so-called "Bechdel" test. That is, they must feature at least two women, both of them with names, and these characters must talk to each other about something other than men (AP 2013).

Serner's unwavering support for gender equity through quotas has had a clear knock-on effect globally. Discussions regarding the role of Telefilm Canada, a crown corporation that manages co-productions on behalf of the Canadian government, administers funds on behalf of the Canadian Media Fund, and seeks to develop screen talent and the industry in Canada, made reference to the Swedish measures. And on November 11, 2016, Telefilm Canada announced its goal of achieving gender parity—amongst directors, writers, and producers—by 2020. Unlike the SFI, the Canadian institution will not be working with quotas, but with a policy of affirmative action:

> Telefilm will now, for projects of equal quality, favour projects that have a woman as director and/or a woman as writer . . . Based on industry recommendations that these two roles require immediate critical attention, gender parity amongst directors and screenwriters was identified as a priority. In September 2017, once Telefilm reviews its survey data . . . the challenges of women producers will be addressed. (Telefilm Canada 2016)

Ranging from personal testimonies by celebrities in the context of global campaigns, through empirical studies by guilds charged with serving the interests of film professionals, to policy decisions by bodies charged with disbursing government funds to the film sector in state-sponsored jurisdictions, the mobilizations are varied, convincing, and backed by serious-minded strategies oriented toward change. Increasingly, then, the sorts of figures that Lauzen has been providing for some time now have an aura of genuine unacceptability about them.

BIER IN THE CONTEXT OF DANISH INITIATIVES

"Film Is Not for Women" is how journalists Anne Jensen Sand and Johanne Mygind (2016) chose to summarize the results of the Danish Film Institute's report on gender in Danish film, published in June 2016 (DFI 2016). Featuring statistics, gathered for the first time, on gender distribution behind the camera, across decision makers, in the programmes at the National Film School of Denmark, amongst actors in Danish films, and across Danish audiences, the DFI's report made for what many considered shocking reading. Christina Rosendahl—chair of the "interest group" known simply as "Danish Film Directors" and the "anchor person" for one of the three action groups charged with articulating recommendations based on the DFI report—describes a tendency leading in the direction of extinction: "The tendency is truly alarming. Our figures show that if this continues there simply won't be any female film directors at all in 2032" (quoted in Sand and Mygind 2016). Unsurprisingly, given her status as an exceptionally successful female director, discussions of the implications of the report, both in the press and in an open forum organized by the DFI (November 2016), made reference to Bier. Sand and Mygind pointed to the paradoxical absence of a positive trend toward greater equity in the wake of Bier's success:

> The fact that one of Danish film's biggest names, Susanne Bier, is a woman, has, paradoxically enough, not led to better opportunities for women in the Danish film industry. On the contrary. In 2004, 40% of the Danish feature films were directed by women. That was the year when Paprika Steen, Hella Joof, Susanne Bier and Annette K. Olesen all had new releases. Since then things have gone downhill. In 2016 the relevant figure is under 14 percent. (Sand and Mygind 2016)

At the open forum at the Danish Film Institute, Jenny Lund Madsen, anchor person for another action group, suggested that the pursuit of equity could be incentivized, through a bonus system that would offer financial rewards for gender diversity, both in front of and behind the camera. She went on to suggest that the sector has been poorly served by blind faith in the power of role models, recurring "talk about Susanne Bier" and her success having been decidedly unhelpful. The sense, clearly, was that, far from fueling a movement toward greater equity, Bier's success had served to create the impression that policy-style interventions are unnecessary. Moderating the forum's discussions, *Berlingske*'s Anne Sophia Hermansen also referred to Bier and to her provocative statements, to the press, to the effect that the personal costs of being a director are high and that this is a reality that women must learn to accept. In the context of current debates about gender equity in the Danish film industry, Bier's views and success are seen as part of a dynamic that is producing results well below the threshold of public acceptability.

The SFI's quota-based approach to effecting change has provided a reference point for the Danish discussions. Thus, for example, Hermansen repeatedly required the three anchor persons to defend the refusal of quotas that was a constant across the three working groups' recommendations. Ulla Hæstrup, the DFI's commissioning editor for shorts and documentaries (with a focus on children and young people) and a member of the DFI's diversity group, also offered a critical view on quotas. Referring to this instrument of change as ultimately having the effect of "creating fear" and "laziness," Hæstrup identified a greater degree of awareness on the part of the film commissioner, as well as an explicit emphasis on diversity by the DFI, as offering a more constructive, and, indeed, creative way forward. Similarly, as far as the DFI's CEO, Henrik Bo Nielsen, is concerned, quotas cannot be part of the solution:

> I do not see quotas as part of the solution, and I do not think that we, at the Danish Film Institute, should be in the business of creating separate points of entry for men and women. I think we have to find a mode of expression and way of talking that is less masculine, and, as I see it, this is not just a question of counting the number of men in senior management. (Sand and Mygind 2016)

How the DFI, in partnership with the industry and other relevant institutions, will effect change in the landscape of Danish film production remains to be seen. What is clear is that the will to change is strong and that it will *not* find expression in quotas.

CAREER LESSONS: GENDER IS TRULY AN ISSUE

Born in 1960, Bier was twenty-seven when she graduated from the National Film School of Denmark and has been actively involved in her profession for some thirty years. In the course of this timeframe, Bier's position on issues of gender has shifted quite markedly. At the height of her career—at a time when her name is being mentioned, for example, in connection with possible new directions for the James Bond franchise—Bier is decidedly more supportive of feminist perspectives on the film industry than she was around the time of her breakthrough film, *The One and Only* (*Den eneste ene*, 1999). In response to a question about gender in the interview book *The Danish Directors*—"Early on in your career, critics hailed you as the outspoken, forceful, female director who was needed in Danish film . . . Are you particularly interested in dealing with questions of gender in your films?" (Hjort and Bondebjerg 2001:

247)—Bier suggested that the struggles for equity were a thing of the past, at least in Denmark: "I've been fortunate, for a lot of women have paved the way for me. As a result of their efforts I've never had to fight for the right to be a woman *and* a film-maker. So in a certain sense I'm not preoccupied by feminist issues. I don't make films because I want to make some political statement about women" (ibid). Referring to nationalism and the Danish "government's policies on refugees and immigrants," Bier noted that she probably "find[s] those problems more acute and urgent in a Danish context than gender-related issues" (ibid).

By 2016, Bier's earlier lack of interest in gender issues had been replaced by a sense that the film industry presents women with challenges that are structural and systemic and thus require a consolidated response that reaches well beyond what any given individual can effect. The American trade publication *Variety* cites Bier as making the following claims:

> There's no doubt that the entire media industry is suffering from not representing the diversity of society.
> [I]n general, female directors get to do a certain kind of material. But female directors are just as good doing traditional male material as male directors. (Dawn 2016)

The same year, in *Vulture*, Bier is quoted as having taken issue with conventional thinking that limits women's creative possibilities: "women directors are stereotyped as making 'intimate dramas,'" says Bier. Asked by Lisa Liebman, in *Vulture*, whether she would consider talking to the Equal Employment Opportunity Commission of the United States in connection with efforts to determine the extent to which directors experience discrimination in film and television, Bier's response is unequivocally affirmative. Liebman's interest in ascertaining the director's views on the nonprofit We Do It Together, the aim of which is to fund the production of female content that is empowering, also prompts expressions of support. Bier, more specifically, indicates that she is "very impressed and very positive about any effort being made to heighten equality." Given the thrust of Bier's statements almost two decades earlier, the concluding exchange with Liebman is especially noteworthy: "I feel very strongly about gender politics. I feel very strongly about fighting for female equality" (Liebman 2016).

Reasons for Bier's change of position are, by the director's own admission, to be sought in her experience of a wider filmmaking world. That is, the experience of making *Things We Lost in the Fire* (2007, with Halle Berry and Benicio Del Toro) and *Serena* (2014, with Bradley Cooper and Jennifer Lawrence) was decisive. Having indirectly attempted, without success, to get Bier to acknowledge that her interest in gender politics has emerged in the course of her career, Simon Johansen takes a more direct approach: "So your position in the debate on equity hasn't changed?" Referencing her experiences in the United States, Bier admits that it has:

> It may well have. I've worked a lot more outside Denmark, in contexts where it is very clear that things are very difficult for women. So I've changed in the sense that I now think there is a very strong need to articulate a clearer agenda around gender politics. As soon as you leave Denmark, you see that things are very different elsewhere, and a lot harder for women. That doesn't mean that things are impossible. But they're harder than at home. (Johansen 2016)

That Bier's newfound commitment to gender politics has a personal dimension and should not be seen as based uniquely on observations of how others are treated becomes evident when listening to an English-language podcast. Reflecting on male chauvinism and prejudice in Hollywood, Bier notes, in connection with the production of the Hollywood film *Serena*, that she found herself thinking, "They would never have talked [to me] that way, had I been a man" (Casey 2014).

Although the encounter with Hollywood undoubtedly prompted Bier's turn towards gender politics, it would be a mistake to overlook the cumulative effect of certain Danish realities. Bier has, for example, increasingly raised objections to the way in which her entire oeuvre, up until the production of the TV miniseries *The Night Manager*, has been seen through a single lens:

> Each time I've made a film, I'm told by a smart studio exec, as if having stumbled across Pythagoras's theorem, that my audience is women between the ages of 20 and 50. For 20 years this "insight" has never changed. All my films have been different: I've made romcoms; I've been political; I've made films about violence and trauma. But because I am a female director they are all treated the same. Anything made by someone who isn't a white male is labeled arthouse and niche. (Bier 2016)

Given the time frame that Bier evokes here, it is fair to assume that she sees the questionable process of categorization as integral to the Danish film industry. What is challenged by Bier is the way in which observations about the director's gender factor out success and a track record of cinematic exploration across genres, yielding constraining expectations regarding future projects.

Bier, it is clear, has found a new sense of responsibility as a result of having encountered obstacles that, tellingly, have persisted even beyond the attainment of the pinnacle of success that a win at the Oscars or Golden Globes represents: "I feel a sense of responsibility in relation to my younger, female colleagues. I feel that they, to a greater extent than I am, are up against habitual thinking, because they don't have as extensive a back catalogue as I do" (Johansen 2016). Such pronouncements suggest the following line of inquiry: How, in recent times, and drawing on a more acute awareness of the relevance of gender politics, has Bier responded to the persisting challenges? And what is the wider effect of the strategies she has adopted? This, as we shall see, is where *The Night Manager* comes into the picture.

A VIRTUOUS CIRCLE: WHEN TV ACCOMMODATES WOMEN AND WOMEN IMPROVE THE QUALITY OF OUR SCREEN CULTURE

Bier's reflections on directing the AMC/BBC Emmy-winning miniseries *The Night Manager* (Bier 2016), consisting of six episodes, emphasize gender to a significant degree. Three strands of gender-related reasoning are of interest, the first having to do with Bier's decision to shift from the large to the small screen, the second with the opportunities that her success with TV production have yielded, and the third with specific aspects of the storytelling that she sees as related to her own gender. Tellingly, Bier's much-cited publication in *The Guardian* is entitled "TV is opening the door to female directors—film needs to catch up." Evoking Jane Campion's murder mystery *Top of the Lake* (2013), Kimberly Peirce's contribution to the atomic-bomb thriller *Manhattan* (2015), and Anna Boden's directing of two episodes of *The Affair* (2015), Bier notes that female directors "have moved from film to TV." This path from film to TV, she claims, is what has facilitated the directors' engagement with "genres [falling] outside of the studio exec's proposed demographic." The small screen, in short, offers a capacious space of moving image production where female directors are given the opportunity to pursue a much wider range of expression. Of critical importance in this regard are the very genres that convention-based thinking within the world of film typically reserves for men. Bier is quick to point out that the freedoms afforded by TV are anything but a matter of "soppy benevolence," being, rather, "a simple case of economic logic." As Bier sees it, intense competition in the TV market makes producers more willing to take risks. The decision to have a woman direct material traditionally seen as falling within the ambit of male expertise is one of the ways in which a heightened appetite for risk fueled by market forces can find expression. Referring to *The Night Manager*, Bier points to the links between risk and innovation:

> TV producers are compelled to take more risks than their film counterparts ... I was chosen by John le Carré's sons, Stephen and Simon

Cornwell, and producer Stephen Garrett, as well as AMC and the BBC, on a leap of faith that, as a woman taking on le Carré, I could bring a unique and fresh vision to a familiar, very male world. (Bier 2016)

For Bier, the shift from film to TV appears to have been an especially creative and stimulating process, for a variety of reasons. There is the pleasure of working within the context of the spy/thriller genre, but TV as a medium, and TV drama at its current stage of development, are also seen as affording exceptionally stimulating creative opportunities. Bier, for example, describes the long form of narration for TV drama, six hours in the case of *The Night Manager*, as "incredibly satisfying and intriguing and challenging in a very thrilling way." What is more, the quality of TV drama productions in recent years is described as setting a standard that promotes continuity between film and TV, with the latter increasingly requiring the "fulfilling" qualities, in terms of "sound," "music," and "imagery," that have traditionally been at the very heart of the truly cinematic experience. TV today, as Bier puts it, "needs to be a cinematic experience" (Galuppo 2016). In addition to bringing cinematic qualities and, arguably, elements of a distinctive style (Redvall, this volume) to *The Night Manager*, Bier, as we shall see, made use of the extended temporality of the miniseries to deliver a number of gender-based innovations, all of them consistent with the freshness of vision that the producers' risk-taking anticipated in a general way. No stranger to success, Bier clearly suggests that *The Night Manager* may well be the work that makes pigeonholing of both her and her moving images within a category of intimate dramas for women a thing of the past: "Yes, I am getting more interesting offers. And I am getting more offers that are less in the traditional female territory" (Liebman 2016).

A recurring argument offered in favor of enhanced equity in the film industry is that women's exclusion or diminished agency entails a significant cultural loss. This kind of reasoning is evident, for example, when Meta Louise Foldager Sørensen (producer of Nikolaj Arcel's *A Royal Affair* [*En kongelig affære*, 2012] and of von Trier's *Melancholia* [2011] and *Antichrist* [2009], and executive producer and CEO of Meta Film, founded in 2010) makes the following claims: "The stories are always colored by the filmmakers' own experiences. So when there are very few women writing and directing many of the films end up expressing men's views on the world, and on gender" (Sand and Mygind 2016). Bier's approach, when directing *The Night Manager*, was consistent with the idea that she, as a woman, had a different perspective to offer on the story and characters, as originally developed by John le Carré. Indeed, an important part of the creative drive appears to have had to do with determining exactly how a gender-based expansion of the story world's depiction of characters, and of the relations and interactions between men and

GENDER EQUITY IN SCREEN CULTURE   145

women, might best be achieved: "We made a conscious attempt to address the white heterosexual boys' club a little bit . . . It is an obligation, I feel, to have female characters be a lot more than an extension of the male imagination. It's about having an overall view that's less stereotyp[ical]" (Dawn 2016). The long form of the TV miniseries had direct implications for the story's supporting characters. Given that many of these originally somewhat "flat" characters are women, the fleshing in of secondary characters has the effect of expanding the women's presence in the story world: "[P]art of what I did is make the female characters real characters. I was adamant that the girlfriend, Jed [Elizabeth Debicki], not be a cliché, that she be a troubled human being with secrets, which is what everybody in the series is" (Liebman 2016). A crucial scene focusing on Jed at the beginning of the second episode helps to pinpoint the process involved in the transformation of the Jed character from mere appendage, trophy girlfriend, and general object of lust into a fully developed character caught between the mistakes of the past, the lure of the good life, and a dawning awareness of the moral costs of extreme wealth. Alone in her room, Jed is shown choosing outfits and applying make-up, when her routine is disturbed by a distressing phone call from her mother who calls her a whore and takes pleasure in cruelly insisting that Jed's son, Billy, no longer asks about her. Jed's distress, expressed through tears, fearful injunctions to her mother not to call her, and, finally, the consumption of a large number of pills, establishes her complexity and the conditions for the spectator's sympathetic/empathetic involvement with her thoughts and actions (Figure 7.1).

The most significant departure from the original novel concerns the intelligence officer who recruits the night manager Jonathan Pine (Tom Hiddleston) for the purposes of bringing down Richard Onslow Roper (Hugh Laurie), an international arms dealer with the reputation for being "the worst man in the world" (le Carré 2013: 19). In the novel, the intelligence officer is Leonard Burr. In the miniseries this officer becomes Angela Burr. What is more, she

Figure 7.1 Jed (Elizabeth Debicki) receives an abusive phone call from her mother. Frame grab, episode two, *The Night Manager*.

is pregnant. While the gender transformation of the English officer was discussed early on in the planning of the series, her pregnant state in the fiction can be attributed to Bier's strong interest in a particular actress and, as it turns out, the happenstance of her being pregnant. Bier recalls having been on the jury at Sundance when Olivia Colman's achievements in *Tyrannosaur* (2011, dir. Paddy Considine) were honored and says:

> Ever since then, I've felt that she has this amazing combination of being *totally* honest, *totally* vulnerable, and yet tough as nails. I just thought she'd be fantastic for his part. Almost one of the first things I did after becoming attached to the project was to meet with her. And she told me that she was pregnant. And I was like, Wow, that's great for the part. But we will have to deal with insurance! I thought it was a real advantage for the part. (Liebman 2016)

The narrative advantages that Bier had in mind are not difficult to imagine. The combination of bodily vulnerability and moral/intellectual toughness in the Burr character is distinctive, creating the conditions for a nuanced and intense process of audience engagement in which multiple emotions are in play. When Burr, in episode two, meets Pine in the Swiss Alps, the night manager asks the intelligence officer about marriage and children. Having indicated that marriage is not to be confused with "a state of bliss," Burr, responding to the question about children, points at her stomach and says "first and last" (Figure 7.2).

Stated with a no-nonsense matter-of-factness, the utterance has the effect of lending a degree of urgency to Burr's plans, heightening the sense of suspense as the action continues to unfold; it also creates an especially strong basis for caring about the character, for an acute awareness of the extent to which threats and retaliations will affect not just a single agent whose risk-filled

Figure 7.2 Angela Burr (Olivia Colman) talks to Jonathan Pine (Tom Hiddleston) about his past, about her marriage, and, pointing to her stomach, her pregnancy. Frame grab, episode two, *The Night Manager*.

career is a matter of personal choice, but the life she carries within her, indeed, her family.

The Night Manager offers a compelling example of what is to be gained by having women participate more fully in the production of moving images for our screens. Hopefully the gendered effects of the "economic logic" (Bier 2016) that currently makes TV production, as compared with film, *relatively* inclusive, will be enhanced across various moving image sectors in the years ahead, through a multiplicity of mutually reinforcing equity-oriented initiatives on a global basis or in specific sites around the world. In the meantime, perhaps *The Night Manager* can offer food for thought in the milieus where conventional modes of thinking continue to exclude and diminish women. The commitment to effecting change, to be sure, is about women, their rights, and what is fair. Ultimately, however, it is also about the quality of the cultures and societies in which women, as the Chinese put it, "hold up half the sky."

NOTE

1. Starting with *Open Hearts* (*Elsker dig for evigt*, 2002), Bier continued to collaborate with Anders Thomas Jensen on *Brothers* (*Brødre*, 2004), *After the Wedding* (*Efter brylluppet*, 2006), *In a Better World* (*Hævnen*, 2010), *Love Is All You Need* (*Den skaldede frisør*, 2012), and *A Second Chance* (*En chance til*, 2014).

BIBLIOGRAPHY

AP (2013), "Swedish cinemas take aim at gender bias with Bechdel test rating," *The Guardian*, November 6, <https://www.theguardian.com/world/2013/nov/06/swedish-cinemas-bechdel-test-films-gender-bias> (accessed November 14, 2017).

Bier, Susanne (2016), "TV is opening the door to female directors—film needs to catch up," *The Guardian*, March 5, <https://www.theguardian.com/commentisfree/2016/mar/05/tv-film-female-directors-susanne-bier-the-night-manager-le-carre> (accessed November 14, 2017).

Casey, Ruairi (2014), "Director Susanne Bier speaks about 'Serena', working with Jennifer Lawrence, and being a woman in Hollywood," Newstalk.com, October 17, <http://www.newstalk.com/Orla-Barry-speaks-to-director-Susanne-Bier-about-Serenity-working-with-Jennifer-Lawrence-and-being-a-woman-in-Hollywood> (accessed November 14, 2017).

Danish Film Institute (2016), "Ny Undersøgelse af kønsfordeling i dansk film," <http://www.dfi.dk/nyheder/filmupdate/pressemeddelelser/2016/ny-undersoegelse-om-koensfordeling-i-dansk-film.aspx> (accessed November 14, 2017).

Dawn, Randee (2016), "Female directors break new ground in TV series," *Variety*, June 14, <http://variety.com/2016/tv/spotlight/female-directors-break-new-ground-tv-1201794653/> (accessed November 14, 2017).

Directors Guild of America (2015), "Feature film diversity report," <https://www.dga.org/The-Guild/Diversity.aspx> (accessed November 14, 2017).

Galuppo, Mia (2016), "Rapid round: *Night Manager* director Susanne Bier on her love of spies and advice for female filmmakers," *Hollywood Reporter*, July 13, <http://www.hollywoodreporter.com/news/rapid-round-night-manager-director-915448> (accessed November 14, 2017).

Geena Davis Institute on Gender in Media (n.d.), "The reel truth: Women aren't seen or heard: An automated analysis of gender representation in popular films," <https://seejane.org/research-informs-empowers/data/> (accessed November 14, 2017).

Heckel, Jodi (2016), "How Sweden took the lead on gender equity in film," *Illinois News Bureau*, April 14, <https://news.illinois.edu/blog/view/6367/350663> (accessed November 14, 2017).

Hjort, Mette, and Ib Bondebjerg, eds. (2003), *The Danish Directors: Dialogues on a Contemporary National Cinema*, Bristol and Chicago: Intellect Books.

Johansen, Simon (2016), "Kvinder kan også instruere til mænd," *Ekkofilm*, April 15, <http://www.ekkofilm.dk/artikler/kvinder-kan-ogsa-instruere-til-maend/> (accessed November 14, 2017).

Lauzen, Martha M. (2016a), "The celluloid ceiling: Behind-the-scenes employment of women on the top 100, 250, and 500 films of 2015," <http://womenintvfilm.sdsu.edu/files/2015_Celluloid_Ceiling_Report.pdf> (accessed November 14, 2017).

Lauzen, Martha M. (2016b), "Women in independent film 2015–16," <http://womenintvfilm.sdsu.edu/files/2016%20Independent_Women_Report.pdf> (accessed November 14, 2017).

le Carré, John (2013), *The Night Manager*, London: Penguin Books.

Liebman, Lisa (2016), "*The Night Manager*'s Susanne Bier on how she directs and the problem with treating women like minorities," *Vulture*, April 20, <http://www.vulture.com/2016/04/director-susanne-bier-on-women-in-hollywood.html> (accessed November 14, 2017).

Sand, Anne Jensen, and Johanne Mygind (2016), "Film er ikke for kvinder," *Weekendavisen* (kultur, week 43), <http://www.weekendavisen.dk/art/film-er-ikke-kvinder> (accessed November 14, 2017).

Telefilm Canada (2016), "Telefilm Canada announces, in partnership with the industry, gender parity measures for feature film production financing," November 1, <https://telefilm.ca/en/news-releases/telefilm-canada-announces-partnership-industry-gender-parity-measures-feature-film-production-financing> (accessed November 14, 2017).

Watson, Emma (2014), "Gender equality is your issue too," September 20, United Nations Headquarters, <http://www.unwomen.org/en/news/stories/2014/9/emma-watson-gender-equality-is-your-issue-too> (accessed November 14, 2017).

PART 3
Authorship and Aesthetics

Part 3 Introduction

The chapters in this part do not provide a definitive portrait of Bier's style; indeed, the diversity of her work would challenge such an effort. Instead, by focusing closely on very particular aspects of specific works, this part's contributions establish aesthetic overlaps among Bier's works while also stressing that the styles of individual works often relate directly to their particular narrative and representational goals. Therefore, they indicate, collectively, that while distinct aesthetic features—most notably, extreme close-ups of eyes—draw attention to Bier's authorship, her tendency as a director is to adapt visual style to the narrative, generic, and psychological concerns that motivate individual works.

Chapter Eight, Mimi Nielsen's "Tracing Affect in Susanna Bier's Dramas," straddles questions of genre and classification as found in this anthology's first part and those pertaining to aesthetics and authorship, the topic of this third part. Despite its framing as a query of genre classification, its claim of two intertwined, extensive themes apparent across much of Bier's oeuvre stresses particular stylistic and narrative traits that significantly contribute to Bier's work being both unique and recognizable. Nielsen, in support of her dual argument that Bier's films evidence a preoccupation with "intensity-as-affect," as it moves "across and through bodies, especially male bodies," draws from four feature films that span much of Bier's directorial career.

With scene analysis of *Freud's Leaving Home* (Freud flyttar hemifrån ..., 1991), Nielsen addresses tendencies already evident in Bier's early cinematography, which in their application elevate Adrian's significance, a character that might otherwise have remained peripheral in a film noteworthy for its strong female portrayals. Nielsen then considers scenes from *Brothers* (*Brødre*, 2004) to substantiate her claim for affect-over-psychology as a primary focus in

Bier's work, a focus particularly evident in her dramas. The role of aesthetics as key to narrative content is then closely considered in scene analyses of *In a Better World* (*Hævnen*, 2010). Finally, in her consideration of *Open Hearts* (*Elsker dig for evigt*, 2002), Nielsen reflects on the prevalence of attention to affect in Bier's work, in this instance its role in a character's self-coherence. She also addresses Bier's preoccupation with male characters and notes how these two themes coalesce and call into question assumptions of containment and self-sufficiency associated with individualism, especially those allied with concepts of masculinity.

Chapter Nine, Danica van de Velde's "Vision and Ethics in *A Second Chance* (*En chance til*, 2014)," addresses Bier's aesthetics in depth. She points out that, despite Bier's insistence that "aesthetics and flashy camerawork are not her primary concern," in a medium such as film, aesthetics are the inevitable consequence of "the linking of cinematography and emotion." Turning her attention to *A Second Chance* as a particularly poignant example because of how it forefronts the "intertwining of image and psychology" so recognizable in Bier's work, van de Velde argues that Bier's approach functions as "a visual strategy that, among other things, highlights the dynamic between spectatorship and ethics." As an example, she explicates the ways in which Bier's use of frequent close-ups of eyes layers the "visual narrative" in such a way that it provokes in the viewer a critical stance, calling into question the reliability of the image and its representation.

In another example of Bier's layering of the visual narrative, van de Velde applies Mary Anne Doane's concept of "the afterimage as a temporal aberration," in which the past—via the image—intrudes on the present, and suggests that Bier inverts its application to different effects. Van de Velde's analysis also provides thought-provoking insight into Bier's use of shots resembling photographic stills and the function of literal photographs in the film, demonstrating how they problematize perception. A compelling observation that van de Velde makes in her analysis of *A Second Chance* is that Bier, through a variety of these aesthetic decisions, "replicates the police investigation at the heart of the narrative," thereby further inciting viewers' critical position. Van de Velde renders visible Bier's visual strategies, showing that while they compel viewer-attention to the characters' inner states, they also ultimately both "disrupt the moral equilibrium of right and wrong" and call into question "the very ethics of spectatorship."

Chapter Ten, the final chapter in this third part, is Eva Novrup Redvall's "The Truth Is in the Eyes: Susanne Bier's Use of Close-ups in *The Night Manager*," which also focuses on one production title, and in the process sheds light on aesthetic strategies apparent in other Bier works. Similarly to van de Velde's conclusion that Bier's stylistic decisions replicate the perspective of a police interrogation, and as such correlate the aesthetics to the film's genre, Redvall points to Bier's decision to frame and interject eyes as a means of aligning the audience with the visual sensibility of a spy. In her analysis of Bier's recent and extremely successful foray into serial television drama, Redvall takes extensive note of Bier's use of close-ups. Applying theoretical discourses on the close-up and studies of Bier's stylistic traits in her previous work, she reflects on the "remarkable array" of eyes, as well as Bier's use of close-ups of objects. Redvall specifies that facial close-ups in particular carry an even greater significance in "dramatic contexts where characters are trying to hide something," while they simultaneously privilege the viewer. After mentioning Bier's intention to employ close-ups as a means to "explore character depth and the spaces between utterances in this timely adaptation of John le Carré's spy-thriller," Redvall thoughtfully analyzes how Bier has utilized them in both "dramatic and intimate moments." She concludes that Bier achieves a high-end mainstream genre production replete with arthouse aesthetics, which forefronts character interiority while highlighting the "complicated tensions" between characters and their circumstances.

CHAPTER 8

Tracing Affect in Susanne Bier's Dramas

Mimi Nielsen

INTRODUCTION

Susanne Bier has repeatedly disavowed melodrama as the appropriate genre designation for her work. In an interview with Jack Giroux in 2011, she states that the stories contained in her film *In a Better World* (*Hævnen*, 2010), "could be very melodramatic, but they're not." She adds, "I perceive them as very real . . . melodrama for me is very much about forcing emotion . . . about pretending that something is emotional and it isn't really." In this same interview, Bier notes, "I think authenticity is kind of what I'm after, but also authenticity and intensity." In a review of *After the Wedding* (*Efter brylluppet*, 2006), Kenneth Turan writes that Bier "mainlines emotion," then adds that, "like all Bier's work, *After the Wedding* is frankly melodrama . . . melodrama that point-blank refuses to acknowledge its being melodramatic, conveying its scenarios with enough intensity, psychological acuity to ignore labels and flat-out overpower audiences." The determination of melodrama, more often than not, implies emotional excess that portends simplistic character development sufficient to undermine both a sense of authenticity and actual affective force (Williams 1998: 58; Doxtater 2012: 10). Yet Turan's phrasing suggests that Bier's insightful character renderings and her work's affective power combine to provide an intensity-laden, evocative experience for audiences that poses a paradox in terms of classification. As such, Turan's statement reflects the longstanding dilemma that the deprecatingly framed feminization of what is simplistically viewed as emotionality poses for genre classification.

In the interview for this anthology, Bier expresses her belief that the assignation of melodrama has much to do with gender and that the criteria applied to her work can be used to classify, for example, Lars von Trier's work as well, but that this is rarely the case. Belinda Smaill similarly claims that Bier's reception has been colored by the historical relationship between gender and genre assignment. She notes that "the terms on which [Bier's] films are negatively assessed frame the popular dimensions of the work pejoratively as feminine" (Smaill 2014: 15). Smaill's conclusion begs consideration of the challenge inherent in engaging with and applying historically grounded discursive practices, as she states that "historical devaluation of women's production [persists] through a conflation with negatively feminized discourses, including genre and emotion" (Smaill 2014: 15).

My intention with this chapter is not to engage in a historical analysis of the ways that the parameters and application of classification have marginalized women's artistic contributions. Rather, I turn to Bier's statement, that she is "after authenticity and intensity" in her work, as an entry point to push back on the rubric of "emotional excess" as a conclusive lens by which to read her body of work. I suggest instead that in Bier's cinematic investigation of human interiority and relationships, psychology, with its focus on ideation and emotions, while crucial, functions more as a means of perceiving and comprehending affect's movements than as the predominant focus. More specifically, in Bier's work, tracing affect-as-intensity and its implications takes primacy over emotional expression per se. Bier covets intensity. In fact, Bier so meticulously guards against the diffusion of intensity that emotions, as they are expressed, represent only a fraction of the productive tension of any one character.[1] Her films sustain intensity and in so doing reveal affect's movement across and through bodies, especially male bodies.

AFFECTIVE STAKES

The spectrum of how affect is considered and applied is broad. I draw on Brian Massumi's assertion that "emotion and affect—if affect is intensity—follow different logics and pertain to different orders" (Massumi 2002: 27). Massumi distinguishes between emotion as "intensity owned and recognized" and affect as "unqualified intensity" (Massumi 2002: 28). However, I also agree with Sianne Ngai's position that affect is not necessarily inherently void of meaning—of psycho-emotional content or form—but that affect and emotion represent two poles on a continuum (Ngai 2004: 27). I find both of these constructs useful in elucidating affect and its role.

Affect theory posits life as radically open; environments and encounters are verdant with affective transfer or, as Massumi writes, "the body is radically open, absorbing impulses quicker than they can be perceived" (Massumi 2002: 29). Consequently, as Sara Ahmed phrases it, "bodies take the shape of the very contact they have with objects and others" (Ahmed 2004: 2). As such, affect theory challenges Cartesian notions fundamental to individualism, with its "masculinist concept of a self-contained, independent subject who is shored up by dualisms of subject/object and mind/body" (Lundeen 2007: xiii), as does Bier's work.

Important to note is the understanding that affective force remains pregnant with potency until, as Spinoza claims, "we form a clear and distinct idea of it" (Adkins 2009: 7). In other words, if we are to act on rather than simply react to affect, we must first perceive it; as Henri Bergson notes, "into our perception, then, something of our body must enter" (Bergson 1911: 310). Without somatic awareness, we are left to reflexively negotiate the affective forces inherent in living according to circumstance and inclination, or as in the case of post-traumatic stress, be at the mercy of a seemingly irresolvable, looping intensity.[2] Bier's astute attention to the radical openness of her characters, and to their bodies, makes affective transfer and its implications visible and palpable.

BUCKING EXPECTATIONS

As a female director, Bier bucks archaic assumptions that female authors focus on women's lives. Instead, her directorial insignia, with its depictions and explorations of men, mirrors the work of famous male directors whose oeuvres have been profoundly focused on women and femininity, either throughout or during particular periods of their careers, such as Woody Allen, Ingmar Bergman, Jean-Luc Godard, and Pedro Almodóvar. Bier's work, like that of these male directors, reflects a passionate preoccupation with the gendered "other." Bier has placed her male characters either at the center of her films, as in *Like It Never Was Before* (*Pensionat Oskar*, 1995), *Brothers* (*Brødre*, 2004), *After the Wedding* (*Efter brylluppet*, 2006), and *In a Better World* (*Hævnen*, 2010); as part of an ensemble cast, such as in *Open Hearts* (*Elsker dig for evigt*, 2002) and *Things We Lost in the Fire* (2007); or at the periphery, as in *Freud's Leaving Home* (Freud flyttar hemifrån . . ., 1991), in such a way as to leave viewers with a sense of directorial preoccupation with men and masculinity.

In this chapter, I discuss the means by which Bier fleshes out the peripheral male character in *Freud's Leaving Home*, then exemplify her use of the psychological backstory as a clarifying context for affective transfer and influence in *Brothers*. Next, I discuss Bier's depiction of the protagonist's skillful engagement with affect, subsequent to an encounter with another father, in the Oscar-winning film *In a Better World*. I end with a consideration of the relationship between affect, emotion, and cognition as depicted in *Open Hearts*. These passages exemplify two significant thematic threads across Bier's oeuvre, both of which weave through her work, often inseparably: her attention to affective transfer and its implications, and her preoccupation with masculinity.

FLESHING OUT THE PERIPHERAL MALE CHARACTER

Already in Bier's first feature-length film, *Freud's Leaving Home*, a film with a strong focus on its female characters, the mise-en-scène and cinematography suggestively foreshadow the increasingly explicit explorations of male characters in her later work. The film follows Angelique Cohen, aka Freud, a graduate student in psychology and a virgin, as she decides to get laid and leave home so as to endure her mother's impending death from cancer. In three brief scenes Freud's newfound boyfriend, Adrian, a seemingly peripheral character in a primarily female-centered family drama, is elevated to more than an instrumental character through Peter Andersson's assuredly physical performance and Bier's mise-en-scène.

In the first of these scenes, Adrian's physicality provides the sensate and emotionally grounded counterpoint to Freud's high-strung pitch. The camera angle, which is slightly in front of and above the two, mimics Adrian's top-down proximity to Freud, a perspective that foregrounds his much larger body as he is closer to the camera and subsequently to the viewer. The solidity of presence that Adrian conveys is carried over into the morning-after scene, as the two lovers lie in bed. Bier retains the same camera-to-character configuration, with Adrian closer to the camera. His body, now bathed in light, occupies much of the shot. In both scenes, Freud's rather manic dissonance combines with the mise-en-scène—placement, languid shots, and lighting—to align the audience with Adrian's presence. His intimate physical approach to bringing Freud into sensate presence provides Freud with a respite from her turmoil. Adrian also affectively cues the audience into embodied awareness of masculine physicality and sensuality. This cue is underscored by his position as the scene's focal center.

A final scene that conveys Adrian's sensate masculinity is one of the few in the film where intimacy and intensity remain sincere, rather than laced with awkwardness or humor. It also solidifies Adrian's role as more than peripheral. As he visits with Freud's bedridden mother, Roshe, the camera cuts to a close-up of Roshe's girlishly attentive face as he reads to her from Gunnar Ekelöf's poem, "I Believe in the Solitary Person." The camera holds Roshe's face for a longer duration against the soothing cadence of Adrian's voice as he recites Ekelöf's ode to solitude and interiority, then cuts to a close-up of his face before cutting back to Roshe as she carefully sits up in bed. After these closely framed shot-reverse-shots, the camera pans back to show Adrian sitting on the edge of Roshe's bed (Figure 8.1). The two of them closely face one another, both on

Figure 8.1 Adrian, witness and confessor to Roshe's scars.

par in relationship to the camera. Their intimacy is tangible. Their positioning shifts the focus from Adrian as the visiting boyfriend of Roshe's daughter, to that of witness and confessor to her scars as she divulges her secret acceptance of post-Nazi German funds. Adrian's presence, while imbued with sensuality, affords Roshe relief and comfort even as it conveys gravitas.

Through these three scenes, Freud and Roshe experience aspects of self as a result of the literal and figurative holding that Adrian embodies. He is Freud's romantic and sexual partner. He is also Roshe's confidant and, via the reading of Ekelöf's poem, her end-of-life adviser. Adrian, who might otherwise have simply remained a peripheral character, is elevated through Bier's use of the mise-en-scène and cinematography and through Peter Andersson's physical acting. Despite the performances' relative brevity and the Cohen family members' more dramatic roles, the presence of Adrian's character palpably lingers even as the credits fade.

PSYCHOLOGICAL BACKSTORY AS A MEANS OF AFFECTIVE COHERENCE

Nowhere is Bier's interest in men and masculinity more evident than in *After the Wedding*, *Brothers*, and *In a Better World*, all collaborations with screenwriter Anders Thomas Jensen. Smaill, in reference to these particular films, which she refers to as a trilogy, notes that Bier "explore[s] how men grapple with the pressure and desire to maintain their roles within conventional patriarchal domestic structures" (Smaill 2014: 13). As Bier tracks multiple and varied configurations of masculinity in these films, she provokes consideration of the consequences of adherence to archaic male gender roles, not only for familial relationships, but also locally and transnationally. Meryl Shriver-Rice, in a comparative study of Bier's *Brothers* and Jim Sheridan's 2009 remake, notes that, while Nordic cinema is associated with psychological and social realism", "What is 'Nordic' for Bier is instead a form of intimate psychological 'realism' that feels *emotionally authentic*" (Shriver-Rice 2015: 152). Bier's minute causal tracing never loses sight of the fact that gender-normative behaviors are experienced within a context of intimate historical affiliations and that even instrumental identities are subject to propagation individual to individual, body to body.

In *Brothers*, Bier, not content to configure the instigation of spectacular violence upon a racial or national "other," provides an earlier, parallel narrative of male triangulation, allegiances, and survival, albeit on a more mundane plane. Bier's rendering of the protagonist Michael Lundberg's family-of-origin dynamics provides a context, a psychological backstory, localizing themes of origination and consequence associated with hypermasculinity within the domestic, both familially and nationally (Nye 2005; Scheff 2006). This contextualizing backstory undercuts what might otherwise appear as gross generalizations associated with racist conventions of "us" versus "them," as it is replete with affective transfers that are relevant to Michael's later actions. Hypermasculinity, as Bier traces it, is shown as a contagion that occurs body-to-body.

Only minutes into the film, Michael is introduced not only as the older brother but also as the good son. He is shown picking up his younger brother Jannik from prison after Jannik has completed a sentence for bank robbery. That evening, at a "welcome home" dinner, their father, Henning, glorifies hypermasculine traits such as stoicism, force of character, and control (Kreiger et al. 2006; Oliffe et al. 2015). In actuality, Henning is a pathetic and petty bully who handles his sense of inadequacy by displacing it onto his younger son, Jannik, while willfully upholding the illusion that he is like his older son, Michael. Yet where the self-aggrandizing Henning is emotionally eruptive and frequently demeaning, Michael, prior to his wartime trauma, quietly asserts control through establishing order by exerting care. It becomes obvious that the brothers are unwittingly caught up in a well-established family dynamic. Michael maintains his position of being the good son (Figure 8.2). While he looks after his brother, he is never shown standing up to Henning, who relentlessly demeans Jannik. Despite the fact that Henning's abusive behavior towards Jannik persists, Michael's later actions in the Taliban camp suggest that his intervening to protect Jannik from Henning's verbal and emotional

Figure 8.2 Welcome home dinner for Jannik.

abuse has not been an uncommon act. All in all, the Lundberg men adhere to the habits delineated by their respective roles. As such, their relationships map the psycho-affective ground that informs the sons' identities as well as their actions under duress. Equilibrium is not only conceptual; selfhood is also a somatic experience comprised of patterns. Fathers and sons such as Henning, Michael, and Jannik do not intentionally set out to be abusive or self-destructive, but are situationally vulnerable as intensity rises and agitates earlier internalized experiences. Affect, as such, does not determine action but lubricates the wheels of inclination (Gould 2010: 30).

In *Brothers*, hypermasculinity's reliance on asserting control and enacting violence becomes an almost unalterable contagion. As Michael is caught by the Taliban and thrown into a dark room with the much younger and emotionally unraveling Niels Peter, the fraught nature of male vulnerability is apparent. Michael, concerned with Niels Peter's wellbeing, attempts to reassure him that they will be rescued. He even intervenes on Niels Peter's behalf while facing off with the Taliban camp's leader. However, following this intervention Michael ultimately becomes exasperated and snaps at Niels Peter to stop crying. As affect theory posits, bodies are radically open to other bodies,[3] and Niels Peter poses an affective challenge in that he is pathetic. Michael's relationship to Niels Peter's despair is therefore complicated, as is evident by his body language after snapping at him: he sits and looks straight ahead, only occasionally casting a quick and hard glance in Niels Peter's direction (Figure 8.3).

Affect remains in the body as a residual intensity unless sensed and acknowledged at the moment it stimulates an emotional response, and even

Figure 8.3 Michael avoids looking at Niels Peter.

then it can continue to reverberate (Brennan 2004: 113). Michael, despite ultimately turning towards Niels Peter, embracing him, and promising him that they will survive, must consequentially carry not only the burden of his position of responsibility to try to ensure Niels Peter's wellbeing, but also the residual affective intensity of his cellmate's terror and defeated self-pity. Michael's body retains the very imprint of what he denies, while he simultaneously carries within himself patterned responses to such states of collapse and hopelessness. None of these responses include yielding.

By establishing Michael's backstory, Bier has laid a map of inclination. The narrative structure, mise-en-scène, and cinematography convey that it is not psychology per se that determines Michael's actions during his subsequent encounter with the Taliban camp's leader, nor even necessarily instinct. Rather, it is the degree and qualities of intensity, acting—within a situation that is interpersonally dynamic—upon a patterned psychophysiology that combine to all but determine the outcome. As Michael is goaded and taunted by the Taliban camp's leader to kill Niels Peter, the shot-reverse-shots mimic the vocal exchanges between the two men (Figure 8.4). They literally scream into one another's faces in a face-off of affective force. As the overwhelming intensity and high stakes of the situation coalesce, Michael adheres to his family-of-origin's male triangulation and his habit of succumbing to Henning's paternal authority. Michael's actions reveal that his position of being the good brother is not only an expression of an ethical and loving brother, but also an investment in survival forged in an abusive family dynamic. As excessive intensity ripples through Michael's system, it channels through neurological pathways of stoicism and compliance vested in overriding collapse at any cost. Simultaneously, Michael's lengthy and claustrophobic closeness to Niels Peter's collapsed affective field remains a potent affective residual. What ensues is scarcely different from playground dynamics associated with bullying, except in its horrific proportion. The patrilineal legacy of hypermasculinity's relationship

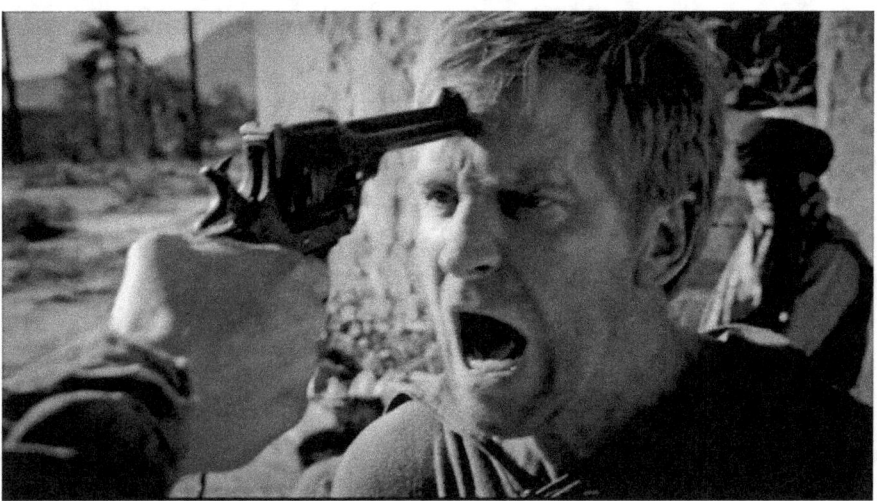

Figure 8.4 Michael screams at the Taliban camp leader.

to violence and survival via compliance at the expense of the weakest remains endemic. It persists even as it varies by degree due to historical, socio-cultural, and economic circumstances. Significant to such scenarios is that "weakness" is not discretely embodied in another. As Michael beats Niels Peter to death in a desperate bargain for survival, he ensures the necessity of confronting his own weakness.

Bier, again and again in her films, traces how intensity travels via our sociality and circumstances, activating and perpetuating cultural-historical and underlying personality patterns. No-one is immune to affective forces or their consequences. Repetition awaits, unless there are means of consciously intervening with affect and its sometimes destructive residual innervation. Shriver-Rice's observation that had Michael acted differently, maybe some alternate possibility would have arisen, is crucial, since without choice, accountability ceases to carry weight (Shriver-Rice 2011: 16). However, as Bier depicts, human vulnerability and our continuously co-constitutive natures are contingent upon the failure to take or to maintain "right action," which is, as Shriver-Rice notes, "a significant catalyst for the person that Michael is to become once back . . . home" (Shriver-Rice 2011: 16).

The affective residual of this traumatic event, coupled with the horror, guilt, and shame of his actions, finds an outlet as Michael re-enacts the intensity of the terrible sequence of events by abusing and threatening to kill his wife, Sarah. However, Michael's behavior is an energetic outlet with no resolution. This conflict-based intensity is in constant need of dispersal (Vanderkolk 1994; Levine 1997), and Michael and his family are caught in a pattern of involuntary repetition. Bier meticulously depicts how the extreme nature of

Michael's experiences at the Taliban camp remains incomprehensible, continuously building, cresting, and overwhelming him.

Bier also touches on the means of skillful intervention in affect's sway over the body and emotions. At the conclusion of *Brothers*, Michael's wife, Sarah, confronts him with an ultimatum: that he needs to begin to talk about what happened in Afghanistan, or he will never see her and the children again. Michael's stoicism yields to his inner turmoil as he begins to talk, providing, if not an assurance of resolution, at least a possibility to intervene in an otherwise always continuously traumatizing past.

AFFECT AND EMOTION AS A CONTINUUM

Bier's close scrutiny of interpersonal and internal processes illuminates the difficulty of differentiating between affect and emotion. Sianne Ngai modifies Massumi's useful but rather binary distinction between affect and emotion, as she formulates their relative indeterminacy:

> My assumption is that affects are *less* formed and structured than emotions, but not lacking form or structure altogether; *less* sociolinguistically fixed, but by no means code-free or meaningless; *less* organized in response to our interpretations of situations, but by no means entirely devoid of organization or diagnostic powers. (Ngai 2004: 27)

What makes Bier's rendering of this more or less fluid affective and emotional dance so discernable is that she turns her gaze so unapologetically to bodies and to the sensory openness of lived materiality. Bier is, as shown, not content with rendering identity as fixed, an already inscribed consequence of inclination and backstory. Rather, she shows the constant interplay and unfolding that occurs through felt experience as it plays out. Agency and indeterminacy, in other words, are inscribed dynamically on bodies. That which unfolds is activating below the surface of emotional specificity, retaining affect's multivalent potential to provoke and evoke, for characters and audiences alike. Bier, in her depictions, establishes affect as primary and inescapable but not irrevocably determinant.

NON-CONFRONTATIONAL MASCULINITY AND THE SKILLFUL MEDITATION OF AFFECT

Bier's 2010 film *In a Better World* provides another means of intervention even as it retains the theme of repetition. *In a Better World* spotlights liberal

Scandinavian ideals of non-confrontational masculinity in the face of nationalistic xenophobia and violence. In a pivotal scene, the protagonist, Anton, a Swedish doctor living in a small seaside town in Denmark when he is not away working for an organization reminiscent of Doctors without Borders, is repeatedly slapped during an encounter with another father, Lars, at a children's playground. His two sons and one of their friends witness the assault. Refusing to respond in kind, Anton leaves, despite the boys egging him on to do *something*. Later, arriving alone at the family summer house on the Kattegat Sea, Anton, noticeably agitated, strides across the yard and out onto the wooden dock, rapidly undressing as he goes. The low evening light reflects on the sea's surface, while Anton becomes merely a dark shape in motion; the briefest of cuts show the contour of his body before he hits and submerges into the placid water, the whiteness of his skin barely visible under the now dark surface.

Anton's purposeful and sure-footed determination conveys masculinity in this scene, but at no time does the cinematography objectify his body in such a way as to overtly sexualize him. His nudity is revealed only from the waist up, and even that only briefly. As Anton surfaces, the camera angle changes, bathing him in ambient light, with the camera moving in for a straight-angle close-up of his face. As he rolls onto his back, floating on the water's viscosity, the camera shifts to a side angle, but again the frame remains focused on Anton's upper body. The camera then languidly moves in for an extended close-up of Anton's face as he lifts his hand to gently caress his slapped cheek (Figure 8.5).

Nudity, while important in this scene as it expresses a stripping of the external with all that it entails, neither de-eroticizes nor overtly eroticizes. Instead, masculinity, eroticism, and emotionality remain indivisible; the embodied and highly charged ground upon which Anton's self-attention meaningfully retains its creative tension. The camera, and therefore the viewer, are brought into

Figre 8.5 Anton floats in the sea, caressing his slapped cheek.

close proximity, compounding the intimacy already inherent in this moment. In this particular scene cinematography and editing mirror the turn of Anton's attention as he seeks out the comfort of the sea to tend his wrought sensations and feelings. Bier's directorial approach is characterized by frequent, purposeful, and often languidly paced alternating medium and close-up shots of bodies and faces—a literal focalizing of attention—to produce intimacy. Yet Bier's languid pacing by no means suggests relaxation; on the contrary, the slowed tempo augments intensity. Sustaining tension is pivotal in Bier's films.

The way in which Anton has been attacked implies de-masculinization: he has been slapped in the face. The purpose of a slap is not only to inflict general physical and emotional injury, but more specifically to demean. Slapping is usually associated with women, punching with men. For a man to slap a man is to render the other's body and person as feminized, signifying their lack. What is commonly expected when a man slaps another man is that the implied denigration of masculinity is reciprocated with a punch. However, as Anton instead walks away, he seeks not merely refuge, but more significantly renewal in the sea—a trope saturated with feminine symbolism—and then tenderly embraces his cheek. Bier confronts crude gender stereotypes by asserting the emotional body as a locus of acts, dependent upon context for destructive or productive assignation.

In this scene, Bier does not simply deconstruct gender, but instead celebrates masculinity as capable of embracing traits commonly considered its antithesis. She employs gender tropes to interrogate, critique, and embrace masculinity. Anton is heralded as a man of humanity, a person capable of great tenderness, which does not entail a capitulation of masculinity. While in Bier's films the male characters are favored, femininity is implied both in the intimate focus and warm quality of her gaze and in the narrative turns. The viewer is shown Anton generating and providing tenderness and love for himself—a role usually assigned a female lover—as his response to being violated. The camera and thus the audience are brought in closely as Anton caresses his cheek. The gaze that the camera conveys suggests a participation in Anton's caress. Intimacy is tangible, both in Anton's relationship with himself and in the audience's proximity to Anton's body, with its sensations and feelings, via the cinematography. As such, this scene exemplifies the indivisibility of style and meaning that inform and distinguish Bier's films.

SENSATE SELF-ATTENTION AS A MORAL PREREQUISITE

Bier's representation of Anton's embodied psycho-emotional and affective process can be understood ideologically. It can be read as a representation of the belief in the capacity to uphold humanistic values; suggesting the indivisibility of sensory, emotional, and mental capacities, in practice if not in actuality. To act ethically is then intrinsically tied to internal access and comprehension. Henri Bergson, in his work on perception and memory, states that "if we take perception as its concrete form, as a synthesis of pure memory and pure perception, that is to say of mind and matter, we compress within its narrowest limits the problem of the union of the soul and body" (Bergson 1911: 325). In this sense, Anton's immersion in the sea and his self-caress as a response to being assaulted signify what Bergson terms "a synthesis of pure memory and pure perception." Anton does not appear to deny the trauma that he has experienced, or its physiological and emotional tracks. Rather than reacting outwardly, he avails himself of an environment that provides pleasurable impressions and supports an inward turning of his attention to sensation and feeling. For Anton's attention to work transformatively, he must by necessity deal with memory, as it is tied to associations and patterned responses. He must do so in a way that allows awareness of all that rises or *is* within him as a consequence of being assaulted, including his reactions, as well as his aim to not necessarily act on them. What Bergson recognizes as mind and body are in a sense unified through embodied internal attention. He notes, "By allowing us to grasp in a single intuition multiple moments of duration, it frees us from the movement of things, that is to say, from the rhythm of necessity" (Bergson 1911: 303).[4] This act of intuition includes awareness of the body-as-thing. In other words, Anton is freed—by consciously directing his attention—from the necessity to otherwise act or react. By attending to what has and is occurring on the level of the psycho-emotional and the body, the *thing*-ness of the body and the *it*-ness of the mind cease to define existence. For those moments that Anton is able to maintain this quality of attention, allowing and attending to "pure perception" and "pure memory," he becomes in a sense indivisible as he transforms the necessity to otherwise act.

AFFECTIVELY CONSTITUTING A SENSE OF SELF

In *Open Hearts*, Bier portrays physical closeness and contact as a necessity for sustaining a sense of self. As such, she elucidates the interplay of affect, cognition, and emotion: how affect, as Nagi suggests, carries meaning. In this context, affect is not necessarily undifferentiated intensity, but, rather, already laden with significance; it exists in the confluence of intensity and emotion. In *Open Hearts*, the female protagonist, Cæcilie, loses her footing following a horrendous accident that renders her fiancé, Joachim, a quadriplegic. When faced with the extent of his injuries, Joachim lashes out and rejects Cæcilie. Increasingly thrown off by Joachim's rejection, Cæcilie, desperate to reach him, shows up in his hospital room. Determined to gain his attention, she

Figure 8.6 Cæcilie desperate for contact with Joachim.

begins to strip. However, he only casts furtive glances her way, assiduously avoiding eye contact. Cæcilie gives voice to her desperation: "You are not going to crush me this way!" Her movements and her words intensify as the camera moves between medium and close-up shots in a shot-reverse-shot pattern. Increasingly distraught, Cæcilie climbs up on Joachim's bed, entreating him to look at her, which he refuses to do. Finally, she lays down on him, with only a momentary sigh of relief, before her panic ensues as neither he nor his body responds (Figure 8.6). With increasing desperation, she realizes that nothing she does will allow her to break through to him. Despite the futility of her situation, she increases her efforts until the nurse and doctor finally pull her off Joachim. The need that motivates Cæcilie's actions is echoed in a subsequent scene. My corresponding analysis will shed light on the layers of meaning this first scene contributes to *Open Hearts*' hypotheses regarding affect and constructs of self.

In this pivotal scene, Cæcilie phones Niels, a doctor at the hospital where Joachim is a patient. It was Niels' wife, Marie, who caused Joachim's injuries. Cæcilie pleads with Niels to come to her apartment, and out of a mixture of guilt, responsibility, and desire, he agrees. Upon his arrival, as Cæcilie hears his knock on her door, she rushes from the sofa bent forward, placing her weight only on the front of her feet—moving more off the floor than on it.

Cæcilie's behavior suggests that she has regressed to a childlike state. As Niels comes into her apartment, Cæcilie, with her head bent down, quickly closes the door and then appears to dive upward into his hesitant embrace—her head still tucked into her chest. Her silence is that of one whose breath is being held to the point of passing out. Seemingly desperate, she begins to wrap her arms around Niels. The sense of desperation is reinforced by Niels' response to her; he appears alarmed. He asks her, "What is going on?" She responds, "Nothing." However, she immediately presses her body into his. As she catches her breath with a sniffle, she says, "Let's just stand here for awhile." With her weight heavily leaning into Niels, she begins to breathe more deeply. Cæcilie's equilibrium slowly reconstitutes through the direct and physical contact with his body. Only then does she become sexual.

In this scene, Cæcilie establishes herself as someone who significantly constitutes a sense of self through intimate, sensate contact with another. Her desperation suggests that it is the intimacy with Joachim that has allowed her to experience herself in an embodied way, although one might also argue that it is the sudden and overwhelming loss, in and of itself, that causes her disassembled state. Either way, Cæcilie is faced with a double loss, of Joachim as she knew him and, through his subsequent rejection, her means of maintaining a sense of self. Out of desperation, she seeks a surrogate to Joachim, another male body through whom she can feel and know herself to exist. Although the scene lends itself to an object relational reading (Ainsworth 1969), my focus is on the relationship between affect and meaning. Cæcilie, unlike Anton, does not have the maturity and skill to directly address her psycho-emotional and sensory experience. But, even so, she knows how to alleviate it. Cæcilie's solution to her profound sense of loss and its subsequent chaos is through the affective transfer that close proximity to another male body makes possible. Cæcilie's dilemma is not purely emotional; it is more primary. She is autonomically struggling to regulate her body without the contact she shared with Joachim prior to his fateful accident. Body, emotion, and cognition are part and parcel of a whole; affect partakes in all its aspects. Bier eloquently depicts affect's potency and variable indeterminacy: how it can act below consciousness and be laden with meaning. If affect in Cæcilie's case did not hold meaning, she would not know how to alleviate her panic. However, she does know that physical proximity—with its affective transfer—allows her to self-regulate in a way that she is not, at this juncture, able to provide herself. Cæcilie's actions do not imply that she necessarily understands the meaning that affect carries in her intimate encounters with men; only that the unbearable intensity she experiences in the wake of Joachim's accident and his refusal to be intimate compels her to act.

Bier's ability to convey what is happening to Cæcilie, even as she does not appear to have language to express her experience, is paramount to *Open*

Hearts' success. Her aesthetic choices place viewers in close proximity to both the minutiae and scope of Cæcilie's despair, as her absolute need for contact is conveyed through attending to its physicality. While Cæcilie is profoundly emotional, affect, not emotion, is the centerpiece of Bier's depiction. Bier's close scrutiny of bodies and their interpersonal contact zones traces affective exchanges and their meanings, portraying the need for intimacy and the productive potential of reflective interiority.

Bier, in *Open Hearts*, also retains the sense of the male body's significance that characterizes so much of her oeuvre. While she trains the camera on Cæcilie in these scenes, her focus is on Cæcilie's preoccupation with two men. Even as Cæcilie ultimately walks away from both men, because her gaze and need at any given time are so intently directed at Joachim or Niels, the impression of directorial preoccupation with male characters remains.

CONCLUSION

In this chapter, I have argued that in Bier's dramas, affect-as-intensity and its implications take primacy over emotion. I have also shown that her preoccupation with intimate representations of embodied psycho-emotional processes should not be reduced to melodrama. I have narrated Bier's passionate and skillful pursuit of moments of intensification and intimacy, made palpable through her use of pace, tone, and proximity, and in relaying their internal content. The scenes I highlight are replete with moments where the camera is allowed to linger, closely trained on a character's state, scenes that successfully reveal internal and interpersonal connection and disconnection as they occur and evolve. It is specifically the richness of frequency and variance in which Bier renders moments of intimacy, alienation, and embodiment palpably evocative and meaningful that distinguishes her dramas. She restricts emotional discharge, thereby retaining intensity's visibility and affective potential. Thus, affect in Bier's dramas becomes not only observable but also experiential for the viewer.

I have also grappled with Bier's preoccupation with male characters by analyzing her depictions of men as she insinuates and celebrates a sort of irreducible masculinity, a kind of physically gendered presence. Considered semantically, Bier pushes on the rubric "masculinity," probing its diverse meanings and implications. By tracing the nebulous lines of affective transfer, Bier continuously whittles away presumptions of self-containment associated with individualism, the bulwark of normative masculinity. Her films delve into the intersection of the body's radical openness and male gender-role expectations, suggestively inferring the need and potential for more relational possibilities.

NOTES

1. I view Halle Berry's performance in *Things We Lost in the Fire* (2007) as an exception to the tendency of retention of intensity otherwise evident in Bier's films. Berry's emotional expression is exhaustive, conveying a sense of complete emptying of tension that is rare in Bier's films.
2. I will use the terms affect and intensity interchangeably.
3. Massumi, for example, writes that "stimulation turns inward, is folded into the body, except there is no inside for it to be in, because the body is radically open" (Massumi 2002: 29).
4. "Pure perception," as I understand Bergson's use of the term, applies to all experiential levels, autonomic, sympathetic, emotional, and cognitive. "Pure memory" encompasses this totality also, although it refracts from a different vantage point, which is variable according to an individual's given history.

BIBLIOGRAPHY

Adkins, Brent (2009), *True Freedom: Spinoza's Practical Philosophy*, Lanham, MD: Lexington.
Ahmed, Sara (2004), *The Cultural Politics of Emotion*, New York: Routledge.
Ainsworth, Mary D. Salter (1969), "Object relations, dependency, and attachment: A theoretical review of the infant–mother relationship," *Child Development* 40, no. 4: 969–1025.
Bergson, Henri (1911), "Summary and conclusion," in *Matter and Memory*, trans. Nancy M. Paul and W. Scott Palmer, London: George Allen and Unwin, pp. 299–332.
Brennan, Teresa (2004), *The Transmission of Affect*, Ithaca, NY: Cornell University Press.
Ekelöf, Gunnar ([1976] 1983), "I Believe in the Solitary Person" ("Jag tror på den ensamma människan"), *Färjesång, Dikter*, Stockholm: Bonniers.
Doxtater, Amanda Elaine (2012), *Pathos, Performance, Volition: Melodrama's Legacy in the work of Carl Th. Dreyer*, Ph.D. dissertation, University of California, Berkeley, <https://escholarship.org/uc/item/97m380jb> (accessed November 14, 2017).
Giroux, Jack (2011), "Interview: Susanne Bier talks bullies and 'In a Better World'," *Film School Rejects Blog*, April 14, <https://filmschoolrejects.com/interview-susanne-bier-talks-bullies-and-in-a-better-world-cf92e5fd294a/> (accessed November 14, 2017).
Gould, Deborah (2010), "On affect and emotion," in J. Staiger, A. Cvetkovitch, and A. M. Reynolds (eds.), *Political Emotions*, New York: Routledge.
Kreiger, Tyson, and C. Dumka (2006), "The Relationships Between Hypergender, Gender, and Psychological Adjustment," *Sex Roles* 54, no. 11, pp. 777–85.
Lane, Anthony (2011), "Time bomb," *The New Yorker* 87.7: 82, <http://www.newyorker.com/magazine/2011/04/04/time-bomb-anthony-lane> (accessed November 14, 2017).
Levine, Peter A. (1997), *Waking the Tiger: Healing Trauma: The Innate Capacity to Transform Overwhelming Experiences*, Berkeley, CA: North Atlantic Books.
Lundeen, Shannon (2007), "Introduction," in A. Jardine, S. Lundeen, and K. Oliver (eds.), *Living Attention: On Teresa Brennan*, New York: State University of New York Press.
Massumi, Brian (2002), *Parables for the Virtual: Movement, Affect, and Sensation*, Durham, NC: Duke University Press.
Ngai, Sianne (2004), *Ugly Feelings*, Cambridge, MA: Harvard University Press.

Nye, Robert A. (2005), "Locating masculinity: Some recent work on men," *Signs* 30, no. 3: 1937–62.

Oliffe, John L., Christina S. E. Han, Murray Drummond, Estephanie Sta. Maria, Joan L. Bottorff, and Genevieve Creighton (2015), "Men, masculinities, and murder-suicide," *American Journal of Men's Health* 9, no. 6: 473–85.

Scheff, Thomas J. (2006), "Hypermasculinity and Violence as a Social System," *Universitas* vol. 2, <http://uwf.edu/dearle/cold%20war/hypermasculine.pdf> (accessed November 14, 2017).

Shriver-Rice, Meryl (2011), "Adapting National Identity: Ethical Borders Made Suspect in the Hollywood Version of Susanne Bier's *Brothers*," *Film International* vol. 9, issue 2: 8–19.

Shriver-Rice, Meryl (2015), *Inclusion in New Danish Cinema: Sexuality and Transnational Belonging*, Bristol and Chicago: Intellect Books.

Smaill, Belinda (2014), "The Male Sojourner, the Female Director, and Popular European Cinema: The Worlds of Susanne Bier," *Camera Obscura* vol. 29, no. 1, 85: 5–31.

Turan, Kenneth (2007), "Insight pierces Danish melodrama," *Los Angeles Times*, March 30, <http://articles.latimes.com/2007/mar/30/entertainment/et-after30> (accessed November 14, 2017).

Vanderkolk, B. A. (1994), "The Body Keeps the Score: Memory and the Evolving Psychobiology of Posttraumatic Stress," *Harvard Review of Psychiatry* 1, no. 5: 253–65.

Williams, Linda (1998), "Melodrama Revised," in Nick Browne (ed.), *Refiguring American Film Genres: History and Theory*, Berkeley: University of California Press, pp. 42–88.

CHAPTER 9

Vision and Ethics in *A Second Chance* (*En chance til*)

Danica van de Velde

The majority of Susanne Bier's films pivot on a symbolic or literal collision, a confrontation that unsettles the emotional trajectory of the film narrative. The collision is metaphorically imagined in *Family Matters* (*Det bli'r i familien*, 1993) through the death of a mother and in *Love Is All You Need* (*Den skaldede frisør*, 2012) through the discovery of adultery, with both events bringing forth larger questions of identity and belonging. However, a car crash in *Open Hearts* (*Elsker dig for evigt*, 2002) and a murder committed under duress in *Brothers* (*Brødre*, 2004) pose violent confrontations that result in psychological crises. In her 2014 Danish-language film *A Second Chance* (*En chance til*), the site of conflict is the encounter between Andreas, a policeman, and Tristan, a heroin trafficker and addict whom Andreas had previously arrested in Copenhagen. When Andreas is called out with his partner, Simon, to intervene in a reported domestic dispute, he is surprised to discover not only that Tristan is living in Funen, but also that Tristan has a baby with his girlfriend, Sanne. After Andreas orders Sanne to move away from a door where she appears to be concealing something, Andreas is confronted by the sight of Tristan and Sanne's son, Sofus. The baby, relegated to a cardboard box on the bathroom floor, is freezing cold as he lies in his urine and feces. Even when juxtaposed with the turbulent interactions between Tristan and Sanne, this image of Sofus carries a resonance that unsettles not only the narrative, but also the sequencing of the film imagery itself. The framing of the shocking sight of the baby through a jarring sequence of jump cuts emphasizes the emotional impact on Andreas. By breaking the cinematographic syntax of the film sequence, this collision in Bier's oeuvre appears as a visual trauma, with the sight of Sofus manifesting as a wound that cannot be sutured.

Played out primarily through familial dynamics, *A Second Chance* contrasts two disparate family atmospheres: the seemingly perfect seaside domesticity of Andreas's life with his wife and son, Anna and Alexander, and the heart-wrenching squalor and abuse that persists in the apartment shared by Tristan, Sanne, and Sofus. The moral dilemma which appears in many of Bier's films occurs, in this case, after the sudden death of Alexander, and Andreas's subsequent decision to break into Tristan and Sanne's apartment and exchange Alexander's lifeless body for Sofus. While maintaining the ardent belief that "It was the right thing to do," the aftershocks of Andreas's decision profoundly affect his family life and the lives of Tristan and Sanne, as they wake from their heroin-induced sleep to discover the body of a deceased baby. Despite Sanne's refusal to believe that the dead baby is Sofus, Tristan stages a fake kidnapping to cover up the death, thereby involving Andreas in a fraudulent missing-person case. Meanwhile, Anna's inability to confront the harsh truth of her role in the head trauma that caused Alexander's death, and the addition of Sofus into their family, results in her suicide. In a similar fashion to Bier's other works, *A Second Chance* focuses on questions of moral judgment within the context of the family unit. However, in this film the exploration of ethics is not rooted in the everyday minutiae of family life, but rather in the details of the police investigation. While domestic scenes remain, they are inflected with overtones of a criminal investigation that reference the police procedural.

Despite the slight shift in genre, *A Second Chance* fits into Bier's auteuristic universe. Specifically, the film's narrative and thematic structuring is in line with Louise Kidde Sauntved's description of Bier's films as "melodramas" in which she "establishes an idyllic world full of love and security and then, seemingly out of nowhere, disaster strikes, shattering the worlds of all involved" (Sauntved 2011: 26). Moreover, the use of the cinema vérité style associated with the everyday realism of the Dogme 95 movement employed in many of Bier's films informs the visual look. Although Bier's use of close-ups, hand-held camerawork, and location shooting does not specifically adhere to the rules outlined in Dogme 95's "Vow of Chastity," *A Second Chance* nonetheless adheres to the rejection of unnecessary cinematic techniques that is enshrined in the Dogme Manifesto and that has carried over into broader Danish cinema (Hjort 2005). As Meryl Shriver-Rice argues:

> The prevalent stylistic conventions of New Danish Cinema complement a focus on intense interpersonal relations. Individuals are investigated by the camera through frequent extreme close-ups that attend to the most minor psychological reactions in facial expression and body language . . . Emotional landscapes are illustrated through intimate camera work at medium to close focus that often takes place in private domestic spaces. (Shriver-Rice 2015: 30)

The close proximity of the camerawork in *A Second Chance* creates an intimacy that lends itself to emotional truth, working to align the image with the psychology of the characters. Moreover, Bier's tight framing of the action cleverly replicates the visual mode of a police interrogation, as the camera's eye gathers evidence to disentangle the multitude of deceptions that exist beneath the surface of the "fake" investigation into the disappearance of Sofus.

Referencing her contribution to the Dogme 95 movement through her film *Open Hearts*, Bier commented in an interview, "I think that the most important role . . . is that of the director not assuming any sort of aesthetics, of not loading the movie with an aesthetic . . . You can't put an aesthetic above psychology" (Wood 2006: 8–9). While Bier has consistently stated that aesthetics and "flashy camerawork" are not her primary concern (Goodridge 2012: 78), her privileging of psychology in a visual medium such as film nonetheless exhibits a form of aesthetics created by the linking of cinematography and emotion. This relationship is particularly evidenced in the intertwining of image and psychology in *A Second Chance*, whereby the sequencing and framing of the film's visuals cut through the narrative to reveal the characters' inner states.

By placing the relationship between cinematography and psychology at the forefront of her film, Bier establishes a visual strategy that highlights the dynamic between spectatorship and ethics. Specifically, this relationship foregrounds the manner in which the structuring and editing of the film's imagery can undermine the interpretation of moral codes by constructing an emotive response from the viewer. The frequent close-ups of the characters' eyes create a secondary visual narrative that underlines the importance of vision and perception, ultimately asking the viewer to question what they are looking at and how they are receiving the image. Indeed, Jane Stadler, in emphasizing that the emotional reception of a film is never a neutral process, posits that "film spectatorship involves the audience in . . . technologically mediated acts of perception and expression, establishing an intersubjective relationship between the audience, the screen characters and the film" (Stadler 2008: 2). In considering the interconnection between aesthetics and emotional truth in *A Second Chance*, this chapter examines how Bier embeds emotion and an ambiguous morality into the very textures of the film image via the cinematography and editing. I argue that the film adopts an investigatory mode of vision that ties in with the genre preoccupations of the police procedural and casts the viewer in the role of a witness who must read the film's imagery to untangle the ethical questions raised by the characters' traumas.

The locus of the trauma in *A Second Chance* is Andreas's first glimpse of Sofus. This moment is replayed twice in quick succession through the insertion of a jarring jump cut that frames Andreas's shocked reaction to the neglected baby (Figure 9.1). The repetition of the extreme close-up of

Figure 9.1 Encounter and afterimage: Andreas finds Sofus.

Andreas's face disrupts the continuity of the film sequence, with the jump cut appearing as a haunting afterimage. The presence of an afterimage, which functions as the residue of a sight that uncannily remains in the mind's eye after it leaves the field of vision, not only emphasizes what is being looked at, but also its emotional impact. Mary Ann Doane refers to the afterimage as a "temporal aberration" whereby the past intrudes into the present through the eye's failure to release a previous sight (Doane 2002: 76). In *A Second Chance* the traumatic sight that impinges on the present is not a repetition of the image of Sofus on the bathroom floor. Instead, the sightlines are inverted, concentrating on Andreas, the traumatized subject, rather than on the object causing the trauma. The significance of Andreas's inner state is thereby prioritized through the framing and camera perspective.

Another afterimage appears when Andreas swaps Alexander and Sofus while Tristan and Sanne lie sleeping in the adjacent room. The doubling of the image takes place after Andreas has undressed both babies and, having put Alexander into Sofus's soiled yellow singlet, begins to wipe the feces collected in Sofus's diaper onto Alexander's face. The jump cut sequence of Andreas with his head in his hands above the babies' bodies re-enacts the framing of his first encounter with Sofus. While Doane provides a provocative reading of the afterimage, claiming that "the eroticism of vision here underlines the fact that the afterimage is accessible only through an experience of intensity, of dazzlement" (Doane 2002: 73), Bier uses it to a different effect in *A Second Chance*, whereby the intensity of the experience does not produce a moment of eroticism, but of trauma. The jump cut signifies Andreas's mental disturbance, thereby dislocating the continuity of the editing and displacing the viewer's attention from the action to focus on the unraveling of his mental stability.

In each of these scenes, Andreas's face is the focus of the jump cut, the camera invasively close. Reflecting on facial close-ups in *A Second Chance*,

Bier commented, "at some point [the] face becomes almost like a landscape. There's also something slightly alienating about the effect and it does something to the moment where you are then within the person's mind and not so much within the person's physique" (We Got This Covered 2014). Bier's allusion to diverting attention away from the physique to the mind suggests that the close-up has the capacity to capture not only the surface expressivity of the face, but also the emotion behind it. In Gilles Deleuze's *Cinema 1: The Movement Image*, he terms the close-up the "affection image," defining it as an image that is capable of "giving an affective reading of the whole film" (Deleuze 2005: 89). According to Deleuze, this process grants the facial close-up "a very special deterritorialisation" (Deleuze 2005: 98), which displaces the viewer's attention away from the central narrative to a secondary space that is associated with the intensity of affect:

> The close-up retains the ... power to tear the image away from spatio-temporal co-ordinates in order to call forth the pure affect as the expressed. Even the place, which is still present in the background, loses its co-ordinates and becomes "any space whatever." (Deleuze 2005: 99)

Deleuze's interpretation of the close-up as exhibiting a loss of spatio-temporal specificity that enables emotional resonance complements Bier's comment on the close-up as a visual form of alienation that centers on the characters' psychological states. Bier additionally employs the close-up to replicate the police investigation at the heart of the narrative, so that the close framing becomes a form of interrogation of the characters' interior lives.

On another level, the intense study of the characters' faces via close-ups isolates parts of their bodies to the point where they resemble photographic stills. These visual pauses, which frequently focus on the characters' eyes, run parallel to the focus on photographs in the diegesis of the film (Figure 9.2). However, while the film imagery that composes *A Second Chance* has a distinctly emotional significance, the photographic objects, which range from family snapshots to police documentation, function as empirical evidence. For example, various scenes stress the authenticity of the image, such as when Tristan films Andreas and Simon on his phone after they forcibly enter his apartment: "You're in my home ... Show me your search warrant ... The police broke into our home." Moreover, when Andreas and Simon's call to social welfare fails to remove Sofus from Tristan and Sanne's custody, Andreas produces a selection of horrific images stating, "This is how he [Tristan] treats his girls ... Book him, or he'll kill them both." As the camera's eye moves across the images placed on the desk, the first photograph captures a blond woman whose face has been severely beaten, followed by close-up images of bruising, battered knees and what appears to be a bite wound. However,

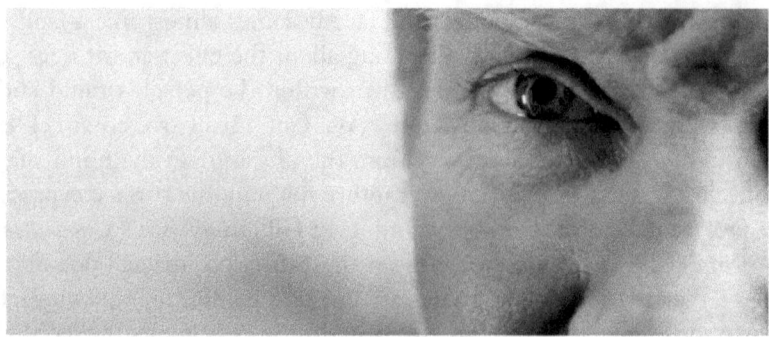

Figure 9.2 Simon sees the truth.

the power of the photographic image as evidence is best encapsulated in the sequence in which Simon begins to question the identity of Andreas's son following an interrogation scene where Andreas mistakenly asks Tristan, "What did you do with Alexander's body?" As Simon looks through the images he had taken of Alexander on his phone, zooming in on details of the baby's face, the comment he made gazing upon Sofus's face (while thinking it was Alexander's) following Anna's death holds the key: "It's almost as if he knows. The look in his eyes has changed." Despite the fact that photographs can be highly constructed, the truth beneath Andreas's deception paradoxically resides within the photographic still.

The connotations of still images in *A Second Chance* relate to Bier's comment in her 2016 Master Class at the Göteborg Film Festival: "In the scheme of big things we tend to be stuck in moments of detail, which is what movie making really is about" (Göteborg Film Festival 2016). The tendency to fixate on details when in the midst of an overwhelming situation echoes the device of the afterimage in *A Second Chance*, which cinematically highlights the visions and moments that haunt Andreas's psyche. Significantly, the use of the afterimage uncannily intersects with the photograph motif during the scene in which Andreas leaves his home with Sofus before retreating to his mother's cottage. As he walks out the door, a framed photograph that features him with Anna and Alexander catches his eye. As in previous traumatic moments, the act of noticing the photograph is played twice, as the camera jump cuts from a medium shot to a close-up of Andreas's face. The photograph that stops Andreas in his tracks is an artifact of loss that underscores the breakdown of the family unit (Figure 9.3). His response to the photograph replicates his earlier reactions to the neglected Sofus and to his act of abduction. Andreas's stark response to the photo also highlights the tenuous construction of the family ideal, as this scene takes place after Andreas discovers that Anna caused their baby's death. The family snapshot is all the more haunting because Alexander's face is not visible in the photograph, which foreshadows his impending absence.

Figure 9.3 The fracture of the ideal family.

The significance of this moment, in which Andreas confronts the ghostly figures of his lost family, cannot be overemphasized. Specifically, the photograph highlights the underlying conceit of the film relating to the interpretation and reception of visual narratives and connects this concern to the crumbling façade of family identity. Susan Sontag writes that:

> Through photographs, each family constructs a portrait-chronicle of itself—a portable kit of images that bears witness to its connectedness. It hardly matters what activities are photographed so long as photographs get taken and are cherished. Photography becomes a rite of family life just when, in the industrializing countries of Europe and America, the very institution of the family starts undergoing radical surgery. As that claustrophobic unit, the nuclear family, was being carved out of a much larger family aggregate, photography came along to memorialize, to reinstate symbolically, the imperiled continuity and vanishing extendedness of family life. Those ghostly traces, photographs, supply the token presence of the dispersed relatives. (Sontag 2008: 8–9)

The photograph of Andreas with Anna and Alexander does not merely hold the spectral traces of his fractured family unit—the essence of *memento mori* that Sontag argues all photographs possess (Sontag 2008: 15)—it presents a moment in the film where vision, perception, and perspective are questioned. Sontag contends that family photographs are taken for their mnemonic and archival capacities; however, this does not necessarily mean that they exist as authentic records of the family. Familial connectedness and contentment, as it appears in the family photograph in *A Second Chance*, is revealed to be merely a construct, a realization that is compounded in Andreas's confession to Simon, "When I'd wake up to his screams at night, he was screaming for help." The breakdown of Andreas's deluded perception of familial bliss through an imagined flashback of Anna violently shaking Alexander undermines everything that the viewer has previously seen and fractures the sharp dichotomy between Andreas and Tristan's respective families. The revelation of Anna's role in Alexander's death set against Andreas's justification for taking Sofus shatters the presumption that they are more suitable caregivers, which instantly draws the viewer into questions of moral reasoning and undermines the implied view that Andreas has saved Sofus from a worse familial situation.

An interest in moral dilemmas and the posing of ethical questions is not limited to Bier's body of work, but is also characteristic of Dogme 95 films, which often question the principles of right and wrong in quotidian environments. Shriver-Rice writes that, "For the Dogme movement, it appears that more 'truthful' film art emerged with the challenge of posing ethical questions within settings of assured verisimilitude" (Shriver-Rice 2011: 11). Although Bier locates parts of *A Second Chance* within everyday settings of domesticity, the engagement with ethics more purposefully questions the very ethics of spectatorship through its editing and cinematography. Specifically, the employment of cinematic imagery to communicate trauma marks the film as a point of departure from Dogme 95 films where aesthetics and visual manipulation are eschewed in the "Vow of Chastity."

The construction of ethical ambiguity via the visual form of film itself also distinguishes *A Second Chance* from Bier's other films. While it is certainly arguable that Bier's films all present moral dilemmas that challenge her characters' values, the interpellation of the viewer into Andreas's point of view in *A Second Chance*, through the use of cinematography rather than plot and dialogue to express emotion, designates the viewer as a witness in a far more direct manner than her previous films. Indeed, the film's English-language promotional poster, which features the tagline "How far would you go?" and captures Andreas at his most emotionally distraught (upon discovering Anna's maternal transgression), encourages sympathy and identification through the direct address of the viewer in the tagline. In this sense, the film's emotive editing aligns the viewer's experience with Andreas's, including his ethically questionable actions and their morally dubious implications.

Ethically questionable actions such as Andreas's, particularly in a film that addresses sensitive issues including infanticide, severe drug addiction, neglect, post-natal depression, and suicide, emphasize the ambivalence of cinematic identification. Identification subsequently renders it difficult for the viewer to objectively ascertain where sympathies belong. Significantly, *A Second Chance* is not the first Bier film that intertwines infanticide and deception. Her award-winning graduate film, *The Island of the Blessed* (*De saliges ø*, 1986), follows a pastor's emotionally and sexually neglected wife, Beate, who becomes pregnant by the pastor's brother. Devastated at the discovery of his wife's betrayal and subsequently questioning his faith, the pastor later kills the baby, believing that this will appease God. When his misdeed is discovered, he allows Beate, who has been silenced by grief, to take the blame and to be imprisoned and executed for his crime.

Despite *A Second Chance*'s handling of similarly complex moral dilemmas, the fact that *The Island of the Blessed* does not use imagery to guide the viewer's sympathies, but instead relies on Beate's voiceover narration, is arguably why it received a better reception. The voiceover technique, which is not afforded to the pastor, instantly places the viewer in an intimate relationship with Beate, whose narration of her decision to engage in sexual relations with her brother-in-law makes her actions more palatable and less reprehensible than those of her husband. Crucially, in *A Second Chance* there are no inner monologues. Sanne and Tristan are not extended a similar level of compassion-inspiring access as Beate has through her voiceover. Instead, the film's insistent invitation to sympathize with Andreas through the re-experiencing of his suffering via afterimages compels the viewer not only to witness, but also to share his trauma. In using this technique, Bier highlights the power of the image to manipulate the viewer's ethical engagement with the film's action. In my view, the almost forceful involvement of the audience, whereby Bier positions the viewer to confront rather than merely view the action, contributed to *A Second Chance*'s polarized reception (Baughan 2015: 12).

A survey of reviews written on the release of *A Second Chance* predominantly concentrate on weaknesses in plot and character development, with critics labeling them "implausible" (Marsh 2016) and "slightly crass" (Bradshaw 2015), as well as weakened by "contrivance" (Hawker 2015) and "one-dimensional characterization" (Debruge 2014). These criticisms, which refer to the extremity of both the film's characters and their actions, do not take into account the manner in which Bier uses visual strategies to deter simple assumptions of right and wrong. The film's difficulty in connecting with audiences stems not only from the narrative's challenging content but also from its distinctiveness in dealing with ethics via visual techniques unique to her filmography. The use of afterimages and affective editing, which serve to highlight the characters' psychological states, potentially creates a reverse effect for viewers, who are not drawn further into the narrative but alienated from it. In this sense, *A Second Chance* presents a double shock that is first experienced through the horrific details of the story, and then reinforced by the purposefully confronting visual techniques. However, in emphasizing the editing of images, Bier forwards an alternative way of "looking" at morality that is cleverly engaged with film's ability to construct and manipulate.

Figure 9.4 Bad parents or victims? Tristan and Sanne's problematic domesticity.

By using the emotional register of the film image to subvert and resist conventional ethics, Bier disrupts the moral equilibrium of right and wrong. Indeed, in one interrogation scene Tristan proclaims, "I'm the victim here," a statement that jolts the viewer to examine the negotiation of victim and perpetrator in the film. Although Tristan is—in that particular instance—the victim, his words have little impact compared to the sensory effect of earlier scenes of him threatening to slit Sanne's throat, neglecting his son, and cooking heroin (Figure 9.4). This tacit demonization is mirrored in Sanne's statement, "You think people like me shouldn't have kids and that I'm a bad mother, but I've never hurt him." However, her proclamation is undercut by scenes of her failing to adequately care for Sofus. Ward E. Jones argues that:

> A spectator's confrontation with a narrative is ethically significant because the narrative (1) manifests an evaluative *attitude* towards its own characters, events, and contexts, and (2) encourages the spectator, through the latter's enjoyment of and satisfaction with the narrative, to adopt a similar attitude. (Jones 2011: 4)

Jones goes on to highlight the complex connection between the formation of one's ethics based on emotions: "This invitation to emotion both reveals the narrative's attitude towards the characters and calls upon spectators to share that attitude, along with the evaluative desires and thoughts that are a part of it" (Jones 2011: 6). The disturbing power of *A Second Chance* is that all the significant characters are morally compromised; therefore, no moral standpoint is ultimately privileged. So while a shift of sympathy may occur when the emotional distress caused by Sanne's separation from Sofus is palpable, the film does not villainize Andreas for his actions. Much like the male protagonists in *After the Wedding* (*Efter brylluppet*, 2006) and *In a Better World* (*Hævnen*, 2010), whose character development subverts initial assumptions established by their roles in society, Andreas's act of kidnapping Sofus undermines any assumptions established by his role as a police detective and committed family man. Adhering to a pattern in many of Bier's films, in which codes of masculinity and ethical expectations are tested, Andreas's moral struggles center on the construction of the nuclear family and the ideation of the perfect domestic space (Smaill 2014: 21).

From the beginning of the film, Bier particularly locates moral ambiguity in relation to Andreas's belief that he and Anna can offer a better domestic environment for Sofus. In the first scene that introduces Andreas and Anna's house, the sense of homeliness is instantly juxtaposed with the detritus of Tristan and Sanne's apartment and the opposing environments offered to the infants within: while Anna is seen stenciling the walls of Alexander's nursery, Sofus is merely afforded a cardboard box. In setting up two irreconcilable versions of home life, Bier addresses the representation of the domestic realm and the presence, or lack thereof, of *hygge* within these spaces to further blur the parameters of right and wrong. *Hygge*, a Danish concept key to successful domesticity, implies sincerity, coziness, and comfort (Linnet 2011: 23) and "mark[s] 'real' family togetherness" (Linnet 2011: 26). The representation of *hygge* within the film gestures not only to cultural ideas about family, but also to their class connotations. The homes they inhabit illustrate Tristan and Sanne's economic and cultural impoverishment and Alexander and Anna's comfortable bourgeois existence. In setting up Andreas and Anna's space as imbued with *hygge* and Tristan and Sanne's as its antithesis, *A Second Chance* appears to justify Andreas's decision for taking Sofus:

> It's not fair. It's not fair that we lose Alexander—while they get to destroy [Sofus]. You can't bear to lose a child, Anna . . . You said you were going to kill yourself. When I met you, you said that all you wanted was a child. He's ours now.

This simple rationalization, which supposedly provides a morally defensible excuse for Andreas's serious act of abduction and his subsequent mishandling of the investigation into Sofus's disappearance, creates the tension within which the moral dilemma pertaining to the kidnapping of Sofus is based. While Anna later refers to Andreas's action as "the perfect crime," his response provides a counterargument, which the film's images and editing support: "It's not a crime. A crime is to let someone like Tristan destroy a child. That's a crime. We're going to save him. I know it's hard to understand right now, honey, but we are." Although Andreas's actions are ultimately concerned with redressing the imbalance within his own domestic space, the revisionist nature of this statement ultimately represents a double contradiction that the film itself never completely unravels. Rather, this ambiguous morality seeps into

Figure 9.5 "Wake up!": Addressing the viewer.

every corner of the film frame, leaving the viewer in a state infused with ethical contradictions.

This chapter has argued that *A Second Chance* implicates the viewer as an active witness charged with not only assessing the ethics of the characters' actions, but also interrogating Bier's construction of imagery. In this sense, the film invites a moral reading of the drama while also calling into question how screen images are interpreted and received. Bier particularly plays with notions of morality by manipulating the camera perspective to draw the viewer into the action, especially in close-up shots of eyes that directly meet the gaze of the audience. For example, when Anna discovers that Alexander has passed away in the middle of the night, her screams to "Wake up" are directed at the camera, instantly engaging the viewer (Figure 9.5). On a metatextual level, Anna's cry to wake up can also be interpreted as Bier's call to action, a demand for the viewer to disentangle the deception of the perfect domesticity encapsulated in the film image. Implicating modes of empathetic spectatorship through the film's imagery, *A Second Chance* not only poses difficult ethical questions, but also demonstrates how editing can impact perception, whereby the theme of vision in the film is cleverly tied to an acute awareness of construction and manipulation through both the cinematography and the focus on still photographs.

In the final scene, Andreas, who has been dismissed from the police force, observes Sanne walking down the aisle of the hardware store where he now works. As he tries to catch a glimpse of her, he is interrupted by a young boy who asks him, "Are you lost?" When Andreas inquires after the boy's name and the reply is Sofus, the narrative comes full circle. During this encounter, however, the film image has regained the stability of its composition and is lacking the fractured jump cuts that marked their first encounter. Moreover, the second chance promised in the film's title appears to have come to fruition for Sanne and Sofus; however, the gaps in the narrative and the manner in which the film suddenly concludes following this meeting leaves the viewer with the difficult task of sorting out the ethics of what they have witnessed. The question "Are you lost?" lingers. Bier has no intention of taking the audience's hand and guiding viewers through her narrative; rather, she leaves them struggling to make sense of what has occurred, and haunted by the film's images.

BIBLIOGRAPHY

Baughan, Nikki (2015), "The reel world," *Index on Censorship* 44 (4): 11–13.
Bradshaw, Peter (2015), "*A Second Chance* review—queasy thriller that does just enough," *The Guardian*, March 20, <https://www.theguardian.com/film/2015/mar/19/a-second-chance-review-susanne-bier> (accessed November 14, 2017).
Deleuze, Gilles ([1986] 2005), *Cinema 1: The Movement Image*, trans. H. Tomlinson and B. Habberjam, London: Continuum.
Doane, Mary Ann (2002), *The Emergence of Cinematic Time: Modernity, Contingency, the Archive*, Cambridge, MA: Harvard University Press.
Felperin, Leslie (2014), "*A Second Chance (En Chance til)*: Toronto Review," *The Hollywood Reporter*, July 9, <http://www.hollywoodreporter.com/review/a-second-chance-en-chance-730737> (accessed November 14, 2017).
Goodridge, Michael (2012), *FilmCraft: Directing*, Burlington: Taylor & Francis.
Göteborg Film Festival (2016), *Live GFF: Nordic Honorary Award Susanne Bier Master Class*, <https://www.youtube.com/watch?v=itnszzETqd8> (accessed November 14, 2017).
Hawker, Philippa (2015), "*A Second Chance* review: Too many twists in the family plot," *Sydney Morning Herald*, September 23, <http://www.smh.com.au/entertainment/movies/a-second-chance-review-too-many-twists-in-the-family-plot-20150923-gjtcfo.html> (accessed November 14, 2017).
Hjort, Mette (2005), *Small Nation, Global Cinema: The New Danish Cinema*, Minneapolis: University of Minnesota Press.
Jones, Ward E. (2011), "Philosophy and ethical signification of spectatorship: An introduction to *Ethics at the Cinema*," in W. E. Jones and S. Vice (eds.), *Ethics at the Cinema*, New York: Oxford University Press, pp. 1–20.
Linnet, Jeppe Trolle (2011), "Money can't buy me *hygge*: Danish middle-class consumption, egalitarianism, and the sanctity of inner space," *Social Analysis* 55 (2): 21–44.
Marsh, James (2016), "Film review: *A Second Chance*—Susanne Bier's bleak drama about grief and parenthood," *South China Morning Post*, July 19, <http://www.scmp.com/culture/film-tv/article/1991666/film-review-second-chance-susanne-biers-bleak-drama-about-grief-and> (accessed November 14, 2017).
Sauntved, Louise Kidde (2011), "Sudden impact," *Film Comment* 47 (2): 24–7.
Shriver-Rice, Meryl (2009), "Adapting National Identity: Ethical Borders Made Suspect in the Hollywood Version of Susanne Bier's *Brothers*," *Film International* 9 (2): 8–19.
Shriver-Rice, Meryl (2015), *Inclusion in New Danish Cinema: Sexuality and Transnational Belonging*, Bristol and Chicago: Intellect Books.
Smaill, Belinda (2014), "The Male Sojourner, the Female Director, and Popular European Cinema: The Worlds of Susanne Bier," *Camera Obscura* 85: 5–31.

Sontag, Susan (2008), *On Photography*, London: Penguin Books.
Stadler, Jane (2008), *Pulling Focus: Intersubjective Experience, Narrative Film, and Ethics*, London: Continuum.
We Got This Covered (2014), "A Second Chance Interview with Susanne Bier and Nikolaj Coster-Waldau," <https://www.youtube.com/watch?v=MAICQlE8-o4> (accessed November 14, 2017).
Wood, Jason (2006), *Talking Movies: Contemporary World Filmmakers in Interview*, London: Wallflower Press.

CHAPTER 10

The Truth is in the Eyes: Susanne Bier's Use of Close-ups in *The Night Manager*

Eva Novrup Redvall

The Emmy-winning miniseries *The Night Manager* (2016) marks the first time that the Oscar-winning Danish director Susanne Bier worked in serial television drama. The series, which was co-produced by the BBC and the American cable channel AMC, is based on an espionage novel from 1993 by acclaimed British author John le Carré. Le Carré's sons specifically chose Bier to direct this prestigious adaptation by screenwriter David Farr. In an interview published by *The Guardian* at the time of the series' release, Bier describes how she was particularly attracted to the material because she wanted to explore "the double depths of the characters, the space between words that makes le Carré's extraordinarily detailed novels so challenging to the time constraints of the big screen" (Bier 2016).

The story of *The Night Manager* is one of questionable loyalties and outright deceit. Everyone has secrets, which compels the characters to constantly search for signs of what is going on inside the minds of others. This chapter will analyze the series' remarkable array of close-ups, of characters' "eye duels" and of particular character's eyes in moments critical to the narrative, as representations of Bier's stated desire to explore character depth and the spaces between utterances. To this end, I will draw on theoretical discussions of the cinematic close-up and studies of stylistic traits in Bier's earlier work.

This chapter highlights examples of how Bier utilizes extreme close-ups during dramatic as well as intimate moments, efficiently employing one of her signature stylistic tools from her arthouse feature films while offering a high-end genre production to mainstream viewers. Bier has stated that with *The Night Manager* she wanted to make viewers feel "intrigued or slightly mystified by what's going on even though they know more than everyone in the story" (Bier quoted in Thompson 2016). Moreover, she wanted the audience to "feel like spies, peeping in through doors and windows, catching the characters unaware in moments of vulnerability," much like the magic trick that the miniseries' villain, Richard Roper, performs at his son's birthday party, where the children have to closely watch the cups to find the hidden ball (Bier 2016).

Bier's use of close-ups in the series is key in facilitating viewers' close proximity to the characters as well as creating the sense that they, too, are spying for details. In *The Night Manager* characters search for the truth as well as mutual understanding in the eyes of others, and as viewers we are offered exclusive access to some of their intimate moments of longing, solitude or self-reflection through a range of images bringing us close to, in particular, their eyes and mouths. The result is an interesting example of a high-end genre series marked by arthouse glimpses that are otherwise not common in mainstream genre productions.

CLOSE-UPS AS THE "SOUL OF CINEMA"

Since the silent film era, film scholars have discussed the close-up as "the technical condition of the art of film" and "the soul of cinema" (Doane 2003: 91). Mary Ann Doane outlines different perceptions of the close-up in film theory, stressing how the close-up has often been linked to "cinema's aspirations to be the vehicle of the presence" (2003: 93). Doane particularly focuses on how the close-up retains an "alliance with a quite particular content," that of the human face (2003: 93). While the possibility of visual closeness offered via the close-up was a revelation in the silent film era and set cinema apart from other narrative art forms such as theater, the close-up of the human face is still regarded as a particularly cinematic feature. Mark Cousins, writing about "cinematic truth," states that "The whole point about cinema, surely, is the close-up of the human face" (Cousins 2004).

Drawing on French film theorist Gilles Deleuze's concept of "faceification," Doane's analysis of the relation between the close-up and the human face stresses how the face is traditionally given three roles: as the privileged site of individualization that embodies each person's uniqueness; as a manifestation of social role or social type; and as the primary tool of intersubjectivity, of relating to or communicating with the other (Doane 2003: 95). Both on and off the screen, the face is regarded as crucial for understanding the personalities of other people and for most human interactions.

According to Doane almost all theories on the face address "the opposition between surface and depth, exteriority and interiority" (2003: 96). Using Danish director Carl Th. Dreyer's spectacular use of close-ups in *The Passion of Joan of Arc* (*La Passion de Jeanne d'Arc*, 1928) as an example of images "that seem to constitute the very revelation of the soul," she argues that "[i]t is almost impossible to see a close-up of a face without asking: what is he/she thinking, feeling, suffering? What is happening beyond what I can see?" (2003: 96). The significance of the facial close-up as inhabiting a sense of "beyondness" carries even greater relevance in dramatic contexts where characters are deliberately trying to hide something, hoping that their faces will not give them away.

Close-ups are versatile, as demonstrated by, for instance, Eisenstein's theories on cinematic montage and working with editing and disproportions from an intellectual perspective. However, mainstream American cinema most often uses the close-up to suggest "proximity," "intimacy," and "knowledge of interiority" (Doane 2003: 107). Close-ups of faces talking, listening, and reacting are naturally integrated in classical Hollywood cinema's continuity editing, as are close-ups that are supposed to draw viewers' attention to a particular story element or object. As an example, Alfred Hitchcock's way of pointing to the knife in a famous dinner scene in *Sabotage* (1936) illustrates how the cuts between close-ups of faces and the dinner knife as a potential murder weapon create suspense by allowing viewers to fill in the characters' thoughts between the gaps.

Close-ups are also prominent in television drama. Traditionally, the soap opera genre has been known for close-ups that convey characters' emotions, but quality television series also increasingly use close-ups as part of particular visual strategies. For instance, one such strategy is to use close-ups to create a sense of disorientation, which Jason Mittell calls "narrative special effects" in his account of complex television drama (Mittell 2006). Rossend Sánchez-Baró argues that *Breaking Bad* (2008–13) uses close-ups and extreme close-ups—for instance, of insects in the bottle episode *The Fly*, or of a worm in the opening of the episode *Grilled*—to take "images out of context, along with constructing undefined and ultimately ambiguous frames" (Sánchez-Baró 2014: 143). The analysis of *The Night Manager* illustrates how Bier, in a few instances, uses disorientating close-ups of objects, such as a water tap, that later turn out to have a particular narrative function as a transitional tool; however, she mainly utilizes close-ups and extreme close-ups to allow viewers to get close to the emotions and reactions in the main characters' eyes.

David Bordwell and Kristen Thompson highlight that the extreme close-up "isolates and magnifies a detail," for instance by focusing on "a portion of the face (eyes or lips)" (Bordwell and Thompson 2001: 219). Addressing a tendency to closer views in modern Hollywood cinema that intensifies continuity, Bordwell argues that rather than using their entire bodies, actors are now primarily faces: "Mouths, brows, and eyes become the principal sources of information and emotion, and actors must scale their performances across varying degrees of intimate framings" (Bordwell 2002: 20). While there are plenty of opportunities to see beautiful bodies and locations in the James Bond-style spy story *The Night Manager*, Bier's focus on mouths and eyes in her first international television drama production will now receive special attention in terms of what this visual strategy adds to the story and how this "six-hour film" relates to her previous work.

THE NIGHT MANAGER AS "A SIX-HOUR FILM"

Several people have wanted to adapt John le Carré's post-Cold War espionage novel *The Night Manager* to film since its 1993 publication. The book is about a former British soldier, now hotel night manager, Jonathan Pine, who gets approached by the British Secret Intelligence Service to go undercover to infiltrate the criminal empire of notorious arms dealer Richard Roper. Paramount optioned the book right after its publication with Sydney Pollack attached to direct, and in a later attempt, Brad Pitt was set to produce and star as Jonathan Pine. However, the rights ended up with le Carré's sons, Stephen and Simon Cornwell, who commissioned screenwriter David Farr to give the novel a contemporary makeover, then produced the miniseries through their London-based production company, Ink Factory (Dalton 2016). The resulting series stars Tom Hiddleston as Jonathan Pine, Hugh Laurie as Richard Roper, Olivia Colman as Angela Burr, and Elizabeth Debicki as Roper's girlfriend, Jed. Changes to the novel include setting the story during the Arab Spring and adapting the male detective, Mr. Burr, to Olivia Colman's pregnant Angela Burr. Also, Richard Roper originally ran his operations from a yacht in the Bahamas, which in the series becomes a beautiful villa on Mallorca, and his shady collaborators are now in Middle Eastern locations rather than among drug cartels in Columbia. The ending was also changed from that of the original novel.

A longtime le Carré fan, Bier describes in several interviews how she was immediately drawn to the material. She comments further that his books "are clear, straight, fantastic thrillers with plots and turns and all the things that classical thrillers have," yet "their characters are also deeply psychologically morally ambiguous and not predictable. I thought, 'I should be doing that.' I do like plots, but I love those kind[s] of characters" (Bier quoted in Thompson 2016). Bier was particularly interested in the adaptation of *The Night Manager* because the opportunity to tell the story in a six-hour miniseries format would enable her "to go into details with the characters in a completely different way" than in a feature film (Bier quoted in Lacuhr 2016). However, while the television format allowed more time to tell the complex story and explore the characters, producer Simon Cornwell insists that "to all intents and purposes" the series was "written and shot as a film—we just hired one director, Susanne

Bier, for all six episodes. I always think of it as a film— just a six-hour one" (Cornwell quoted in Jones 2016).

Similarly, when offering his opinion of the series to the BBC, le Carré referred to the series as a "movie" (le Carré 2016). He had no problem with the adaptive changes, and expressed what he liked best about the series as "how Susanne Bier goes on chewing at the bone of the drama long after other directors would have given up; and how, in this back-and-forth interaction between film and book, a two-way process occurs, as I begin to spot in her film things she herself may not be aware of, just as she has spotted things in my novel that I may not have been aware of" (le Carré 2016).

Bier approached the making of the series in much the same way as when working for the cinema screen. And stylistically, *The Night Manager* shares similarities with her feature films that might not be noticeable to the average viewer, but are remarkable to those with knowledge of her history of conveying emotions through extreme close-ups.

THE EXTREME CLOSE-UP AS A STYLISTIC FEATURE

Film scholars and critics have highlighted how a notable feature in the films of Bier is "her willingness to deal seriously and unapologetically with the strongest possible emotions" (for example, Thuran in Monggaard 2007). Family is a recurring theme in her work, as is an interest in exploring "male power dynamics as her characters try to parse doing the right thing in a world where that is not always clear or possible" (Thompson 2016). *The Night Manager* is different from Bier's internationally acclaimed Danish dramas such as the Dogme film *Open Hearts* (*Elsker dig for evigt*, 2002), *Brothers* (*Brødre*, 2004), the Oscar-nominated *After the Wedding* (*Efter brylluppet*, 2006), or the Oscar-winning *In a Better World* (*Hævnen*, 2010), because it is a thriller plot rather than a relation-based family drama, and it does not possess the lighter touch or humorous interludes of her breakthrough romantic comedy *The One and Only* (*Den eneste ene*, 1999) or *Love Is All You Need* (*Den skaldede frisør*, 2012).

However, while the espionage plot of *The Night Manager* is not directly about family or personal relations, it does contain both elements in the way that Richard Roper runs his criminal activities as a tight family operation built on trust. When Pine gets accepted as one of the gang, he is welcomed to "the family," and when Roper visits his military camp with soldiers from all over the world, he cheerfully stresses how this is the real United Nations: "one big happy family." The importance of family is also evident in the way that Pine enters Roper's network by appearing to rescue Roper's son, thereby winning a special status and gratitude. Jed's absent son also has a part to play, as has Angela Burr's unborn son, who is repeatedly put at risk because of Angela's commitment to punishing Roper for making business out of the tragic deaths of women and children. Family does matter in the series, and even if family issues don't take center stage, they are a crucial part of the drama.

As for personal drama, Bier definitely focuses on the many complicated interpersonal relations in the story, even if the bottom line is whether Burr and Pine will manage to defeat Roper or not. Bier's films often focus on conflicts between people who have difficult relations although they ought to be close, and she has never shied away from showing the emotional moments in those kinds of stories. As she has stated, "You can't be ashamed of big emotions if you make cinema" (in Hoggard 2013). In several of her feature films, the camera captures these big emotions by moving very close to the characters. Meryl Shriver-Rice analyzes how Bier often shows "disembodied eyes" or "roaming close-ups of body parts during intense emotional moments" (2015: 31). According to Shriver-Rice, "Bier's editing and camerawork invites the spectator to become absorbed into each character's emotional state" (2015: 31).

In an analysis of "Susanne Bier's Living, Breathing Body of Work," Sonia Lupher describes Bier's camera in *After the Wedding* as "yearning," focusing on how it lingers "on her main characters as shocking family secrets spill out into the open" (Lupher 2016). Lupher also highlights Bier's interest in "the micro-gestures that are revealed in close-ups on expressive body parts (an eye, a mouth, a hand)" and how shots of such micro-gestures are "inserted in her films like punctuation" (ibid.). In Lupher's opinion, "[t]hese intimate details bring her characters to life, revealing their interiority amid the situations unraveling around them" (ibid.). Bier herself has called the close-up her most effective "tool," stressing that, for her, "filmmaking is a lot of what's happening in the face" (Bier quoted in Thompson 2016).

Reviews of *The Night Manager* have not been marked by specific comments on Bier's use of close-ups, but there has been widespread praise for the production values of the series, not least its use of spectacular locations and charismatic stars. However, comparing *The Night Manager* to Bier's previous work illustrates how she employs close-ups, in particular extreme close-ups, in the series to play with the spaces between words where the eyes indicate the often complicated tensions between the characters' exteriority and interiority.

CLOSE-UPS AS NARRATIVE MARKERS

Scholarship on close-ups often stresses their attention to emotions in the human face, but close-ups can also fulfill important narrative functions by making viewers focus on particular story details. This is a classical use of the close-up that Bier naturally also uses to convey crucial story information. For example, when Jed spies to get the code for Roper's safe, we see these four digits closely, and when Pine copies Roper's papers for the mysterious Sophie Alekan (Aure Atika), close-ups of the list of weapons demonstrate Pine becoming aware that these papers contain information about an arms deal.

Soon after, Pine's mouth is framed in extreme close-up while he calls his British friend to ask questions about Mr. Hamid (Figure 10.1). This strategy of showing mouths as they are pronouncing important names or character relations is used several times in the series. When Sophie refers to Richard Roper as "the worst man in the world," we see her say his name in an extreme

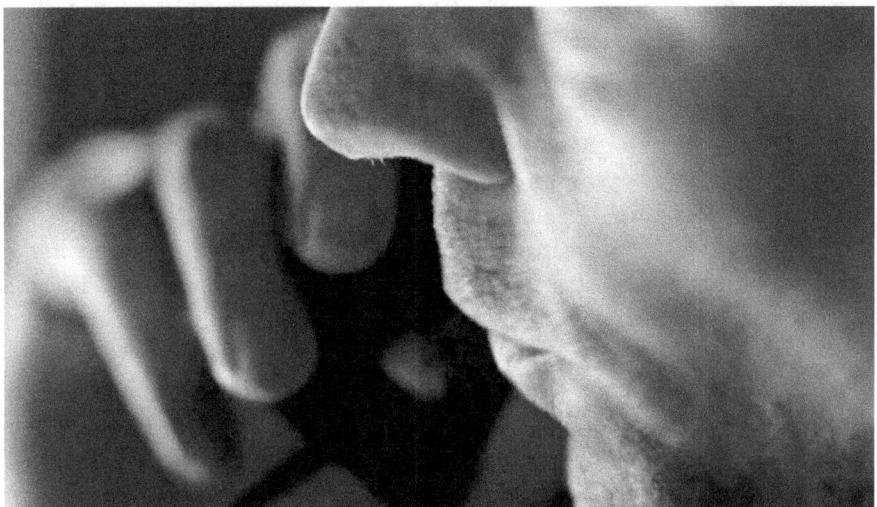

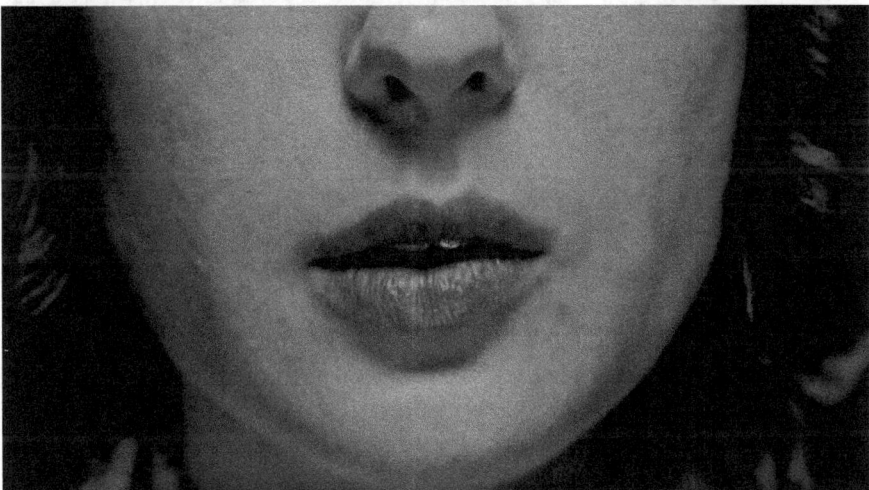

Figure 10.1 Jonathan Pine (Tom Hiddleston) asking questions about Mr. Hamid on the phone in episode one; and the mouth of Marilyn (Hannah Steele) explaining that "he never said who he was" (from *The Night Manager*, episodes one and two).

close-up of her mouth. When Roper's son is kidnapped in episode two, he is not only a criminal but also a father when we see his mouth announcing that "yes, he is my son." We also nearly taste the words when Marilyn (Hannah Steele), the young woman with whom Pine has an affair while creating a convincing criminal backstory for himself in the U.K.—testifies that "he never said who he was" (Figure 10.1). Later, after Roper gives Pine the name "Andrew Birch," we see Pine's mouth in an extreme close-up when he uses the alias to transfer money on his phone. When images zoom in on names and dialogue in this way, viewers are encouraged to pay particular attention to what is said. Moreover, using close-ups in this manner can also be a way to show how another character is intensely listening. Thus, when Roper explains that there was "a minor issue at the Syrian border" in episode six, a close-up of Roper saying these words is followed by an extreme close-up of Pine's eyes taking in this information. This use of close-ups is not Bier's particular trademark, but these examples of close-ups as narrative markers illustrate the range of functions close-ups fill in *The Night Manager*.

Episode two features a remarkable use of close-ups to orient viewers in the timeline of the episode, which opens on the crisis in which Pine rescues Roper's son in a seaside restaurant in Mallorca. In the dramatic opening, viewers do not know Pine is at the scene. At the height of the drama, when the pretend kidnappers have taken Roper's son, a close-up of Pine's eye reveals him peeping through a hole in the door. This image is followed by a flashback to six months earlier, which opens with an extreme close-up of a tap dripping. We have no way of understanding this image until the end of the flashback sequence, when we learn that the dripping tap appears in a blood-covered kitchen where a fake murder in Pine's cover story has taken place (Figure 10.2).

The image of the tap dripping takes us back to the interrogation of Marilyn—who is the main witness to Pine's fake murder—while the repetition of the close-up of Pine behind the door brings us back to the drama in the restaurant. Since these two close-up images visually stand out and are hard to interpret when we first encounter them, they serve as helpful transitional markers. At first sight, they create a sense of disorientation, but the images are used as narrative special effects even if the story quickly moves on to create contexts so that they end up primarily serving as time markers in the story; the tap was back then, the eye behind the door is the now of the story, thus efficiently taking viewers back to the episode's dramatic opening.

While the image of the tap stands out in relation to the rest of the series, the eye behind the door contributes to Bier's emphasis that the drama hinges on who sees what and who is spying on who. In this way, the close-ups of eyes and mouths not only convey characters' emotions and facilitate intimate atmospheres; they also serve other purposes in the narration and portrayal of characters in the series.

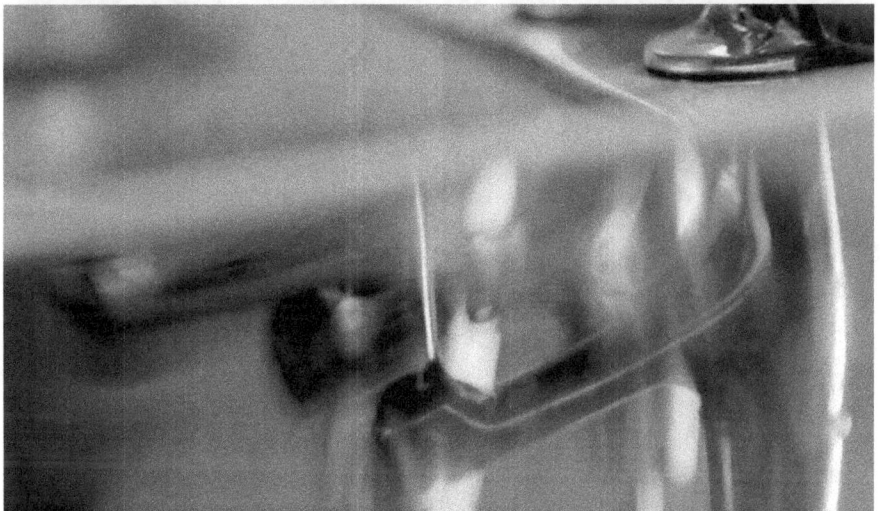

Figure 10.2 The image of Jonathan Pine's eye spying behind a door during the attempt to kidnap the son of Richard Roper (Hugh Laurie) reappears at the end of the flashback as a visually remarkable transition back to the drama at the restaurant in Mallorca (from *The Night Manager*, episode two).

BATTLES OF TRUST AND SPYING EYES

Throughout the series, the camera moves close to the eyes of characters, and the dialogue repeatedly plays with lines about seeing or not seeing—as when Roper's right-hand man, Corkoran (Tom Hollander), refers to Roper as "the blind man who cannot see." In this espionage story, close-ups of eyes often feature in scenes in which characters have to decide whether they can trust each other or not. When Burr and Pine meet in London in episode two, they need to figure out whether this undercover set-up will work, and they look for the answer in each other's eyes. This is not an uncommon feature in, for instance, the film noir genre, which similarly uses close-ups to draw attention to the face in stories that are often about deceit and being let down by people who were regarded as trustworthy. However, in *The Night Manager* this "theme of seeing" is explicit on many different levels in the story itself, and Bier's strategy is often to allow viewers privileged access to character information by allowing the audience to see reactions in "the spaces between words" that are not visible to other characters. There are "eye duels" where characters test each other, but there are also intimate moments of character concern being conveyed through images of their eyes that only we as viewers get to share.

Roper and Pine have several "staring showdowns" during their complicated relationship, which from the very outset is marked by Roper's natural suspicion. In the opening of episode two, close-ups show Roper trying to figure Pine out by looking him in the eyes, and they later have an intense showdown on a plane in episode five after Roper finds out that Burr got hold of a list with the names of his collaborators. Roper states that anyone can betray anyone, and asks whether Pine is the traitor, while watching him carefully. When Pine first passes the test of his inquisitive gaze, Roper pretends to go to sleep—only to immediately re-open his eyes to see whether Pine shows any sign of relief when thinking that Roper is no longer watching (Figure 10.3). Later in the episode, Roper watches Pine intensely after Corkoran's death. He does not verbalize his suspicion, but—standing behind Pine—the close-up of Roper's eyes shows his careful observation of Pine's reaction (Figure 10.3).

While the intense eye duels represent characters trying to see or conceal the truth in a world where everyone has good reasons to lie, the eye images also provide access to character thoughts and emotions that other characters are not aware of. In several scenes, close-ups of eyes reveal emotions for the viewers only, as when Pine wakes up beside Marilyn in the episode two flashback and seems to have some kind of plan of which she is unaware. Later, when he is recovering from his injuries at the restaurant kidnapping and people are talking by his bed, viewers see his eyes registering information, while no characters in the story have knowledge of this happening. On a very basic level, then, the eyes show us secret reactions that other characters are unaware of, such as when Roper announces that "nothing is quite as pretty as napalm in the night" at the military camp in episode five, and a close-up of Pine's eyes indicates his disagreement.

The integration of biometric eye scans into the series' close-up strategy literalizes the aphorism that the eyes reveal the truth. In episode four, Pine as Andrew Birch undergoes a biometric eye scan to access the bank account used

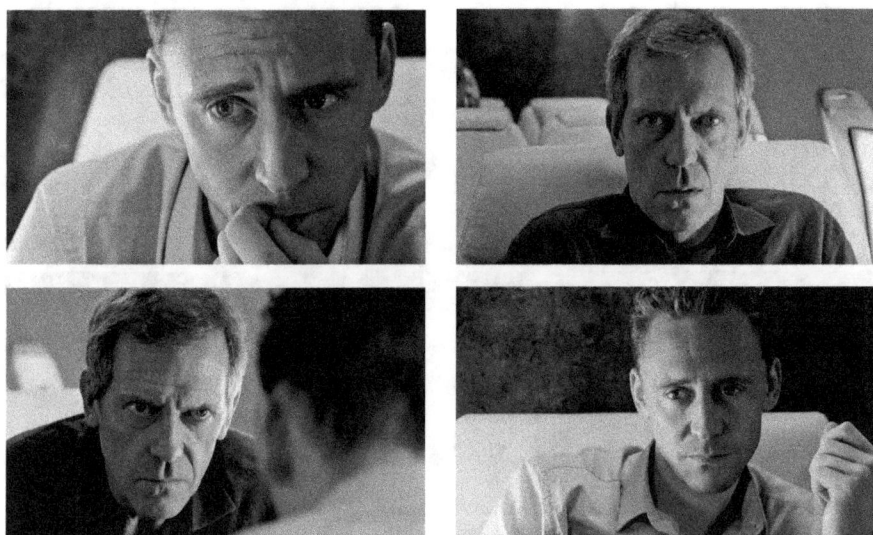

Figure 10.3 Richard Roper and Jonathan Pine/Andrew Birch in one of their "eye duels" when Roper tries to figure out whether Pine can be trusted by looking him intensely in the eyes (from *The Night Manager*, episode five).

in the arms deal. The eye scan ensures that the person accessing the account is really who he claims to be, thus naturally leading to a number of close-ups of Pine's eyes confirming the money transfer, for instance episode four's harbor scene (Figure 10.4a).

The biometric eye scan is central to the plot, which ends up revolving around Pine being able to "cheat with his eyes" while no one is watching, thereby messing up the criminal scheme. Fundamentally, Pine's eyes execute an essential plot function. As Roper jokingly comments during a money transfer in episode six, "Don't mess it up, Andrew. A lot of people depending on that beautiful iris of yours." This line of dialogue is one of many that highlight the importance of eyes in the story (Figure 10.4b).

However, the most interesting use of eyes in the series, and the one that most clearly links *The Night Manager* to Bier's previous work, is in extreme close-ups that create a sense of intimacy between characters that seems to perpetually fascinate Bier.

THE EXTREME CLOSE-UP AND CHARACTER INTIMACY

As described by Doane and others, close-ups often create a sense of proximity and intimacy that invites the audience to access the unspoken thoughts and feelings of characters, which filmmakers, unlike novelists, must show rather

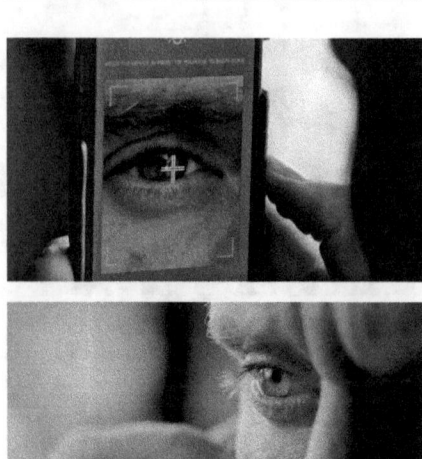
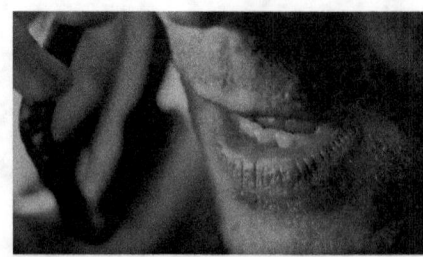

Figure 10.4a The biometric eye scan is central to the plot of *The Night Manager* and makes Pine's eyes execute an essential plot function (from *The Night Manager*, episode four).

than describe. Bier efficiently aligns viewers with characters' inner lives in dressing situations, when close-ups emphasize how they put on a façade to meet the world. In such private and vulnerable moments, viewers simply watch the characters and reflect on what they may be thinking. For example, episode two opens with close-ups of Jed getting dressed, and the scene is intimate in the details and body parts shown. In the previous episode, Pine was shown putting on his façade as the night manager in Switzerland, the perfection of his appearance masking the complexity behind the immaculate suit.

Writing about Danish cinema, Shriver-Rice has argued that showing characters when they are alone is a general trend in recent Danish films, and she has particularly highlighted how Bier for instance works with portraying moments of solitude and self-reflection in a feature film such as *In a Better World* (Shriver-Rice 2015). In the case of *The Night Manager*, Bier offers intimate moments of solitude with Jed and Pine, who both have to keep up appearances in order not to give away their true selves. As illustrated in the screenshots from the scene with Jed in episode two (Figure 10.5), parts of these moments are portrayed in extreme close-ups, particularly of her eyes, before showing the rest of her body and her surroundings.

SUSANNE BIER'S USE OF CLOSE-UPS   199

Figure 10.4b "A lot of people depending on that beautiful iris of yours." Jonathan Pine (Tom Hiddleston) "cheats with his eyes" in the final showdown (from *The Night Manager*, episode six).

From the beginning of the series, Bier's camera also focuses on details to show how characters are drawn to each other. There is only a short time in episode one to establish a passionate relationship between Pine and Sophie, and close-ups are an important part of this: from the close-up of Sophie's cigarette in their first meeting, to multiple extreme close-ups of their eyes and mouths, and finally, to the horrified look on Pine's face when he finds Sophie's dead body in the hotel room. Pine and Sophie develop an intimate relationship in a very short period of time—in story as well as screen time—and close-ups exoticize and eroticize the relationship's evolution (Figure 10.6).

Similarly, the relationship between Pine and Roper's girlfriend Jed culminates in a scene where extreme close-ups demonstrate that they only see each other in a casino full of other people. When Jed asks Pine who he is and comments that everyone is attracted to him, the camera moves close to their eyes as they give in to their attraction to each other and go to her hotel room together. Interestingly, the camera keeps a distance while they have sex, as if their eyes meeting beforehand is more important than the meeting of their bodies (Figure 10.7).

According to Bier, one of *The Night Manager*'s main assets from the beginning was Tom Hiddleston's eyes: "There's a certain incredibly enigmatic quality to his eyes. You aren't sure you can trust him, but you are sure there is a pain there that he doesn't show. He's so immaculate and fun and elegant and charming, and there is somewhere inside of him a painfulness, which I think for most women, is irresistible" (Bier in Thompson 2016). While the

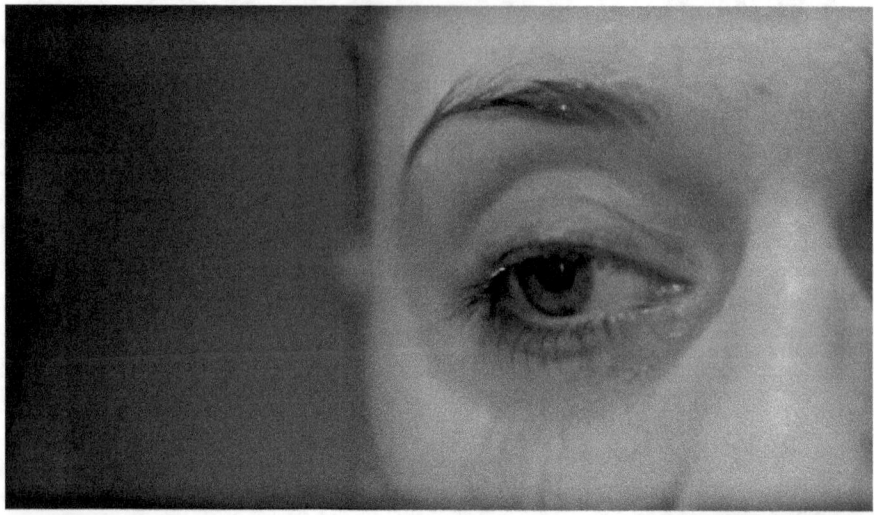
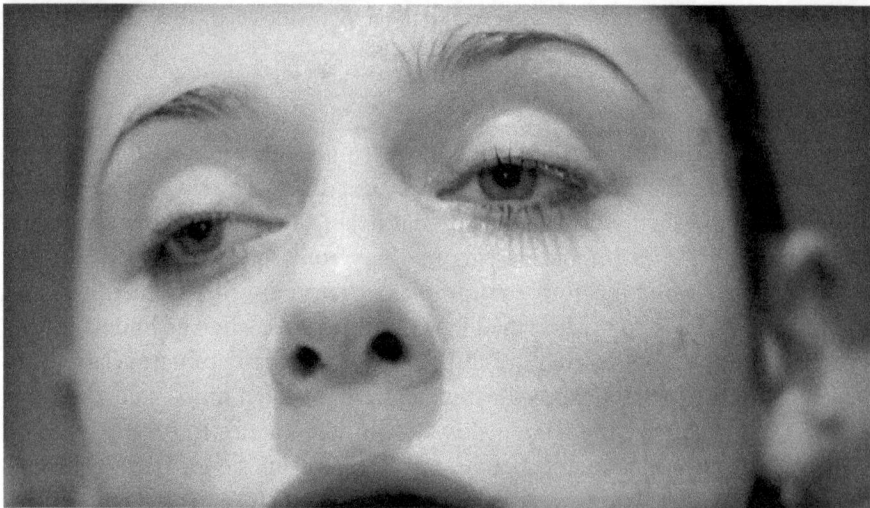

Figure 10.5 Jed (Elizabeth Debicki) showering and dressing up for a new day before a phone call makes viewers aware that she also has a secret of which Roper is unaware (from *The Night Manager*, episode two).

landscapes and impressive locations of the series have an obvious visual grandeur, production value—as well as drama and emotion—can also be found in the uniqueness of the human faces or eyes of characters, to which Bier has always been attracted in her filmmaking. *The Night Manager* employs microgestures and disembodied mouths and eyes in ways that are similar to her previous work in Danish filmmaking, while telling a spy story that perfectly fits Bier's interest in zooming in on complex relationships and creating visually interesting and intimate portrayals of complicated characters.

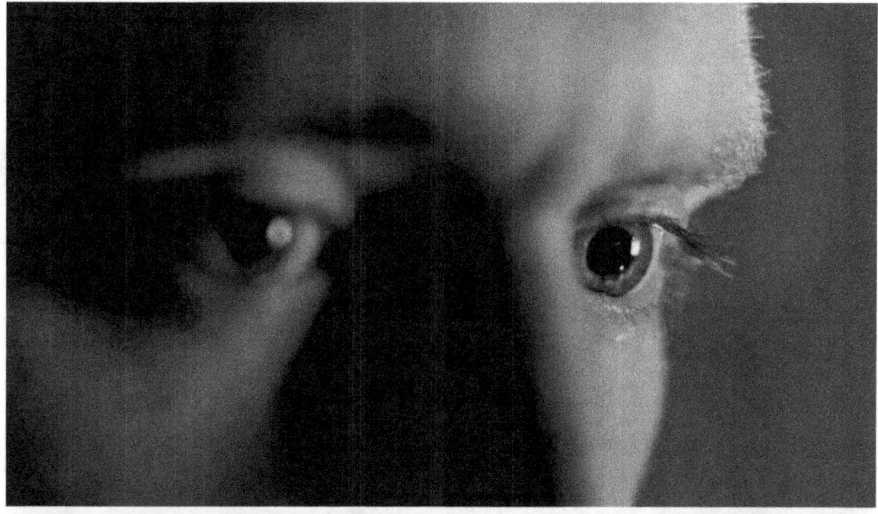

Figure 10.6 Jonathan Pine (Tom Hiddleston) taking in the beaten face of Sophie Alekan (Aure Atika) (from *The Night Manager*, episode one).

CONCLUDING REMARKS

In *The Night Manager*, first-time television series director Susanne Bier successfully managed to incorporate remarkable stylistic motifs from her previous cinematic work into a mainstream miniseries. The story and characters of *The Night Manager* fit neatly with Bier's interest in working with the close-up as her main "tool," since the plot centers on people trying to figure out what is going on underneath the surface of other characters and contains a number

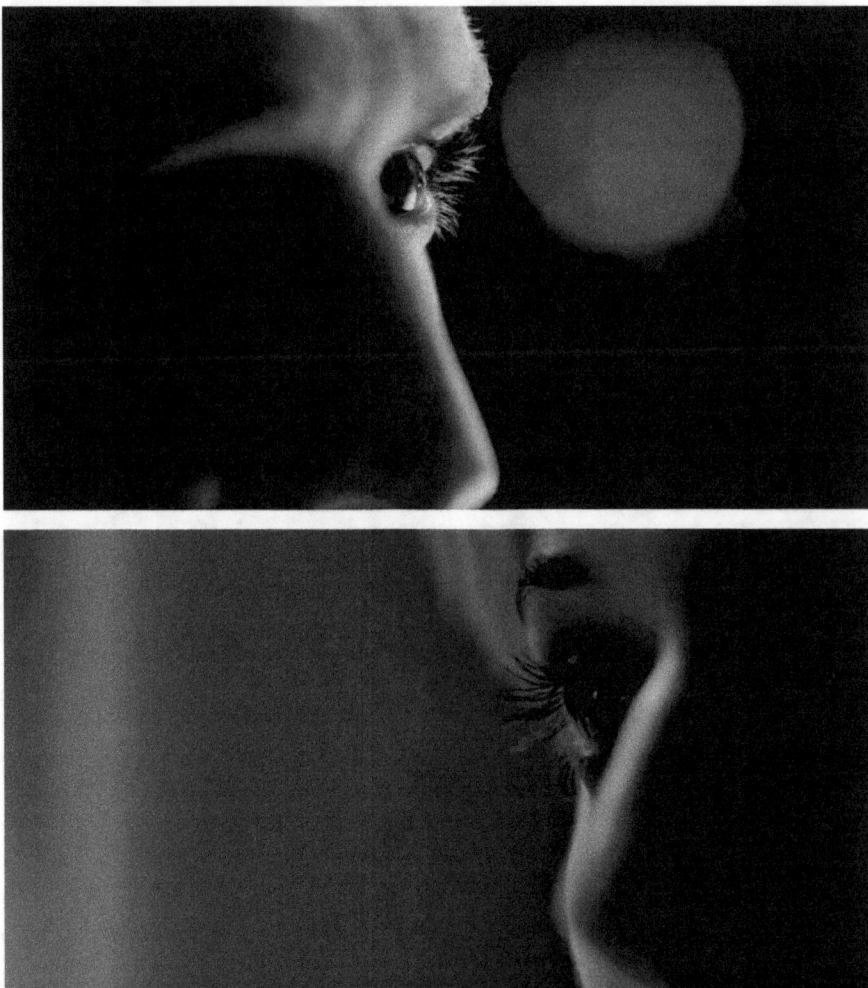

Figure 10.7 "Who are you? Everyone is attracted to you . . ." Jonathan and Jed only seeing each other before going to her room (from *The Night Manager*, episode four).

of complicated relationships in which issues of trust and deceit, longing and passion, all play a part. The espionage plot naturally builds on conflicts between the exterior and interior of characters, and the use of close-ups and extreme close-ups is an efficient strategy for exploring these conflicts and for giving audiences the sense of spying on characters. As described above, viewers often get close to characters in ways that no other characters in the story do, both in vulnerable private moments and in social situations when crucial story information appears in their eyes. The close-ups also create special bonds between characters and convey a strong sense of longing that is essential in a story where characters put their lives at risk because of their attraction to or love for others.

As Bier states, she likes plot, but she loves characters. *The Night Manager* offered her the opportunity to explore le Carré's characters in a six-hour television format that she approached as a long feature film. The analysis above has uncovered how getting close to the faces of the main characters in the story, particularly to their mouths and eyes, is an important element of exploring not only their actions and reactions, but also the sense of "beyondness" that film theorists have discussed in relation to the close-up as the soul of cinema. In the series, viewers as well as characters look for the truth in the eyes of others, and in the end, the whole plot converges on the eyes of Jonathan Pine/Andrew Birch bringing down Richard Roper.

Bier's feature films have been discussed as simultaneously demonstrating properties of art cinema and popular genre cinema (for example, Agger 2015; Smaill 2014). Sonia Lupher states that "[Bier's] film's melodramatic tendencies put her at odds with the art film crowd, but her careful attention to visual composition keeps her films out of the strictly commercial realm" (Lupher 2016). *The Night Manager* contains art cinema glimpses through its use of particularly extreme close-ups that briefly make viewers see visual details in a way that is not common in mainstream film or television. One can regard these extreme close-ups as part of Bier's attempt to capture "the double depths of characters" and "the spaces between words" in the work of le Carré. However, the series is fundamentally an efficient and entertaining piece of high-end television, and its impressive viewing figures, positive reviews and Emmy win all point to how working with micro-gestures and disembodied eyes does not disturb the overall appeal of this "six-hour film" for either the targeted primetime audiences, or the television critics and Susanne Bier fans.

BIBLIOGRAPHY

Agger, Gunhild (2015), "Strategies in Danish Film Culture—and the Case of Susanne Bier," *Kosmorama* 259 (March 11), <http://www.kosmorama.org/Artikler/Susanne-Bier.aspx> (accessed November 14, 2017).

Bier, Susanne (2016), "TV is opening its doors to female directors—Film needs to catch up," *The Guardian*, March 5, <http://www.theguardian.com/commentisfree/2016/mar/05/tv-film-female-directors-susanne-bier-the-night-manager-le-carre> (accessed November 14, 2017).

Bordwell, David (2002), "Intensified continuity: visual style in contemporary American film," *Film Quarterly* 55(3): 16–28.

Cousins, Mark (2004), "Cinematic truth lies in the close-up," *Prospect Magazine*, June 20, <http://www.prospectmagazine.co.uk/magazine/5992-widescreen> (accessed November 14, 2017).

Doane, Mary Ann (2003), "The close-up: Scale and detail in the cinema," *Differences* 14(3): 89–111.

Dalton, Stephen (2016), "*The Night Manager*: Berlin review," *The Hollywood Reporter*, February 18, <http://www.hollywoodreporter.com/review/night-manager-berlin-review-867287> (accessed November 14, 2017).

Feinstein, Howard (2007), "Susanne Bier on *After the Wedding*," Filmmakermagazine.com, March 30, <http://filmmakermagazine.com/4867-susanne-bier-after-the-wedding/#.WAVw9NxH_Gw> (accessed November 14, 2017).

Hjort, Mette (2000), "Interview with Susanne Bier," in Mette Hjort and Ib Bondebjerg (eds.) (2003), *The Danish Directors: Dialogues on a Contemporary National Cinema*, Bristol and Chicago: Intellect Books.

Hoggard, Liz (2013), "Susanne Bier: You can't be ashamed of big emotions if you make cinema," *The Guardian*, April 14, <https://www.theguardian.com/theobserver/2013/apr/14/susanne-bier-love-all-you-need> (accessed November 14, 2017).

Jones, Emma (2016), "How the 'risk' of making *The Night Manager* paid off," *BBC News*, March 25, <http://www.bbc.com/news/entertainment-arts-35884333> (accessed November 14, 2017).

le Carré, John (2016), "John le Carré on The Night Manager on TV: they've totally changed my book—but it works," The Guardian, February 20, <https://www.theguardian.com/books/2016/feb/20/john-le-carre-the-night-manager-television-adaptation> (accessed November 14, 2017).

Lupher, Sonia (2016), "Susanne Bier's living, breathing body of work," Btchflcks.com, April 4, <http://www.btchflcks.com/2016/04/susanne-biers-living-breathing-body-of-work.html#.WAVMlmCAow1> (accessed November 14, 2017).

Mittell, Jason (2006), "Narrative complexity in contemporary American television," *The Velvet Light Trap* no. 58 (Fall 2006): 29–40.

Monggaard, Christian (2007), <https://www.information.dk/christian-monggaards-blog/2007/10/things-we-lost-in-the-fire> (accessed November 14, 2017).

Sánchez-Baró, Rossend (2014), "Uncertain beginnings: *Breaking Bad*'s episodic openings," in David P. Pierson (ed.), *Breaking Bad: Critical Essays on the Contexts, Politics, Style and Reception of the Television Series*, Lanham, MD and Plymouth: Lexington Books, pp. 139–54.

Schwarzbaum, Lisa (2007), "Things We Lost in The Fire," *Entertainment Weekly*, October 17, <http://www.ew.com/article/2007/10/17/things-we-lost-fire> (accessed November 14, 2017).

Shriver-Rice, Meryl (2015), *Inclusion in New Danish Cinema: Sexuality and Transnational Belonging*, Bristol and Chicago: Intellect Books.

Smaill, Belinda (2014), "The Male Sojourner, the Female Director, and Popular European Cinema: The Worlds of Susanne Bier," *Camera Obscura* vol. 29, no. 1, 85: 5–31.

Smith, Kyle (2007), "Going down in flames," *New York Post*, October 19, <http://nypost.com/2007/10/19/going-down-in-flames/> (accessed November 14, 2017).

Tartaglione, Nancy (2016), "*The Night Manager* ends UK run on ratings high," Deadline.com, March 28, <http://deadline.com/2016/03/night-manager-ratings-finale-bbc-second-season-james-bond-1201727140/> (accessed November 14, 2017).

Thompson, Anne (2016), "*The Night Manager* is thrilling and boasts one director: Susanne Bier," *Indiewire*, April 18, <http://www.indiewire.com/2016/04/the-night-manager-is-thrilling-and-boasts-one-director-susanne-bier-289742/> (accessed November 14, 2017).

PART 4

Transnational Reach

Part 4 Introduction

The fourth and final part of this collection features the global nature and transnational reach of Bier's film practices and reception. The transnational nature of Bier's work has been highlighted and discussed at length in many of the chapters of this book as one of the most definitive elements of her oeuvre. In this final part, Bier's transnational reach is examined by Belinda Smaill, Cath Moore, and Meryl Shriver-Rice using three different approaches.

In Chapter 11 Smaill employs a feminist lens to situate women filmmakers within a wider global context in which all women's cinema can be considered to be "world cinema," set apart from local contexts that fail to encompass women's film practices in terms of resources, space, and mobility. Advocating a perspective advanced by Patricia White in *Women's Cinema, World Cinema*, Smaill proposes that women filmmakers should be viewed within "whole world approaches" that comprehensively address the context of production, circulation, representation, and image of each director. This chapter first looks at Bier's specific national and transnational production milieus as they relate to her films' representations of the world, before situating her films and directorial agency against the industrial strategies and films of other significant women directors, including Claire Denis, Katheryn Bigelow, and Jane Campion. While tracking the mobility of female directors, Smaill points out that while it is difficult for women to achieve employment as feature directors in the U.S., it is even more difficult to gain access to the industry from outside the U.S. Hollywood is an exclusive domain, making Bier's transnational American work a critical site for investigation. Thus, Smaill takes a closer look at *Serena* to investigate the narrative and aesthetic traditions that locate Bier's work in gendered paradigms of representation. As an example of world cinema that cuts across traditional film categories (such as art and commercial cinema, or auteur and mainstream film), there is an unresolved tension surrounding *Serena*'s address to the audience, especially in the film's appeal to mainstream expectations. *Serena*, Smaill concludes, represents a complex manifestation of world cinema.

In Chapter 12 Cath Moore draws attention to the unique Danish co-writing process that most Danish directors employ, in which a director and screenwriter collaborate on scripts and share writing credit. Bier's most successful films have been co-written with Anders Thomas Jensen, who also works with actors during the writing process, rewriting lines of story and dialogue after collaborative reading sessions. With a focus on the Bier/Jensen trilogy, Moore delineates the creative divergences between Bier's solo work and Jensen's dark satirical and absurdist self-written and directed films. Moore argues that the trilogy's preoccupation with fathers and sons stems from Jensen's male perspective, but is bolstered by Bier's distinctive take on male characters. This masculine emphasis distinguishes her dramas from what is often expected of women directors, as many view a woman director's work expecting an immersive, inclusive site of feminized concerns. Moore asserts that the critical and commercial success of the unparalleled Bier/Jensen oeuvre is a result of their preference for highly dramatic stories focused on personal conflict that transcends the local domestic space of Denmark. These transnational storylines, she believes, utilize different national settings as an important facet of story construction to visualize a shared humanity. In this way, disparate realities are bound together to challenge the belief that, as Bier phrases it, "the third world is away from us . . . and that's not true, it's really part of our own world." For Moore, this use of—and emphasis on—Danish domestic space anchors Nordic concerns regarding childhood, masculinity, and violence. Using examples from *After the Wedding* and *In a Better World*, Moore contends that the gendered presentation of childhood is a distinct component of Bier/Jensen world-building, one that mirrors a Nordic preference for depicting relations on screen between sons and parents more frequently than parents and daughters. The metanarrative in these storylines examines violence as gendered and perhaps the inevitable, instinctive result of intergenerational transfer.

In the final chapter of this collection, Shriver-Rice interprets *Brothers, After the Wedding*, and *In a Better World* in terms of the shared trope of the white male sojourner who travels from Denmark to locations that feature non-white, non-Western citizens to, respectively, assist the NATO-led coalition in Afghanistan, feed and house Indian orphans, and provide medical care in the South Sudan. This chapter situates the Bier/Jensen trilogy within a wider trend of contemporary Scandinavian narratives of guilt. In assessing potential critiques of the trilogy on postcolonial grounds, Shriver-Rice argues that the "elsewheres" of these films do not ignore geographic locations and cultural contexts in order to assert a universalizing morality. Instead, the ethical trajectories of these films are not universal, and the idea that universalist ethics will inevitably fail takes precedence. Though universal in reach and successfully aimed at global audiences, these three films do not alienate Danish audiences: instead, they star Danish actors, are scripted in Danish, and depict Danish families on Danish soil. Consequently, Bier's drawing from non-industrialized, non-Western space has more to do with speaking to the privileged-world guilt in the Danish viewer, and reminding him or her of the world at large beyond Western space. Essentially, Shriver-Rice sees these films as concerned with a cosmopolitan outlook that is diagnostic of the current age in which rapid epistemic ruptures have been pointing not towards a privileged and irresponsible detachment, but towards a normative stance in dealing with one's guilt that supports political action.

CHAPTER 11

Cinema of the World and Women's Film Culture: Susanne Bier's Transnational Cinema

Belinda Smaill

In recent years the popular press has drawn attention to gender disparity in the film industry. With a focus on establishing which women are the exceptions at male-dominated awards ceremonies or how few achieve director credits on top grossing films, this attention has, paradoxically, resulted in more and more women directors gaining visibility. Susanne Bier has directed fifteen feature films and one miniseries—her success has been considerable against any measure, but especially so in light of the statistics regarding female directors. Bier's profile, however, has been slow to come to prominence in both the public sphere and film studies circles, including feminist film studies. This may be because her body of work is thematically diverse, does not cohere around a particular approach to questions of gender, and, from a production perspective, traverses nations and continents. Rather than perceiving these issues as an impediment to analysis, I am interested in how the intricacies and perceived incongruities of Bier's profile and film work might be seen through a feminist optic and scholarly approaches to the female director.

Bier's film work makes a rich contribution to the interrelated movements of New Danish Cinema, the transnational Nordic film industry, and the avant-garde film phenomena Dogme 95. Accounting for Bier's films on these terms and within these contexts allows for fruitful analysis, in particular for national cinema scholarship. National and regional contexts cannot, however, tell the whole story of the female director. An accurate mapping of women and film culture can only be achieved by looking beyond local considerations to identify cultural and industrial links with other female practitioners in ways that not only acknowledge the increasingly international tenor of film production, but also account for broader histories of women's filmmaking and the systemic changes that shape women's careers at a global level.

In her book *Women's Cinema, World Cinema: Projecting Contemporary Feminisms*, Patricia White explores how films circulate given a range of factors including the value bestowed on men's versus women's genres, the formulation of the director's public persona, and the uneven international commercial terrain that distinguishes the influence of different cinemas. White argues that in the age of global mass media, "women have a crucial role as producers of [a] public social vision, not only as media consumers and representational supports" (White 2015: 3). In this vein she attends to "the terms of public debate about who controls images of the world" (White 2015: 4). White's methodology is underpinned by the proposition that "women's cinema should always be seen as world cinema" (White 2015: 4). The understanding of world cinema that White invokes with this claim draws on Lúcia Nagib's definition of world cinema as polycentric, rejecting Hollywood as the defining center of film production because "once notions of a single centre and primacies are discarded, everything can be put on the world cinema map on an equal footing, even Hollywood, which instead of a threat becomes a cinema amongst others" (2011: 1). Nagib's notion of world cinema places emphasis on "cutting across film history according to waves of relevant films and movements, thus creating flexible geographies" (2006: 35), suggesting how "world cinema" might function as an analytical tool for understanding a range of cinema formations.

Also asking how it is possible to build a more precise picture of women's film production, Kathleen McHugh historicizes contemporary film feminisms by investigating the social and industrial structures of opportunity that have enabled the careers of women practitioners. The structures she describes encompass the diverse effects of globalizing movements and feminist legacies. McHugh suggests that women's film production has been marginalized, in part, by the manner in which it has been catalogued and represented, particularly in the schema of reference books that describe individual female directors on the terms of personal success, dehistoricized from wider political movements and initiatives. Their contributions are typically catalogued alphabetically in encyclopaedias of "women filmmakers" or of "women in film," or in books that distinguish their topics by country—"women directors in Mexico, Australia, Japan"—or by region—"Middle Eastern or South Asian women filmmakers." The former are reference formats, useful but ahistorical, while the latter limit women's place in cinema to a subgenre of national or regional cinemas, belying transnational influences and relationships (McHugh 2009: 115).

McHugh calls for a "whole world" approach that recognizes women's troubled relation to the nation—women have been historically marginalized in the nation state (in the domestic sphere) and have "no-place" (McHugh 2009: 112). Less contained or defined by the nation, their place must be "the whole world." Notably, McHugh establishes this point with reference to Virginia Woolf's famous quote: "As a woman I have no country; as a woman, I want no country; as a woman my country is the whole world" (Woolf cited in McHugh 2009: 111). The articulation of women's relationship to the space of the nation is the starting point for McHugh's analysis of women's film practice and its legacies by way of the problem of gender, resources, space, and mobility.

The scholarship of McHugh, White, and Nagib offers an important whole-world approach that comprehensively addresses the context of production, circulation, representation, and the image of the director. It informs my central question: if all women's cinema is world cinema, what kind of women's cinema is Susanne Bier's? In order to address this question, I focus on three considerations: a) the impact of specific national and transnational production milieus on Bier's cinema's "images of the world"; b) the alignment of her practice with that of other significant female filmmakers to establish her place within feminist legacies to come; and c) an investigation of which narrative and aesthetic traditions locate her films in gendered paradigms of representation. I begin with an account of Bier's profile and the development of her film practice before turning to focus on one of her more recent films, *Serena* (2014), mapping both through the multiple flows and contexts that constitute Bier's relationship to transnational women's cinema.

BIER'S CINEMA IN CONTEXT

Bier's biographical narrative and identity as a filmmaker has never been singularly aligned with Danish nationhood. She studied comparative religion and set design for three years at the University of Jerusalem and architecture in London before attending the National Film School in Denmark. Bier is also part of the second-generation post-war Jewish diaspora—her father fled Nazi Germany to arrive in Denmark in 1933, while her mother's family escaped a Russian pogrom. Bier's films were transnational productions from the outset, and her early works can be characterized most aptly as transnational Nordic comedies. Her first film, *Freud's Leaving Home* (Freud flyttar hemifrån . . ., 1991), was a Swedish/Danish production set in Sweden. Her next film, *Family Matters* (*Det bli'r i familien*, 1993), was a Swedish/Danish/Portuguese production. These films were at the forefront of a movement towards transnational financing and exchange of personnel, particularly across Denmark and Sweden, that was to become ubiquitous. In an interview with Mette Hjort, Bier notes, "when we made *Family Matters* co-productions were very much in their infancy" (Bier quoted in Hjort 2001: 243). As Hjort notes in *Small Nation, Global Cinema: New Danish Cinema*, a particular mode of transnationalism emerged in the mid-nineties, one that was culturally flexible in that it did not demand that the onscreen representation of cultural specificity be proportionate to the funding offered by different nations. The resulting model allowed for the greater "circulation of ideas, people, money and films" (Hjort 2005: 179). Thus, Bier's early films were forerunners of the intensification of Nordic transnational cinema.

If Bier's early films display a strong interest in transnational production, they also frequently explore themes that revolve around family, border crossing, and the problem of identity formation. How might this be understood in relation to film feminisms when Bier's claims about her work have been more focused on the question of cultural identity than gender? During the 2001 interview, Hjort describes how critics in the early part of the director's career described Bier as the "outspoken, forceful, female director who was needed in Danish film" (Hjort 2001: 247). Yet, in response to questions of gender in her films, Bier states:

> I don't make films because I want to make some political statement about women. I do make films in which I say a lot about women, because they're what really interests me. If I were to identify an issue on which I take a radical stance, it would be nationalism, and that issue can of course hardly be said to be irrelevant to gender politics. (Hjort 2001: 247)

Bier's response is compelling, not because it plays down her interest in gender, but because it stresses the intersectionality of gender and nationalism and the accompanying issues she describes, such as racism and migration. She prefaces her statement by noting that "I've been fortunate, for a lot of women have paved the way for me. As a result of their efforts I've never had to fight for the right to be a woman *and* a filmmaker" (Hjort 2001: 247). In observing this intersectionality and making reference to feminist predecessors, Bier implicitly acknowledges the feminist legacies of post-war globalizing women's movements.

While Bier does not identify a strong feminist agenda in her work, at the time of this interview her oeuvre had been predominantly composed of family and romantic comedy genre films (and narratives that often veer towards tragedy). *Freud's Leaving Home*, for example, revolves around Freud, the Swedish daughter of Jewish Holocaust survivors. *The One and Only* (*Den eneste ene*, 1999) tells the story of two Danish couples (one including an Italian spouse) and the web of infidelity that ties them together. Her 2012 film *Love Is All You Need* (*Den skaldede frisør*) returns to the romantic comedy genre and is an intensely international production (Denmark, Sweden, Italy, France, Germany). Written by Anders Thomas Jensen, the predominantly Danish- and English-language film stars Pierce Brosnan and Trine Dyrholm and follows the story of Ida, a hairdresser who has recently undergone treatment for breast cancer. After finding her husband has been unfaithful, she travels to Italy for her daughter's wedding and becomes romantically involved with the groom's father. *Love Is All You Need* emphasizes intergenerational bonds between women, the experiences and subjectivity of women in middle age, and extends the domestic sphere across continents and across sexual orientation. Telling women's stories focused on women's experiences of family relationships, Bier's comedies are oriented towards the popular feminism of women's genres. The question of genre is pivotal to an understanding of Bier's cinema, whether it is drama or comedy. The feminist nuances of her films are apparent in the relationship between genre and the transnational address of the films. In order to map this relationship it is necessary to offer further background to Bier's early career, the development of her thematic focus on drama, and the context for the circulation/production of her more recent film work.

Between 1991 and 2000 Bier directed six feature films, which demonstrates that her profile as a director and her aptitude for negotiating the industrial landscape were quickly consolidated in the early part of her career. This occurred, paradoxically, when the material state support for women's filmmaking in many national contexts had recently diminished. While no specific feminist infrastructure existed in Denmark at the time, the women's film units, film funds, and television initiatives that developed in the 1970s and 1980s in countries such as Germany, Australia, and Canada[1] gave way to the forces of economic rationalism by the early 1990s. There was a confluence of factors in play at this time—initiatives that supported gendered representation were on the wane;[2] the imperative for success at the box office put pressure on national film finance programs; and second-wave feminism as a social movement was experiencing a powerful backlash. It is perhaps testament to the legacies of Nordic feminism that in the 1990s and 2000s New Danish Cinema produced a strong cohort of female directors, such as Lone Scherfig, Paprika Steen, Annette K. Olesen, and Lotte Svendsen.

In 2002 Bier directed the acclaimed Dogme 95-inspired work, *Open Hearts* (*Elsker dig for evigt*). This film marked a turn from comedy towards drama. I bracket the films that follow *Open Hearts* as transnational Nordic dramas, including in this grouping three films that I have referred to elsewhere as a trilogy due to their focus on a male sojourner who traverses international borders: *Brothers* (*Brødre*, 2004), *After the Wedding* (*Efter brylluppet*, 2006), and *In a Better World* (*Hævnen*, 2010) (Smaill 2014: 16). *A Second Chance* (*En chance til*, 2014) is a more recent addition to her body of Nordic dramas. All of these films are products of Bier's collaboration with Thomas Jensen.

With her extensive body of work, Bier has been a pivotal figure in mobilizing and sustaining the transnational flows of Danish cinema. At the height of Dogme 95, Bier's filmmaking was overshadowed by the male-dominated auteurism of the movement. Nevertheless, as White observes, she is one of the most prolific and acclaimed members of the group and the only one of these directors to have a film win an Oscar with *In a Better World* (2015: 6). From another vantage, Bier's cinema not only made a significant contribution to, but was also supported by, intensifying cross-border flows. Her films have enjoyed particular commercial success and wide distribution because they were congruent not only with Nordic transnationalism, but the rationalism of contemporary European cinema industries. In Europe since the 1990s, Thomas Elsaesser writes, "co-productions have become the norm, rather than the exception, and contemporary auteurs feel neither called upon to be 'artists' nor play the role of nationally representative figureheads" (2005: 491). For Elsaesser the director's status is no longer strongly tied to the nation; what matters instead is how well the director's local/national provenance can communicate with global/transnational audiences (Elsaesser 2005: 491). The dramas I noted above employ what Meryl Shriver-Rice refers to as a Nordic style of "psychological realism" (2011: 10) in her discussion of *Brothers*. Yet as Shriver-Rice also observes, "like her *Dogme* work, Bier's *Brothers* is 'non-nationalist' in that it favours a global audience over an emphasis on Danish local culture and inclusion" (2011: 14). The example of *Brothers* is particularly instructive because it was remade in the U.S. in English, scene by scene, which testifies to the perceived translatability of its audience appeal.[3]

While the forms of expression that communicate to audiences across national divides can be explicated in a number of different ways, genre is one of the most prominent mechanisms for augmenting transnational accessibility. The success of classical Hollywood cinema relied upon genre's capacity to draw audiences to the theater based on the promise that their shared needs and expectations would be fulfilled. At its most schematic, "the genre film celebrates our collective sensibilities, providing an array of ideological strategies for negotiating social conflicts" (Schatz 1981: 29). While it is not my intention to deem Bier's Nordic or European cinema a product of Hollywood influence and genre repetition, I wish to acknowledge the enduring audience appeal of generic codes (if not fully fledged genre films) inside and outside the Hollywood system to illuminate the various layers of genre and gender in Bier's cinema. Usually contemporary genre categories are most evident in popular, entertainment (often Hollywood) cinema rather than arthouse cinema. As I have noted elsewhere, however, popular cinema is not a fixed category, and this is exemplified in the case of Bier's Nordic dramas (Smaill 2014). Her work may address a mass audience in Denmark or even France, but a subtitled version will cater to the niche structures of art cinema in the U.K. I suggest that Bier's films are successful in appealing to different audiences in different markets, in part, because they retain the internationally recognizable traces of genre codes, while marking them with a degree of Nordic specificity.[4] I have already described Bier's comedies as women's genres. Many of Bier's dramas engage a different aspect of women's cinema—they convey settings, themes, and narrative sensibilities associated with melodrama.

Brothers, *After the Wedding*, and *In a Better World* are consistently preoccupied with the conflicts and affective charge of extended family relations, and the expectation and crisis of gender roles that come with this. In this respect, their plots recall aspects of the family melodramas of 1950s Hollywood. Yet the trilogy refuses the tight focus on family structures, a focus that, as David Rodowick writes, "is attentive only to problems which concern the family's internal security and economy, and therefore considers its authority to be restricted to issues of private power and patriarchal right" (1987: 270). If melodrama, in its classical incarnation, views the family as a microcosm of the social, working through ideological issues without representing the public sphere, Bier's trilogy connects familial power struggles more explicitly to the social world. The films' domestic settings are squarely located in everyday life in small-town or suburban Denmark. Yet the melodrama is tied to geopolitical concerns, as the films' plotlines extend the action beyond Danish borders. *Brothers*, *After the Wedding*, and *In a Better World* all follow a character's journey to international sites of humanitarian relevance: a U.N. peacekeeping mission to Afghanistan, an orphanage in India, and an African refugee camp respectively. Yet rather than focus on women's experiences of patriarchy, the men in Bier's trilogy are thrown into situations where they must grapple with the tangled expectations of masculinity, class, and ethnicity, and situations of moral uncertainty that revolve around these. If, as I note above, Bier has stated her interest in questions of nationhood, race, and migration, in all of these films this interest is conjoined with the fallibility of masculinity and masculine authority more specifically. In many respects, Bier's strategic approach to genre hinges as much on male melodrama[5] as family melodrama, questioning male patriarchal and at times Western authority by straddling the everyday environments of home and the developing world of the global south.

Consequently, Bier might be seen alongside not only her Danish female contemporaries, but also European transnational filmmakers such as Claire Denis or Monika Treut. However, while Denis and Bier share an interest in the politics of race and migration, Bier's films have much more in common with the genre films of Kathryn Bigelow than the art cinema of Denis. Although Bigelow began her career working on feminist-informed independent cinema, she has found great acclaim directing popular genre cinema. White invokes Bigelow's Academy Award-winning *The Hurt Locker* (2009) to suggest, "it has topical relevance purportedly lacking in most women's films, too often stereotyped as aimed at audiences who are domestic in both senses" (2015: 4). White describes *The Hurt Locker* as a film that explodes stereotypes of women's filmmaking by speaking to audiences about the worldliness of war and the public sphere, thereby transcending the domestic typology of female audiences. Bier's dramas, like many of Bigelow's, bring worldly problems to mainstream audiences, and they do so by offering contemporary versions of long-standing genres. Both directors have also enjoyed a measure of success at the Academy Awards that is rare for female directors. As I noted above, *In a Better World* won the Oscar for Best Foreign Language Film in 2011, but was not selected to screen at Cannes. This fact does not definitely indicate an industry schema of recognition, but supports a certain codification that categorizes Bier's work as closer to Hollywood than arthouse expectations. Like Bigelow, Bier has enjoyed significant success on North American awards and festival circuits, specifically for films exploring settings and themes that emphasize masculine conflict and psychology. However, Bier's films have also been successful with European awards. She has won awards at many European festivals and has been successful in the prestigious Bodil and Robert awards[6] for, in particular, her comedies and her early drama *Open Hearts*. It is these films that have enjoyed the most critical success in Europe, marking out the different parts of her oeuvre with a division between the male melodramas which succeed as global arthouse films and the comedies, which succeed[7] as a domestic/regional cinema.

Bigelow may present images of the world, eschewing the perceived domestic conventions of women's filmmaking, but the diverse composition of Bier's body of work in terms of location, financing, and genre make it a truly varied cinema of the world. Moreover, her oeuvre produces an increasingly broad transnational address to its audience. Her dramas in particular offer an example of the way women's feature filmmaking might forge a relationship with women's genres, such as melodrama, while expanding the precepts and thus the relevance of the narratives to issues of homosocialty, nationhood, and global politics. While an increasingly transnational European production and distribution environment has facilitated Bier's career trajectory, her interest in genre and its imaginative possibilities invites a consideration of her films through a feminist lens. As I explore below, Bier's movements into the sphere of American cinema herald a further context to her women's cinema, adding another set of considerations to the European transnationalism of her work.

TRANSNATIONAL AMERICAN CINEMA: *SERENA*

The two films that I bracket as Bier's transnational American cinema, *Things We Lost in the Fire* (2007)[8] and *Serena*, convey emotional intensity and focus on characters in times of crisis, elements reminiscent of her Nordic dramas. However, both *Things We Lost in the Fire* and *Serena* are English-language films, presenting story worlds in distinctly American settings. While Bier's previous dramas were couched in transnational networks that enabled them to find at least a limited audience in the U.S., *Things We Lost in the Fire* and *Serena* might be perceived as films located more squarely within the

Hollywood paradigm of production and distribution. Yet a closer look reveals a complex relationship to transnational networks and associations.[9] While both films are important within Bier's body of work, I focus on *Serena* because it is one of her most high-budget, high-profile, and, perhaps, notorious films, making it highly significant to her career. It is Bier's least successful film, both critically and commercially, and for this reason it is challenging to address as part of her oeuvre. *Serena* is, nevertheless, an intriguing example that sits at the intersection of mainstream Hollywood and world cinema, women's mobility and gendered representations.

Crucially, American cinema (independent cinema and Hollywood) has always been engaged in cross-border exchange, its history characterized by multidirectional flows of capital, personnel, and films, albeit frequently in ways that reinforce Hollywood imperialism. One of the most visible manifestations of this is the mobility of the director; European directors have enriched American filmmaking throughout history with prominent examples including Fritz Lang, Roman Polanski, Miloš Forman, and Bernardo Bertolucci. While many male directors have made their names in different parts of the world before gaining access to the institutions of Hollywood and American independent cinema, few women have followed this same path; notable exceptions include Jane Campion, Gillian Armstrong, and Niki Caro. Accounting for the mobility of the female director recognizes that while it is difficult for women to achieve employment as feature directors in the U.S., it is even more difficult to gain access to the industry from outside the U.S. Hollywood is an exclusive domain, making Bier's transnational American cinema a critical site for investigation.[10]

Based on the novel of the same name by Ron Rash, *Serena* is set in the Smokey Mountains of North Carolina during the Depression. Against the backdrop of the fledgling logging industry, an emerging timber baron, George Pemberton (Bradley Cooper), marries Serena (Jennifer Lawrence). The industry is brutal for the workers, who are frequently injured or killed, and this violence is set against the couple's ambitions for the business to succeed at all costs. As the narrative progresses they begin to face crises—there is pressure from local authorities to turn the land into parkland, and the couple's fortunes turn with the stock market crash.

In some respects, *Serena* presents a distinct move away from the Nordic dramas that directly preceded it; rather than the preoccupations of contemporary Danish life and international humanitarian landscapes, this film is a lavish period drama. The setting is intensely American, as it takes on the recognizable historical iconography of a Depression-era logging town. Despite the differences, *Serena* is, like the earlier dramas, interested in psychological realism and the psychodynamic of human relationships. While the plot is propelled by the financial desperation brought with the onset of the Depression, it is the

Figure 11.1 Serena's descent into madness is exacerbated following her miscarriage.

relationship between the two protagonists, George and Serena, that focuses the film's drama. In contrast with the Nordic trilogy's accent on masculinity and male sociality, Serena and George are rendered with equal importance, and the film offers an aesthetic and narrative platform for contemplating gendered typologies. Centered on Serena and George (and George's illegitimate son with another woman), the film emphasizes the family's internal workings and domestic life, the machinations of which are clearly rendered with the affective intensity and moral conflicts that are a marker of melodrama. But like Bier's earlier films, the social world is clearly rendered as a force that impacts the vicissitudes of personal relations.

Determined to build a timber empire, George embodies entrepreneurial masculinity, making great sacrifices in order to maintain possession of the land and the business, including murdering his duplicitous business partner, Mr. Buchanan. It is Serena's character arc, however, that motivates the plot's spiral into calamity. When newly married Serena takes a keen interest in the industry, showing herself to be a shrewd businesswoman, George encourages her involvement, to the irritation of Buchanan. Events take a turn when Serena suffers a miscarriage and learns she can no longer bear children. From this point her descent into madness begins (Figure 11.1). George has an illegitimate son, Jacob, conceived before he met Serena, and Jacob's presence fuels Serena's paranoia. Jacob represents, in part, the promise of the continuation of patrilineality, which Serena can no longer fulfill.

The film can be located in a tradition of film and literature that explores the relationship between mental illness and women's experiences, especially in the confines of domesticity.[11] The most apt film associations are Jane Campion's early films *Sweetie* (1989) and *An Angel at My Table* (1990), which feature female protagonists dealing with mental illness, albeit in markedly different ways. Yet *The Piano* (1993) offers the most important reference point. Like *Serena*, it centers on the psychology and interior world of a female protagonist negotiating a male world, and the viewer's knowledge of this interior world is informed by the dark, Gothic landscape that surrounds her. Gothic settings in nature frequently infuse narratives with threat and uncertainty,

Figure 11.2 The opening shots of the film establish the location: the eerie Smokey Mountains of North Carolina.

Figure 11.3 Transitions between scenes in *Serena* consistently return to images of the mountains, reminding the viewer of their constant presence.

inferring that something is out of kilter and exacerbating a character's isolation as they navigate unfamiliar places and situations. Both Ada in *The Piano* and Serena are newcomers to their environments and, in both cases, the nonhuman environment includes fecund forested mountains which provide a malevolent landscape that augments the increasing desperation of their experiences.

The eerie Smokey Mountains are a constant presence in *Serena*'s mise-en-scène—not only is the small logging town set at the base of the mountains, transitions between scenes constantly cut to the expanse of trees, mountains, and the mist that covers them (Figure 11.2, Figure 11.3). The topography of the natural environment looms above and surrounds the couple and the workers at the camp, offering a sense of both isolation and quiet darkness (Figure 11.4). The setting informs the almost preternatural sensibility that infuses the interaction between human activity and the nonhuman environment in *Serena*. The early scenes are rendered from George's perspective; in the opening sequence, the audience is introduced to George while he is out hunting (Figure 11.5). He only comes across bobcats, and he tasks Galloway, known for his "gift of vision," to find him the mythical panther living in the hills. Hunting scenes weave through the plot (including the determined search for the panther), and it is when the two are hunting a bear that George shoots and kills Buchanan. The forest, moreover, is a source of danger to the workers, whether via rattlesnakes or industrial accidents.[12] In the film's

Figure 11.4 The small logging town is set at the base of the mountains, and the topography of the natural environment looms above and surrounds the couple and the workers.

Figure 11.5 *Serena* begins as a story told from George's (Bradley Cooper) perspective, and the viewer first encounters him when he is out hunting.

Figure 11.6 Serena and Galloway hunt down Jacob and his mother, Rachel, first slitting the throat of the child's babysitter. They hunt at night, moving from cabin to cabin.

final act, Serena, with Galloway as her accomplice, hunts down Jacob and his mother, Rachel, first slitting the throat of the child's babysitter (Figure 11.6). They do so at night, and as they move from cabin to cabin, the threat posed by Serena's resolve permeates the dark forested mountains.

In *Serena*, George and Serena both experience fear and desperation, yet for different reasons—George fears the loss of his business and then his son (at the hands of Serena), and Serena fears that she will lose George, her status and belonging due to the existence of Jacob. It is significant that, in comparison with women in Campion's films and many other explorations of female subjectivity in crisis, Serena is not as confined by domesticity or patriarchal repression—indeed, her agency reflects the freedoms that women of her class were experiencing during the liberal 1920s. Her psychosis seems to be partly historical (her family was killed in a fire and she is the only survivor, casting doubt on her involvement in the tragedy), partly triggered by the trauma of losing a child. Yet, as with George, her ambitions are great, and her miscarriage marks a certain failure to actualize the potential of her status both in terms of family and capital. In the face of this failure, she becomes ruthless and single-minded.

The film was produced by 2929 Entertainment, a U.S.-based company, but co-financed by French "mini-major" Studiocanal with a budget of $25–30 million. *Serena* was largely produced at Prague's Barrandov Studio and shot on Czech locations (Hopewell 2012). The film went through multiple edits, and was shelved for two years before it was released in 2014. Film critics and audiences responded unfavorably to *Serena*, and it only returned a fraction of its budget—$176,391 domestically and $4,899,231 internationally (*Serena*, Box Office Mojo). There was much industry press speculation about the difficulties in securing a successful edit of the film, and this was heightened by the involvement of Cooper and Lawrence, both high-profile actors.

While the film is centrally preoccupied with female subjectivity and can be couched in relation to traditions of women's filmmaking, most notably the work of Jane Campion, *Serena* also aspires to an epic tradition, with events and characters playing into familiar morality tales. The plot and characters make clear references to Shakespeare's *Macbeth*, a story that also revolves around the folly of ambition; Serena's ruthlessness and downfall are evocative of a 1920s Lady Macbeth. Employing the recognizable vernacular of the Shakespearean tradition is a move that sits well with the film's transnational production context—if *Serena* was designed to resonate with Western audiences outside as much as inside the U.S., the universal themes it conveys offer an avenue for achieving this.

In his discussion of world cinema, Elsaesser describes a grouping of films in which

> the traditional line between national and international, as well as between art cinema and commercial cinema, is no longer as clear cut as it was during the confrontation between Europe and Hollywood between 1945 and roughly 1990. All these cinemas are more adept at mixing idioms, more transnational in their styles, as well as having more of a crossover appeal. (2005: 498)

Indeed, there is much evidence to suggest that *Serena* was intended to find its success in just such a productive blurring of boundaries as Elssaesser describes, since it brings an arthouse sensibility to high-budget commercial cinema. In an article for *Variety*, John Hopewell describes the financing model for *Serena* as one that "has created a kind of hybrid: the auteur mainstream movie." He deems *Serena* "a classic example of how U.S. productions are taking advantage of European financing opportunities." While, arguably, such opportunities have been in place for some time (and Hollywood's reach has always relied upon global distribution), *Serena* belongs to a mode of production in which the co-financing model is employed to produce wide appeal both in Europe and in the U.S.

With a French funding partner, a Danish director, and a Czech shooting location, there is much to support the notion that *Serena* is, in a significant sense, a European film. Notably, there is further similarity with *The Piano* here, which was co-produced by French company Ciby 2000. Both *Serena* and *The Piano* might be seen as part of a French tradition in which costume drama has developed as a significant second-order genre since the post-war period.[13] Further locating the film within women's filmmaking traditions, Lawrence brought with her, at the time of casting, an aura of American women's independent filmmaking, having just appeared in *Winter's Bone* (2010), directed by Debra Granik. This film is also set in a rural mountainous area, the Ozarks, and revolves around Lawrence's seventeen-year-old character, Rae.[14] At this time Lawrence was yet to make *The Hunger Games* (2012) and was more firmly associated with independent cinema. Moreover, Bier had to convince producers to cast Lawrence and Cooper. She describes the relevance of this casting choice: "But we cast them both and, in the interim, they became these huge stars, and that changed the expectations around the movie. It was always a dark, dark, love story. Never a mainstream film" (Maher 2014). Bier's assertion that *Serena* was never meant to be a mainstream film suggests, perhaps, that she anticipated it to be more aligned with European popular costume drama or American independent cinema of the kind Lawrence was previously associated with. However, the film's budget required mainstream appeal to make a return on investments.[15] Moreover, because the setting is quintessentially American, *Serena* (especially without considering the context of production) can be persuasively deemed as first and foremost an American film principally making use of global distribution.

Even as an example of a world cinema that cuts across traditional film categories (such as art cinema and commercial cinema, or auteur film and mainstream film), there is an unresolved tension surrounding *Serena*'s address to the audience, especially in the film's appeal to mainstream expectations. This is apparent in the film's amalgamation of an epic (Shakespeare-inspired) costume drama with the dark psychology of a Gothic sensibility reminiscent of *The Piano*. The film nonetheless offers an example of how the flows of women's filmmaking practice are not outside but rather directly infuse the mixing of idioms and transnational style that Elsaesser refers to. With *Serena*, Bier cements her place as a director who takes on the world by lending her authorial signature to a complex manifestation of world cinema.

While most of Bier's films are, at least in part, set in Denmark, they focus on the local (including distant locales) in ways that emphasize personal conflicts, emotions, and moral dilemmas rather than cultural specificity. Thus, rather than non-nationalist, her films rework the markers of national cultural representation in order to address an expanded audience. This is achieved through an adherence to certain genres that accentuate the politics of selfhood: the romantic comedy and the melodrama. Her romantic comedies are more clearly female-oriented in their focus on female characters and their appeals to the audience. But it is her dramas, including *Serena*, that grapple with the subtleties of the human condition, especially as it manifests at the intersection of social expectation and family crisis.

In couching her discussion of women's cinema and the world in relation to Virginia Woolf's well-known claim that "as a woman my country is the whole world," McHugh is careful to point out that while these words indicate women's troubled relation to the nation, they also articulate a privileged form of desire. Well after Woolf was writing, such a claim to the world, as McHugh notes, "has come to exemplify the privileged and ethnocentric universalism of second-wave feminism" (112). This consideration is instructive when accounting for Bier's work and the politics of location because her position is a privileged one—a career that begins with the enabling context of Nordic cinema (and Nordic feminism) is very different to the context of, for example, third- or fourth-world cinemas. This should not undercut the importance of Bier and her cinema as a site of feminist film studies investigation, but rather offers a further perspective that informs an understanding of her place in women's film culture. I have endeavored to show how Bier's cinema has worked in tandem with an intensification of transnational finance and distribution at a time when women's filmmaking is more reliant on its potential for commercial success than state support. Bier's cinema is an exemplar for successfully navigating the demands of transnational production. More than this, her film work should also be viewed alongside the legacy of other first-world women filmmakers who have occupied privileged positions on the world filmmaking stage, such as Kathryn Bigelow and Jane Campion.

Clear parallels can be drawn between Bier's work and the films of these prominent female filmmakers, whether it is in terms of style, theme, or genre/industry categorization. There are also important distinctions between these directors—Bier did not train and begin her career in an Anglophone national cinema context, and her filmmaking practice came of age at a different industrial moment, providing the different structures of opportunity that I have outlined. All of these factors distinguish her transnational women's cinema from that of Bigelow and Campion. A lucid understanding of the female director must be attuned to observing how women's film might function as a shared culture while also mapping differences across contexts, films, and career pathways. In closing, I wish to stress that the question should not be whether and why, as scholars, we should devote attention to women directors. Rather, the task at hand is to offer rigorous consideration of *how* and with what tools we account for the diverse work and experiences of female filmmakers. Important scholarship continues to focus on the changing status of the director and the politics of auteurism[16] while focusing almost exclusively on films directed by men. A response to this omission should not offer analysis of token female directors. An antidote to the normalization of masculinist approaches requires a wide view of film culture that encompasses the world of women's film production, histories, and audiences and the factors that enable and limit this world. Susanne Bier's world cinema provides a rich and nuanced example that underlines the value of such an approach.

NOTES

1. See McHugh (2009) for a discussion of this infrastructure in Australia particularly, and Elsaesser (1989) for detail about the German context.
2. There has been a recent return to initiatives to address gender equity in the industry in Australia (the Gender Matters initiative introduced in 2016) and the U.K. (the Three Ticks initiative introduced in 2014). For an analysis of the gender quotas that have been in place in the Swedish film industry since 2006, see Jansson (2017).
3. See Shriver-Rice (2011) for a fuller discussion of the implications of this process of remaking.
4. See Ramon Lobato and Mark David Ryan (2011) for an insightful study of distribution and contemporary genre studies.
5. See Janet Staiger (2008) for a discussion of the male melodrama that, while focused on the genre of film noir, is relevant to Bier's cinema.
6. The Bodil Awards are Danish film awards decided by the Danish Film Critics' Association, and the Robert Awards are the national industry awards decided by the Danish Film Academy each year.
7. A particularly interesting example in this respect is *Love is All You Need*. While the film was largely shot in Italy and financed by multiple European sources, it made more than $7 million of its total $10 million globally at the box office in Denmark. It made $1.6 million in the U.S. (Box Office Mojo). The film also won the Robert Audience Award for comedy in 2013 and was selected as best comedy film at the 26th European Film Awards, highlighting its European/Danish success.
8. *Things We Lost in the Fire* stars two well-known actors, Halle Berry and Benicio del Toro (one African American and one Spanish). While the film was distributed by DreamWorks Pictures, it was produced by director Sam Mendes' British production company, Neal Street Pictures, and shot in Canada. *Things We Lost in the Fire* is set in the U.S. city of Seattle. It explores intimate relationships within families, the plot revolving around the experiences of a widow who invites her husband's troubled best friend to live with her and her two children as he recovers from a drug addiction. The film circles around the consequences of loss and is intensely character-driven.

9. For example, while both films failed to achieve commercial success relative to their budgets, they found more receptive audiences, at least in terms of box-office measures, outside of the U.S.
10. If few non-U.S. women directors have access to the Hollywood industrial machine, very few also have access to budgets on the scale of *Serena*. It is, however, comparable to Sofia Coppola's *Marie Antoinette* (2006) at $40 million and Catherine Hardwicke's *Twilight* (2008) at $37 million.
11. *The Yellow Wallpaper* by Charlotte Perkins Gilman and Sylvia Plath's *The Bell Jar* are perhaps the most well-known literary examples.
12. Notably, in both *The Piano* and *Serena*, the forest or bush is the scene of physical impairment caused by the blade of an axe. Ada's finger is cut off by Alisdair Stewart, and Galloway (a logging worker) slips against a tree, his hand accidentally cut off by an axe. Serena saves him with a tourniquet, and their futures become intertwined from then on.
13. See Susan Hayward (2008) for an account of this genre.
14. Bier states in an interview that she had "seen Jennifer in *Winter's Bone* and just thought she was an incredible performer. I knew she would be right for the lead role in *Serena*" (Johnson, 2014).
15. Also supporting the film's intended mainstream status is the fact that the scriptwriter appointed to write the novel-to-film adaptation for *Serena*, Christopher Kyle, worked with Oliver Stone on the script for *Alexander* (2004) and notably also worked on the scripts for *The Weight of Water* (2000) and *K-19: The Widowmaker* (2002), both directed by Kathryn Bigelow. All are high-budget films with strong genre designations.
16. For just one example see the recent collection edited by Seung-hoon Jeong and Jeremi Szaniawski, titled *The Global Auteur: The Politics of Authorship in 21st Century Cinema* (2016).

BIBLIOGRAPHY

Elsaesser, Thomas (1989), *New German Cinema: A History*, New Brunswick, NJ: Rutgers University Press.

Elsaesser, Thomas (2005), *European Cinema: Face to Face with Hollywood*, Amsterdam: Amsterdam University Press.

Hayward, Susan (2008), "Reviewing quality cinema: French costume drama of the 1950s," *Studies in French Cinema* 8.3: 229–44.

Hjort, Mette (2003), "Susanne Bier," in Mette Hjort and Ib Bondebjerg (eds.), *The Danish Directors: Dialogues on a Contemporary National Cinema*, Bristol and Chicago: Intellect Books, pp. 240–8.

Hjort, Mette (2005), *Small Nation, Global Cinema: The New Danish Cinema*, Minneapolis: University of Minnesota Press.

Hopewell, John (2012), "Serena: New model for co-finance," *Variety*, February 8, <http://variety.com/2012/film/markets-festivals/serena-new-model-for-co-finance-1118049901/> (accessed Novermber 14, 2017).

Jansson, Maria (2017), "Gender equality in Swedish film policy: Radical interpretations and 'unruly' women," *European Journal of Women's Studies* 24.2.

Jeong, Seung-hoon, and Jeremi Szaniawski (2016), *The Global Auteur: The Politics of Authorship in 21st Century Cinema*, London: Bloomsbury.

Johnson, Mark (2014), "Serena director Susanne Bier gives NFTS Masterclass," *Screen Daily*, October 23, <http://www.screendaily.com/home/blogs/serena-director-susanne-bier-gives-nfts-masterclass/5078966.article> (accessed November 14, 2017).

Lobato, Ramon, and Mark David Ryan (2011), "Rethinking genre studies through distribution analysis: Issues in international Horror movie circuits," *New Review of Film and Television Studies* 9.2: 188–203.

Maher, Kevin (2014), "Jennifer Lawrence was the star . . . So what could possibly go wrong?" *The Times*, October 22, <http://infoweb.newsbank.com/resources/doc/nb/news/1511F2EBB0B73CB8?p=AWN> (accessed March 12, 2017)..

McHugh, Kathleen (2009), "The world and the soup: Historicizing media feminisms in transnational contexts," *Camera Obscura*, no. 72: 111–50.

Nagib, Lúcia (2006), "Towards a positive definition of World Cinema," in Stephanie Dennison and Song Hwee Lim (eds.), *Remapping World Cinema: Identity, Culture and Politics in Film*, London: Wallflower Press, pp. 30–7.

Nagib, Lúcia (2011), *World Cinema and the Ethics Of Realism*, New York: Continuum.

Plath, Sylvia (1971), *The Bell Jar*, New York: Harper & Row.

Rodowick, David N. (1987), "Madness, authority and ideology: The domestic melodrama of the 1950s," in Christine Gledhill (ed.), *Home is Where the Heart Is: Studies in Melodrama and the Woman's Film*, London: BFI Publishing.

Schatz, Thomas (1981), *Hollywood Genres: Formulas, Filmmaking and the Hollywood System*, New York: Random House.

Serena, Box Office Mojo, <http://www.boxofficemojo.com/movies/?page=main&id=serena.htm> (accessed November 14, 2017).

Shriver-Rice, Meryl (2009), "Adapting National Identity: Ethical Borders Made Suspect in the Hollywood Version of Susanne Bier's *Brothers*," *Film International* vol. 9, issue 2: 8–19.

Smaill, Belinda (2014), "The Male Sojourner, the Female Director, and Popular European Cinema: The Worlds of Susanne Bier," *Camera Obscura* vol. 29, no. 1, 85: 5–31.

Staiger, Janet (2008), "Film noir as male melodrama: The politics of film genre labeling," in Lincoln Geraghty and Mark Jancovich (eds.), *The Shifting Definitions of Genre: Essays on Labeling Films, Television Shows and Media*, Jefferson, NC: McFarland, pp. 71–91.

Stetson, Charlotte Perkins (1892), "The Yellow Wallpaper: A Story," *The New England Magazine* 11.5: 647–57.

White, Patricia (2015), *Women's Cinema, World Cinema: Projecting Contemporary Feminisms*, Durham, NC: Duke University Press.

CHAPTER 12

From Local to Global: The Bier/Jensen Screenwriting Collaboration

Cath Moore

Denmark, as a small filmmaking nation, has gone through multiple transformations since garnering consecutive Oscar wins in the 1980s.[1] Such creative mutability is largely a result of constraint-based artistic approaches that grew out of the Dogme 95 manifesto and the pivotal mid-1990s industrial overhaul under which the New Danish Cinema movement emerged. As Mette Hjort suggests, regeneration of this sort is dependent upon cinematic representations that transcend national borders and consciousness, narratives that intertwine through commonality of story or shared language, one not based on dialect but discourse (Hjort 2005: 39). While Hjort's comment affirms the value of universal creative exchange, it also reflects Denmark's industrial sensibility.

While Danish directors, such as Lars von Trier, Thomas Vinterberg, Lone Scherfig, and, more recently, Nicolaj Arcel and Tobias Lindholm, have swept film festival awards and attained international visibility, collaboration rather than singularity defines contemporary Danish cinema. One of the major differences between Danish cinema practices and other film industries is the focus on writer/director partnerships and story collaboration. This approach has provided Danish film practitioners with a distinct and visionary approach to creative development that is unlike any other national film industry. Susanne Bier's work with the prolific screenwriter Anders Thomas Jensen best reflects the transnational capacities of this cultural model. Over the past fifteen years, the duo have co-written six feature films and provide a clear example of the *collaborative auteur* approach to development[2] that is increasingly seen as a unique feature of Danish cinema (Redvall 2010: 76). A successful writer/director in his own right, Jensen's body of work expresses a vastly different sensibility than Bier's. Indeed, any synergy between the two may have originally seemed unlikely. However, their filmography is the result of one of the most critically acclaimed and commercially successful partnerships to straddle both domestic and international markets.

ANDERS THOMAS JENSEN'S DARK COMEDIES

In contrast to Bier, Jensen's writer/director sensibility is far more focused on the local than the global. His films are in Danish with Danish actors and characters and rely on shared notions of Danish culture. As a director, Jensen is somewhat unusual as he bypassed the National Film School of Denmark, yet still managed to forge a prolific output as an independent screenwriter and director. His self-written and directed comedic films possess a distinct style that is unburdened by film school expectations or institutional styles, not unlike how Wes Anderson's cinematic style has evolved unimpeded by the demands of film theory or institutional expectation. Unlike Bier's predilection for drama situated in the everyday, Jensen's films are filled with the strange and the unlikely. The critical acclaim Jensen receives for his ability to "at once repulse and amuse us at almost every turn" (Maksimiuk 2016) endorses such eccentric excess. As Shriver-Rice notes, Jensen's cinematic world is marked by the perverse and absurd (Shriver-Rice 2015: 45), which is arguably dependent upon his preference for male sociality and behavior as the vehicle for conflict and comedy. Marked by a playful amalgamation of genres, his darkly absurdist comedies tap into a distinctly Danish sense of humor. Bestowed with a biblical fatalism, Jensen's narratives often take the shape of modern-day fables. Like Bier, his characters are often struck by misfortune or overcome with desire, but lack the self-awareness that might provide resolution or relief. Often loud, brutish, or unsophisticated, Jensen's male characters exude a physicalized presence; their limited worldview generates indifference and highlights their ignorance of the world at large.

More obviously than many of his Danish contemporaries, Jensen deliberately chooses to use a hybridized genre form, and in doing so reconfigures traditional ideas about the use of genre. In interviews, he has been forthcoming on this strategy, stating:

> I usually want to make films in which I embrace all genres. I like stories, which play with the idea of genre. I need to check if I can mix slapstick with horror, drama and comedy, every time. Finding the right balance is the key. (quoted in Maksimuik 2015)

Jensen's willingness to experiment with form reiterates the risk-taking ethos that underpins New Danish Cinema, where conventional thinking is not a prime consideration. In many ways, Jensen's oeuvre reiterates film style as an aesthetic informed by thematic and structural principles (Hjort 2012: 9). His approach also aligns with the collaborative and egalitarian spirit of contemporary Danish filmmaking as he also works with actors as part of the development process. As he explains it:

> I have the basic idea and I do like a flash draft with the structure in it and the basic elements of the characters, but I'll send that out to the cast and we'll read it. I'll meet with them and we'll do readings and I'll rewrite. I like to create the characters along with the actors. I always try it when I do a Susanne Bier film . . . I really like to implement all of their stuff because they're really talented actors, so why not let them work along with you? (quoted in Saito 2016)

Though Jensen's work consists predominantly of Danish-language films, his prolific capacity and talent has attracted attention from Hollywood. Directed and co-written by fellow Dane Nicolaj Arcel, Hollywood's *Dark Tower* (2017) is a continuation of Stephen King's novel series of the same name. It seems fitting that Jensen should be a part of the film's screenwriting team, given the multi-genre framework traverses fantasy, Western, action, and horror.

BIER'S SCREEN WORLD

When trying to establish the creative dimensions of this unique partnership, examining their aesthetic preferences as individual practitioners becomes an important consideration. For Bier, a Jewish heritage that involves her father being forced to flee Germany and to later flee Denmark with Bier's mother clearly exists as a creative preoccupation with abrupt irreversible change. The disquieting nature of Bier's screen worlds, where bad things happen to good people, arguably reflects a cultural heritage shaped by betrayal. A cautionary apprehension that tomorrow may not be as it is today is, as Bier reiterates, "very much a Jewish thing" (quoted in Gold 2007). Her first foray into Hollywood with *Things we Lost in the Fire* (2007) depicts a family fractured by the unexpected death of their husband/father and the emotionally fraught path to recovery. Yet the empathetic spirit that persists throughout offers a hopeful subtext, one that reflects Bier's personal approach to reconciling loss.

Bier's Jewish heritage and reverence for family have also afforded her access to forms of communication within families (quoted in Hjort and Bjondberg 2003: 242) and a desire to portray humanity without an overarching sense of cynicism. Indeed, belonging to a minority culture has arguably provided some relativity with which to revise what might be intrinsically Nordic about Bier's way into the screen story. In contrast to the realism and restraint associated with greater Scandinavian cinema, her films explore the psychodynamics of family and intimate relationships through bold yet nuanced performances. Bier actively challenges the subdued nature of Nordic expression, wary of what she sees as "an intellectual timidity," and insists that "you can't be ashamed of big emotions if you make movies" (quoted in Hoggard 2013).

Bier's adherence or belonging to any particular mode of film genre such as "melodrama" is complex, rendering her work as drama that involves comedy. We would benefit from viewing her work not only as a result of collaboration, but also as a hybrid of various genre modes (drama, melodrama, romantic comedy, etc.). One example of Bier's genre mixing is *The One and Only* (*Den eneste ene*, written by Kim Fupz Aakeson, 1999). This romantic comedy plus drama provided Bier with her initial domestic success, as it became one of the most popular Danish films of the 1990s. Her ability to imbue comedy with a sense of pathos facilitated a passage into the medium of TV with the BBC/AMC drama series *The Night Manager* (2016). As executive producer Simon Cornwell expressed, Bier's other comedy, *Love Is All You Need* (*Den skaldede frisør*, 2012), demonstrated her capacity to produce drama with a lightness of touch (quoted in Saner 2016) that could provide dimension to the series. While *The Night Manager* (2016) was critically acclaimed, stepping into preconceived projects is not always easy to navigate, as Bier's second American feature, *Serena* (2015), demonstrates. Bier has conceded that the film lost itself in post-production amidst the growing trajectories of its leads Jennifer Lawrence and Bradley Cooper, and what was essentially a psychologically dark love story was inaccurately billed as a mainstream romance (Jagernouth 2014). From an industrial perspective, the film's lukewarm reception indicates the difficulties of working inside Hollywood. Such Hollywood-style hierarchical systems are far removed from the collaborative egalitarianism present throughout the Danish chain of production, which has heavily contributed to the success of the Bier and Jensen partnership.

This small-nation Danish context may also provide a better context for Bier to flex her directorial skills with actors. Bier's ability to understand and articulate the lived experience has been noted in her reputation as an actor's director. The reciprocity she fosters during production provides a shared resonance that supports authentic performances. As Danish actor Mads Mikkelsen attests, she is "aware of human nature in general and can tell when it's not there . . . it's comfortable to know that we're not leaving the scene until it feels right" (quoted in Gold 2007). Knowing what is "right" is also a question of creative authorship and directorial intuition. As Swedish actor Mikael Persbrandt suggests, "She knows what she wants to say and you can be confident in that [as an actor] and enjoy it, and do complicated stories about human beings" (quoted in Saner 2016). Bier's aesthetic approach to emotions and intimacy also adds a

Figure 12.1 The use of close-ups has become an important marker of Bier's screen aesthetic (Stine Fischer Christensen as Anna in *After the Wedding*).

sense of complexity (Figure 12.1). With a proclivity for the lingering close-up, her frame consistently focuses on sensual body parts such as the hands, eyes, and lips (Lupher 2016). This tactic infuses her work with an erotically charged tension, providing a dramatic pendulum that swings between apprehension and release. As Danish producer Sidsel Hybschmann comments:

> Susanne's close-ups have a kind of sensual and delicate allure that makes them quite effective emotionally. In terms of what makes it [her films] powerful—well she is very good at her craft. She knows how to make the most of her actors and has a very acute sense of exactly what each scene and shift is about and what the effect of particular details will be. (2015)

The presentation of masculinity is another important distinction regarding Bier's directorial preferences. As director for hire, her American films *Things We Lost in the Fire* (2007) and *Serena* (2014) are defined by intimate relationships between couples, but still concentrate on single masculine points of view. The ease with which Bier speaks to and about her male protagonists (Smaill 2014: 10) is an instinct that she says naturally intersects with Jensen's ease with men:

> I always feel very comfortable in a world of men, more so than in a world of women. Anders Thomas writes the script, and he's a man. I think he feels a lot more comfortable in a world of men than in a world of women. I could definitely describe a woman as well, but I feel very comfortable and very curious describing men. (quoted in Feinstein 2007)

This masculine world reconfigures her dramas away from what is often expected of women directors, as many critics view a woman director's work and expect an immersive, inclusive site of feminized concerns towards cinematic space, as defined by Pam Cook (cited in Gledhill 2012: 3).

Though the Bier/Jensen filmography is often characterized as intimate and insightful portrayals of intense catastrophe, their narrative arcs largely reconcile loss or moral transgression with hope. This sense of trauma acknowledges the dramatic pendulum that swings between fear and hope and, as Jensen acknowledges, the "humanness" Bier attains by immersing herself within a character's unrelenting reality. Ultimately all Bier/Jensen characters are at the mercy of existential fears and human failings. Bier's focus on personal forgiveness, integrity, and compassion imbues her films with a humanism that is at once strikingly compassionate while still managing to convey a sense of dramatic restraint.

Significantly, dramatic restraint of this type recognizes the limitations of personal transformation within the narrative timeline of a feature film and reflects a kind of cinematic secularism. In Denmark, a country where the Lutheran church is usually seen as a cultural rather than religious entity, the absence of a more transcendent narrative arc like those often associated with Christian doctrine is expected. Hollywood productions, by comparison, tend to reflect a national psyche bound to Christian morality. In these circumstances, the morally corrupt must either go through a complete metamorphosis or be killed. Within the Bier/Jensen screen story, virtue, or the attainment of its moral equivalency, is never deliberately imposed. Rather, a sense of moral fortitude persists within the protagonist, delivering a bittersweet narrative completion that may well be the inevitable existential tension of twenty-first-century individuals torn between local responsibilities and global forces.

The harmony and, sometimes, dissonance provided by these two creative dances—chaos and possibility, as well as the recognition of human imperfection—at the intersection of intimate local sensibilities and overwhelming global problems, draw on thematic connections between childhood, masculinity, and violence. In order to better frame this, let us look at Bier/Jensen narrative practices and more closely analyze their film texts. A unique production context is central to this creative collaboration, which finds its subtlety and power in narrative patterns and aesthetic sensibility.

DANISH STORY WRITING COLLABORATION AND THE BIER/JENSEN NARRATIVE MODEL

The Bier/Jensen partnership is a primary example of a particularly Danish approach to screen story development and creative practice. The duo are situated within a wider collaborative context that includes Kim Fupz Aakeson and Pernille Fischer Christensen (*En Familie/A Family*, 2010; *En du elsker/Someone you Love*, 2014), Nikolaj Arcel and Rasmus Heisterberg (*Man som hatar Kvinnor/The Girl with the Dragon Tattoo*, 2009; *En kongelig affaere/A Royal*

Affair, 2012; *Fasandraeberne/The Absent One*, 2014); and Thomas Vinterberg and Tobias Lindholm (*Submarino/Submarino*, 2010; *Jagten/The Hunt*, 2012).

Story collaboration approaches filmmaking as a multiplicative process, one that utilizes problem-finding and -solving as a key developmental strategy (Redvall 2010: 52). While one might see the co-story credit as a particularly Danish approach to script development, the critical and commercial success of the Bier/Jensen oeuvre is largely unparalleled. Their preference for highly dramatic stories focused on personal conflict that transcends the local domestic space of Denmark (Livingston 2012: 77) has become a thematic codifier for their work in which the interplay between emotion and ethics provides a deliberate means of chaos.[3] Though the Bier/Jensen creative process lacks formality, there is a consistent pathway into the story, as Bier explains:

> We'll build the story little by little . . . We never have a synopsis. We don't do treatment either. We can't actually make the movie until we have the matter of the characters. (quoted in Saner 2016)

As a female director with a proclivity for male characters, Bier's films often service a feminist discourse on gender representation. Yet, I would argue, this inclination is best observed as part of the collaborative sensibility she shares with or expresses most with Jensen. Her interest in masculine tropes plays out in her male characters' flaws, and the ways in which she ties violence and childhood to masculine education and action.

VIOLENCE AND CHILDREN IN *A BETTER WORLD*

In terms of Danish industrial policy and production's shift from the local towards the global, film critic Kim Skotte attributes significant demarcation value to the 2010 global success of *In a Better World* (Skotte 2011). In his role as doctor, protagonist Anton travels between Denmark and a medical station, serving refugees in South Sudan. The film's binational setting supports an intensification of the unfolding narrative's range of ideas, which includes themes pertaining to revenge, violence, and justice. Bier's interest in narratives that reach beyond discrete national borders was already articulated through her earlier film with Jensen, *After the Wedding* (*Efter brylluppet*, 2006), which thematizes global mobility from a Danish perspective (Smaill 2014: 10) through the Danish aid worker Jacob (Figure 12.2). While responsible for an orphanage in India, Jacob learns that he has a daughter in Denmark, and he must subsequently come to terms with prioritizing familial responsibilities between the two spaces. The presence and utility of an alternate setting in the global south deposits the protagonist into the chaos and misfortune of others.[4]

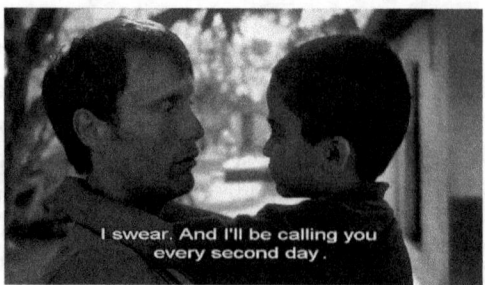

Figure 12.2 Jacob (Mads Mikkelsen) says goodbye to Indian orphan Pramod (Neeral Mulchandani), promising he will return from Denmark in time for the boy's birthday (*After the Wedding*).

Figure 12.3 A South Sudanese refugee begs Anton (Mikael Persbrandt) not to help the barbaric Big Man, an injured warlord who has just arrived for treatment. Bier's acknowledgment of a problematic and persistent first-/third-world divide is clearly reflected in the mise-en-scène and separation of characters.

As the external third world, India is rendered as a problematic space, one that can only be "fixed" or at least managed by the authority of a Western outsider. This world sits in contrast to Denmark, the personalized world, where redemption and a sense of agency are found. The tonal quality of *In a Better World* and *After the Wedding* rests largely with the interrogation of unease that lies between these realms, which provides an acknowledgment of inequity rather than a narrative quest to resolve injustice (Figure 12.3).

The inclusion of India and South Sudan as alternate national settings draws protagonists Anton and Jacob out into the world at large. The subsequent spatial tension is emblematic of the ethical dilemma that drives the Bier/Jensen story engine, but it also engages a key thematic question: how does one navigate both spaces and also forge a coherent identity? Jacob has access to both settings, yet he is unable to inhabit either on a permanent basis without a significant sacrifice. Similarly, Anton in *In a Better World* must reconcile his need to implement his Scandinavian values in a third-world space. Despite a commitment to pacifism, he finds himself struggling with his own aggressive impulses, and finally gives in and allows them to play a decisive role in another man's demise. When the injured warlord Big Man arrives in the camp where most of his dead or injured victims are being treated, Anton's moral code is destabilized. He shoves the incapacitated warlord out of the medical station, knowing full well that the refugees will seek vengeance. Sanctioned by Anton's lack of intervention, they kill Big Man in a cathartic, primal act of collective wrath. In this appropriation of justice, Anton's role as bystander becomes a violently charged position that goes against his pacifist beliefs.

Both films utilize different national settings as an important facet of story construction to tie together a visualization of a shared humanity. In this way, disparate realities are bound together to reveal Bier's desire to challenge a belief that "the third world is away from us . . . and that's not true, it's really part of our own world" (quoted in Douglas 2011). This use and emphasis on Danish domestic space can be seen as anchoring the Nordic concerns regarding childhood, masculinity, and violence. A gendered presentation of childhood is a distinct component of Bier/Jensen world-building, one that mirrors a Nordic preference for depicting relations on screen between sons and parents more frequently than parents and daughters (Martinsson 2014: 40). This is evidenced in *After the Wedding* through a first/third world parallel: impoverishment in India with Jacob's favored male orphan, Pramod, and affluence in Denmark with Jørgen's twin boys. Jacob's special bond with Pramod is threatened when he returns to Denmark to secure much needed funding from Jørgen, a wealthy benefactor (Figure 12.4). Here we see Jørgen playfully put his twin boys to bed at their country mansion. While overtly bourgeois, this presentation of a comfortable first-world setting becomes an entry point for transnational audiences through an implicit "elsewhere" (Smaill 2014: 21) both on and off screen. Expressions of childhood in these two films confirm the efficacy of Ib Bondebjerg's theory of the Bier/Jensen double narrative strategy (Bondebjerg 2014: 36), whereby global issues are mirrored against localized conflicts. In both films, the application of this strategy allows the audience to be of the world at large while simultaneously being privy to distinctly Danish

Figure 12.4 In contrast to the sparse Indian orphanage, Jørgen (Rolf Lassgard) reads a bedtime story to his twin boys, Martin and Morten (Frederik and Kristian Gullits Ernst), in their opulent country mansion (*After the Wedding*).

concerns. For example, in *In a Better World*, Anton's son Elias is bullied at school because he's a gawky teenager who speaks with a Swedish accent. The "you are not from here" conflict is universal, the context cultural. Similarly, a plot-based division between childhood and adulthood reinforces an idealization, and subsequent disillusionment, that children, regardless of gender, often experience as a rite of passage.

In both films, thematic threads concerned with masculinity bind the parallel narratives together. These themes include patriarchal responsibility, aggression as a masculine attribute, and the agency to cause negative or positive change. All three themes are learned by the male children. Also, they must all learn to reconcile loss. In *After the Wedding*, Pramod chooses to let go of Jacob as a father figure, while Elias's friend Christian finally submits to the grief of losing his mother. Elias, in dealing with his parents' separation, jokes to his father Anton: "I bet mum would love it if you weren't such a wimp." Not aware of his father's infidelity, Elias attributes his parents' separation to what he perceives as Anton's passivity, which has been presented as a liberal ideal of nonviolence. Grown-ups and their dysfunctions establish a particularly filmic tension between child and adulthood.

Bier's lived experience of Jewish culture, with the concomitant understanding that bad things happen to good people, resonates through relational transactions between fathers and sons and the transference of guilt and retribution between them. *In a Better World* elaborates on such ethics, which underpin notions of violence and revenge. For instance, teenage Christian's worldview is framed by perceived injustice. Having lost his mother to cancer after a wrenchingly slow death, then suddenly leaving London and beginning life anew in Denmark, followed by seeing Elias bullied, causes Christian to betray everything his father has taught him about violence. This is tied directly to the fact that he believes his father lied to him about his mother's illness. His radical response to the chaos he feels is one of extreme violence. He savagely bashes the school bully with a bike pump and holds a knife to his throat. Christian's violent actions undercut previous images of emotional sterility that frame his privileged world of wealth. Despite this affluence, the same base instinct that overcomes Anton in Africa prevails. Christian's survivalist logic in the face of an unforgiving reality is evident in his response to his father's acute concern about his violent actions. His father exclaims, "If you hit him and he hits you then it never ends. Don't you see? That's how wars are started." Christian responds, "Not if you hit hard enough the first time.'

Violence, in these films, is used as a tool to both destroy and to build relationships. In a gesture of comradeship, Christian gifts his special knife to Elias, who is thrilled. But this conspiratorial act also strengthens their destructive union. When Lars, an aggressive mechanic, assaults Anton, the boys decide to blow up his van. While violence in this case is justified by

Figure 12.5 Bier's framing highlights the legacy of violence between children and adults. Elias (Markus Rygaard) and Christian (William Johnk Juels Nielsen) watch as Anton attempts to defuse an altercation with the aggressive mechanic Lars (Kim Bodnia) (*In a Better World*).

Christian as a restorative measure, it also speaks to Bier's emphasis on realism as rendered through the moral complexities of human desire. Elias, in contrast to Christian, resorts to destructive behavior as a means of attaining much-needed companionship. There is a strange conversation between the boys when they talk about death: Christian says his mother was burnt, that "corpses rot and seep into the groundwater." It is disturbing to frame the death of his mother with such a blunt dissection of decay, but it astutely highlights Christian's intimate experience of death and the feelings he has suppressed concerning the tragic loss of his mother. While this transaction counters more sanitized versions of childhood, it also reflects Bier's wariness of becoming too "comfortable" (Gold 2007) within the filmmaking process for fear of the prescriptive or predictable.

Thematic expressions of violence have often been employed within discourses on altered depictions and expectations of manhood (Armengol 2014: 139) (Figure 12.5). The metanarrative in these storylines examines violence as gendered and perhaps the inevitable, instinctive result of intergenerational transfer. While Anton's wife Marianne and the African village women demonstrate a capacity for violence, it is primarily expressed through male cultural counterparts: the sadistic warlord in Africa who butchers pregnant women, the aggressive Danish mechanic Lars who talks with his fists, the schoolyard bullies who tease Elias, and Christian, whose grief manifests through violent episodes and a preoccupation with death. Violence is magnified in the third world through acknowledgment of a grim third-world order at play. As one of the refugees simply states to Anton: "everyone has killed here; man, woman, children." Given that this line is presented before Anton's violent act, the interplay between black and white men feels like an important thematic transaction, positioning violence not so much as a test of manhood (Armengol 2014: 135) but as a fundamental aspect of humanity writ large.

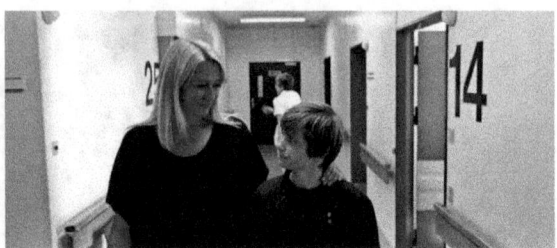

Figure 12.6 Marianne (Trine Dyrholm) escorts Christian to see her son Elias, who is recovering in the hospital after the boys' car bomb explosion (*In a Better World*).

CONCLUSION

Though childhood is often expressed as a traumatic rite of passage into a complex adult world, the use of male children in Bier/Jensen storylines nevertheless highlights Bier's directorial ethos, one in which "hope is just as real and just as intrinsic to who we are" (quoted in Robson 2016) (Figure 12.6). In this way, child characters are used to tap into universal ideals about the enduring legacy and sense of transformative redemption that lies waiting beyond the frame. As a body of work, the Bier/Jensen filmography has much to tell us about mechanisms of cinematic mobility and the dimensions of screen stories that travel beyond the national frame. Perhaps the most salient feature of the partnership is the collaborative development of both screen idea and subsequent story. As a system of knowledge exchange, this dynamic expresses a wider cultural sensibility that fosters strong writer/director teams and a value system that embraces creative inquisition. The active role Bier as director plays in narrative development also raises questions as to how we interpret and research the role of storyteller.

In regards to the discourse on national cinemas, the partnership demonstrates a particularly Danish interplay between cultural landscape and the strategic articulation of age and gender as transnational story components. Moving away from the expressive constraints of naturalism most commonly associated with Scandinavian cinema, one might suggest that the scale of emotional expression within the global drama has always suited Bier's disposition (Esther 2011), all the while imbuing her work with a cinematic transmutability. What makes Bier an accomplished practitioner has less to do with marketability than with her perceptive interrogation and expression of the human experience.

Though having always expressed a disinterest in the political, Bier inadvertently articulates the importance of positioning Denmark within a larger socio-cultural frame, rather than focusing on domestically oriented stories defined by parochial concerns or aesthetics. The Bier/Jensen gaze focuses on the humanist rather than religious or political dimensions within the narrative and imbues their films with a far-reaching accessibility that celebrates life as a complicated, interwoven humanity.

NOTES

1. *Babette's Feast* (*Babettes gaestebud*, 1987), written/directed by Gabriel Axel, received the award for Best Foreign Language film at the 2007 Academy Awards, followed in 2008 by the Danish/Swedish co-production *Pelle the Conqueror* (*Pelle Erobreren*, 2007), co-written/directed by Bille August.
2. The collaborative auteur theory was established by Vinca Wiedemann. Within this approach, the director drives the project forward, but through collaboration with key creatives involved in the storytelling process. See Redvall 2010: 76.
3. This combination is often considered as a gateway to an international audience (Dancyger 2001: 199).
4. This includes war in Afghanistan, as examined in *Brothers* (*Brødre*, 2004).

BIBLIOGRAPHY

Armengol, Josep (2014), "Alternative masculinities in Richard Ford's Fiction and/versus Susanne Bier's *In a Better World*," in J. Armengol and A. Carabi (eds.), *Alternative Masculinities for a Changing World*, New York: Palgrave Macmillan, pp. 131–44.
Bondebjerg, Ib (2014), "Regional and Global Dimensions of Danish Film Culture and Film Policy," in Mette Hjort and Ursula Lindqvist (eds.), *A Companion to Nordic Cinema*, Malden, MA and Oxford: Wiley Blackwell, pp. 19–40.
Dancyger, Ken (2001), *Global Scriptwriting*, Burlington, VT: Focal Press.
Douglas, Edward (2011), "Exclusive: Susanne Bier lives in a Better World," *Comingsoon.net*, March 29, <http://www.comingsoon.net/movies/features/75479-exclusive-susanne-bier-lives-in-a-better-world> (accessed November 14, 2017).
Esther, John (2011), "*In a Better World*'s Susanne Bier: Senseless and sensitivity," *UR Chicago Journal*, March 28, <http://www.urchicago.com/interviews/2011/3/28/in-a-better-worlds-susanne-bier.html> (accessed November 14, 2017).
Feinstein, Howard (2007), "Susanne Bier on *After the Wedding*," *Filmmaker Magazine*, March 30, <http://filmmakermagazine.com/4867-susanne-bier-after-the-wedding/#.WGhahLFh3eR> (accessed November 14, 2017).
Gledhill, Christine (2012), "Introduction," in Christine Gledhill (ed.), *Gender Meets Genre in Postwar Cinemas*, Urbana, Chicago, and Springfield: University of Illinois Press, pp. 1–12.
Gold, Sylviane (2007), "A director comfortable with catastrophe," *The New York Times*, March 25, <http://www.nytimes.com/2007/03/25/movies/25gold.html?pagewanted=all> (accessed November 14, 2017).
Hjort, Mette (2003), "Susanne Bier," in Mette Hjort and Ib Bondebjerg (eds.), *The Danish Directors: Dialogues on a Contemporary National Cinema*, Bristol and Chicago: Intellect Books, pp. 240–8.
Hjort, Mette (2005), *Small Nation, Global Cinema*, Minneapolis: University of Minneapolis Press.

Hjort, Mette (2012), "Introduction: The film phenomenon and how risk pervades it," in Mette Hjort (ed.), *Risk and Film*, Detroit: Wayne State University Press, pp. 1–30.

Hoggard, Liz (2013), "Susanne Bier: You can't be ashamed of big emotions if you make movies," *The Guardian*, April 14, <https://www.theguardian.com/theobserver/2013/apr/14/susanne-bier-love-all-you-need> (accessed November 14, 2017).

Hybschmann, Sidsel (2015), in-person interview, November 21.

Jagernauth, Kevin (2014), "Susanne Bier says *Serena* was 'never a mainstream film,' talks 'anxious' Bradley Cooper and Jennifer Lawrence," *Indie Wire*, October 22, <http://www.indiewire.com/2014/10/susanne-bier-says-serena-was-never-a-mainstream-film-talks-anxious-bradley-cooper-jennifer-lawrence-271078/> (accessed November 14, 2017).

Livingston, Paisley (2012), "Spectatorship and Risk," in Mette Hjort (ed.), *Risk and Film*, Detroit: Wayne State University Press, pp. 73–96.

Lupher, Sonia (2016), "Susanne Bier's living, breathing body of work," *Bitch Flicks*, April 4, <http://www.btchflcks.com/2016/04/susanne-biers-living-breathing-body-of-work.html#.WGzHDrFh3eR> (accessed November 14, 2017).

Maksimiuk, Magdalena (2016), "Interview: Anders Thomas Jensen on *Men & Chicken*," *Slant Magazine*, April 19, <http://www.slantmagazine.com/features/article/interview-anders-thomas-jensen-on-men-and-chicken> (accessed November 14, 2017).

Martinsson, Terese (2014), *Beyond the Habitual: Studying the Gender Balance in the Nordic Feature Film Releases of 2012*, B.A. Thesis, University of Gothenburg, <http://www.ewawomen.com/uploads/files/martinssontbachelor.pdf> (accessed November 14, 2017).

Redvall, Eva Novrup (2010), "Scriptwriting as a creative, collaborative learning process of problem finding and problem solving," *Mediekultur, Journal of Media and Communication Research*, 25.46: pp. 34–55, <http://ojs.statsbiblioteket.dk/index.php/mediekultur/article/view/1342> (accessed November 14, 2017).

Robson, David (2016), "Meet Le Carré's smiley Danish connection," *The Jewish Chronicle*, February 25, <https://www.thejc.com/culture/tv/meet-le-carré-s-smiley-danish-connection-1.60528> (accessed November 14, 2017).

Saito, Stephen (2016), "Anders Thomas Jensen on birthing the delightfully deranged *Men & Chicken*," moveablefest.com, April 20, <http://moveablefest.com/moveable_fest/2016/04/anders-thomas-jensen-men-chicken.html> (accessed November 14, 2017).

Saner, Emine (2016), "Susanne Bier: I would probably cut off my right ear to do James Bond," *The Guardian*, June 3, <https://www.theguardian.com/film/2016/jun/03/susanne-bier-i-would-probably-cut-off-my-ear-to-do-james-bond> (accessed November 14, 2017).

Shriver-Rice, Meryl (2015), *Inclusion in New Danish Cinema: Sexuality and Transnational Belonging*, Bristol and Chicago: Intellect Books.

Skotte, Kim (2011), "A New Phase for Danish Cinema," *Danish Film Institute Official Website*, <http://www.dfi.dk/service/english/news-and-publications/news/march-2011/new-phase-for-danish-cinema.aspx> (accessed November 14, 2017).

Smaill, Belinda (2014), "The Male Sojourner, the Female Director, and Popular European Cinema: The Worlds of Susanne Bier," *Camera Obscura* vol. 29, no. 1, 85: 5–31.

CHAPTER 13

Danish Privilege and Responsibility in the Work of Susanne Bier

Meryl Shriver-Rice

Susanne Bier is both wildly praised and vaguely dismissed by film critics and the Danish public alike for the accessibility, and hence popularity, of her films. Ask a random Dane at a bar in Copenhagen about Susanne Bier and you are likely to hear the phrase "popular movies," while Americans who are familiar with her work are likely to label her films "art cinema." This polarizing split is Bier's reception conundrum in a nutshell. Not quite fitting the definition of intellectual European art cinema, and not quite Hollywood, Bier's work straddles a unique space that garners both popular reception and critical praise. This space breaks with the expectations of film critics, who implicitly possess the predisposition that films that are praised for being aesthetically innovative and psychologically or socio-politically heavy hitting are seldom widely loved by the general Hollywood-blockbuster-inclined public. Never mind that Alfred Hitchcock, Alfonso Cuarón, Quentin Tarantino, Gus Van Sant, Guillermo del Toro, Spike Jonze, Alejandro González Iñárritu, Lasse Hallström, Wes Anderson, Sophia Coppola, Tom Hooper, Jane Campion, Ang Lee, and others are all critically acclaimed yet widely popular filmmakers whose works, while generally released in small-town America, also line film school canon lists. Bier's conundrum essentially places her amongst respectable cinematic company—a fact that Hollywood and the BBC have not missed—as she (like her Danish colleague Lone Scherfig) is continuously invited to direct films and television for major English-language production studios.

Arguably Bier's greatest global cinematic successes are what Belinda Smaill refers to as her "male sojourner trilogy," which includes *Brothers* (*Brødre*, 2004), *After the Wedding* (*Efter Brylluppet*, 2006), and *In a Better World* (*Hævnen*, 2011) (Smaill 2014)—so named because in all three films a Western white male protagonist moves between Denmark and formerly colonized or currently militarized locations. These three protagonists feel an ethical responsibility towards non-Danish people who include Afghan refugees (*Brothers*), Indian orphans (*After the Wedding*), and sub-Saharan medical refugees (*In a Better World*). These men actively choose to spend large portions of their lives abroad as soldiers, orphanage directors, and *Médecins Sans Frontières*. Each white male protagonist's career choice appears to be fueled in part by the guilt of being born in a privileged developed nation, which each protagonist exhibits differently in their feelings towards the critical need for international policing (Michael, *Brothers*), scorn for their affluent place of birth (Jacob, *After the Wedding*), and adopting and embodying a universalist cosmopolitan sense of personal ethics (Anton, *In a Better World*).

THE PRIVILEGED WELFARE NATIONS

Bier and co-writer Anders Thomas Jensen's trilogy is not unique amongst recent Nordic cinema, nor amidst Danish film, for narratives that evoke privileged-nation guilt; instead the trilogy is part of a wider trend in twenty-first-century Nordic entertainment to incorporate people and spaces that lie outside of the relative stability and affluence of northern European social democratic nations. Within Scandinavian cinema, Swedish directors Lukas Moodysson and Roy Andersson are known for narratives that portray intense experiences of palpable privileged-world guilt. Comparing these two Swedish filmmakers, one can get a glimpse of the wide-ranging styles and genres that have incorporated notions of privileged-world guilt. Moodysson's films are dark, intense "melodramas of demand" that invoke shame in the spectator (Nestingen 2008), while Andersson's work relies on dry, Scandinavian existentialist humor in his Ingmar-Bergman-meets-Monty-Python-style comedies (Yang 2013).

In the Danish context, an explosion of films since 2005 has dealt with issues of industrialized-nation guilt, particularly in terms of immigration and citizenship. Films such as *Chinaman/Kinamand* (Henrik Ruben Genz, 2005), *Little Soldier/Lille Soldat* (Annette K. Olesen, 2008), *Brotherhood/Brøderskab* (Nicolo Donato, 2011), and the Academy Award-nominated *A War/Krigen* (Tobias Lindholm, 2016) dive head first into issues of belonging, identity, race, class, and citizenship. These films invite questions such as: who embodies the Other, and who deserves Danish citizenship? For those not familiar with Danish film, it should be pointed out that this inclination towards examining issues of inequality is somewhat expected from a country known for story-driven rather than profit-driven films mostly directed by alumni of the socio-politically informed National Film School of Denmark. In the past fifteen years Denmark has demonstrated the viability of film to be used as a vehicle to negotiate and reinforce cultural ethics and political values, while also navigating the ongoing and mounting forces of digital communication and globalization (Shriver-Rice 2015). There has been little reason for Danish directors to tone down the social justice issues in their narrative content, since for many Danish directors, such as Bier, embracing politically or ethically charged content has not diminished their films' critical success at highly visible film festivals like Cannes and Berlin. As the rise of exclusionist, populist, and isolationist Western governments occurs in the second decade of this century (Brexit in the U.K., the election of Trump in the U.S.A., the rise of populist parties in Netherlands, France, Denmark, and so forth), screen narratives that contend with issues of migration and resource allocation and address the "us versus them" paradigm speak to the historical moment.

"SCANGUILT"

In this chapter I will first review the postcolonial criticism that can be aimed at Bier and Jensen's trilogy, then move on to examine other theoretical frames of understanding in which to view these films, and finally, I will argue that these films are part of a larger trend in New Danish Cinema in which cinematic narratives act as sites of ethical negotiation and epistemic rupture for spectators in the position of privileged welfare state citizens. I suggest viewing these films through the lens of wider twenty-first-century Scandinavian guilt, a highly noticeable trend within Scandinavian entertainment that has resulted in the implementation of a multi-year cross-disciplinary research group labeled "Scanguilt" that is housed at the University of Oslo. Scanguilt is funded by the Research Council of Norway (2014–19). The Scanguilt project thesis states:

> We live at a moment in time when most Scandinavians are extremely privileged. Time and again we are acclaimed as the richest, happiest and most egalitarian nations in the world. At the same time, globalization brings us into close contact with non-privileged Others. Through media and migration we are confronted on a daily basis with an awareness of suffering Others—child laborers, victims of trafficking, war refugees, etc. The Other lives side-by-side with us; often they even contribute (more or less directly) to our affluence. Numerous contemporary narratives indicate that this sense of global inequality does not simply lead to Scandinavians' counting themselves lucky for their unusual privileges; they also feel uncomfortable and suffer from what we call "Scandinavian guilt feelings." (Oxfeldt 2014)

For Danish children who grow up attending an educational system in which local, regional, and international equality and global social justice issues are integrated into everyday teachable moments, it comes as no surprise that many Danish adults are chronically beset with varying degrees of privileged-nation guilt. Self-awareness of privilege in a postcolonial world is a cornerstone of Danish contemporary cosmopolitan identity. Within Danish cinema, this cosmopolitanism does not exhibit the qualities Martin Roberts refers to in his description of the global imaginary of Euro-American film in which "conscious cosmopolitanism of the international avant-garde engage in forms of detached, sardonic observation of an increasingly transnational world order and cultural change associated with directors and characters alike self-consciously constituting themselves as nomads and postmodern descendants of Baudelaire's flâneurs, rootless cosmopolitans threading their way around the globe in search of something new and different" (Lopes 2010: 5). Instead, the constant self-awareness of privilege is so ever-present in the Danish cultural imaginary as to be mocked and satirized in mainstream Danish comedy, as is epitomized in Hella Joof's wacky *Almost Perfect/Sover Dolly på ryggen?* (2012). In this romantic comedy, the lead protagonist decides that a "perfect" romantic interest is boring and lacking sexual charisma due to the fact that he is too "perfect," as as a man who spends his Christmas holidays giving gifts to lower-class children, frets over heterosexual norms and buys gender-neutral dolls, runs marathons, and sponsors orphan children from other countries in his spare time.

This is a comedic tradition that does not readily translate as humorous to less socially conscientious international audiences, and within American popular culture can only be compared to the mocking of "hipster" authenticity and social awareness in satires like the television series *Portlandia* (2011–). The dramatic films of contemporary Danish psychological realism direct less playful mockery at the unvirtuous and self-interested, who openly ridicule other characters' attempts to be socially conscious citizens. This form of mockery is rampant in two films that I discuss later in this chapter. The protagonist of *Little Soldier* (2008) is cruelly taunted by her father for trying to save the world by becoming a soldier and going off to Afghanistan, and even further for having a bleeding heart over the fate of her father's African sex workers. In *Brotherhood* (2010), neo-Nazi characters openly deride anyone who, like the Danish majority, believes in human equality between different racial and ethnic groups.

Bier and Jensen's trilogy does not self-reflexively mock or acknowledge its sincerity; instead, its protagonists embody earnest humanitarian aid workers who profoundly believe in the benefits of their actions. As Smaill has pointed out, these Western protagonists represent

> neither the colonizer nor the tourist, but rather constitutes the new figure of the new aid worker or peacekeeping soldier. He embodies the projection

of humanitarianism that, in Fuyuki Kurasawa's words, "has become one of the principal manifestations of the liberal democratic project in the post-Cold War world. The project that facilitates the transnational flow of workers and soldiers from affluent nations also signals an expanding mode of liberal democratic humanism based in empathy and a discourse of human rights." (Smaill 2014: 24)

Sincerity aside, these films, when viewed from a postcolonial perspective, can also be seen as narratives starring "white savior" figures who attempt to save non-white individuals who cannot save themselves. Cath Moore has weighed in on this resemblance to the white savior figure in the films of Bier's trilogy, stating:

> As a woman of colour I hover in my personal attitudes towards these films and the postcolonial diatribe at play within. Certainly, they reflect a continuing paternalism in the world outside the frame: both white, male protagonists are inevitably protected by the privilege of their first-world position, most notably by leaving the unreconciled chaos of the third world behind. Accordingly, mortality as a conceptual construct holds a different value within each world, weighted to reflect or investigate the emotional concerns of the first-world characters over the more dire conflicts that secondary (dark skinned) characters in the third world face, such as poverty, war, death and disease . . . Cynically, one may suggest that the instability of the third world renders it ultimately disposable within the storyline. The function of the third world is then to allow a separate space for the protagonist to confront conflict and gain a new-found sense of clarity, before returning to a more reconciled space that the permanence of the first world offers. (Moore, 2015: 372)

POSTCOLONIAL SHORTCOMINGS

In short, one could loosely contend that this trilogy falls into the neocolonialist trap of exhibiting the suffering of racialized Others who lack subjectivity within dangerous, victimized non-Western space in order for a benevolent Western protagonist to emerge from the narrative as a hero-like figure. Hollywood is best known for this type of white savior neo-imperialist narrative. Exemplars include the ultimate 1980s masculine hero in *Rambo* (George Cosmatos, 1985); the xenophobically appalling *Indiana Jones and the Temple of Doom* (Steven Spielberg, 1984), which is especially inexcusable given that the protagonist is an archaeologist; sports narratives where white men and women lead or help African American athletes to greatness, such as *Hardball* (Brian Robbins, 2001),

Figure 13.1 White, blue-eyed Scandinavian protagonist.

Glory Road (James Gartner, 2006), and *The Blind Side* (John Lee Hancock, 2009); teachers who rehabilitate non-white students in films such as *Dangerous Minds* (John N. Smith, 1995) and *Freedom Writers* (Richard LaGravenese, 2007); and the quintessential Hollywood, white male reluctant and imperialist heroes in *The Last Samurai* (Edward Zwick, 2003) and *Avatar* (James Cameron, 2009). Viewed through the lens of postcolonial thought, it is difficult to escape the fact that in all three films of the trilogy, white Scandinavian men travel to non-industrialized locales in overtly benevolent roles, and in all three films the subjectivity of non-Western, non-white individuals, while touched upon, is not highlighted or investigated, and all of the main characters with agency and subjectivity come from privileged Nordic space (Figure 13.1).

Within these films there are several illustrations of Danish space as idyllic and safe while juxtaposed in stark contrast to dangerous, non-industrialized space. A prime example of this crosscutting technique occurs within the opening scenes of *In a Better World*. Bier has been highly praised for her ability to interweave different geographic spaces through scenic juxtapositions of privileged, developed-world homelands and characters set in non-industrialized locations. This technique intricately intertwines the two spaces, often employing overlapping, non-simultaneous sound. In one of the opening scenes of *In a Better World*, a clean, orderly English funeral commences as dust-covered children play in the dirt pretending to make a makeshift grave at an indeterminate African location (Figures 13.2 and 13.3). This scene crosscuts back to English space within a regal stone church and shows an audience seated in clean, crisp formal attire. Death in the Western world space is marked by the voicing of a poem that overlaps with visuals of a dirt-covered child crying in a starkly arid South Sudan setting as the words "grass is always green" are heard. From this funeral scene, the film cuts to a large farmhouse in wide open Danish countryside, where a sweet, happy-faced grandmother says to her bereaved grandson, "There's so much space, lots of peace and quiet. The internet has been installed for you, and you can choose which room you want." While the English church fittingly sets the stage for safe, clean, and

Figure 13.2 Clean, orderly Western space juxtaposed against Anton's South Sudan workplace in *In a Better World*.

Figure 13.3 A young girl cries in a dust storm in South Sudan before a shot of children playing with a makeshift grave in the dirt.

formal space, the film's arrival in Denmark is markedly idyllic, technologically and architecturally privileged, without financial concern, and mostly homogenous in racial and ethnic terms. On a superficial level, a viewer of this series of scenes from *In a Better World* and others like it from the trilogy could assume that Danish space is exclusively white, ethically sound, and morally superior to the racialized, chaotic, poor, dirty, and uncontrolled Afghanistan, Indian, and African settings in the trilogy.

However, there is a tendency in New Danish Cinema to avoid fully closed ethical or moral systems in order to complicate ethical choices, and Bier's work is no exception. The best example of this open ethical stance can be seen in the opening scene of *Brothers*. The voiceover states: "Life is neither right or wrong. Good or bad." From the opening of the film, the voiceover unties the narrative from fixed posts of meaning and accords value to an intrinsic singularity that mobilizes the force of ethical interrogation (Shriver-Rice 2011). In *In a Better World*, Bier and Jensen showcase the possibility of any space and/or any person as potentially dangerous, and universalist ethical systems as fatally flawed. The picturesque Danish farmhouse setting becomes the site of a bomb-making lab; the bereaved grandson who is being coddled by his father and grandmother becomes the maker of said bomb. And Anton, the would-be hero-father-doctor figure who attempts to embody pacifist beliefs for his children, does not prevent his own son from setting off a bomb, nor is he able to stick to his Hippocratic oath to medically treat all patients the same regardless of their personal behavior outside of the operating room. Despite its idyllic depiction of Denmark, *In a Better World* enforces the notion that one is not safe anywhere, and that human violence is not only delivered by outsiders, but also by fellow Danes, including the protagonist's own son.

In *Brothers*, *After the Wedding*, and *In a Better World*, Bier focuses on the protagonists' inner struggle to negotiate their ethical decisions rather than fixed notions of right or wrong that are reinforced by the narrative logic and common hallmarks of the "white savior" narrative. In *Brothers*, Michael also breaks with his own ethical beliefs and commits violence against another Dane in order to stay alive. Once back on Danish soil the film leaves the viewer doubtful that Michael's family would question his choice to survive, yet by this point in the narrative Michael has abandoned all notions of inner ethical coherence. This one action causes his entire Danish-ordered moral world to come loose at the seams. This theme of multivalent morality is ever present in Bier's realistic fiction, and as I will demonstrate below, it is a characteristic of wider psychological realism films within New Danish Cinema.

However, Bier's films do not entirely evade the embodiment of a positioned politics of representation that is determined by national context—as it is mainly Danish protagonists and their Danish family members who possess subjectivity and agency. *After the Wedding* offers one exception in Jacob's adopted son figure, Pramod. Though he garners little screen time, Pramod is allowed to make his own decisions concerning the trajectory of his future. After Jacob realizes that he must remain in Copenhagen, he does not wrench his son from India to save him from "third"-world atrocities. Instead, Jacob travels back to India, places little Pramod at eye level, and presents him with the choice of whether to stay in India without his father figure, or return with him to Denmark (Figure 13.4). Sadly for Jacob, Pramod chooses to stay in India now that funding from a self-serving billionaire has rendered the orphanage to be

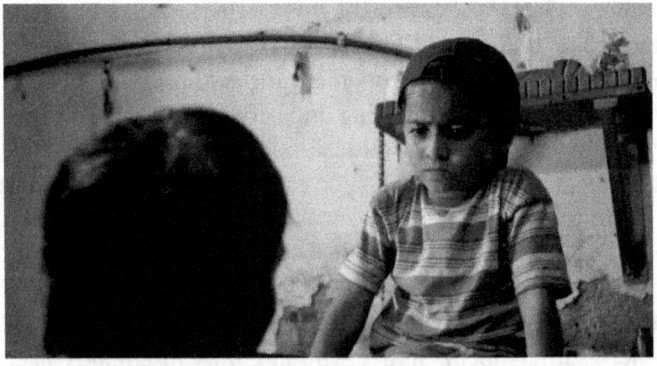

Figure 13.4 Jacob and Pramod meet at eye level in *After the Wedding*.

"so good here now." The film thus avoids a neo-colonialist ending in which a non-white child is saved from former colony backwardness and relocated to be saved in superior, white Western space. The failure to live by a fixed universalist set of standards and triumph as a moral hero figures prominently in all three narratives in the trilogy. In Pramod's father's case, Jacob believes he is a failure for being unable to leave his entitled native country, which he views with scorn, and for being unable to dedicate the rest of his life to Pramod and the other Indian orphans who have been his life's greatest concern for twenty years.

While some critics have argued that the "elsewhere" of these films ignores geographic location specifics and cultural contexts in order to assert a universalizing morality, I argue that the ethical trajectories of the films are not universal—instead, the idea that universalist ethics will inevitably fail takes precedence. The interweaving of formerly imperial and formerly colonized spaces around funeral imagery in the opening of *In a Better World* is less about safe and unsafe space, and more about enforcing the universality of human mortality. Mortality features as a constant presence in these films, and one is not so much left with a white benevolent hero by each film's close as one is left with the feeling that death is possible at any moment for any person, and that maintaining a universal system of ethics is a painful and angst-ridden impossibility.

Benevolence implies ethical or moral perfection and the sense that an individual is unwaveringly certain of the correctness of his or her actions. Instead of such self-aggrandizing self-righteousness, I argue that Bier and Jensen's trilogy aims for a humanistic sense of humility, one that critiques the certainty and benevolence of stereotypical Western white male sojourners. This humility hinges on the simple reminder that humanity's place in the world is as one life form among many, all of which share the common fate of death. Bier often cuts from dramatic action to calming landscapes or nature scenes in her trilogy, and while these cinematic moments certainly act as emotional breaks or as tension release points within her narratives, the lingering of the camera on the eyes of dead foxes in fields and decaying plants in the wind in *After the Wedding* is not calming. These moments are rife with discomfort. Within a horror film or a psychological thriller, these moments would build tension and suspense as a prelude to violence, yet in Bier's work they subtly invest subjectivity onto the dead animals to remind viewers that death visits us all, and is the one fate that all life forms share. At several points in *After the Wedding* her unflinching camera probes the eyes of murdered trophy animals mounted on the wall of a wealthy white Western man (Jørgen; Figure 13.5). As spectators, we are unsettled by the deathly stare of these once vivacious creatures, and are reminded that the dying man upstairs had no qualms about taking these animals' lives in order to make trophies from their faces. Bier's close-up on

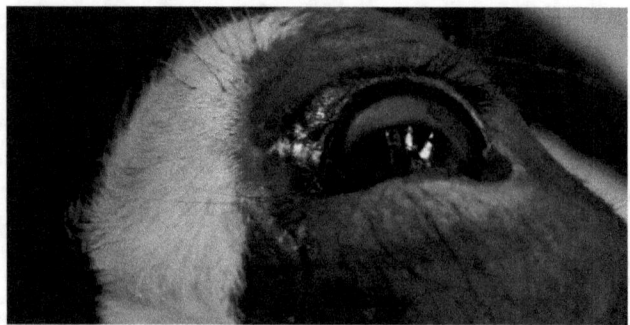

Figure 13.5 Close-up of unseeing animal eyes on Jørgen's walls in *In a Better World*.

these unseeing animal eyes reminds the viewer of the overt cruelty and selfishness of colonial pursuits and the irony that no man, no matter how many times over a billionaire or a killer of fierce beasts, can escape from his own mortality. By the end of *After the Wedding*, both male protagonists appear far from heroic; Jørgen must suffer from a total lack of control as a mere dying animal, and any interior forms of benevolence Jacob might have harbored are dismantled when he realizes just how selfish his refusal to travel to industrialized nations has been in his twenty-year efforts to gain resources for his orphanage.

As Smaill points out, Bier is explicitly concerned with transcending cultural specificities so that audiences "get the point," which has enabled her to reach not only a regional but also a global audience (Smaill 2014: 12). While her films are aimed at a global audience, they do not ignore her Danish viewers—they star Danish actors, are in Danish, and depict Danish families on Danish soil. Consequently, Bier's drawing from non-industrialized space has more to do with speaking to the privileged-world guilt in the Danish viewer, and reminding him or her of the world at large beyond Western space—a world that the Danish are not cut off from. This narrative strategy is used to reach audiences who are aware of difference, but who are perhaps unwilling to submit two hours of their lives to a social documentary; simply put, if the suffering of a distant Other is beyond comprehension, audiences can easily claim distance or strangeness as a reason for not understanding (Rovisco 2013: 155). Bier and Jensen did not set out to make films that depict the experiences of, and the agencies of, Others in non-Western spaces; they set out to make films that ask such questions as: what does one do with the guilt that stems from living privileged lives while many do not? In what ways should such guilt be acted upon? What does it mean to make life decisions that involve attempts to aid people in "third"-world places? In the same way that humanitarian and environmental media campaigns attempt to avoid "emotionally numbing" viewers, Bier is careful not to overwhelm her viewers with more than she believes they can handle (Linville 1991). Not that her cinematography shies away from the bloody beating of a man with a pipe in *Brothers*, or the on-screen horrific evidence of Big Man's knife slashes upon a young woman; but we do not see Big Man commit the bloody act in *In a Better World*. And in *After the Wedding*, the positive changes to Jacob's orphanage are explicitly shown within the visuals of the narrative to provide the spectator with at least some relief from "first-world" guilt.

Rather than criticize this trilogy, as so many critics of black cinema did of Spike Lee for offering up innovative descriptions of racism in *Do The Right Thing* (1989) but not offering up solutions, I propose reading this type of Western-oriented film as a stepping stone in the forward move towards processing privileged-nation guilt and the range of options available to privileged citizens who want to find ways to use their resources to help. Without *Do the Right Thing*, it is doubtful that *Get Out* (Jordan Peele, 2017) would have been released in the past year, and certainly there would have been no *Moonlight* (Barry Jenkins, 2016) to win 2017's Academy award for Best Picture. There are many ways one can criticize Bier's depiction of non-industrialized nations; however, these films are not about non-Western subjectivity. They are about Danish family values and what it means to be a privileged-nation citizen aware of/and experienced with the less privileged areas of the world. Despite the white/benevolent and darker-skinned/victim dynamic, these films are deeply concerned with the issues of less privileged nations and manage to successfully engage their (mainly) developed-world audience through the lens of Western humanistic values.

ONTOLOGICAL SHIFTS AND COSMOPOLITANISM

There has been a push by Scandinavian scholars in the past decade to describe the ever-growing transnational nature of their "small-nation" filmmaking, which has become beset by the forces of globalization (Hjort 2005; Hjort and Petrie 2007; Nestingen and Elkington 2005; Gustafson and Kääpä 2013). This need arose from the increasingly multi-national production teams and shooting locations used by Scandinavian and other "small-nation" European projects. As this dialogue concerning transnational productions took focus, other scholars writing at this time suggested that this cosmopolitan move in practice did not only mark a turn in globalized production, but also signaled an ontological shift in representation and narrative focus. In his work on cosmopolitan filmmaking, Denilson Lopes designates transnational productions as those that employ "multilingual scripts, multi-country shooting locations, multi-national production companies and crews, and multi-national actors" (Lopes 2010: 5). The trilogy arguably falls into this designation with its use of Danish, English, and Arabic and its dual-country shooting locations.

Brothers was shot in both Denmark and Spain, while *After the Wedding* was shot in Denmark and India, and *In a Better World* was filmed in Denmark and Kenya. All three films rely on Danish actors and settings, but also include multi-national casts, crews, and shooting locations. Bier and Jensen's comfort with such transnational production contexts is showcased in the film that followed the trilogy, a comedy titled *Love Is All You Need/Den skaldede frisør* (2012). This wildly successful film was a Danish-, Italian-, and English-language production shot in Denmark and Italy with English, Danish, and Italian actors.

Maria Rovisco has further pointed out that cinematic cosmopolitanism is also often marked by both the identity of a filmmaker as migrant or diasporic, and the cinematic representation in their films of individuals and social groups caught up in conditions of greater interconnectivity and mobility (2013: 149). For Rovisco, cosmopolitan cinema is both a *mode of production* and a *cross-cultural aesthetic practice* that is capable of generating serious public dialogue. It does so by self-consciously engaging in denouncing the violation of human dignity in a transnational public sphere (2013: 154, emphasis my own). As many chapters in this collection examine, Bier's Jewish heritage plays a strong role in her filmmaking choices. As she has described in multiple interviews, her parents met while fleeing from the persecution of Jews during World War II, and she attended Hebrew University in Jerusalem, studying architecture there and in London prior to deciding to move back to Denmark and apply to the National Film School of Denmark. She sees herself as Danish, but also her sense of belonging falls outside of typical Danish culture to identify with the Jewish diaspora, who refuse to forget the trauma of the recent past (Hjort and Bondebjerg, 2003; Bier quoted in Molloy, Nielsen, and Shriver-Rice 2016).

Expanding on this notion of cosmopolitanism within narratives, Torill Strand contends that current, emerging cosmopolitanism differs from earlier, turn-of-the-millennium globalization in the ideas that it produces. He believes that the contemporary cosmopolitan turn in art, cinematic narrative, and literature signifies an innovation in global awareness and new habits of thought, and may be characterized as globalization from *within*. Rather than existing in a *cosmopolitan condition* that claims universality while reflecting a Westernized social order, this cosmopolitan turn embodies a *cosmopolitan outlook* that is a "way of seeing the world as entrenched in global awareness" (Strand 2010: 234, emphasis my own). This cosmopolitan outlook signifies a new way of seeing the world and a radical paradigm shift towards social and political analysis. In short, Strand believes that this cosmopolitan outlook is diagnostic of the current age, in which rapid epistemic ruptures have been pointing towards a normative stance that supports political action rather than a privileged and irresponsible detachment (Strand 2010: 233). He points out that while people from New York to Beijing have long been living in existing relations of interdependence, "what's new is not forced mixing but *global awareness* of it, it is self-conscious political affirmation, its reflection and recognition before a global public via mass media, in the news and in the global social movement of blacks, women, and minorities" (Strand 2010: 234, emphasis original). Bier's trilogy engages with this cosmopolitan outlook, in which countless current political, cultural, and educational discourses are generating ontological shifts in the ways that individuals see their place in the world.

This shift has been further propelled by increasing interest in and educational discourse around postcolonial studies, the familiarity with which tends to trigger feelings of guilt in Western individuals; this guilt arises from a sense of accountability for the violations of human dignity produced through and during the aftermath of various forms of colonial occupation. However, postcolonial discourse does not always address how to live with these feelings of guilt, or what it means to live as an agent of change. Fiction film can be a springboard for cosmopolitan imagination as it stages a discursive ethical space where a range of interlocutors including filmmakers, audiences, creative personnel, and critics can enter into conversation with each other about issues of human worth and dignity, and their violation—to achieve a shared understanding of what constitutes a human being in the contemporary world (Rovisco 2013: 153). The first film of the trilogy, *Brothers*, garnered awards from multiple film festivals and was so talked about that Hollywood rapidly invested $26 million into its remake (Jim Sheridan, 2009). Bier and Jensen undoubtedly kept this visibility in mind when they set out to craft the storylines of the next two films. Both films notably close not with Danish space, but with highlighting children as signifiers of the future in less privileged world spaces. Each film's concern with industrialized world responsibilities are reinstated by closing with shots of Anton near the medical tents interacting with Sudanese children in *In a Better World*, and the credits rolling to Indian music and scenes of life outside the orphanage with open markets and people on the street in *After the Wedding* (Figure 13.6).

Figure 13.6 *After the Wedding*'s credits roll in India.

AFRICAN SEX TRAFFICKING, QUEER NAZIS, AND WAR FILMS

Beyond the trilogy, New Danish Cinema of the last decade boasts a fleet of films that bluntly deal with the concerns of privileged-nation guilt. These films draw attention to various tensions between industrialized (and formerly imperial) and non-industrialized nations and individuals, and focus on issues such as prejudice and violence against immigrants, contemporary forms of slavery, the difficulty of securing citizenship in Western nations, and the militarization of nations by Western countries. *Little Soldier* (written by Kim Fupz Aakeson) is the story of an ex-soldier who has returned from a recent tour of duty in Afghanistan. Her father runs an illegal prostitution firm of African women, and he decides to make his soldier-daughter, Lotte, the personal bodyguard of his favorite prostitute, Lily. Lotte bonds quickly with Lily over the daughter that Lily has left behind in Africa. As a daughter who was herself left behind, Lotte decides to "free" Lily by stealing her passport back and giving her money for a plane ticket. The film complicates this white savior narrative through Lily's continuous declaration that she is happy and well taken care of. From a Western world perspective, Lily's life is abhorrent; she must prostitute herself to necrophiliacs and continuously sleep with her boss. However, when Lotte attempts to point out that Lily has a dismal life, Lily refutes this by stating that she is "lucky because she gets to live with the boss, does not have to pay rent, or have to drink piss and things like the other girls." When Lotte informs Lily that she wants to "free" her, Lily does not respond with gratitude. Instead Lily shakes her head angrily at Lotte's naïveté and sense of "first-world" entitlement to make decisions for her. *Little Soldier* makes it readily apparent that even the most subjugated of individuals may not want to be told what to do by yet another white Westerner, no matter the good intentions.

Brotherhood, co-written by Rasmus Birch and Nicolo Donato, follows Lars and Jimmy, two ex-army men who get involved with a neo-Nazi, anti-immigrant white supremacy group. For the brotherhood, true Danes follow the "laws of nature," and consequently Lars and Jimmy's queer feelings and identities are both hidden and sublimated. *Brotherhood* simultaneously examines the fear of the racial Others by merging it with the fear of non-heteronormative masculinity. An outward performance of masculinity is required to become a member of the brotherhood. This performance includes violence and open prejudice directed towards anyone who is not a heterosexual ethnic Dane. *Brotherhood* deconstructs the psychological reasons that individuals choose to exclude others, and provides commentary on the current conservative political backlash over immigration, Danish citizenship, and belonging.

A number of the most forceful examples of cosmopolitan filmmaking and postcolonial guilt appear in films about war. In an attempt to give voices to Danish soldiers and Afghan refugees who have had first-hand experience of the trauma of the war in Afghanistan, writer-director Tobias Lindholm shot *A War* with a cast composed almost entirely of actual Danish soldiers and Afghan refugees. The film starred only three professional actors and was filmed in Turkey and Denmark. Lindholm's film is exemplary of an attempt by a film crew to reduce social distance from those subjects whose stories it wanted to tell (Rovisco 2013: 157). Pilou Asbaek, who plays *A War*'s protagonist commander, Claus Michael Pedersen, publicly stated that he believes that *A War* "heralds a new type of war film—one where there are no heroes" (Jones 2016). A BBC article covering *A War* stated, "Unusually, *A War* also shows Pedersen's wife at home in Denmark, played by Swedish actress Tuva Novotny. Struggling to bring up her three children at home alone, Novotny says that for the first time, 'a woman left at home has her point of view told'" (Jones 2016). Interestingly, Lindholm cited *The Deer Hunter* (1978) as his inspiration for the narrative, yet Bier's widely seen *Brothers* focused on Danish soldiers in Afghanistan (though these were played by actors) and framed war as without heroes. Furthermore, *Brothers* is the film in which Bier honed her skill of interweaving white, industrialized and non-white, less privileged spaces together as she juxtaposed the protagonist soldier's life in Afghanistan with his wife's existence back in Denmark. Lindholm ignoring *Brothers* appears willful, as well as odd, given that most Danes and, one could reasonably assume, all Danish directors had seen the film as its adaption by Hollywood under the same title, with nearly the same script and a cast full of A-list actors, was well covered by the Danish press.

Lindholm's choice not to mention Bier's film may reflect his desire to distance himself from a woman director whose work is continuously labeled by the wider press and critics with the gendered (and frequently diminishing) term "melodrama," despite the fact that her oeuvre has run the gamut of genres. Susanne Bier's dramas appeal to a popular audience, yet should never be confused with profit-driven mainstream cinema. The narratives of her trilogy navigate transnational and cosmopolitan ethics of action at the individual level, repeatedly asking the question: what does it mean to be a responsible Western citizen in this age of globalization? As these examples have demonstrated, the socially critical films of Susanne Bier are a significant contribution to the growing body of contemporary cinematic commentary on privileged-world guilt. While these films privilege Danish storylines and priorities, they also articulate notions of responsibility through the banal wisdom contained in the decisions of realistic life, where financial decisions and career choices are also a story about our contemporary global society.

BIBLIOGRAPHY

Gustafson, Tommy, and Pietara Kääpä, eds. (2013), *Transnational Ecocinema: Film Culture in an Era of Ecological Transformation*, Bristol and Chicago: Intellect Books.

Hjort, Mette (2005), *Small Nation, Global Cinema: The New Danish Cinema*, Minneapolis: University of Minnesota Press.

Hjort, Mette, and Ib Bondebjerg, eds. (2003), *The Danish Directors: Dialogues on a Contemporary National Cinema*, Bristol and Chicago: Intellect Books.

Hjort, Mette, and Duncan Petrie, eds. (2007), *The Cinema of Small Nations*, Bloomington: Indiana University Press.

Jones, Emma (2016), "No heroes for Denmark's A War movie," *BBC News*, January 17, <http://www.bbc.com/news/entertainment-arts-35250491> (accessed November 14, 2017).

Linville, P. W., and G. W. Fischer (1991), "Preferences for separating and combining events: a social application of prospect theory and the mental accounting model," *Journal of Personality and Social Psychology* 60: 5–23.

Lopes, Denilson (2010), "Global cinema, world cinema," *E-Compós*, Brasilia, vol. 13, no. 2: 1–16.

Moore, Cath (2015), "Riding the wave—creative preferences, spatial tension and transnational story components in the collaborations of Susanne Bier and Anders Thomas Jensen," *Journal of Screenwriting* vol. 6, no. 3: 363–78.

Nestingen, Andrew K. (2008), *Crime and Fantasy in Scandinavia: Fiction, Film, and Social Change*, Seattle: University of Washington.

Nestingen, Andrew, and Trevor G. Elkington, eds. (2005), *Transnational Cinema in a Global North: Nordic Cinema in Transition*, Detroit: Wayne State University Press.

Øksdal, Alf (2017), "Scandinavians can learn from feelings of guilt," University of Oslo: Department of Linguistics and Scandanavian Studies website, January 9, <http://www.hf.uio.no/iln/english/research/news-and-events/news/2017/scandinavians-can-learn-from-feelings-of-guilt.html> (accessed November 14, 2017).

Oxfeldt, Elisabet (2014), "Scandinavian narratives of of guilt and privilege in an age of globalization (Scanguilt)," University of Oslo: Faculty of Humanities website, January 31 <http://www.hf.uio.no/english/research/theme/scandinavian-narratives-of-guilt-and-privilege/index.html> (accessed November 14, 2017).

Oxfeldt, Elisabet, ed. (2016), *Skandinaviske fortellinger om skyld og privilegier i en globaliseringstid*, Scandinavian University Press, open access book: <https://www.idunn.no/file/pdf/66913321/skandinaviske-fortellinger.pdf> (accessed November 14, 2017).

Rovisco, Maria (2013), "Towards a cosmopolitan cinema: Understanding the connection between borders, mobility, and cosmopolitanism in the fiction film," *Mobilities* 8(1): 148–65.

Shriver-Rice, Meryl (2011), "Adapting National Identity: Ethical Borders Made Suspect in the Hollywood Version of Susanne Bier's *Brothers*," *Film International* vol. 9, issue 2: 8–19.

Shriver-Rice, Meryl (2015), *Inclusion in New Danish Cinema: Sexuality & Transnational Belonging*, Bristol and Chicago: Intellect Books.

Smaill, Belinda (2014), "The Male Sojourner, the Female Director, and Popular European Cinema: The Worlds of Susanne Bier," *Camera Obscura* vol. 29, no. 1, 85: 5–31.

Strand, Torill (2010), "The Making of a New Cosmopolitanism," *Studies in Philosophy of Education* vol. 29: 229–42.

Yang, Julianne Q. M. [楊秋凌] (2013), *Towards a cinema of contemplation: Roy Andersson's aesthetics and ethics*, thesis, University of Hong Kong, <http://dx.doi.org/10.5353/th_b5016281> (accessed November 14, 2017).

Yang, Julianne Q. M. (2015), "Swedish post-war guilt and imperialism in Roy Andersson's *Songs from the Second Floor* and *A Pigeon Sat on a Branch Reflecting on Existence*," paper delivered at the annual meeting of the Society for Scandinavian Studies, May 8, Columbus, OH.

POSTSCRIPT

A Conversation with Susanne Bier

November 3, 2016 at ShaBaz Kaffebar og Køkken in Copenhagen
Missy Molloy, Mimi Nielsen, and Meryl Shriver-Rice

Shriver-Rice: We're here as academic scholars who are putting together the first book that focuses on your body of work. We've noticed that other prominent Nordic directors have had multiple books written on their work. Is there anything in particular that you would like us to address about your work that you feel may have been ignored, or even misconstrued by popular press?
Bier: I've been approached about my work before, and I haven't really wanted to collaborate for a number of reasons, mostly because it hasn't been that serious or it hasn't been sufficiently convincing. But also, I think one of the reasons is that I think I sit somewhere in a place where I'm too popular. In Denmark, I'm too commercial to be considered arthouse, and obviously, in the English language I am pretty arthouse. So I'm sitting somewhere in a space where it hasn't been scholarly at a level that I've been sufficiently interested in.
Shriver-Rice: And is there anything about your work that you feel has been misconstrued?
Molloy: . . . by the popular press? Have you read any of the scholarship on your work?
Bier: I don't tend to read too much about myself. Because this is an industry where your vanity is being fed like nowhere else, and I don't particularly want to get into that. And I'm fairly narrow-minded about wanting to work without being disturbed and then having [the time] to be with people I'm close to, my family and all that, and I don't really want to mess it up. I read reviews sometimes by reviewers I respect a lot just because it can be very educational, but I

Figure P.1 Susanne Bier.

don't tend to read, in general, press about myself. And I don't tend to look too much at images. I don't want to be outside of myself. And I really don't want to feed that intrinsic vanity that I suppose we all have. You have to try to control it, doing what I'm doing.

Molloy: We're going to ask questions having to do with points that are coming up in different chapters, which begin to create some sort of picture, "Susanne Bier is a filmmaker who. . ." Do you have an idea of what your logline would be for a book on your work?

Bier: I have an idea about what my very specific area of expertise is, what it is that I'm doing particularly well. I think I can create moments of extreme presence, of extreme intimacy; not just in intimate scenes, but also in bigger scenes, there are moments of extreme, intimate presence. Often when scenes don't necessarily lend themselves to it, I still create that. And I think it's because, possibly, this is who I am, and this is also who I am in my private life. I can't do small talk. I kind of get bored with anything that doesn't have a real sense of intensity. And I know it's kind of an abstract thing, but that's probably a very extreme strength I have, which is pretty visible in all my work. Even in the works that are not entirely successful, there are still moments of that very strong presence. And then in the works that are less successful, there are less of those moments. [*Bier laughs*]

Molloy: While you were talking, I was thinking of *The Night Manager* when Roper takes everyone out in the desert to basically explode his weapons; the scene has this sort of presence that you wouldn't expect. We've also been curious about your perspective on representing identity. Has it changed over the course of your career?

Bier: What do you mean exactly by "identity"?

Molloy: We mean "identity" on two levels: How your own identity impacts your cinema, and how you approach your characters' identities—the situations they experience, the social identities they inhabit, and how those are navigated in the films.

Bier: What you're basically asking is how does the fact that I'm Danish, a woman, Jewish, a whole lot of formal things, how does that impact the nature of the work, but also the identities of the characters. There's a traditional understanding of art where you kind of go, "well, this is a female director, and obviously the female protagonist or even antagonist are going to be stronger," because one tends to translate identity as a one into another one. It doesn't work like that. There are way more factors that play in, which are not necessarily part of one formal identity. I have always felt that I as easily identify with men as with women. To an extent, actually, it's been easier for me to identify with men. I've always had male friends since I was young; I've always played with boys, and I've always had male friends. Even now I often have an easier time, in a way, talking to men than I do to women. You know, our identity is very much . . . it comes down to the way you were brought up; it comes down to a whole lot of tiny, tiny factors, like how long we are allowed to be up when we were kids, a whole lot of things that then gradually shape our understanding of the world. I have a brother a year younger, and I think I have been brought [up] quite equal and in a way more like a boy than a girl. So I think I've always had an easy time identifying with men.

But also, being Jewish, in a way, has impacted to quite an extreme extent everything I've done, not because I'm religious—I am from a religious family—but because being Jewish today you are always part of a history of a potential catastrophe, and an undercurrent of anxiety. And there is a kind of intrinsic awareness that everything can end, that everybody can turn upside down. And I think that has to an extreme degree influenced everything I've done, and not necessarily just in terms of the actual storytelling, but also in terms of even just shaping a scene and a character's physical movements, understanding that there is an underlying nervousness or something. I think that all my characters have that, at all times.

Molloy: Then it's interesting that in your most popular films, you haven't explicitly addressed Jewish identity—not since the nineties. Do you see yourself doing so more explicitly in the future, or is that just something that drives you?

Bier: I feel that I'd have to be more interested in it. It doesn't interest me more than other stories. I'm driven by great stories; I'm driven by being touched by a story. I'm driven by a certain, sort of moral conscience, but I'm not particularly driven by Jewish stories. But I think it has impacted the way I understand the world in a very profound way.

Shriver-Rice: Do you feel a responsibility as a successful filmmaker to represent characters and situations that are different from what people tend to see in mainstream media?

Bier: I don't think moviemaking is about education. I don't think moviemaking or television is about teaching people things that they don't necessarily want to learn. But I do think it's about seduction, and I do think seduction will then allow me to emphasize things that I personally think are important. I'm probably more driven by a sense of ethics, a sense of morality, than politics. I am interested in politics, but I find it less translatable into cinema or television than more core questions. I do think at times political cinema tends to be, there is a certain danger of it being predictable that I don't particularly like, or that I'm not particularly attracted to. I just think that movies and television are not necessarily the best media for abstract ideas. Literature is way better for that. That's what I kind of feel, politics sits somewhere in between. I mean the seventies were full of amazing political films, but they still have very strong, definite storytelling. My main thing is that I'm always driven to story. I'm always driven to surprising, interesting characters.

Nielsen: By the same token, your close attention to the male characters and gender roles, how they negotiate their masculinity, becomes—because you attend so much to the detail of what it's like to be a singular man in a certain moral dilemma—a political critique. In a sense, they become a social critique of gender roles, too, because that's what is conveyed through the characters . . . I think your films are very political.

Bier: Yes, I mean, it's always political. I think that's definitely impacting the gender relationships and the gender attitudes, and also I do occasionally have fun with a certain kind of . . . For example, if you look at Roper in *The Night Manager*, you can say he's a racist; you can also say he's definitely a male chauvinist, but it's not in a very obvious way because he's also super charming and quite respectful. He does have a girlfriend who is not the token . . . girlfriend or whatever; she's quite complicated, and so yes, it's definitely there, but I don't really like it to be the engine. The engine is story, and everything then comes into it, but I'd rather sneak it in and have it sort of subtly there.

Nielsen: It's where the personal becomes political.

Bier: Yes.

Molloy: Have you had moments where you felt surprised by the way the public was receiving the film, or you thought that they were picking up on something you hadn't intended?

Bier: There have been a number of years that—all my movies have been huge in Denmark. Huge. For example, *In a Better World*, which went on to win a Golden Globe and an Oscar, but didn't win the Danish film award and wasn't even nominated for it. I can't remember whether the movie was nominated or I was nominated; I can't remember anymore. There has always been a sense of arrogance on behalf of the reviewers, as if you can't be sophisticated, or it can't be innovative, if it hits such a big audience. I have to say, I find it more funny than anything else. It doesn't bother me, I just register it, and I do find it quite funny. It shows a tendency [that is] incredibly anachronistic, which I also find at the European film festivals, which is like, "Hey, wake up. Realize that you are actually addressing an audience." There's nothing particularly attractive in making a movie so complicated and so sophisticated that you get an audience of ten in a select cinema. I'm not talking about everything being a major, huge studio thing, I'm just saying, recognize that part of what you're doing as a director is actually communicating. And if you have important stories to tell, if you have an important point of view, doing it in a way where you actually address it to an audience is way more important than—and I always feel, "come on, festivals, don't have 80% of the selections for the competition be completely uninteresting to an audience." It just doesn't work. I also think it just completely defies the purpose. I think it's so wrong.

Molloy: Well, it's upholding that high culture/popular culture divide, undercutting popular culture.

Nielsen: There's a long-standing use of popularity as a way to undercut value. Particularly when it comes to women there's a whole different magnitude of stigma. Your focus on men is very similar to Michelangelo Antonioni's, Woody Allen's, and Pedro Almodovar's focus on female characters.

Bier: That's right.

Nielsen: And they're very popular, art film directors, and there's a real consideration of them as *auteurs*, but here again, I recognize the pattern in the arguments from nineteenth-century literature in the reception, and it's still the same issues. So women directors, who straddle the popular and the artistic, are received and judged very differently.

Bier: Yes, but I think that's a fundamental female thing. I remember when I was in film school, we'd go to these festivals, and I'd be sitting with film school students from other countries, and they'd be so cool, and they'd be wearing black, and they'd be talking so pompously about their own work. And then you saw what they did, and it was just shit. I think women just tend to be less pompous about what they do, and more about the actual work.

Molloy: Well, we're not given the latitude to do that.

Bier: That's right. And we don't really want to do it. You can't help finding it rather ridiculous. You sit through programs and see directors being interviewed, and then it's like "come on."

Molloy: What he says the film does doesn't actually match anything that you see.

Bier: Yes.

Molloy: We've been particularly interested in the melodramatic label because in a lot of writing on your films, people tend to use that word. And they use it differently, we feel, than when they apply it to, specifically, male directors who also work in melodramatic modes. How do you feel about that label applied to your work, and in which sense do you consider your work melodramatic?

Bier: That depends on how you understand melodrama. Because if melodramatic implies a certain fakeness, I don't like it, and I don't find I can identify with it in any sort of way because I feel that what I do and what I'm aiming at is actually very truthful. But it has always been applied to my films. I've also been criticized for manipulating, which is in the same vein, and I kind of think, "okay, if a director's not manipulating, what is it exactly that a director is doing?" Because in my world, that *is* what we are doing, we *are* manipulating: we're manipulating the audience's emotions, the amount of knowledge we are leaving for them at certain times—I mean, that's the job, it is to manipulate.

Of course, if you feel manipulated in an uncomfortable way, then it doesn't work. I often go and see very big films, and I do feel manipulated in an uncomfortable way; I kind of feel, "Can they not tell me everything before the music?" It's sort of the difference between seduction and rape. As an audience, you don't want to be raped into feeling stuff, but you do want to be seduced. Are they harsher on me because I'm a woman? I don't know, and I want to say, I don't care. I mean, I do care whether there is a gender prejudice, but I don't care personally because I think it's a stupid criticism. Of course I'm manipulative. What do they expect?

Molloy: So if you consider your work melodramatic, in what sense?

Shriver-Rice: I think that we understand melodramatic as a very complicated academic notion, and that writing about your work in the popular press often overlooks that complexity.

Bier: I think when it's been written about in popular press, it's been understood as some sort of shallow, manipulating thing, so you're supposed to feel a whole lot. But I mean, so is Ibsen then melodramatic? I know it's a pretentious comparison, and I don't want to compare myself to Ibsen, but you know, you want to go and see classical drama. Is Chekhov melodramatic, or whatever? It's not withdrawn. It's not. And I've completely embraced that. I'm not particularly interested in withdrawn. I kind of get bored if it's too withdrawn.
Nielsen: I think you're working with such intense ethical issues, characters in really intense situations, especially in what we refer to as your transnational melodramas. And to me, those films are very prescient; they're ahead of their time. They're anticipating the instability of the world that we're experiencing at this very moment. They intimate that we *should* have intense feelings. What's going down is scary, it's intense, and I think you were ahead of your time in the way that you brought the emotionality of these very dramatic, very catastrophic situations to the audience.
Shriver-Rice: Your point being that it would be unacceptable to not have that reaction in those circumstances.
Nielsen: Yes, to not feel, to not have intense feelings in those situations is suspect. And yet you get judged for being melodramatic because it is highly emotional.
Molloy: On a related note, in academic work, and in the popular press to a certain extent, your work also attracts the label "transnational." We were wondering how your focus on stories and place, and on reaching out to the larger world to build the story, relates to the trajectory of your career and to opportunities you have had to work in certain production contexts.
Bier: I don't think it starts there; I actually do think it ties into being Jewish. I think being Jewish, you don't feel necessarily restrained to being part of just one country. My father was a refugee; I'm basically a second-generation immigrant here. Being Jewish [carries with it] a kind of global awareness which is part of who I am. There might be a connection with working more internationally, but it's not driven by that. It's not driven by a desire to do that; it's driven by a notion of our world becoming more and more difficult to isolate in the geographic sphere. That actually what is happening in other places has a direct impact on our life, in a completely different way even from ten years ago. It has happened so rapidly and is definitely very different from twenty-five years ago.
Molloy: And industrial changes have also changed so that financing a film can involve budgets culled from a bunch of different . . .
Bier: Yes, but my movies have not been financed in a way where we had to—you know, some European films are financed in such a way that you have to shoot some of it somewhere—that has not been the case. It hasn't been the case that they've been financed in a manner where we've actually had to shoot

certain places. It was the opposite; we kind of figured we wanted to shoot here or there and then found out we could finance it some way because it [involved] more than one nation. But I want to say that with my action movies, you don't really get any money out of shooting in Kenya, you don't get any money out of shooting in India, you don't even get money out of shooting in Italy. So that hasn't really been the case.

Molloy: But you're saying that your sense of the world as already global, and the local as interconnected with the global, has impacted you from the beginning, not just in these films that became very popular for that reason.

Nielsen: I have a related question: Do you identify then with the sense of being a diasporic citizen?

Bier: Yes. I mean my first film was *Freud's Leaving Home*, and also it was shot in Stockholm. I mean, I'm not Swedish; my parents were there, both of them, during the war. But ever since I've started, I've been quite comfortable working out of my own country, and I like the sense of isolation while working that is . . . In a way, being a foreigner and shooting somewhere else, or being a foreigner working somewhere else, you have a very accurate sense of the environment. Almost more accurate than . . .

Molloy: People that live there.

Bier: Yes.

Molloy: And do you feel that you had that in Copenhagen growing up?

Bier: Yes. And I also . . . I do feel very proudly Danish, but there's always a sense where I don't necessarily feel like I belong anywhere.

Molloy: We know that you consider yourself as having an "other" perspective on Danishness, so we were wondering if you could elaborate on that. But we also have a question regarding what the Danish film industry is known for (particularly since New Danish Cinema): collaborations and creative risk-taking. Do you feel that your work illustrates these qualities, or do you think that it's different or alternative?

Bier: *Open Hearts* is a Dogme film, and it did sort of comply with the Dogme rules. It also created a massive conflict with Lars Trier and a whole lot of discussion about whether . . .

Molloy: . . . you broke the rules.

Bier: Yes, because there was music, but she was actually, we did have the music, but—

Molloy: Is it diegetic or non-diegetic? Because [Cæcilie's] listening to it.

Bier: She's listening to it, and we had it on set, so it was all recorded, but of course it was . . . I didn't even think about it. I was just thinking, "how can I do that so that it actually works?" And it did something to her acting, and it did something to the whole scene, and it enabled us to actually have music.

So yes, I am part of it, but I've always also, for the very reason you mention related to melodrama, had the sense that my work has been, in a way, possibly

too American for what has been considered good taste. Certainly, if I am to mention my favorite directors, most of them are going to be American.
Molloy and Shriver-Rice: Can you mention them? [*laughter*]
Shriver-Rice: Just because we're curious. It's actually one of our questions.
Bier: I'll do that, but most of them are going to be American, and I think if you look at other directors, I think a lot of them are going to be non-American. If you're very European and if you're militant, it might not be artistic enough, it might be too commercial.
Molloy: There might be a contradictory sense in what is successful about recent Danish cinema because there's an idealization of certain types of art, and then there's the conscious use of genre to appeal to audiences by a lot of the directors, and I think the American influence is very clear. So there's kind of a mixed message.
Bier: I think *Festen* is a masterpiece, but are you going to tell me it's not a melodrama? And I think if you look at the mechanics of it, it's going to completely do all the right things at the right time.
Molloy: And some of the first Dogme films were definitely genre films.
Bier: Definitely.
Molloy: There have been particularly harsh reactions to [*Open Hearts*] and *Italian for Beginners* and to your breaking of the Dogme rules as opposed to others, and also critiques of the fact that the films sold more tickets than the other ones.
Bier: But all the movies that have sold a lot of tickets have been heavily criticized, and you kind of go "All right" . . . I just think it's ridiculous.
Molloy: Another notable feature of Danish cinema is the collaborations from the time you're in the National Film School, the connections that you make that you maintain throughout your career. Could you give us a sense of your approach to cinematic co-authorship and collaboration and to what extent that aligns with Danish cinema?
Bier: Part of the advantage of going to film school is creating collaborators whom you grew up with and have an immediate understanding with. And I have those—you know, I've been working with the same people forever and ever. And in the last couple of years, that has changed a bit, which I think comes naturally in life; you know, maybe your relationships with friends change, even if you are still close. And in a lot of cases there have been transitions with no regrets, you know, from anyone.
Shriver-Rice: And which filmmakers have influenced your style?
Bier: I love Michael Cimino, Coppola, I love all the seventies films, when they began to make real . . . *Dog Day Afternoon*, I love all the Billy Wilder, all the comedies. I love the sort of very melodramatic comedies. [*laughs*]
Molloy: You mean from the Classical Hollywood period, then the [New] Hollywood period?

Bier: Yeah. Scorsese, probably Coppola more than Scorsese. I love Lucas . . . I love *Star Wars*. [*laughs*] I probably like all the strong male protagonist-driven films. [*laughs*]

Molloy: We were also wondering which contemporary filmmakers you feel your career resembles or aligns with? Where you see their films and recognize something you're experimenting with?

Bier: There's quite a lot, actually. Because I was Oscar nominated twice, I tend to follow the directors who have also been Oscar nominated. I don't necessarily feel that I have a familiar language or that there's anything artistic, I'm just curious about them. At the moment, I think Werner Herzog has managed to be one of the most interesting directors and has always been. Actually, at the moment I really enjoy Asian films. I see a lot. At the moment I'm watching a lot of television.

Molloy: What's something you really loved most recently, television-wise?

Bier: *Veep. Transparent.* I enjoy *Modern Family*. I watch [that] a lot. I think *Veep* is just brilliant.

Molloy: [Julia Louis-Dreyfus'] performance is just . . . She's my favorite actress now.

Shriver-Rice: Many of your films feature queer characters, but all of them are male, and we were wondering if that was the result of a conscious decision or the product of how a narrative takes form?

Bier: I've been working with the same screenwriter, Anders Jensen, for a number of projects, and you can't exactly take him out of being responsible for the scripts. He definitely prefers writing for men than for women. It's kind of funny, the sort of sense of humor he has with men . . . he's so accurate. And I don't think he enjoys it as much writing for women.

Molloy: He doesn't think they're as funny?

Bier: Well, they aren't. [*laughter*]

Molloy: He did write *Love Is All You Need*.

Bier: Yes, which I loved, but which he's a bit mystified by.

Nielsen: In what sense?

Bier: It's just so different from everything else he's written.

Molloy: Maybe it's the only film he's ever written that's largely focused on a female character.

Bier: Yes.

Molloy: People disagree a little bit about *Open Hearts* because you could say it's from [Cæcilie's] perspective, but it's more of an ensemble piece. And this is like . . . [Ida's] the lead.

Bier: *Open Hearts* is both; it has both. I still think possibly the male characters as written . . . I mean, then there are actresses, once you start shooting it, [they become] so forceful that you don't really notice. But if you read the script, you'd probably find that the male characters have slightly more fun lines.

Molloy: Like Joachim has great lines, and the same actor [Nikolaj Lie Kass] has great lines in *Brothers*.
Bier: Yes.
Molloy: So the queer characters aren't really your responsibility, is what you're saying?
Bier: No, I think they are my responsibility, but I think it has to do with my collaborations. But when I read scripts, in general—you know, I'm reading so many scripts right now—I don't tend to be particularly interested in . . . I do get a number of very conventional female projects, and I don't tend to be particularly interested in those.
Molloy: Like romantic comedies?
Bier: Yes. I do like romantic comedies, but they have to have some kind of edge. I tend to get any amount of period dramas, with the unmarried girls who really want to meet a boyfriend or want to meet a potential husband, and I have to admit that I do have a bit of a hard time engaging. I just don't find it particularly . . .
Nielsen: Interesting.
Bier: I'm not being arrogant; it just doesn't trigger me. I'd rather do war films.
Molloy: We were going to ask you about genre because we have several people writing about genre. You mentioned Herzog, who has experimented successfully with a number of genres, and you have also experimented. You've recently moved into television, and also into the action genre, so now that you're looking at new scripts, what are you looking for in your next project? What's a genre that you haven't worked in that you would love to experiment with?
Bier: At the moment I'm quite tempted to do more action, actually. Just because I found that balance between creating those moments of something profound within something which is way more fluid, I just found it interesting and intriguing and stimulating. I can't say, "this is the genre I'd like to do." I can say that, even working in different genres, it's not the genre itself which is attracting me, it's the story. I do want to do more spy stuff. I think it's really fun and surprisingly meaningful. I quite like the fact that you can actually tell something meaningful, but it's not labeled as being important; it's labeled as being entertaining, and then it has an undercover.
Shriver-Rice: Many of our contributors are analyzing your most notable stylistic strategies, and we wanted to ask you about two specifically. One is your tendency to insert images of nature as transitional elements, and the second relates to a statement you made several years ago about your use of the camera as erotic. We were wondering how that manifests in your editing and cinematography?
Bier: The nature, I don't think they're transitions. I think that they are very much part of the moment, and they are certainly not meant to go "hey, now

it's a new chapter." Of what I've done until now, that's not how they work. They are very much there to enhance the moment, make the moment more magical, and I love that there are no characters in it, or that the characters are really small. I like everything which doesn't stop the stream of the storytelling.

And the camera being erotic has to do with [the fact that] I think the camera needs to be infatuated with the characters. I think the camera needs to have that love of the characters and wanting to touch the characters. So yes, it is erotic, but probably very different from the way a man would do it. Those words coming out of a man, I would probably go "ew, go away." And I don't mean [the camera] to disrespect actors' boundaries, I just mean it to be very affectionate and actually very loyal. But erotic is probably still the most accurate word because it needs to be vibrant. It can't just be caressing; it needs to be sexy in a funny way.

Nielsen: But you don't objectify. And also the warmth; there's this tremendous warmth.

Bier: I want to say that the warmth, just to go back to the melodrama, part of [that label] is also because everything I've done has always been quite warm. And I can't *not* do that because that's probably who I am. But warmth does not necessarily play well into fine art.

Molloy: There's a notion of critical distance as key to the work of other well-received filmmakers. But that's been eroding—in the last twenty years, a lot of the more critically acclaimed film directors have been much less distant from their subjects. Because there is a tactile quality to a lot of editing and camera work that has become popular, and yet it's used in all these different ways.

Bier: But it's not just the camera work, it's also the way you treat the characters. It's the essence of the piece. It's funny, talking about Herzog; Herzog is a weird mixture because he's very intellectual in a way, but I also think that there's an extreme amount of warmth. He might not be comfortable with it, and he might fight it, but it's still there.

Molloy: There's also a fascination—he's obviously fascinated with all the work he does.

Bier: Obsessive. Yes.

Molloy: And he doesn't take distance from his subjects. He's always inserting himself, and that's part of the interest, I think.

Bier: Yes.

Molloy: Have you had difficulties in any particular production context, and is there a certain kind of story or character that you've had trouble getting close to representing with the warmth you're talking about?

Bier: My most troubled production has probably been *Serena*. It might possibly be that a character who does such horrific things and is played by someone as lovable as Jennifer Lawrence . . . it was difficult making that whole story work. And the same thing with Bradley Cooper. Because I do tend to want to work with actors that I kind of fall in love with, and I think having them be characters who are doing such unforgivable things is just a tricky cocktail.

I think the production was relatively—not completely, but relatively—easy, but then what happened was . . . We shot it after they shot *Silver Linings* and after she'd shot *Hunger Games*, but none of the movies had come out. So we edited as she became this major, major star. And I think that a lot of people suddenly believed that this movie could do different things from what it could and through editing—we must have done 120 edits or something. And I can't edit that much. I can probably do ten edits. Part of what I've got is a compass [for what] is right or wrong, and with an audience, I can tell if the beats are working or not. And that sort of intuitive, sharp sense of "Is this working?" goes away. You kind of go, "I don't know." And I was numb. After edit number eight I was completely numb. And I think [the film] was edited for like two years. [*laughs*]

Molloy: It's interesting because it is a sort of feminist book on one level. It is focused on a female character for sure. So what was attractive to you about telling that story? It might not have come through, but what was it that you really wanted to tell?

Bier: It was her, but it was also the destruction of nature, but I think what happened was the reason for making the movie in the entire post-production just dispersed, and nobody could remember why we actually wanted to make that movie by the time . . . [*laughs*] Which has been hugely educational. I think it was probably one of the things [that] has [taught] me the most because I'm never going to do that again. I'm never going to venture into something and then end up in a process where I can't remember why I wanted to do it.

Molloy: And with *The Night Manager*, you made it relatively quickly.

Bier: Yes.

Molloy: So what production context, material conditions . . . what works best for you?

Bier: Everything quickly. I am like that, I can't do it; I get bored so quickly. I also can't stay at a party long. I might have fun for two hours and then I have to go. My daughter told me that in the entire world, she doesn't know anyone as impatient as me. [*laughter*]

Molloy: Well, it's great in a director . . .

Bier: . . . but it might not be as great in a mom.

Nielsen: Intensity comes back to presence and substance.

Bier: Exactly.

Nielsen: One of the things that I find so beautiful in your work—and I think the nature scenes also are part of that—is your anchoring presence into something other than doing. You studied religion in Israel; this transcendent presence comes through in your work, this interiority of being. How much have Kabbalistic teachings influenced your work?

Bier: There's no doubt that religious studies have influenced me. And you can say that in that sense of nature, there is a sense of something intangible, something in the moment, which is not the narrative, is part of the characters, but also part of something else. So it's definitely there. But I always worry about talking too much about it because it becomes quite banal once you put it into words, but I'm definitely influenced by it. I'm not a religious person though, but it has an impact.

Molloy: We're interested in your background in that you've said before that you don't have the traditional biography of a lot of film directors, like, "I'm a cinephile. From the time I was ten, I was watching everything . . . " You were obviously interested in other things, and in your biography on Wikipedia, it says, "and then suddenly Bier goes to the Danish Film School." Where did that come from? You were doing architecture, doing religion, moving around, then you were in the Danish Film School.

Bier: That's more or less how it was. [*laughs*] I did architecture, I did become interested in set design, and then I realized, trying to design stuff, I became more interested in, "I wonder who those characters are?"—the characters moving around within the things I was supposed to design. It was gradual, but it was over quite a short time. But I want to say that if you look at religion, and if you then look at architecture, then filmmaking is not necessarily . . . You know, you can make a triangle, and it makes sense. I just don't come out of a family where anybody was a filmmaker, or an actor, or anything like that.

Molloy: So it wasn't immediate.

Bier: No, it wasn't. But I went onto a set with a friend of mine who was at film school, and I just thought it made a lot of sense. I always thought I was creative, and I couldn't sing and wasn't an actor. I was always super shy actually, and so you're searching for "what is the outlet for that creativity?" And you try various things.

Molloy: It's difficult to get into that school though, isn't it?

Bier: It's very difficult.

Molloy: How did you manage that?

Bier: I did photographs. I submitted quite a strong photographic portfolio.

Molloy: Related to your architecture, or just what you were interested in?

Bier: Some of them related, but some were actually mini-movies out of photographs; I'd just taken sequences of photographs. [They were] things [that] were actually quite cinematic.

Molloy: Do you remember what they were?

Bier: One of them was an open-air swimming thing near the airport, and I did a love story of two people walking there, like in *Last Year at Marienbad*. It was very sort of lonely, two people looking at each other—actually lots of landscape, and lots of room around them. In a way, I mean, definitely things that are still in my movies which I was obsessed with at the time. I think all directors have certain obsessions, and they never go away. But if I look at it today, it was not exactly devoid of being pretentious. [*laughter*]

Molloy: But come on, you were twenty-something, it's hard not to be.

Bier: My finishing film from film school was also fairly heavy-handed. *The Island of the Blessed* is sort of Bergman-like. It's definitely Scandinavian, and there's a priest in it.

Molloy: So it was a big shift, then, to *Freud's Leaving Home*?

Bier: Yes.

Molloy: You said that some directors have an obsession. I'm writing about *Things We Lost in the Fire* and *Serena*. *Things We Lost in the Fire* is almost *Brothers* told again with different narrative emphases. So there are certain elements in your films that recur, certain attractions to certain types of situations. In that particular film, were you considering the similarities to *Brothers* while you were trying to tell the story of *Things We Lost in the Fire*? Do you think that led them to consider you as the right director for the project?

Bier: It's interesting, I hadn't actually thought about it until you said it, but you're absolutely right. You don't think it's just because it's two men, and their friendship is like a brotherhood?

Molloy: One of them socially does everything right, and the other one's the not-do-right—

Bier: And they switch—

Molloy: And one of them is taken away, and his whole relationship to the world shifts, so he gets to test out other social roles, and the woman's kind of in the axis.

Bier: But with *Things We Lost in the Fire*, I actually did think it should have been a love story. And it was so much not part of the project, and the producers and the writers . . . when I came into it, it was not a love story, so it wasn't an argument I could really win. I actually think it should have been more of a real love story.

Molloy: In *Brothers* it was the same?

Bier: In *Brothers* it *is* a love story.

Molloy: But it has the withholding of tension, in that moment after Michael got arrested and she's in the shower . . .

Bier: But they do actually have a proper love story. It is a kind of consummated love story. I guess I just don't believe in unconsummated love stories. I just don't think it's real. I think if people have strong passions, then it's really hard to avoid them.

Molloy: So *Things We Lost in the Fire* ends up being an alternate take on that love story?

Bier: You could say that, yes.

Molloy: And I felt that the impact of the close-ups on Benicio del Toro's eyes were really effective.
Bier: Yes.
Molloy: So you maybe fell in love with that character?
Bier: With Benicio, definitely. I mean, that's very hard not to do.
Molloy: We were also curious about the weird English-language translations of the titles. I feel like a lot of the irony is lost somehow, really explicitly in the titles, like *Love You Always* to *Open Hearts*, and *The Bald Hairdresser*.
Bier: *The Bald Hairdresser*, definitely. Basically, the distributor decides what they're going to call it. And it's very hard for small distributors because if you have a title, you don't—I mean, except for the very aficionado audience, broader audiences don't necessarily know anything about those films, and they will see them for the first time at a festival, or have heard about them from the festival or read a positive review, and if it has a title that audiences might think is too scary, they're just not going to go to that. So they tend to go for softer titles, always.
Molloy: It's funny that they soften them because a title does do something to you as a viewer; it gives you a signpost to the film before you go into it, and so it's like they take the edge out of your films a bit with the titles.
Bier: Yes.
Shriver-Rice: And that might be gendered as well, the same way that women's novels' covers are often made very feminine, even if the content is highly dark and dramatic.
[*A woman interrupts to thank Susanne Bier for her work, which she praises, adding, "du er så smuk."/"you are so beautiful." Susanne thanks her profusely.*]
Molloy: Which film are you most proud of? What can you watch again and again?
Bier: I don't ever watch my films again. I don't watch them after . . .
Nielsen: Why? Are you critical of them?
Shriver-Rice: That's fairly common, actually, for people to not watch them.
Bier: Because after the mix, you can't really do anything more. And it's so frustrating. Because I sit there and watch and go "Shit! We should have taken four frames out here." It doesn't stop for me, and I can't do it. It just becomes really painful for me. Even at premieres, I can't . . . I sneak out the back.
Molloy: But what would you change? I don't think there's anything you could change about *Den eneste ene* to make it a better screwball comedy.
Bier: It's not objective, it's just a sense. And also, I might be right, that it makes no difference in the bigger scale of things.
Molloy: What was weird about *The Night Manager* premiere, by the way?
Bier: There was a woman asking Tom Hiddleston about what it felt like being naked or something . . .
Molloy: Earlier, [Mimi] said [that you don't] objectify anyone, but in *The*

Night Manager, there is a sense of Tom Hiddleston being more the object of lust than the female characters.
Bier: But she's also . . .
Molloy: She's beautiful, but viewers really [responded to] the moment when they see his ass—all the British papers wrote about it.
Bier: I mean, regarding that question, I kind of go, "It's very hard to have sex without actually unzipping your trousers." [*laughter*] It's actually not objectifying anyone. It's just making a sex scene that is remotely real.
Molloy: It was actually really different from the sex scene in the first episode with the woman who dies.
Bier: It was meant to be very different.
Molloy: What's the reasoning behind the difference?
Bier: Because the first is sort of idealized—it's his dream of an amazing love story. And then with Jed it's a bit later, and it becomes more real, and also it's more forbidden. And they have a very short time.
Molloy: So it's more like a single take, and the other a montage?
Bier: Yeah.
Shriver-Rice: We have a question from another contributor curious about your collaborations with Jonas Gardell. Can you tell us more about the process of making *Like It Never Was Before* (another strange title change)?
Bier: That was a long time ago . . . Jonas Gardell is an amazing writer. I'm not sure what to say about it—I mean, it was a lot of fun doing it. First we did *Pensionat Oskar*, which I'm not sure—what is that called in English?
Nielsen: *Like It Never Was Before*.
Bier: *Like It Never Was Before*. And the next one—we did two films together. I'm not sure what the English title is of that.
Molloy: *Once in a Lifetime*.
Nielsen: *Livet är en schlager*.
Bier: Oh good, yes. You know, he has a funny, very extreme mix of poetry and humor, and so it's probably one of my most stylized movies. And that was because the script invited a certain style; it was quite stylized. I think probably that story is more cohesive than the next one. The next one the story is possibly too big for a feature film, I think. I can't really remember all the detail.
Molloy: Most of the published writing on your work covers releases post-2000, so we're trying to cover more of the work from before then . . . but these are probably old to you. There was also the film called *Sekten*—was that originally made for TV?
Bier: No, no, that was made for film. I made a couple of movies that absolutely didn't work, that being one of them. It's weird, because the first two thirds are actually quite good, I think, or at least decent, and then the last third makes absolutely no sense. And I think there are a couple of movies like that.

Molloy: Since you say that you work best in short time intervals and at a fast speed, then you must be willing to risk that something doesn't work.

Bier: Well, experience does help, and I want to say that I've always had quite strong script instincts, and I made a decision that I will be quite true to them. Because I do think that I by now have a sense of what it takes for a script to be successful.

Molloy: So your instinct to remain loyal to the story . . .

Bier: Yes.

Molloy: As written?

Bier: No, not necessarily. Instinct as to when the story actually works, and when a story does deliver what it sets out to. And possibly that's where I'm most conventional artistically because I do feel that for living images, the story has to have a certain natural [quality]; everything that doesn't have it, for me doesn't really work.

Molloy: So it has to follow a certain kind of dramatic structure?

Bier: Yes. I know a lot of directors really love it when there's no story, or when it's more arbitrary, or whatever. I get bored. I'm quite conservative.

Shriver-Rice: You've received a lot of praise for your ability to direct actors. Do you approach directing actors in Hollywood productions differently to Danish productions?

Bier: No. I don't.

Molloy: You mentioned something about Anders having difficulty writing for female characters?

Bier: I don't think he has difficulty writing for female characters; I think he's just naturally more interested in men. Anders Thomas can write anything. If he were to sit down and say, "Okay, I'm going to write a teenage girl story," he would do it, and it would be entirely successful. I just can't imagine him really being excited about it. He's so talented that he can write whatever he likes, but in general he's been more interested in men, and he's been quite interested in the darker side of men. And so I've probably been the one that has pulled it a bit, in a way, to the lighter [side].

Molloy: I find in *Brothers* the daughter's perspective is very strong, and also in *After the Wedding*, the daughter's perspective is very strong. There tends to be a female character in each film whose perspective is strongly felt that might not have been.

Shriver-Rice: Is that a result of your editing?

Molloy: Or your directing or your tendency . . .

Bier: Anders Thomas has a strong compassion for kids, so that is definitely part of it. I mean, there are kids in all the stories, and they're quite strong characters always. I think possibly the daughter—you know, it's always been very easy for me to identify with the daughter, for obvious reasons. So it's probably a combination.

Nielsen: And Marianne's a really strong character in *Hævnen*. We don't get a lot of her but—especially the schoolroom scene, when she's so angry that the teachers are part of this systemic violence that's occurring to her son.

Bier: Yes, I'm not saying that the female characters aren't strong; I'm just saying that he has easier access to what he knows about men than he does about women.

Molloy: Is there any story you've told that you feel most personally identified with?

Shriver-Rice: You can absolutely say no if you'd like.

Bier: It's very hard to say because it changes a bit. I come back quite frequently to *After the Wedding* when I think about things I'd like to do more of. I don't think it's necessarily my favorite film because I don't think I have one. It was really successful, but I don't feel that I'm quite finished with it. I'd like to do something more in that vein.

Molloy: So maybe it has to do with the kind of story you're obsessed with or attracted to telling, that's unfinished?

Bier: Yes, but also it has a sense of a wrought family, and a very extreme, narrow conflict. There's something about the set-up which I find intriguing.

Molloy: What is the ethical question that you think you're driven to by focusing on Denmark and elsewhere?

Bier: You know, what are our problems? Can you put hierarchy to problems? Yes, in a global scale you can: you can say that people suffering is more of a problem than someone not being able to buy a car. But for the individual, the fact that a person can't buy a car is a real issue, or can be a real issue. So it's this whole thing of, who are we to judge? Do we have any right to have any opinion on . . . The daughter's problem is as real as the father's problem. It's about addressing that. It's about having some kind of modesty or humility. It's also having a human sense of compassion and understanding.

Molloy: You're saying you can take these problems that are global and you can take these problems that are local, but they're all relative to the characters, so showing that—the value lies in that.

Bier: Yes.

Molloy: One contributor is directly dealing with your work parallel to Lars von Trier's, not because of your work per se, but because of your personas and your statuses as perhaps the most prominent Danish directors on an international scale, and also as a result of the comments he's made about you that have been critical. So I was wondering, when you were developing the story for *Open Hearts*, did you notice the relationship between that and *Breaking the Waves*, or was it just a coincidence that there are certain plot similarities?

Bier: I didn't remotely think of it. To be completely honest—you know, I like Lars von Trier, but *Breaking the Waves* is not one of my favorites at all.

Molloy: What's your favorite?

Bier: I liked the one where all the people were . . .
Molloy: *The Idiots.*
Bier: I loved *The Idiots.* I thought that was really funny. He has a very complicated relationship to me; I don't really have a complicated relationship to him. Our daughters are best friends, and I want to say that part of what might have annoyed him is that I don't really give a fuck, honestly.
Molloy: He was trying to provoke you, and you didn't want to bite?
Bier: Yes.
Molloy: So you weren't actually commenting on his work; you're not inspired by his work, it's just something that's there.
Bier: Yes. You know, I have tremendous respect for him; I think he's an amazing artist. I do my own thing, and I'm not that interested.
Nielsen: The world's big enough for both of you.
Molloy: Well, it had better be! [*laughter*] Of the Danish directors of your generation, is there one that you do identify with more than the others?
Bier: Anders Thomas. But also his work is so different. And I so much enjoy his films, I just really love them.
Molloy: It's funny because you're using a lot of the same actors, too.
Bier: Yeah, but they are very . . .
Molloy: very different films.
Bier: And I think it's quite enjoyable that there is no merging or anything. And I like that they're so bizarre.
Molloy: He doesn't seem to focus too much on children in his films. They're mainly focused on adult men.
Bier: They're mainly focused on really bizarre adult men. [*laughter*] And really embarrassing.
Nielsen: Are there any female directors that you relate to or really value?
Bier: Jane Campion. I really like her work.
Nielsen: She's similar to you in the pacing, the taking time with the picture and setting.
Bier: I think Kathryn Bigelow is great.
Molloy: Did you see *Top of the Lake* before you did *The Night Manager*?
Bier: Yes.
Molloy: The movement into longer-form narrative in television, how has that changed your process, maybe by offering new opportunities in pacing . . . ?
Bier: It's so interesting, so much fun. It's like getting a whole new set of tools.
Molloy: I'm very interested in this length of narrative right now. When you see *Top of the Lake*, when you see a season of *Fargo*, when you see what people can do with a six to eight episode format . . .
Bier: It's amazing. It's so interesting. You actually get that through film and reading a novel, you get into the characters, and it feels very short—like making a feature film, it also feels kind of exciting, it just feels very short

suddenly. Two hours, it's almost over. And I almost feel when I'm watching it, I don't want to watch a feature film; I want to watch something where I know there are many, many episodes.
Molloy: Well, it lets you get that exposure to the character, like you peel back the layers. You don't want to leave [the characters], you want to keep going with them. But it is also finite—it's not a serial.
Bier: No, it doesn't go on.
Molloy: It has a dramatic structure similar to a feature-length film. But it's difficult to adapt a novel to be a feature-length film.

Figure P.2 Susanne Bier with the volume editors.

Bier: It's more like a short story. A short story is like a feature film, and a novel is like a series. But I think what's interesting about six hours, because it's three acts, the acts are just longer. So I think there's that natural arc, which is also like for two hours.
Molloy: You can have the same dramatic structure, but it allows you to take more time with the people, with the world, with the situations.
Bier: Yes.

Filmography of Susanne Bier

De saliges ø / The Island of the Blessed (Den Danske Filmskole), 1986
Director

I Fridtjof Nansens fodspor over Indlandsisen / The Track (Columbus Film), 1988
Documentary. Screenwriter

Himmel og helvede / Heaven and Hell (Metronome Productions), 1988
Casting assistant

Notater om kærligheden / Notes on Love (Jørgen Leth Film, Columbus Film), 1989
Assistant director, writer (additional dialogue)

Songlines (independent), 1989
Collection of short films. Director, *Summer Rain*

Freud flyttar hemifrån . . . / Freud's Leaving Home (Sandrew Film & Teater AB, Crone Film, Omega Film & Television), 1991
Director
Writer: Marianne Goldman

Brev til Jonas (Film & Lyd ApS), 1992
Director
Writers: Lars Kjeldgård, Philip Zandén

Luischen (DR [TV-Fiktion]), 1993
Director

Det bli'r i familien / Family Matters (Svensk Filmindustri, Zentropa Entertainments, Grupo de Estudios e Realizaçoês, Nordisk Film), 1993
Director
Writers: Lars Kjeldgård, Philip Zandén

Abra kedabra (Peter Bech Film), 1995
Music video. Director

Pensionat Oskar/Like It Never Was Before (Sveriges Television TV 1), 1995
Director
Writer: Jonas Gardell

Sekten/Credo (Zentropa Entertainments), 1997
Director, co-writer
Writers: Jacob Grønlykke, Peter Asmussen, Juliane Preisler (novel)

Den eneste ene/The One and Only (Metronome Productions), 1999
Director, writer (story)
Writer (screenplay): Kim Fupz Aakeson

Hånden på hjertet/Once in a Lifetime (Nordisk Film Production, Sonet Film), 2000
Director
Writer: Jonas Gardell

The One and Only (TF1 International), 2002
Executive Producer, director, writer (story)
Writer (screenplay): Kim Fupz Aakeson

Elsker dig for evigt/Open Hearts (Zentropa Entertainments), 2002
Director
Writer: Anders Thomas Jensen

Brødre/Brothers (Zentropa Entertainments), 2004
Director, writer (story)
Writer (screenplay): Anders Thomas Jensen

Efter brylluppet/After the Wedding (Zentropa Entertainments), 2006
Director, writer (story)
Writer (screenplay): Anders Thomas Jensen

Things We Lost in the Fire (DreamWorks Pictures), 2007
Director
Writer: Allan Loeb

Hævnen/In a Better World (Zentropa Entertainments), 2010
Director, writer (story)
Writer (screenplay): Anders Thomas Jensen

Den skaldede frisør/Love Is All You Need (Zentropa Entertainments), 2012
Director, writer (story)
Writer (screenplay): Anders Thomas Jensen

En Chance Til/A Second Chance (FilmFyn, Zentropa International Sweden, Film i Väst), 2014
Director
Writer: Anders Thomas Jensen

Serena (2929 Productions), 2014
Producer, director
Writer: Christopher Kyle, Ron Rash

The Night Manager (BBC), 2016
Television miniseries. Executive producer, director
Writers: David Farr, John le Carré

Acknowledgments

First and foremost, we would like to thank the contributors to this volume for their resounding enthusiasm for the project and their intellectual generosity, and Susanne Bier for inspiring all of our efforts through her innovative and provocative works. Bier and her production assistants, Ida Hesseldal Windfeld-Hansen and Maximillian Birger Grønholdt, also supported this volume by making time for our interview and providing difficult to access resources. Much gratitude also goes to the EUP staff, who has made this process extremely rewarding, and we especially thank Gillian Leslie, Richard Strachan, Eddie Clark, and Rebecca Mackenzie for their competence and support.

The Society for the Advancement of Scandinavian Study (SASS) supported our earliest scholarship and research on Bier, without which this collection may not have taken form. In addition, the welcoming and collaborative Scandinavian Studies Scholarly Interest Group at the Society for Cinema & Media Studies, along with our conference pal Johnny Walker, helped us North American scholars connect with needed resources and contacts across the pond—many of whom joined the project as contributors. Thanks to Victoria University of Wellington for supporting this collection through a research grant and the allocation of a research assistant, Hannah Parry, whose attention to detail we are particularly grateful for.

Missy would additionally like to thank Leo Juhasz Molloy and Guillaume Cailleau for generously accepting her commitment to this volume; the US Department of Education's FLAS awards for funding four years of Danish language and cinema studies; Mona Mounzer for introducing her to many aspects of Danish culture and for the open invitation to Copenhagen; Maureen Turim for consistently supporting her research on Bier; and finally her sisters, Irene, Cathryn, Mary Clare, and Ann Molloy, and parents, Ed and Linda Molloy, who have made advanced study possible. Mimi thanks Andrew Nestingen for including Bier in his auteur syllabus and for his thoughtful and enthusiastic support, Sarah Ross for her inspired input on Bier's cinematography, Meryl Shriver-Rice for taking her on this first wild ride of co-editing a book, Missy Molloy for being such a passionate collaborator, and Al Nelson, whose whole-hearted support continues to carry her forward. Meryl would personally like to thank her fiancé Hunter Vaughan for his intellectual sparring and partnership, her mother Rebecca Shriver (Paulsen) for continuously sharing and engaging with her family's Danish heritage, and her sister Allyx Shriver-Rice for her compassionate anthropological debates.

Index

Note: f indicates a figure and n an endnote

Aakeson, Kim Fupz, 42, 232
   Little Soldier/Lille Soldat, 244, 246, 256
Aakeson, Kim Fupz and Christensen, Pernille Fischer
   En Familie/A Family, 234
   Someone you Love/En du elsker, 234
Aalbæk Jensen, Peter, 115, 122
Abbott, Stacey, 39
Abrams, Nathan, 118
aesthetics, 175, 180, 240
affect theory, 155–70
   emotion, 164
   meaning, 169
   psychological backstory, 159–64
   sense of self, 167–70
After the Wedding (Efter brylluppet), 57, 70
   awards, 6
   camera work, 192; close-ups, 29, 192, 251–2
   childhood, 237
   contrast, 63, 64f
   ethics, 250–1
   family structure, 217
   gender, 279
   global mobility, 235–6
   idealism, 238
   interconnections, xiv
   male characters, 76n7, 124, 157, 243–4
   masculinity, 62, 159, 238
   as melodrama, 155
   morality, xiv, 251
   mortality, 251–2
   "potential catastrophe," 116
   psychological realism, 4, 20, 23, 25
   "supra-diegetic" motifs, 31, 33
   transnationality, 5, 21, 114, 217, 254, 255
   traumas, xiv, 4
   violence, 251
   vulnerability, 63
Agger, Gunhild, 6, 29, 61
   The Europeanness of European Cinema: Identity, Meaning, Globalization, 41
Ahmed, Sara, 156–7
AIDS, 103, 110
Akerman, Chantal, 91–2
Allen, Woody, 157, 265
Almodóvar, Pedro, 157, 265
Altman, Rick, 31
AMC (American cable channel), 4, 144, 187
American cinema, 219; *see also* Hollywood
Anderson, Wes, 230, 243
Andersson, Peter, 159
Andersson, Roy, 244
anti-Semitism, 82, 120, 121, 125
Antonioni, Michelangelo, 265
Arcel, Nicolaj, 229, 234
   Dark Tower, 231
Aristotle, 23, 34n4
Armstrong, Gillian, 219
Aronofsky, Darren, 72

art films, 19, 20, 36, 216
  ambiguity in, 27–9
  categorization of, 61
  in English, 37, 114
  European films as, 41
"artistically valuable" films, 3
Asbaek, Pilou, 257
Atika, Aure, 193, 201f
August, Bille, 127n1
  Pelle the Conqueror (*Pelle Erobreren*), 241n1
Australia
  Gender Matters initiative, 226n2
  women's film units, 215
avant-garde, and cosmopolitanism, 246
awards
  Academy Awards (Oscars), xiii, 1, 6, 60, 70, 135, 142–3, 157, 191, 215, 218, 229, 253, 265, 270
  Bodil award, 6, 218
  Emmys, 135, 203
  European Film Awards, 47
  Golden Globes, 135, 142–3, 265
  Guldbagge Awards, 128n24
  Robert award, 6, 128n24, 218
  Sundance, 135, 146
  see also prizes
Axel, Gabriel: *Babette's Feast*, 241n1

Badley, Linda, 123
Bainbridge, Caroline, 123
Bald Hairdresser, The see Love Is All You Need
Barda, Jeanne-Pierre, 102
Baron, Lawrence, 118
Bazin, André, 23
BBC, 4, 125, 144, 187, 191, 243, 257
Bechdel Test, 68, 138
Bergman, Ingmar, 123, 157
Bergson, Henri, 157, 167
Berry, Halle, 6, 56, 67, 171n1, 226n8
Bertolucci, Bernardo, 219
Bhabha, Homi, 120
Bier, Rudolf Salomon (S. B.'s father), 84, 115, 213, 231
Bier, Susanne, 262f, 281f
  background, 4, 213, 225, 254, 274–5
Bigelow, Kathryn, 218, 225
  Hurt Locker, The, 59–60, 217
  K-19: The Widowmaker, 227n15
  Top of the Lake, 280
  Weight of Water, The, 227n15
Birch, Rasmus and Donato, Nicolo:
  Brotherhood, 256
Bird Box, 76

Björk, 115, 122
Boden, Anna, 143
Bodnia, Kim, 48, 239f
Bogdanovich, Peter: *What's Up, Doc?* 39–40
Bondebjerg, Ib, 114, 237; *see also* Hjort, Mette and Bondebjerg, Ib
books: film adaptations of, 72–3, 75–6
Bordwell, David, 27, 32, 189
Braff, Zac: *Garden State*, 92
Breaking Bad (TV drama), 189
Brennan, Teresa, 161–2
Bronski, Michael, 99, 100
Brooks, Peter, 62
Brosnan, Pierce, 47, 50f, 214
Brothers (*Brødre*), 6, 10, 16, 26f, 28f, 56, 57, 71, 76n7
  awards, 255
  budget, 70
  characterization, 23–4, 25
  cinematography, 162
  close-ups, 27, 29
  comedy, 62
  contrasts, 21–2
  ethics, 249, 250
  female characters, 74, 278
  genre, 33, 39, 257, 276
  masculinity, 62–3, 67, 124, 129n41, 157, 159, 243–4, 271
  mockery, 246
  morality, 250
  psychological realism, 4, 20, 162
  supra-diegetic motifs, 31
  transnationality, 36, 215, 216, 217, 254
  trauma, 4, 62–3, 163
  violence, 160–4, 173, 253
  voiceover, 249
  Von Trier's criticism of, 115
  vulnerability, 161, 163
budgets, 5, 57, 61
  Brothers, 70
  Dogme 95 movement, 2–3
  and funding schemes, 114
  Hollywood production model, 70–1
  Night Manager, The, 6
  Serena, 223–4
  see also financing

camera work, 9, 170, 174, 192
  After the Wedding, 29, 192, 251–2
  afterimages, 152, 176, 178, 181
  erotic, 272
  Freud's Leaving Home, 85, 86, 90, 158–9
  In a Better World, 31, 165–6

camera work (*cont.*)
  Night Manager, The, 195–6, 199–200
  Open Hearts, 168, 170
  Second Chance, A, 174–5, 175–8, 184
  von Trier, Lars, 129n27
  see also cinematography; close-ups
Cameron, James: *Avatar*, 248
Campion, Jane, 219, 225, 243, 280
  Angel at My Table, An, 220
  Piano, The, 220, 221, 224, 227n12
  Sweetie, 220
  Top of the Lake, 143
Canada
  films shot in *see Serena*
  Telefilm Canada, 138
  women's film units, 215
Caro, Niki, 219
Cavani, Liliana, 66
celluloid ceiling, 134, 136
childhood
  double narrative strategy, 237–8
  gendered presentation of, 237
  and violence, 235, 238–9
Christensen, Casper
  Klovn forever, 39
  Klovn—the Movie, 38–9
Christensen, Pernille Fischer, 3; *see also* Aakeson, Kim Fupz and Christensen, Pernille Fischer
Churchill, Winston: "Sinews of Peace" speech, 53n6
Cimino, Michael, 269
cinema vérité, 174; *see also* realism
cinematography, 151
  Brothers, 162
  and editing, 180, 272
  and emotion, 175, 252–3
  Freud's Leaving Home, 158
  In a Better World, 165, 166
  and psychology, 175
  Second Chance, A, 173, 180, 184
  women and, 136
  see also camera work
close-ups, 174, 188–90, 233
  After the Wedding, 251–2
  Brothers, 29
  Deleuze on, 177
  extreme, 191–2, 193, 197–201
  film noir, 29
  as narrative markers, 192–3
  Night Manager, The, 187–8, 189, 192–4, 195f
  Open Hearts, 27
  Second Chance, A, 176–8, 184
  television drama, 189
  Things We Lost in the Fire, 276
co-productions, 213, 216
Cohen-Olivar, Jerome: *L'Orchestre de minuit (Midnight Orchestra)*, 92, 93
collaborations: writer-director, 229–30, 232, 233, 234–41, 249–50, 252, 254, 255, 268, 269, 270, 277–8
Colman, Olivia, 146, 146f, 190
comedies, 4, 6–7, 33n1, 36–52, 216
  awards, 47, 218
  British tradition, 40
  Danish tradition, 37–9, 246
  dialogues in, 39
  Hollywood tradition, 39, 40
  Jensen, Anders Thomas, 230–1
  and Jewish heritage, 116
  and language, 45, 47
  lies in, 24
  masculine, 38–9
  music and, 39
  names in, 44
  queer, 39
  romantic, 39, 61, 225, 246, 271; *see also Love Is All You Need*; *One and Only, The*
  screwball, 39, 40, 44
  situation *see Freud's Leaving Home*
  and social issues, 92
  see also humor
commercialism, 58
Considine, Paddy: *Tyrannosaur*, 146
Cook, Pam, 233
Cooper, Bradley, 5, 57, 71, 73, 219, 222f, 223, 224, 232, 273
Coppola, Francis Ford, 269, 270
Coppola, Sofia, 243
  Marie Antoinette, 227n10
Cornwell, Simon, 143, 187, 190–1, 232
Cornwell, Stephen, 143, 187, 190
cosmopolitanism, 246, 254; *see also* transnationality
Cousins, Mark, 188
Credo see Sekten
criticism, 60, 75
Cuarón, Alfonso, 243
Curtis, Richard, 44, 53n7
  Love, Actually, 40

Dahl, Henrik, 45
D'Amore, Marco, 47
Danish film
  awards, 6, 218

Danish language, 60, 114
definition, 113
Hollywoodization of, 114–15
transformations, 229
see also Dogme 95 movement; New Danish Cinema
Danish Film Institute, 3, 52, 113, 114, 139, 140
Danish Film School see National Film School of Denmark
Danish Metronome Productions, 42
Danishness, 268
Love Is All You Need, 49–50, 51
Dawn, Randee, 141
Debicki, Elizabeth, 145, 145f, 190, 200f
del Toro, Benicio, 6, 56, 70, 226n8
del Toro, Guillermo, 243
Deleuze, Gilles: *Cinema 1: The Movement Image*, 177
Denis, Claire, 217
diegesis: "supra-diegetic" motifs, 20, 31, 33
digital technologies, 2, 245
disabilities, 102–3
Doane, Mary Ann, 176, 188–9, 197
Dogme 95 movement, 37, 175, 211, 229, 268
aesthetics, 180
and genre film, 269
and New Danish Cinema, 3
production strategy, 2–3
"Vow of Chastity," 174, 180
Donato, Nicolo see Birch, Rasmus and Donato, Nicolo
drama
definition, 19
family see *Freud's Leaving Home*
Nordic, 215, 216
period, 271
television, 189, 243, 270, 281–2; see also *Breaking Bad*; *Night Manager, The*
see also melodrama
DreamWorks Pictures, 76n2, 226n8
Dreyer, Carl Th., xiii, 123
Day of Wrath (Vredens dag), xiii
Passion of Joan of Arc, The (La Passion de Jeanne d'Arc), 188–9
Duchovny, David, 6
Dyrholm, Trine, 48, 214, 240f

Ebert, Roger, 69–70
Edelstein, David, 129n38
Edholm, Rafael, 42, 43f
egalitarianism, 3, 231, 232, 245
Egelind, Molly Blixt, 48

Egelind, Søs, 42, 43f
Eisenstein, Sergei, 188–9
Ekblad, Stine, 47, 111n5
Ekelöf, Gunnar, 158
Elkabetz, Ronit and Shlomi: *Shiva*, 92
Elsaesser, Thomas, 216, 223
English language, 41–2, 52, 61, 71, 113, 114, 276
Englishness, 51
eroticism, 68, 176, 199, 272
ethics, 180, 279–80
After the Wedding, 250–1
Brothers, 249, 250
cultural and political, 244–5
and emotions, 235
In a Better World, 238, 244
Second Chance, A, 174, 180, 181, 182
and spectatorship, 175, 180
ethnic films, 128n21; see also Jewish directors
ethnicity, 137; see also Jewish identities
Eurimages, 114
Europeanness, 41–2
Eurovision Song Contest, 98, 102, 103–4

Faber, Alyda, 123
families
dysfunctional, 86
and gay identity, 98–9, 100–1, 102, 106
Jewish, 84; see also *Freud's Leaving Home*
Night Manager, The, 191–2
photographs, 179
psychodynamics of, 22, 25–6, 232
Serena, 220
see also *Brothers*; *Family Matters*; *Second Chance, A*; *Things We Lost in the Fire*
Family Matters (Det bli'r i familien), 5, 92, 115, 128n19, 173, 213
Farr, David, 187, 190
feature films, 3, 115, 211, 215, 218, 281–2
femininity, 123, 124, 166
feminism, 141, 212, 214–15, 235
Nordic, 215
second-wave, 225
Festen see Celebration, The
festivals, 265, 266
Berlin, 245
BFI London, 72
Cannes, 122, 127, 245
Göteborg, 178
Munich Filmschool, 5, 115
Toronto, 6
women's representation, 136
film noir, 29, 196

financing, 7, 213, 215, 223–4, 225, 267–8; see also budgets; funding schemes
Flickering Lights (*Blinkende lygter*) (Jensen), 38
Foldager Sørensen, Meta Louise, 144
Forman, Miloš, 219
Four Weddings and a Funeral (Newell), 40, 44
Frampton, Edith, 89
Freud, Sigmund, "The Family Romance," 83
Freud's Leaving Home (*Freud flyttar hemifrån*), 36–7, 83–95, 157, 214
  awards, 84, 119
  camera work, 85, 86, 90, 158–9
  as comedy, 4, 61–2
  funding, 114
  homosexuality, 86–7, 94
  intimacy, 158–9
  Jewish themes, 117, 118–19, 126
  male characters, 158–9
  "potential catastrophe," 116
  satire, 89
  solitude, 158
  stereotypes, 86
  transnationality, 5, 213, 268
  trauma, 86–7, 94, 118
Frye, Northrup, 23, 33n3
Fuchs, Thomas, 25
funding schemes, 3, 114, 137–8; see also budgets; financing

Gardell, Jonas, 97–8, 99, 102–3, 277–8
  Don't Ever Wipe Tears Without Gloves (*Torka aldrig tårar utan handskar*), 103
Garrett, Stephen, 144
Gartner, James: *Glory Road*, 248
gay/queer identities
  Like It Never Was Before), 94, 97, 98–101, 110, 128n19
  Love Is All You Need, 81, 97, 98, 105–7, 110
gay rights, 98–9
Gehring, Wes, 39–40
gender, 123–4, 214, 264–5
  and childhood, 237
  in comedies, 39
  of directors, 5, 58–9, 60, 157
  inequalities, 60, 136–8, 139, 238
  initiatives, 226n2
  politics, 135, 141–3
  quotas, 138, 140, 226n2
  stereotypes, 141, 166, 217
  transgender "libidinal" identifications, 124

  see also femininity; feminism; masculinity; women
genre films, 36, 51, 61, 232
  Danish, 114
  Dogme 95 and, 37, 269
  English, 37
  feminist, 218
  Swedish, 114
  transnationality, 216
  see also art films; comedies; drama; melodrama
Genz, Henrik Ruben, 244
Germany
  conquest of Denmark, World War II, 84
  women's film units, 215
gestures, 192
Gilman, Charlotte Perkins: *The Yellow Wallpaper*, 227n11
Giroux, Jack, 155
Gledhill, Christine, 62
global mobility, 235–6
globalization, 2, 245, 253
Godard, Jean-Luc, 157
Goffman, Erving, 23
Goldman, Marianne, 84, 89, 117, 118, 128n24
González Iñárritu, Alejandro, 243
Goodridge, Mike, 44
Gouri, Vanessa, 43–4
Gråbøl, Sofie, 44
Granik, Debra: *The Winter's Bone*, 224
Greenberg, Udi E., 129n30
Grodal, Torben, 32
Guardian, The (newspaper), 143, 187
guilt
  postcolonial, 255, 257
  privileged-nation, 244–5, 256, 257
  "Scanguilt," 245–7, 252–3
Gullits Ernst, Frederik and Kristian, 237f

Hæstrup, Ulla, 140
Hallström, Lasse, 243
Hancock, John Lee: *The Blind Side*, 248
Hardwicke, Catherine: *Twilight*, 227n10
Hartvigsson, Niels, 53n3
Hawks, Howard, 39
HeForShe campaign, 137
Heisterberg, Rasmus, 234–5
Hermansen, Anne Sophia, 139, 140
Herzog, Werner, 270, 271, 272
Hiddleston, Tom, 145, 190, 193f, 195f, 197f, 199f, 201f, 277
Higson, Andrew, 40

Hirsch, Marianne: *The Mother/Daughter Plot: Narrative, Psychoanalysis, Feminism*, 95
Hitchcock, Alfred, 243
  Sabotage, 189
Hjort, Mette, 3, 41, 60, 68, 114, 229
  Small Nation, Global Cinema: New Danish Cinema, 128n17, 213–14
Hjort, Mette and Bondebjerg, Ib (eds.): *The Danish Directors*, 140–1
Høeg, Peter: *Borderliners (De måske egnede)*, 45
Hoggart, Liz, 47
Hollander, Tom, 195
Hollywood
  Academy Awards (Oscars), xiii, 1, 6, 60, 70, 135, 142–3, 157, 191, 215, 218, 229, 253, 265, 270
  Brothers remake, 255, 257
  close-ups, 189
  gender politics, 142, 219
  and genre, 216
  hierarchies, 232
  influence, 2, 16, 32, 40, 57, 114–15, 243, 269–70
  Jewish influence, 117–18
  morality, 234
  neo-imperialism, 247–8
  populism, 60–1
  production model, 70–1
  and world cinema, 212
Hollywood Reporter, The (newspaper), 73
homosexuality
  Beginners, 92–3
  Freud's Leaving Home, 86–7, 94
  gay rights, 98–9
  Like It Never Was Before, 94, 98–9
  see also identities: gay/queer
Honeycutt, Kirk, 69–70
Hong, Nathaniel: *Occupied: Denmark's Adaptation and Resistance to German Occupation 1940–1945*, 84
Hooper, Tom, 243
Hopewell, John, 223–4
human bodies
  affect theory, 156–7, 161–2, 164
  male, 170
  norms of, 107
  nudity, 165–6
  self-attention, 166–7
  see also close-ups
human face: close-ups, 188

humanitarianism, 23, 246–7
  In a Better World, 217
humor, 61–2
  existentialist, 244
  Jewish, 87
  see also comedies
Hybschmann, Sidsel, 233
hygge, 183

idealism, 23, 24, 32, 269
  After the Wedding, 238
  children and, 240
  of family, 178
  and masculinity, 165, 240
  Night Manager, The, 277
  von Trier, Lars and, 123
identities, 81–2
  and disability, 102–3
  gay/queer, 86–7, 92–3, 94, 97–110, 256; *Like It Never Was Before*, 98–101, 110; *Love Is All You Need*, 105–7, 110; *Night Manager, The*, 108, 110; *Once in a Lifetime*, 102–4, 110
  Jewish, 84, 86, 113–27, 263–4, 267
  and marginalization, 103
  non-normative, 102
  see also gender
In a Better World (Hævnen), xiii, 1, 20, 29–31, 36–7, 235–7
  awards, 6, 215, 218, 265
  camera work, 31, 165–6
  contrasts, 21
  criticism, 129n38
  crosscutting, 248–50
  double narrative strategy, 238
  ending, 25–6
  ethics, 238, 250, 280
  female characters, 279
  humanitarianism, 217
  intimacy, 166
  male characters, 23–4, 74, 124, 157, 182–3, 215, 243–4
  masculinity, 60, 62, 129n41, 159–60, 164–6, 238
  melodrama, 155, 217
  morality, 237
  solitude, 198
  "supra-diegetic" motifs, 31
  transnationality, 114, 255
  traumas, 4, 25, 164, 167
  violence, 20, 60, 165, 238–9, 250
  visual layering, 30
  vulnerability, 31

Ink Factory (production company), 190
intimacy, 20, 26, 29, 32, 58, 71, 232–3, 263
   close-ups, 189, 197–201
   Freud's Leaving Home, 158–9
   In a Better World, 166
   Open Hearts, 94, 169, 170
   Second Chance, A, 175
   Sekten, 68
   Things We Lost in the Fire, 62
Island of the Blessed, The (*De Saliges ø*), 5, 37, 115, 116, 180–1, 275

Jäckel, Anne, 41
Jenkins, Barry: *Moonlight*, 253
Jensen, Anders Thomas, 2
   Adam's Apples (*Adams æbler*), 38
   collaboration with Bier, 6, 7, 20, 33, 47, 67, 75, 116, 134, 159, 214, 232, 233, 234–41, 249–50, 252, 254, 255, 270
   comedies, 230–1
   on European and American film industries, 56, 70, 115
   Flickering Lights (*Blinkende lygter*), 38
   and gender, 278–9
   Green Butchers, The (*De grønne slagtere*), 38
   In China They Eat Dogs (*I Kina spiser de hunde*), 38
   Men & Chicken (*Mænd og høns*), 38
Jensen, Peter Aalbæk *see* Aalbæk Jensen, Peter
Jermyn, Deborah, 39
Jerslev, Anne, 59
Jessen, Sebastian, 48
Jewish culture, 238; *see also* Yiddish language
Jewish diaporas, 84, 88–9, 93, 116, 117, 213
Jewish directors, 92–3
Jewish heritage, 81, 87–9, 91, 92–3, 116, 118, 231, 254; *see also* Judaism
Jewish identities, 84, 86, 113–27, 267
   von Trier, Lars, 113, 119–22, 125–6, 127n3
Johansen, Simon, 142
Jolie, Angelina, 72
Jonas, Hennie (S. B.'s mother), 84, 115, 213, 231
Jones, Ward E., 182
Jonze, Spike, 243
Joof, Hella, 3, 44, 98, 139
   Almost Perfect (*Sover Dolly på ryggen?*), 246
   Oh, Happy Day, 39
   Shake It All About (*En kort, en lang*), 39
Judaism, 115

Kaalund, Lars, 42
Kass, Nikolaj Lie, 271
Kiang, Jessica, 111n6
Kidman, Nicole, 122
Klein, Melanie: "Notes on Some Schizoid Mechanisms," 89
Knudsen, Sidse Babett, 42, 43f, 46f
Kosmorama (magazine), 56
Kovács, András, 32
Krasnik, Martin, 125
Kulyk, Laëtitia, 42
Kurasawa, Fuyuki, 247
Kyle, Christopher, 72, 227n15

LaGravenese, Richard: *Freedom Writers*, 248
Lang, Fritz, 219
Langkjær, Birger: *Realismen i Dansk Film*, 59
language
   Danish films, 113
   English, 41–2, 52, 61, 71, 113, 114, 276
   and humor, 45
   Jewish, 87, 120
   and Otherness, 238
   and transnationalism, 253
   Yiddish, 87, 120
Larsen, Gorm, 25
Lassgård, Rolf, 22f, 237f
Laurie, Hugh, 145f, 190, 197f
Lauzen, Martha M., 136
Lawrence, Jennifer, 5, 57, 71, 72, 73, 219, 223, 224, 232, 273
Lawson, Terry, 59
le Carré, John: *The Night Manager* (novel), 190, 191
Lee, Ang, 243
Lee, Spike: *Do The Right Thing*, 253
Letter to Jonas (*Brev til Jonas*), 37, 116
Levy, Shawn: *This is Where I Leave You*, 92
Liebman, Lisa, 141
Like It Never Was Before (*Pensionat Oskar*)
   collaboration with Gardell, 277–8
   disability, 102–3
   gay/queer identities, 94, 97, 98–101, 110, 128n19
   male characters, 157
   premiere, 6
   promotional poster, 99, 100f, 107
   "supra-diegetic," 31
   transnationality, 36
Lindegaard, Bo: *Countrymen: The Untold Story of How Denmark's Jews Escaped the Nazis*, 84

INDEX 293

Lindholm, Tobias, 229, 235, 257
  A War/Krigen, 244, 257
Liz, Mariana, 41
locations, 4, 225
  Serena, 74, 218, 219, 221, 223
  Things We Lost in the Fire, 226n8
Lopes, Denilson, 246, 253
Louis-Dreyfus, Julia, 270
Love Is All You Need (*Den skaldede frisør*), 4, 5, 6, 41, 47–51, 101f
  awards, 6, 47, 226n7
  collisions, 173
  color, 50–1
  Danishness, 49–50, 51
  eroticism, 68–9
  female characters, 68, 74, 270
  feminism, 215
  gay/queer identities, 81, 97, 98, 105–7, 110
  genres, 15, 16, 44, 61, 62, 191, 214–15, 232, 254
  Italianness, 48–50, 51, 52
  stereotypes, 49–50
  translation, 276
  transnationality, 36–7
  vulnerability, 51
Lucas, George, 270
Luischen, 6, 37
Lupher, Sonia, 203
  "Susanne Bier's Living, Breathing Body of Work," 192
Lutheran church, 234
lying, 23–4, 25

McHugh, Kathleen, 212–13, 225
Madsen, Jenny Lund, 139
mainstream films, 3, 6, 29, 36–7, 41, 52, 60, 61, 187, 188, 201, 208, 217, 224, 232, 246
  close-ups, 189
  human bodies, 107
  queer characters, 82, 98, 103–4, 108
  transnational, 114–15
  see also popular cinema
"male sojourner trilogy" *see After the Wedding*; *Brothers*; *In a Better World*
marginalization, 103
  and disability, 102–3
  and gay/queer identities, 82, 98, 106, 108, 110
  von Trier and, 124, 126
  of women, 212–13
marketability, 2, 3, 40, 57, 143, 216

Martiny, Didier: *Pique-nique de Lulu Kreutz* (*Lulu Kreutz's Picnic*), 92
masculinity, 7, 233, 264
  After the Fire, 62, 159, 238
  and aggression, 129n41
  Brothers, 62–3, 67, 124, 129n41, 157, 159, 243–4, 271
  configurations of, 160
  dilemmas of, 62, 63
  and ethics, 238
  hyper-, 160, 161, 162–3
  and idealism, 240
  "impaired," 66
  In A Better World, 60, 62, 129n41, 159–60, 164–6, 238
  and individualism, 170
  Jensen and, 230
  and legitimacy, 60
  and melodrama, 20–1, 217
  and morals, 183
  Night Manager, The, 264
  non-confrontational, 164–6
  non-heteronormative, 256
  and responsibility, 124
  Serena, 220, 233
  stereotypes of, 45
  Things We Lost in the Fire, 63, 66, 233
  and violence, 60, 239
  and vulnerability, 63–4, 67, 124
  see also men
Massumi, Brian, 156
Mayer, Louis B., xiii
MEDIA Programme, 114
melodrama, 7, 29, 58, 174, 203, 216, 232, 266–7
  Danish compared with American, 33
  and emotion, 155
  and family dynamics, 62, 217
  and gender, 59, 155–6
  male, 20–1, 123–4
  "melodramatic modality," 62
  Moodysson, Lukas, 244
  and realism, 20, 22–4, 59, 74
  storytelling and style, 20–2, 32
  and warmth, 272–3
memory
  Holocaust, 91
  and perception, 167
men
  as directors, 157
  male body, 170
  male characters, 158–64, 191, 235
  see also masculinity

Meta Film, 144
migration, 214, 217
Mikkelsen, Mads, xiv, 22f, 28f, 232, 236f
Miller, Alice, 91
Mills, Mike: *Beginners*, 92–3
mimesis, 23, 33
misogyny, 122–3
Mittell, Jason, 189
Moddelmog, Debra, 106
Moodysson, Lukas, 244
   Show Me Love (*Fucking Åmål*), 98, 103
Moore, Cath, 247
morality, 250, 264
   After the Wedding, xiv, 251
   Hollywood, 234
   In a Better World, 237, 249
   Second Chance, A, 184
mortality, 251–2
Mulchandani, Neeral, 236f
multiculturalism, 128n17
music, 21, 144, 268
   Indian, 255
   and Jewishness, 88–9, 93
   schlager, 102
   see also Eurovision Song Contest
Mygind, Johanne, 139

Nagib, Lúcia, 212, 213
National Film School of Denmark, 3, 4, 23, 115, 134, 139, 238, 274
nationalism, 141, 214
naturalism, 33, 75
nature images, 271–2
Neal Street Productions, 76n2, 226n8
Netflix, 76
New Danish Cinema, 1, 2, 19, 29, 114, 211
   appeal of, 3
   Brothers as a catalyst for, 39
   and Dogme 95 movement, 3, 229
   and female directors, 215
   as a mirror of Danes, 38
   morality and ethics, 41, 249
   and privileged-nation guilt, 256
   stylistic conventions of, 174
   and transnationalism, 213–14
New Danish Screen, 230–1
New Queer Cinema, 98, 103
Ngai, Sianne, 156, 164
Nielsen, Connie, 26f
Nielsen, Henrik Bo, 140
Nielsen, William Johnk Juels, 239f, 240f
Night Manager, The, 232, 273
   adaptation from novel, 72
   budget, 6
   camera work, 195–6, 199–200; close-ups, 187–8, 189, 192–4, 195–203
   Emmy award, 60
   eroticism, 199
   families, 191–2
   gender, 144–7, 190, 277
   identities, 263, 265; gay/queer, 97, 108, 110
   male characters, 63
   masculinity, 264
   popularity, 4, 5, 6, 61, 75
   risk and innovation in, 143–4
   as a "six-hour film," 190–1
   social justice, 111n6
   solitude, 188, 198
   vulnerability, 63, 146, 188, 198, 202
Night Manager, The (novel), 190, 191
Nørby, Ghita, 128n24
Novotny, Tuva, 257

Olesen, Annette K., 2, 139, 215, 244
Olesen, Niels, 42, 43f
Once in a Lifetime (*Livet är en schlager*), 6, 101f
   collaboration with Gardell, 277
   disability, 103
   female characters, 76n7
   gay/queer identities, 81, 97, 102–4, 105, 110, 128n19
   gay rights, 98
   transnationality, 36
One and Only, The (*Den eneste ene*)
   as comedy, 19, 33n1, 36, 42–7, 51–2, 61, 214
   female characters, 76n7
   genre mixing, 232
   popularity, 1, 4, 6, 38
   satire, 51
   stereotypes, 45–6, 51, 52
   taboo issues, 128n19
Open Hearts (*Elsker dig for evigt*), 6, 19–20, 26–7, 28f, 56, 65f, 76n7, 167–70, 215, 218
   as an art film, 36, 58
   authorial control, 75
   camera work, 168, 170; close-ups, 27
   contrasts, 21
   and Dogme 95 movement, 268, 269
   ending, 25
   female characters, 68, 74
   gay/queer identities, 94
   gender, 270–1

intimacy, 94, 169, 170
lying, 23
male characters, 63–4, 157
realism, 27, 59
violence, 173
vulnerability, 63–4
Otherness, 238, 244, 245, 247, 252, 256
Out of Africa, 75, 76

Pearl, Monica, 103
Peele, Jordan: *Get Out*, 253
Peirce, Kimberly: *Manhattan*, 143
Persbrandt, Mikael, 30f, 232, 236f
Petrone, Cire, 47
Philipsen, Heidi, 29
photographs, 152, 177–9, 275
Pitt, Brad, 190
Plath, Sylvia: *The Bell Jar*, 227n11
Polanski, Roman, 219
politics, 265
  and ethics, 244–5, 264
  of gender, 135, 141–3
  of race, 217
Pollack, Sydney, 190
popular cinema, 58–62, 216, 265; *see also* mainstream films
postcolonialism, 45, 208–9, 246, 247–53, 255
prizes, 41
  anti-prizes, 122
  see also awards
production strategies, 2–3, 61
psychology, 15, 24, 175
  Brothers, 162
  and conflict, 218
  Piano, The (Campion), 220–1
  Second Chance, A, 175, 177
  Things We Lost in the Fire, 68
  see also realism: psychological

queer film *see* New Queer Cinema
Quigly, Paula, 123

race: politics of, 217
racism, 160, 214, 253
Rash, Ron, 72
realism, 19–20, 33
  British, 40
  and melodrama, 20, 22–4, 59, 74
  Open Hearts, 27, 59
  psychological, 4, 23, 24, 160, 216, 219, 246
  social, 23
  see also cinema vérité
Redvall, Eva Novrup, 3, 56

Refn, Nicolas Winding, 126, 127n1
Reinfeldt, Fredrik, 98
religion, 274; *see also* Judaism; Lutheran church
Reza, Yasmina, 92
Richter, Sonja, 28f
risk, 61, 75, 143–4, 268
Robbins, Brian: *Hardball*, 247
Roberts, Martin, 246
Rodowick, David, 217
Roe, Anabelle Honess, 40
Röör, Gunilla, 128n24
Rosendahl, Christina, 139
Rovisco, Maria, 254
Russo, Vito, 108
Rygaard, Markus, 239f

Sánchez-Baró, Rossend, 189
Sand, Anne Jensen, 139
Sandgren, Åke, 2
Sandrew Metronome (distribution company), 42
satire, 246
  Freud's Leaving Home, 89
  One and Only, The, 51
  von Trier and, 122
Sauntved, Louise Kidde, 20, 29, 174
"Scanguilt" (research group), 245
Schatz, Thomas, 216
Schaumburg-Müller, Christiane, 48
Scherfig, Lone, 2, 3, 127n1, 215, 229, 243
  Italian for Beginners, 58, 269
Scorsese, Martin, 270
screenwriting, 3, 115, 138; *see also* collaborations: author-director
scripts, 23, 278
Sebastian/När alla vet (Wamb), 98
Second Chance, A (En chance til), 6, 20, 173–80, 181–5, 215
  aesthetics, 175
  afterimages, 176, 178, 181
  camera work, 174–5; cinematography, 173, 180; close-ups, 176–8, 184
  characterization, 63
  criticisms, 181
  ending, 25
  ethics, 174, 180, 181, 182
  identification, 180
  intimacy, 175
  lying, 23–4
  morality, 184
  nature images, 31
  photographs, 152, 177–9

Second Chance, A (En chance til) (*cont.*)
   "potential catastrophe," 116
   psychology, 175, 177
   social markers, 21
   traumas, 173, 174, 175–6, 181
   violence, 180
Sekten/Credo, 6, 23n1, 64–5, 66f, 68, 277
Serena, 57, 59, 60, 61, 71–4, 141, 221–5, 222f, 232
   appeal, 224–5
   authorial control, 75, 224
   budget, 223–4
   characterization, 72–4, 223
   critical reception, 76n140
   editing process, 73, 273
   epic qualities, 33
   financing model, 223–4
   gender, 142, 219, 222–3
   location, 74, 218, 219, 221, 223
   masculinity, 220, 233
   mise-en-scène, 222
   psychological realism, 219–20
   transnationality, 5, 37, 218–19
   trauma, 74
   violence, 219
   vulnerability, 72, 73
Serena (novel), 72–3
Serner, Anna, 137–8
Shakespeare, William: *Macbeth*, 223
Sheridan, Jim, 71, 160
Shriver-Rice, Meryl, 20, 29, 41, 94, 160, 163, 174, 180, 192, 198, 216, 230
Silver Linings Playbook (Russell), 72, 76n3
Silverman, Kaja, 57, 66, 124
Skotte, Kim, 235
Smaill, Belinda, 22, 29, 32, 41, 57, 61, 62, 67, 123–4, 156, 159–60, 243, 246–7, 252
   "The Male Sojourner, the Female Director, and Popular European Cinema: The Worlds of Susanne Bier," 59
Smith, John N.: *Dangerous Minds*, 248
social justice, 111n6, 245–6
Sontag, Susan, 179
Spinoza, Baruch, 157
Springall, Alejandro: *Morirse está en Hebreo (My Mexican Shiva)*, 92, 93
Stadler, Jane, 175
Steele, Hannah, 193f, 194f
Steen, Paprika, 2, 3, 42, 48, 139, 215
stereotypes
   gender, 141, 166, 217
   Jewish, 86, 120, 121, 122, 124, 125
   national, 49–50, 51, 52
   queer, 110
   romantic, 45–6
Stevenson, Jack: *Dogme Uncut*, 58–9
Stone, Oliver, 227n15
Strand, Torill, 254–5
Studiocanal, 223
Svendsen, Lotte, 215
Sweden
   English language films, 42
   films set in, 5, 6, 117, 268
   gay rights, 98
   gender quotas, 226n2
   Jewish community, 84, 117
   queer film, 98
   rating system, 138
Swedish Film Institute, 137, 140
Swedish language films, 36, 114

taboo issues, 116
Tarantino, Quentin, 243
television
   drama, 189, 243, 270, 281–2; *see also Breaking Bad*; *Kingdom, The*; *Out of Africa*
   miniseries, 72; *see also Night Manager, The*
   sitcoms, 86
   women and, 143
terrorism, 87
Things We Lost in the Fire, 6, 56–7, 60, 61, 64, 65f, 70–1, 92, 141
   as an art film, 37
   Berry's performance, 171n1
   characterization, 66–9, 232n8
   close-ups, 276
   compared with *Brothers*, 275, 276
   criticism, 59, 74
   intimacy, 62
   location, 226n8
   loss, 231
   male characters, 124, 157
   masculinity, 63, 66, 233
   praise for, 70
   production, 232n8
   promotional poster, 67
   psychology, 68
   signature features, 33
   transnationality, 218
   vulnerability, 63, 64–5, 66–7
Thomas, Anders, 280–1
Thompson, Kristen, 189
Thomsen, Ulrich, 26f
titles: translations, 276

transnationality, 5, 135, 160, 213–16, 224–5, 257, 267–8
After the Wedding, 5, 21, 114, 217, 254
American cinema, 219
Brothers, 36, 215, 216, 217, 254
definition, 41
and Europeanness, 41–2
female filmmakers and, 41
Freud's Leaving Home, 5, 213, 268
genre films, 216
and globalization, 253
In a Better World, 114
and language, 253
Like It Never Was Before, 36
Love Is All You Need, 36–7, 47, 226n7
Once in a Lifetime, 36
plurality of, 114–15
queer themes, 97
Serena, 5, 37, 218–19
Things We Lost in the Fire, 218
"transnational turn," 113–14
world cinema, 223
see also cosmopolitanism
traumas, xiii, 4, 62, 67, 142
After the Wedding, xiv
AIDS, 110
Brothers, 62–3, 163
cause of, 25
cinematic imagery, 180
Freud's Leaving Home, 94, 118
In a Better World, 25, 164, 167
Open Hearts, 36, 58
post-traumatic stress, 157
and restraint, 234
Second Chance, A, 173, 174, 175–6, 181
Serena, 74
Treut, Monika, 217
Trier, Carl-Henrik, 129n28
Trier, Ulf, 115, 119
Turan, Kenneth, 155

U.K.
comedies, 40
realism, 40
relationship with Hollywood, 40
Three Ticks initiative, 226n2
U.S.A.
co-productions, 40
Directors Guild of America (DGA), 71, 137
Equal Employment Opportunity Commission, 141
films shot in *see Things We Lost in the Fire*

Geena Davis Institute on Gender in Media, 137
see also Hollywood
Universal (film company), 40

Van Sant, Gus, 243
Variety (journal), 141, 223–4
Vinterberg, Thomas, 2, 127n1, 229, 235
The Celebration (Festen), 23, 269
Vinterberg, Thomas and Lindholm, Tobias: *Submarino*, 244
violence, 208, 237
After the Wedding, 251
Brotherhood, 256
Brothers, 160–4, 173, 253
and childhood, 235, 238–9
In a Better World, 20, 60, 165, 238–9, 250
and masculinity, 239
and misogyny, 122
New Danish Cinema and, 256
Open Hearts, 173
Second Chance, A, 180
Serena, 219
von Trier, Lars, 61, 127n1, 229, 268
Antichrist, 122, 123, 124, 130n47
Boss of It All, The (Direktøren for det hele), 122
Breaking the Waves, 114, 122, 123, 129n27
camera work, 129n27
Dancer in the Dark, 114, 129n27, 130n47
Depression trilogy *see Antichrist*; *Melancholia*; *Nymphomaniac*
Dogville, xiii
Element of Crime, The, 113, 120
English-language films, 127n5
Europa, 114, 120, 121, 125, 128n24, 129n28
genres, 37
and Hollywood, xiii, 114–15
idealism, 123
Idiots, The, 280
Images of a Relief (Befrielsesbilleder), 121
and Judaism, 113, 119–22, 125–6, 127n3
Kingdom, The (Riget), 129n27
Melancholia, 124, 125, 127, 130n47
and melodrama, 156
and misogyny, 122–3, 126
Nymphomaniac, 124
Orchid Gardener, The (Orchidégartneren), 120–1, 129n28
outsider status, 113
satire, 122

vulnerability, 15, 24–6, 31, 33
　After the Wedding, 63
　and aggression, 125
　Brothers, 161, 163
　In a Better World, 31
　Love Is All You Need, 51
　and masculinity, 63–4, 67, 124
　Night Manager, The, 63, 146, 188, 198, 202
　Open Hearts, 63–4
　Serena, 72, 73
　Things We Lost in the Fire, 63, 64–5, 66–7
Vulture (journal), 141

Waldron, Darren, 105
war films, 257, 271; *see also* Bigelow, Kathryn: *Hurt Locker, The*
Watson, Emma, 137
We Do It Together (production company), 141
Weinstein, Harvey, 122
White, Patricia, 213, 215, 217
　Women's Cinema, World Cinema: Projecting Contemporary Feminisms, 212
Wiedemann, Vinca: collaborative auteur theory, 241n2
Wikipedia, 57
Wilder, Billy, 269
　Some Like It Hot, 24
women
　female characters, 67–8, 76, 137, 145–7, 265, 270, 278–9
　as filmmakers, 41, 75, 81, 135–8, 141, 142, 144, 211–12, 213, 215, 219, 224, 225–6, 233, 266
　and intersubjectivity, 89
　Jewish matriarchs, 118
　marginalization, 212–13
　and mental illness, 220–1
　mobility, 207, 219
　mother–daughter relationship, 95
　powerful, 74
　and television, 143
　see also femininity; feminism; misogyny
Woolf, Virginia, 212–13, 225
Working Title (film company), 40
world cinema, 212, 219, 223
World War II
　German occupation of Denmark, 84
　Holocaust, 91, 95
　Jews, 84
Wright, Rochelle: *The Visible Wall: Jews and Other Ethnic Outsiders in Swedish Film*, 84, 117

Yiddish language, 87, 120

Zandén, Jessica, 128n24
Zandén, Philip, 111n5
Zentropa (production company), 122, 125, 126, 134
Zwick, Edward: *The Last Samurai*, 248

EU representative:
Easy Access System Europe
Mustamäe tee 50, 10621 Tallinn, Estonia
Gpsr.requests@easproject.com

www.ingramcontent.com/pod-product-compliance
Lightning Source LLC
Chambersburg PA
CBHW070234240426
43673CB00044B/1789